Method
Engineering

IFIP – The International Federation for Information Processing

IFIP was founded in 1960 under the auspices of UNESCO, following the First World Computer Congress held in Paris the previous year. An umbrella organization for societies working in information processing, IFIP's aim is two-fold: to support information processing within its member countries and to encourage technology transfer to developing nations. As its mission statement clearly states,

> IFIP's mission is to be the leading, truly international, apolitical organization which encourages and assists in the development, exploitation and application of information technology for the benefit of all people.

IFIP is a non-profitmaking organization, run almost solely by 2500 volunteers. It operates through a number of technical committees, which organize events and publications. IFIP's events range from an international congress to local seminars, but the most important are:

- the IFIP World Computer Congress, held every second year;
- open conferences;
- working conferences.

The flagship event is the IFIP World Computer Congress, at which both invited and contributed papers are presented. Contributed papers are rigorously refereed and the rejection rate is high.

As with the Congress, participation in the open conferences is open to all and papers may be invited or submitted. Again, submitted papers are stringently refereed.

The working conferences are structured differently. They are usually run by a working group and attendance is small and by invitation only. Their purpose is to create an atmosphere conducive to innovation and development. Refereeing is less rigorous and papers are subjected to extensive group discussion.

Publications arising from IFIP events vary. The papers presented at the IFIP World Computer Congress and at open conferences are published as conference proceedings, while the results of the working conferences are often published as collections of selected and edited papers.

Any national society whose primary activity is in information may apply to become a full member of IFIP, although full membership is restricted to one society per country. Full members are entitled to vote at the annual General Assembly, National societies preferring a less committed involvement may apply for associate or corresponding membership. Associate members enjoy the same benefits as full members, but without voting rights. Corresponding members are not represented in IFIP bodies. Affiliated membership is open to non-national societies, and individual and honorary membership schemes are also offered.

Method Engineering

Principles of method construction and tool support

**Proceedings of the IFIP TC8, WG8.1/8.2
Working Conference on Method Engineering
26–28 August 1996, Atlanta, USA**

Edited by

Sjaak Brinkkemper
University of Twente
The Netherlands

Kalle Lyytinen
University of Jyväskylä
Finland

and

Richard J. Welke
Georgia State University
Atlanta, USA

Published by Chapman & Hall on behalf of the
International Federation for Information Processing (IFIP)

CHAPMAN & HALL
London · Weinheim · New York · Tokyo · Melbourne · Madras

Published by Chapman & Hall, 2–6 Boundary Row, London SE1 8HN, UK

Chapman & Hall, 2–6 Boundary Row, London SE1 8HN, UK

Chapman & Hall GmbH, Pappelallee 3, 69469 Weinheim, Germany

Chapman & Hall USA, 115 Fifth Avenue, New York, NY 10003, USA

Chapman & Hall Japan, ITP-Japan, Kyowa Building, 3F, 2-2-1 Hirakawacho, Chiyoda-ku, Tokyo 102, Japan

Chapman & Hall Australia, 102 Dodds Street, South Melbourne, Victoria 3205, Australia

Chapman & Hall India, R. Seshadri, 32 Second Main Road, CIT East, Madras 600 035, India

First edition 1996

© 1996 IFIP

Printed in Great Britain by TJ Press Ltd, Padstow, Cornwall

ISBN 0 412 79750 X

A catalogue record for this book is available from the British Library

Printed on permanent acid-free text paper, manufactured in accordance with
ANSI/NISO Z39.48-1992 and ANSI/NISO Z39.48-1984 (Permanence of Paper).

CONTENTS

Editors' Preface

Research and development in the area of Method Engineering is concerned with the design, construction and evaluation of methods, techniques, and support tools for information systems development. Over the years, numerous development methods, based on a variety of paradigms, have been proposed. Of these a substantial number are currently applied in industry, with mixed success. Both generic and method-specific specification techniques have been designed for use within various development approaches. These methods are constantly adapted and extended to meet the changing needs of the practice and to reflect new technological and organizational insights. The advent of Computer Aided Software Engineering (CASE) tools has increased the turbulence in the field by making the underlying methods and techniques more apparent to their users, while, at the same time, reducing their ability to adapt to changing needs. Recent methods based on new paradigms, such as object-orientation, or new application types, as workflow management and client-server architectures, reveal the trend towards modular methods with generic, interchangeable components. The need for a new vision on methods and tools has manifested itself.

The conference organisers are very proud to be instrumental to producing the first book in the area of Method Engineering. We gave this conference the subtitle: *Principles of Method Construction and Tool Support*. The work in the area of Method Engineering comprises many research topics, and is influenced by several reference disciplines, such as organisation theory, software engineering, logic, and management science. The proceedings of this first Method Engineering conference shows this variety, as the following topics can be distinguished:

- Method representation formalisms, Meta-modelling
- Meta CASE, CASE adaptability and CAME tools
- Repositories, Tool integration
- Situational methods, Contingency approaches
- Terminology and reference models, Ontologies
- Organizational issues and impact
- Usability and experience reports
- Generation and evaluation of CASE tools
- Method construction paradigms
- Research methods and methodological frameworks

Method Engineering'96 would not have been possible without the assistance of many people. We are indebted to the program committee members and additional reviewers for preparing thorough reviews in a very tight schedule. The authors are thanked for their efforts in making an excellent scientific contribution to this new and challenging field. Finally, the organisers wish to thank all persons involved in making of the Method Engineering'96 conference into a success.

May 1996

Sjaak Brinkkemper
Kalle Lyytinen
Richard J. Welke

Officers, Program Committee Members and Additional Referees

General Conference Chair:

Kalle Lyytinen, University of Jyväskylä, Finland

Program Committee Chair:

Sjaak Brinkkemper, University of Twente, the Netherlands

Organizing Chair:

Richard J. Welke, Georgia State University, USA

Program Committee:

David Avison, UK
Sue Conger, USA
Jurgen Ebert, Germany
Antony Finkelstein, UK
Alan Hevner, USA
Shuguang Hong, USA
Matthias Jarke, Germany
Peri Loucopoulos, UK
Leon Osterweil, USA
Naveen Prakash, India
Motoshi Saeki, Japan
Arne Sølvberg, Norway
John Venable, New Zealand
Tony Wasserman, USA
Stanislaw Wrycza, Poland

Janis Bubenko, Sweden
Alan Davis, USA
Gregor Engels, The Netherlands
Brian Henderson-Sellers, Australia
Gezinus Hidding, USA
Juhani Iivari, Finland
Heinz Klein, USA
Lars Mathiassen, Denmark
Barbara Pernici, Italy
Colette Rolland, France
Olivia Sheng, Hong Kong
Paul Sorenson, Canada
Yair Wand, Canada
Trevor Wood-Harper, UK

Program Assistance:

Rolf Engmann, University of Twente, the Netherlands
George Steenbekke, University of Twente, the Netherlands

Additional Referees:

C. Cauvet, France
G. Grosz, France
T.R. Henriksen, Norway
P. Kerola, Finland
J. Rekers, the Netherlands
H. Rønneberg, Norway
D. Turk, USA
C. Wei, Hong Kong
E. van der Winden, the Netherlands

L.P.J. Groenewegen, the Netherlands
B.A. Farshchian, Norway
J. Kajava, Norway
V. Plihon, France
H. Render, USA
I. Tervonen, Finland
S. Volkov, USA
J.R.G. Wood, UK
A. Zamperoni, the Netherlands

A PRIMER TO METHOD ENGINEERING

J. J. Odell
James Odell Associates
1315 Hutchins Avenue
Ann Arbor, MI 48103 USA
Tel: +1 313 994-0844
email: 71051.1733@compuserve.com

INTRODUCTION

> A *methodology* is a body of methods employed by a discipline.
>
> A *method* is a procedure for attaining something.
>
> *Method engineering* is the coordinated and systematic approach to establishing work methods.

Traditional methodologies for information system (I.S.) development are—by nature—general purpose. As such, they contain an ideal set of methods, techniques, and guidelines that in reality can never be followed literally. They must be tuned to the situation at hand. Steps are sometimes omitted, added, or modified. Guidelines are often modified or ignored to fit special circumstances, such as technology, development expertise, the application, and external factors. [Harmsen, 1994]

To complicate things further, numerous methodologies exist for I.S. development—each with its own set of tools and techniques. Comparing and selecting an approach from a multitude of methodologies is confusing and difficult. To aid in this selection, various comparison standards have been proposed for object-oriented methodologies, such as those documented by the OMG [Hutt, 1994a; 1994b]. Some approaches attempt to harmonize several methodologies—forming yet another rigid methodology [Coleman, 1994]. Other methodologies provide a choice of options, or *paths*, that the user can select depending on the circumstances. In short, an I.S. project can choose from three basic methodologies, as depicted in Fig. 1.

Figure 1 Methodological approaches fall into three categories (adapted from Harmsen [Harmsen, 1994]).

METHOD ENGINEERING

Flexibility without control can hardly be considered a methodology, since any systematic and coordinated approach to establishing work methods is absent. For such an approach to be systematic and coordinated requires method engineering.

Method engineering produces methodologies. For I.S., a methodology is a body of methods employed to develop automated systems. In turn, a method defines the steps needed to automate a system—along with the required techniques and tools and the anticipated products. Adapting a methodology to the needs of a particular project is sometimes called *situational method engineering*. For I.S., situational method engineering designs, constructs, and adapts I.S. development methods.

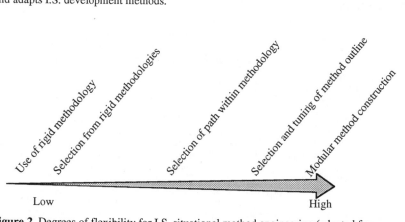

Figure 2 Degrees of flexibility for I.S. situational method engineering (adapted from Harmsen [Harmsen, 1994]).

As indicated in Fig. 2, method engineering has various degrees of flexibility. These are as follows:

- *Use of a rigid methodology.* At one extreme, using a rigid methodology permits virtually no flexibility. Such methodologies are based on a single development philosophy and thus adopt fixed standards, procedures, and techniques. Project managers are typically not permitted to modify the methodology.

- *Selection from rigid methodologies.* Instead of permitting only one rigid approach, this option allows each project to choose its methodology from one of several rigid methodologies. This makes possible the selection of an approach that might be more appropriate for the project. However, this is a bit like buying a suit without having it altered. You make the best of what is available, despite the fact that the chosen methodology will probably not fit the project perfectly. Furthermore, each methodology involves additional purchase and training costs.

- *Selection of paths within a methodology.* Many methodologies permit more flexibility by providing a choice of predefined paths within the methodology. Typical development paths include *traditional* and *rapid* application development. Some methodologies now include paths that support development aspects, such as package selection, pilot projects, client/server, realtime, knowledge-based systems, and object orientation. A common disadvantage, however, is that it may not be possible to combine some options. For instance, realtime, knowledge-based projects may not be supported.

- *Selection and tuning of a method outline.* This option permits each project to both select methods from different approaches and tune them to the project's needs. Typically, this involves selecting a global method process and data model. These models, then, are further adapted and refined by the project. This option is best supported by an automated tool.

- *Modular method construction.* One of the most flexible options is to generate a methodology for a given project from predefined building blocks. Each building block is a method fragment that is stored in a method base. Using rules, these building blocks are assembled based on a project's profile. The result is an effective, efficient, complete, and consistent methodology for the project.

  An automated tool is recommended for this option. Here, a project's methodology can be generated automatically and then adapted and further refined by the project manager. Performing the entire activity manually would require much work and time. Such an option is illustrated in Fig. 3.

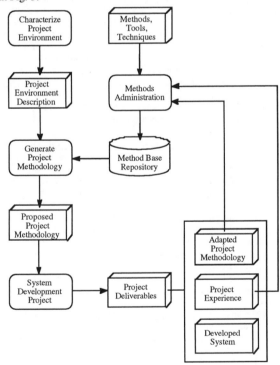

Figure 3 An object-flow diagram specifying the process of modular method construction.

COMPUTER-AIDED METHOD ENGINEERING

Computer-Aided Software Engineering (CASE) automates automation. In contrast, Computer-Aided Method Engineering (CAME) automates the assembly of methods. A CAME tool should support the following activities [Harmsen, 1994]:

- *Definition and evaluation of contingency rules and factors.* In order to choose the right method fragments for a project, rules and factors for selecting the proper method fragments must be defined. Method engineers are responsible for these definitions. Given the project profile and method base, the CAME tool selects and assembles the appropriate methodology.

- *Storage of method fragments.* Selecting and assembling a methodology from method fragments requires a *method base*. This method base is the repository from which method engineers and the CAME tool can select various method fragments. As new methodologies arise, they can also be incorporated into the method base.

- *Retrieval and composition of method fragments.* Certainly, for a CAME tool to generate a methodology from a method base, retrieval operations must be available for method fragments. However, total automation of methodology generation may never be completely feasible. A more realistic scenario could involve both automatic generation and a method engineer. The method engineer should be able to manipulate and modify method fragments within a methodology.

- *Validation and verification of the generated methodology.* The CAME tool should not only support selecting and assembling a methodology, it should also check the results. The tool, therefore, should incorporate guidelines to ensure that the correct set of method fragments has been selected. Furthermore, the tool should ensure that the fragments are assembled in a consistent manner. In other words, the CAME tool should ensure, or assist in ensuring, the quality of the generated methodology. (After all, generated methodologies must meet the same standards as standards methodologies.)

- *Adaptation of the generated methodology.* The method base should also accumulate the experience of previous projects and their methodologies. This experience should be used to improve method fragments, along with their contingency rules and factors. (Also illustrated in Fig. 4.) In other words, practical experience should be used to adapt future methodologies.

- *Integration with a meta-CASE tool.* CAME and CASE tools should eventually be integrated. When a methodology is generated for a particular project, the appropriate supporting tools should also be integrated. Adapting a CASE tool in this fashion would require configuring the CASE tool to support the resulting methodology. In other words, a meta-CASE tool would be required so that techniques and diagrammatic representations can be defined based on the methodology. Such a tool would be similar in nature to the CAME tool. Within this meta-CASE tool, CASE fragments would have to be defined. Additionally, it would require the ability to retrieve and compose new conceptual fragments.

- *Interface with a method base.* This method base is the repository for the various method fragments from which method engineers and the CAME tool can select.

To support CAME, the I.S. organization requires two additional roles—the *method engineer* and the *method administrator*. The method administrator is responsible for the contents of the method base. The method engineer is responsible for generating the right methodology for each project. Both support and are supported by the CAME tool—and are part of a larger framework called *process management*.

CAME tools are being developed by many organizations around the world. They are currently available from companies such as, James Martin & Co and Ernst & Young. While still in their infancy, the CAME tools from these two companies support many of the properties described above.

PROCESS MANAGEMENT

To support applications systems, the repository must—of course—contain information about the *product* of I.S. development. This includes information regarding analysis results, such as structural and behavioral models, business rules, and so on. For design and implementation, the repository would include information such as design templates, application data structures, programs, and interfaces. Additionally, the development repository must also contain *process*-related information, such as intermediate results, human agents, tools involved, process plans, design decisions, and steps taken to execute them.

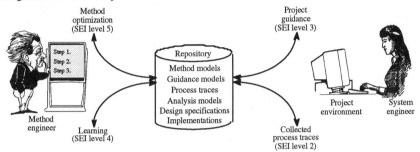

Figure 4 An environment for process management.

SEI support

The Software Engineering Institute (SEI) has been influential in the movement toward high-quality products. Its framework proposes five levels of process maturity: initial, repeatable, defined, managed, and optimizing [Paulk, 1993]. This same framework can be applied to process management.

Jarke recommends several kinds of SEI-related actions be performed that will ensure a high-quality process management environment [Jarke, 1994]. These are illustrated in Fig. 4. At the *initial* level, an organization does not provide a stable environment. Here, no repository exists. At the *repeatable* level, policies for managing a project and procedures to implement those policies are established. The planning and management of new projects is based on experience with similar projects. This is aided by capturing process traces, as indicated in the lower right of Fig. 4. At the *defined* level, an organization standardizes both its system engineering and management processes. Such an organization exploits effective software-engineering practices when standardizing its processes. Furthermore, an organization's process standards are tailored for each project to develop their own *defined* processes, as indicated in the upper right of Fig. 4. Once this has been established, the organization can introduce procedures for measuring the actual process execution. At this *managed* level, the organization learns to predict trends in processes and product quality. This action is depicted in the lower left of Fig. 4. Finally, at the *optimizing* level, the entire organization is focused on continuous process improvement (upper left of Fig. 4).

CAME TOOLS

CAME tools are being developed by many organizations around the world. As discussed above, CAME tools automate and control the application development processes, enabling the method engineer to develop fast, fluid, and flexible processes. These tools should increase planning, management, and development efficiency by providing tighter controls over each development project as it evolves. Furthermore, CAME tools ensure that methods are designed to be reusable and can be continually revised and improved through integration of best practices from previous projects.

A CAME tool is typically used for process management in four distinct modes—defining the process, planning the project, delivering the project, and improving the process.

• *Defining the process*—method components are created based on specific enterprise needs and characteristics. This ensures a successful foundation for a project. New method components can also be added to the library. The focus is on reusability and the intent that the processes will be used by project teams.

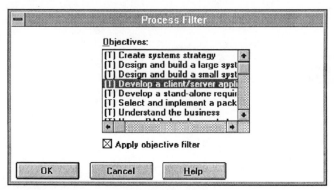

Figure 5 A screen that offers a choice of project objectives. Based on these objectives, the CAME tool can generate an appropriate methodology (Architect, James Martin & Co.).

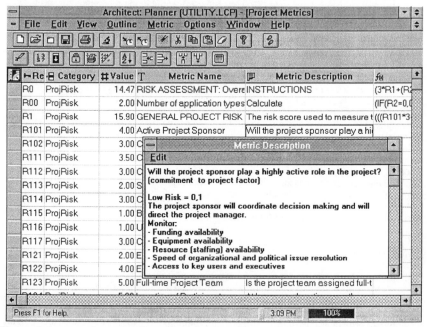

Figure 6 A screen that maintains and reports on various project metrics, such as duration and risk (Architect, James Martin & Co.).

- *Planning the project*—project managers are assisted in planning by assembling the necessary methodology for a particular project. Since the method base repository is constantly being improved from many different projects, project managers always have the most successful method components available to them. The methodology is tailored according to constraints of the individual project. Currently, both Ernst & Young and James Martin & Co offer such a tool. For example, Fig. 5 depicts a "process filter" screen from James Martin & Company's CAME tool called Architect. This screen helps Architect to select the appropriate method segments based on the objectives selected in the right side of the window. Once the methodology is generated, the project can be estimated and its risk assessed. Figure 6 depicts an Architect project metrics screen.

- *Delivering the project*—system development work assignments can be assigned to individuals and to development tools. CAME tools can then guide the workflow of a project by ensuring that the right task is being completed by the right person, using the right tools.

- *Improving the process*—continuous improvement is key to process management. Using measurable quantitative feedback from each project, the method components used are re-evaluated to determine what worked and what did not. Here, method components are modified, added, or deleted to reflect the best practices and lessons from SDLC projects.

REFERENCES

Coleman, Derek, Patrick Arnold, Stephanie Bodoff, Chris Dollin, Helena Gilchrist, Fiona Hayes, and Paul Jeremaes, Object-Oriented Development: The Fusion Method, Prentice Hall, Englewood Cliffs, NJ, 1994.

Harmsen, Frank, Sjaak Brinkkember, and Han Oei, "Situational Method Engineering for Information System Project Approaches," Methods and Associated Tools for the Information Systems Life Cycle, A. A. Verrijn-Stuart and T. William Olle, eds., Elsevier, Amsterdam, 1994, pp. 169–194.

Hutt, Andrew T. F., ed., *Object-Oriented Analysis and Design: Comparison of Methods*, Wiley-QED, New York, 1994a.

Hutt, Andrew T. F., ed.,*Object-Oriented Analysis and Design: Description of Methods*, Wiley-QED, New York, 1994b.

Jarke, Matthias, Klaus Pohl, Colette Roland, and Jean-Roch Schmitt, "Experience-Based Method Evaluation and Improvement: A Process Modeling Approach," *Methods and Associated Tools for the Information Systems Life Cycle,* A. A. Verrijn-Stuart and T. William Olle, eds., Elsevier, Amsterdam, 1994, pp. 1–27.

Martin, James, and James J. Odell, *Object-Oriented Methods: Pragmatic Considerations*, Prentice Hall, Englewood Cliffs, NJ, 1996.

Paulk, Mark C., Bill Curtis, Mary Beth Chrissis, and Charles V. Webber, "Capability Maturity Model, Version 2.1," *IEEE Software,* 10:4, 1993, pp. 18–27.

2

Structural Artifacts in Method Engineering: The Security Imperative

Richard Baskerville
Copenhagen Business School and
Binghamton University
Binghamton, New York 13902 USA
Tel +1 607 777 2337 Fax +1 607 777 4422 Email baskerville@cbs.dk

Abstract

The organizational structure has to do with human relationships, and is distinguished from the various artifacts (like information technology, systems development methods, and other mechanical products) that reflect those relationships. Information technology represents a first-level artifact and systems development methods represent a second-level artifact. This paper explains and illustrates a theory in which method engineering introduces third-level structural artifacts in organizations. A demonstration is included that uses security as one of the system imperatives that must be captured by third-level structural artifacts such as method engineering. This demonstration shows how method engineering may produce methods that are more complete and more harmonized with the organizational situation.

Keywords

Information Systems Development, Systems Development Methods, Software Engineering, Organizational Structure, Information Systems Security

1 INTRODUCTION

There are a large number of widely varied methods available for information systems developers. These include structured approaches (*e.g.,* Yourdon 1989), prototyping approaches (*e.g.,* Connell and Shafer 1989), information engineering (*e.g.* Finkelstein 1989), soft systems (*e.g.,* Checkland and Scholes 1990), sociotechnical (*e.g.,* Mumford 1983), object-oriented (*e.g.* Embley, Kurtz and Woodfield 1992), *etc.* Many of these methods have been comparatively analyzed in books (*e.g,* Olle *et al.* 1988 or Avison and Fitzgerald), and journal articles (*e.g.* Jackson and Keys 1984, Jayaratna 1988 or Hirschheim and Klein 1992). Despite a fairly large body of work concerning the details of systems development methods, there is still a very poor understanding of how such methods are actually used in practice (Wynekoop and Russo 1993) or even whether these are ever used at all (Baskerville Travis and Truex 1992).

Method engineering (Kumar and Welke 1992) represents the effort to improve the usefulness of systems development methods by creating an adaptation framework whereby methods are created to match specific organizational situations. The goals of this adaptation framework include at least two possible objectives. The first objective is the production of contingency methods, that is, situation-specific methods for certain types of bounded organizational settings. This objective represents method engineering as the creation of a multiple choice setting. For example, in a systems consulting-firm situation, method engineering might be used to create a number of alternative predetermined methods, and each new client's situation might be analyzed to select one of the methods which would be most appropriate for use. The second objective is one in which method engineering is used to produce methods "on-the-fly". Each systems development project begins with a method definition phase where the development method is invented on the spot. In this second objective, method engineering is a mechanism for coping with the uniqueness of each development setting. Organizational change is involved because it contributes to this uniqueness. The mechanism operates by lifting the systems structures to a higher (third) level of abstraction, such that the actual development structures become "selectable" (or definable), and importantly, the determination of these selections itself becomes more highly structured.

The purpose of this paper is to explain and illustrate a theory of method engineering which is oriented toward these third-level structural artifacts in organizations. Third-level artifacts represent to the imperatives of the method engineer. This purpose is addressed by four major sections. In the remainder of this first section, we will define several key terms. The second section will analyze the relationship between information systems and organizational structures in terms of structural artifacts. The third section extends this analysis to the new artifacts demanded by the new level of abstraction introduced by method engineering. Following this, the fourth section illustrates the rather positive nature of these new artifacts using information systems security as an example. The final section summarizes the demonstration and discusses some research issues that are opened by the analysis.

It is not the purpose of this paper to directly propose method engineering techniques and structures like tool selection heuristics, notation inventories or analytical techniques directed toward the target organizational situation. The paper will not attempt to survey the various imperatives to which method engineers must respond. Rather, an analysis is presented which can frame a better understanding of how such proposals will interact with human organizations, information systems, and system development methods. However, the analysis is illustrated using an outline of possible security notation and criteria which would be appropriate in method engineering.

For the purposes of this paper, the term information technology (IT) will suggest a broader view than "just computers", including telecommunications and office technologies like photocopiers. Also IT is not bound to machinery, but includes conceptually-grouped technologies (*e.g.,* object-oriented or prototyping concepts). It is arguable whether definitions of information systems and information technology may encompass each other. In this paper, these are separate but closely related concepts, information systems (IS) refers to the systematic development, operation and management of IT as well as the IT itself. We are especially concerned with this "systematic development" component in IS, and we will use the term information systems development (ISD) to refer to the analysis, design and implementation components embedded in our definition of IS.

Both Oxford and Webster's dictionaries primarily define the term "*method*" as meaning "the procedure for obtaining an object." The secondary definitions fasten on such ideas as "orderly," "systematic," "regularity," and "regimen." Method is clearly a concept of process rather than representation. This paper will avoid the term *methodology* altogether, for in the field of IS, the original meaning of this term (the study of method) has become confused, and is either used as a simple synonym for method (*cf.* Olle *et al.* 1988, p. 1) or to create a hierarchy of methods (*cf.* Jayaratna 1993, Wynekoop and Russo 1993) which has been shown to be rather strained when closely examined: It is a higher-order version of the same construct: "a method of methods" (Oliga 1988, p. 90)

The concept of "artifact" is especially important in this work. An artifact is an object made by people, usually with skill, for subsequent use. Its common archeological and anthropological usage also implies that the object is from an earlier time or cultural stage. This implies that an artifact has a physical persistence These connotations are important, because these distinguish the making of the object from its use, imply that such objects are cultural icons, and that their existence may endure through later periods of time and cultural stages.

Information systems security is used to illustrate the points below regarding IS organizational artifacts. For this paper, "security" is defined broadly to include not only features that prevent intentional losses, such as fraud and vandalism, but also unintentional losses such as natural disasters and errors. Thus security encompasses system integrity and reliability. Security is presented as one "imperative" of systems development methods. Such imperatives are fundamental goals of the systems development that motivate the inclusion of certain absolutely-necessary features into a method's design. For example, imperatives like maintainability or reusability motivate features like encapsulation or inheritance in an object-oriented method.

2. STRUCTURAL ARTIFACTS OF ORGANIZATIONS

The information system has an important relationship with organizational structure. The development methods are also directly or indirectly elements of this relationship. This implies that there is also a relationship between method engineering and organizational structure.

There is a clear distinction between the structure in a human organization and the artifacts which reflect that structure. It is possible for the human organization to conflict with its structural artifacts. For example, in many organizations the CEO's secretary wields real power, like autonomously making decisions in assigning responsibilities further "down the line". Every person in the organization will be aware of this line authority, yet it almost never appears in the organizational chart or position descriptions. The human organization differs in reality from the artifacts that supposedly define it.

This important distinction between the structure of the human organization and the artifacts intended to reflect that structure requires a precise terminology. The terms "organization", "structure" and "system" will appear below as icons for fairly strict dictionary concepts. *"Organizations"* is a term that regards people who are dividing their work together for some common purpose. *"Organized"* is a term that regards something formed into a whole consisting of interdependent or coordinated parts especially for united action. Organization is defined recursively: A group of persons or smaller organizations organized for some end or work. This paper will use the term organizational structure to regard the persistent relationships between the people (or smaller organizations) in organizations. "Persistent" regards repeated instances of relationships that occur with regularity.[1]

2.1 IT And Other Structural Artifacts

There are widely varied viewpoints about the relationship between IT and organizational structure. However, many of these seem to assume that the information technology is somehow an elemental part of the organizational structure. (Five of these viewpoints are surveyed in the appendix to illustrate how each relates to this assumption.) However, organizational structure regards persistent *relationships between people*. While the IT might enable or reflect this relationship, it does not embody the relationship itself. It is important to carefully distinguish organizational structure (human relationships) from the IT artifacts (mechanical products) that reflect those relationships. (In this point we are carefully distinguishing between IT, which is artifactual in our definition, and IS which may be seen as a "web" or "institution" that is inherently embedded in the social context which is using the IT, and therefore may not be artifactual in our definition.)

Together with IT, there are many different artifacts that people create which reflect their organizational structures. Table I lists some examples of these artifacts. These artifacts reflect, or encode the organizational structure, but should not be construed to *be* the organizational structure. These artifacts represent the different rules and protocols by which the members of the organization may choose to behave. The accuracy of these representations is, of course, variable. These rules and protocols have been likened to grammars in languages (Wand and Weber 1995). The grammar metaphor is useful as an analogy because linguistic grammars vary among communities, undergo change, naturally conflict among versions and may be accurately or inaccurately represented by grammatical texts. These organizational artifacts may vary among the organization's communities, undergo change, naturally conflict among themselves and may be accurately or inaccurately represented by structural artifacts.

---

[1]To a specific degree, these concepts are based on the roots of the terms, the original Latin and Greek ideas. Organization comes from the same Greek and Latin root as organism and organic (an individual life form) but most commonly meant "tool" or "device", and in this sense was also applied to "living" body organs. Our sense of the term is a natural, living device with a purpose. Structure arises from the Latin word *structure*, meaning something put together, taken from the verb *struere*, to put together. Structure implies the act of organizing, the assembling of the people, and the connections made between the individuals in the organization.

Table I. Examples of artifacts that people create which reflect their organizational structures.

1 *Organization charts*, which graphically depict organizational members and their different kinds of relationships
2 *Personnel policies*, which define reporting lines (who is whose boss), job descriptions, rewards structures and payroll policies
3 *Union agreements*, which reflect the relationships between union members and others in the organization
4 *Standard Operating Procedures (SOPs)*, which are typically detailed functional policies that define important coordinated actions in the organization.
5 *Resource access policies*, such as travel justification, modes of travel (private jet or tourist-class), company cars, cellular phones, etc.
6 *Workspace division*, which includes the size of an individual or group workarea and the collocation of organizational members (whose office is next to whose).
7 Workarea attributes and resources, such as decoration and furniture quality, quantity or size; privacy (e.g., corner-office or open-plan cubical); and dining facilities.
8 *Information Systems* which determine access to information resources such as computer accounts, LAN membership, automatic channelling of inputs and outputs, and screen and paper form designs.
9 *Methods* for developing information systems, which determine who sets the goals, who participates in the design, what issues are considered and how the system elements are represented.

2.3 Conflicting Versions of Organizational Structure

The different structural artifacts overlap, and will sometimes encode the organization's structure in conflicting ways. For example, the payroll policies, personnel policies and organization chart (Table I) may encode an individual without influence in organizational strategy; yet the workspace division, attributes and information system may encode a structure in which that same individual bears essential responsibility for shaping organizational strategy. Neither artifact *is* the organizational structure, that structure is defined by the relationships between the individuals, not by any particular set of organizational artifacts. When the artifacts suggest conflicting versions of the structures, the reflection of the real structure is blurred and the determination of its shape is made more difficult.

The organizational artifacts may tell different stories about the organizational structures. Conflicts between these stories seem to arise most often when the organizational structure differs in reality from an "official" version of the organization. These "official" organizational artifacts reflect the version of the organizational structure story as told by a particularly privileged class of organizational members: usually relatively senior management. Similarly to the priest-class in a theocracy, this class of individuals is widely accepted to own the authority to determine organizational structure. Accordingly, this class controls a large set of overt organizational artifacts.

However, when the structural story suggested by these "official" artifacts conflicts with the structural story suggested by many other organizational artifacts, then the reality of organizational structure is indistinct. Artifacts that may be beyond the influence of the "priesthood" in management may include those that are too menial for official control, such as workspace collocation; those that can be replaced by alternative artifacts (such as a lower-authority policy taking effect even though it contradicts and countermands a higher-authority policy); or those in which important functional artifacts ignore the specification artifacts, such as when the real information flows violate operating policies.

2.4 Conflicting Realities of Organizational Structure

An important aspect of conflicting artifactual reflections of organizational structure is the broad acceptance of "official" artifacts even when these conflict blatantly with the majority of other artifactual representations. This aspect regards the important, almost priestly power of the privileged organizational classes to interpret and pronounce organizational reality. As a result, management itself and many organizational scientists will not look beyond such privileged organizational artifacts, and sanction organizational structure to be, in reality, as officially declared by a certain subset of organizational artifacts.

The process by which an imaginary belief becomes accepted as being real, is the well-known thesis of Berger and Luckmann (1967) in the social construction of reality. Their thesis, applied here, suggests that the structural reality of organizations arises from routine relationships that become habitualized and explained in a symbolic universe. This symbolic universe in organizations may be strongly influenced by a powerful set of managers (the priestly class), and which can justify the relationships symbolically even when these become unnecessary or harmful (*e.g.*, government clerks following patently absurd bureaucratic rules because these justify some other part of the bureaucracy).

2.5 Emergent organizations

Organizational artifacts may also temporally reflect multiple versions of the reality of organizational structures. Each of these versions must be seen as being dynamic to a certain degree. That is, the relationships between organizational members (being social) are continuously changing. Emergent organizations are always seeking, but never quite achieving a regular pattern of behavior (Truex and Klein 1991). The most recent changes are less likely to be reflected in the organizational artifacts, and this means that such artifacts will be more-or-less out of sync with the reality of organizational structure. If the pace of change is fast in an organization, usually in response to fast-paced changes in its environment, then one should expect less fidelity and more conflict in its organizational artifacts with regard to its structure.

From this perspective, the issue runs deeper than merely conflicting versions of the reality of organizational structures, or indeed multiple organizational realities, and develops the possibility that no matter which artifacts one chooses to believe, that reflection of organizational structure is inevitably out of sync with the realities. This suggests that all organizational artifacts should be viewed with a degree of suspicion, especially in a setting with rapid change (a frequent characteristic in ISD). Each artifact tells a particular version of a particular set of organizational structures at a particular time. Indeed, such artifacts may have been entirely invented to match a desired organizational structure that may, or may not, have been realized at a later time. The relationship between these artifacts and current organizational structures is always open to question. As a consequence, contingency theories (*e.g.*, Davis 1982) provide an overly confining framework for ISD (Baskerville, Travis and Truex 1992).

3. THE CHALLENGE TO METHOD ENGINEERING

The problems of conflict between structural artifacts and emergent organizations is found at two levels of abstraction within the IS literature. At the first level, the IS community must deal with the potential conflict between the information technology, itself a structural artifact, and the emergent organization. At this fundamental level, one discovers IT that is ineffective in various ways, outdated, misplaced, or altogether unused because it conflicts with the present organizational structure. This conflict is dealt with, although somewhat indirectly, by the literature on IS failure, (*e.g.*, Bostrom and Heinen 1977, Ginzberg 1981, Lyytinen 1988 or Lyytinen and Hirschheim 1987), end-user development (*e.g.*, McLean 1979, Sumner and Kleer 1987, Galletta and Heckman 1990, or Amoroso and Cheney 1992) and software maintenance (*e.g.*, Schneidewind 1987 or Schnebeger 1995).

At the second level of abstraction, the IS community must deal with the potential conflict between the emergent organization and the development method (also itself a structural artifact) used to determine the structural artifact of information technology. At this level, one also discovers the IT development approaches are ineffective similarly to the IT itself, outdated, misplaced or altogether unused. This conflict is dealt with, also a bit indirectly, as a problem in need of solution by contingency approaches (*e.g.*, Davis 1982), prototyping approaches (*e.g.*, Naumann and Jenkins 1982), participative approaches (*e.g.*, Kyng 1991), and object-oriented approaches (*e.g.*, Coad and Yourdon, 1991). This conflict has been more directly dealt with in research which has shown that methods may not be entirely succeeding as a paradigm for the development of information technology (*e.g.*, Baskerville, Travis and Truex 1992, Wynekoop and Russo 1993, or Naur 1993).

Method engineering introduces a third level of abstraction, a method for creating methods. Indeed, method engineering may be a reaction to the structural conflicts which have (perhaps inevitably) accompanied the first two levels. The inability to discover suitable structural artifacts at the first level leads the search for suitable structures at the second level. That is, consistent failures at structuring IT as a match to organizations has demanded a search for successful structures for the structuring process. This idea is related to Giddens' (1984) social structuration theory, and has been explored directly in the IT context (Orlikowski and Robey 1991). Method engineering raises the problems of conflicts between structural artifacts and organizations to a higher level. See Figure 1.

However, it may be possible that this third level of abstraction will enable IT researchers to consider ever more essential structural artifacts regarding IT development and IT systems. If the methodical (the predefined, repetitive process) is abandoned to the second level, what structural artifacts remain for method engineering? Among the most prominent are notation and criteria.

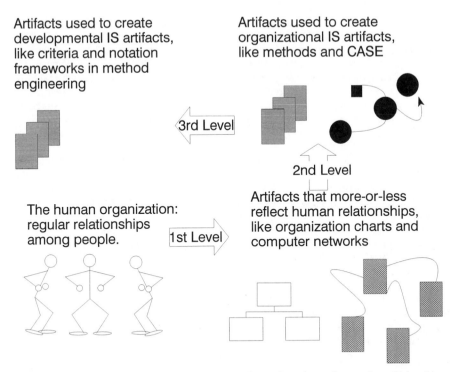

Artifacts used to create developmental IS artifacts, like criteria and notation frameworks in method engineering

Artifacts used to create organizational IS artifacts, like methods and CASE

3rd Level

2nd Level

The human organization: regular relationships among people.

1st Level

Artifacts that more-or-less reflect human relationships, like organization charts and computer networks

Figure 1. Three levels of information systems abstraction above the regular relationships in human organization.

The notation used in ISD methods varies widely: examples include data flow diagrams, data dictionaries, rich pictures, root definitions, and entity-relationship diagrams. The selection of the set of notation to be used in a system development project is among the most critical, since this decision will determine what concepts can (and what concepts cannot) be represented in the formal specification and design (Gause and Weinberg 1989). Conflicting representational schemes have also been explored in comparative methods studies, such as the work arising from the CRIS working conferences using the so-called IFIP case as its benchmark (Olle *et al.* 1988). Indeed, the empirical work by Bansler and Bødker (1993) suggests that the notation may be the only durable component of a systems development method.

The criteria regards the underlying rationale of the method, the details of its major aims, purposes and scope. The authors of the various methods are usually quite clear in explaining their criteria, but only in the context of each element of their method. As a whole, these criteria indicate what the method's authors believed would characterize a successful ISD project. But like philosophical assumptions, the discovery and general classification of these abstract criteria are problematic because these are conflated with the features of the method (*cf.* Coad and Yourdon, 1991 with Checkland and Scholes, 1990). However, there are examples of comparative work that has focussed on the features of methods (*e.g.* Olle, *et al.* 1983), and also work which has considered the underlying criteria (*e.g.* Olle *et al.* 1982).

At the third level of abstraction, namely method engineering, it will be necessary to introduce new structural artifacts. These new artifacts are likely include elements for selection of notation and criteria at the second level (ISD methods). Comparative studies of both notation and criteria will be prominent in formulating these new, third-level structural artifacts. However, the analysis should move beyond the description of the present structural artifacts of ISD, and also consider the real human organization and the way ISD unfolds in these organizations. Clearly, studying "methods" is not adequate for studying the reality of "ISD" (*cf.* Parnas and Clements, 1986, Baskerville, Travis, & Truex, 1992, Bansler & Bødker, 1993, Naur, 1993, Wynekoop & Russo, 1993). In other words, before building new artifacts that reflect the old ones on a new level of abstraction, one should question the old artifacts. In what ways do the structural artifacts of ISD conflict with the real organization?

There are a number of ways to prescriptively approach this issue. At one level, one can ask what criteria and notation might be available to capture conflicts between organizational structural artifacts (*e.g.,* when customer service policies and trouble-call operational procedures disagree), or to capture conflicts organizational structural artifacts and the organization itself (*e.g.,* when customer service policies and the actual social behavior of the service representatives disagree).

At another level (the method engineering level), one may ask what criteria and notation might be available to capture ever-present change in requirements. These elements would regard the need to follow an emergent organization through the course of an ISD project, especially considering the limited accuracy of all structural artifacts that purport to represent the organization in such settings.

4. NOTATION AND CRITERIA EXEMPLAR: SYSTEMS SECURITY

Systems security is an example of the problematic issues that arise from these challenges. Despite widespread agreement about the importance of privacy, reliability and integrity in information systems, explicit security constructs are extremely rare in ISD methods (Baskerville 1993a). Perhaps this is not so surprising considering that security features will typically conflict with the functionality of the system (Baskerville 1992). Also, security features are designed to prevent unpredicted organizational behavior, and will typically embody an uncomfortable constraint on emergent organizations (Baskerville 1993b). Finally, security features have been shown to create recursively security problems on their own (Baskerville 1995).

Not surprisingly, there are many examples of security problems in information systems (Neumann 1995). Perhaps it is more surprising that, despite the lack of consideration by ISD methods, the majority of information systems have security safeguards in place (albeit minimum), such as data backup and simple password schemes (*cf.* Hitchings 1995, Wood 1995). While this does not mean that existing security is entirely adequate for most information systems, it does mean that security features are being constructed into systems despite the lack of explicit structures in most ISD methods.

There are two implications that arise in this commonplace design of security features outside of explicit method artifacts. First, this design activity suggests that the structures of current ISD methods do not represent the reality of this aspect of ISD design. Second, this design activity might be better enabled if the structures of the ISD methods agreed more explicitly with the behavior of ISD analysts and designers.

These two implications comprise the security imperative for method engineering. This imperative regards the demand for explicit structures for developing system security in most ISD methods. On the one hand, this demand is founded on the unstructured design activity that is ignored by the criteria and the notation within IS design. On the other hand, this demand is founded on the need to reduce the substantial damage encountered by many organizations due to the lack of adequate security safeguards properly designed into their information systems.

The security imperative would entail, at a minimum, the inclusion of explicit security criteria and notation at the third level of abstraction. That is, method engineering should have structural artifacts that prescribe various criteria for security design and development, and alternative sets of notation for explicitly capturing security risks and protective features in the system.

These criteria and notation do not to be entirely invented. A survey of various security analysis and design notation is described by Baskerville (1993a), and book-length security methods exist (*e.g.*, Fisher 1984, Lane 1985). There are also surveys of criteria (*e.g.* Neugent 1982), and the European initiative on criteria for security of information technology is a "harmonization" of several national policies on such criteria (Commission of European Communities 1990). However, these resources provide only contrasting descriptions of second-order notation and criteria. These must be further analyzed in order to draw out frameworks for comparing and choosing among competing notations and criteria.

4.1 Notation

As a basis for one third-level notation framework, for example, the following security literature regarding methods for security safeguards specification was reviewed and analyzed using a limited inductive classification approach (*cf.* Sandman Klompus and Yarrison (1985). The framework below provides one initial possible framework for structuring the selection of security notation. The publications underlying this limited analysis are Browne (1979), Krauss (1980), Fisher (1984), Lane (1985), Baskerville (1988), Hutt *et al.* (1988), Fitzgerald and Fitzgerald (1990), Farquhar (1991), Ozier (1992), Forcht (1994) and Neumann (1995). Because of the heterogeneous nature of this body of literature, many other competing frameworks are possible. However, this example demonstrates the feasibility of such frameworks. The framework consists of three types of notation that comprise security features in ISD: Representation of security elements, security analysis and design, and security maintenance and management. This framework is illustrated in Table II.

This framework of security notation exemplifies a third-level structural artifact for organizational IS. Other related artifacts in method engineering might include heuristics for selecting a complete notational set, perhaps matching characteristics of the IS setting (captured in still another artifactual notation), or against the security criteria.

Table II. Third-level security notation framework for method engineering.

Security element representation notation.
The three elements organized for analysis in security design methods are typically the risks that threaten the system, the system assets requiring protection and the potential safeguards that might be erected to protect the system assets. Representation tools must be capable of representing inventories of these elements. Each of these inventories will need a classification system and a notation framework to permit analysis if they are to be practical. Examples of these classes and frameworks:

Risk
    Categories: natural disasters, malfunctions, criminal acts, errors
    Framework: probability, cost of damage, degrees of impact
Assets
    Categories: computers, communications, storage, personnel
    Framework: location, value, visibility, accessibility
Safeguard
    Categories: operating integrity, backup, access control, error detection
    Framework: implementation details, costs, second-order problems

Security Analysis and Design Notation
The notation must also capture the rationale leading to the implementation of safeguards. For the purposes of both designing and maintaining the safeguards, the notation should capture the risks against asset mapping process, and the safeguards selection process in the sense that one should be able to implosively and explosively audit the design. For example, one should be able to trace each safeguard to the risks it protects against and the assets it is protecting. Likewise risks and assets should be mapped to the safeguards, or alternatively the notations should demonstrate that the benefit of safeguards were trivial and unnecessary. Examples of such notation:
    Risk ranking notation
    Asset ranking notation
    Risk-asset-safeguard mapping
    Safeguard ranking notation
    Safeguard selection and design integration details

Security Maintenance and Management Notation
Under the assumption that organizations are emergent, and that system security is yet another form of structural artifact in organizations, safeguards maintenance and maintenance of security may imply additional necessary notation. Examples of such notation:
    Security maintenance frameworks
        Risks review and update process and routine
        Safeguards validation process and routine
        System maintenance security validation reviews

    Disaster planning frameworks
        Computer center loss plan
        Communication loss plan
        Cross-training plan

4.2 Criteria

The security criteria is another third-level structural artifact that represents the security characteristics which method engineering might instill in the ISD method. An example of such third-level criteria was developed in a workshop sponsored by the INFOSEC Standards and Initiatives group of the Communications Security Establishment for the purposes of commenting on a federal guideline for risk management of computer information systems in the Government of Canada. The working group that regarded managerial considerations was particularly concerned with adopting a risk management method that was equally relevant in large, complex installations (*e.g.,* an air base), as well as small, simple installations (*e.g.,* a small, remote police post).

Rather than seek a single method, dictated from the central government security establishment, the working group concentrated on distributed security decision-making. That is, instead of completely defining the risk assessment process to be universally applied throughout the Government of Canada, the exact decision would be deferred to the localized agencies responsible for the computing elements. This deferral takes on some characteristics of third-level method engineering. The summary of the recommendations appear in Verrett and Hysert (1993).

The approach recommended by the working group was oriented toward centralized criteria-setting, rather than centralized control. The central authority would set the criteria for the process of risk assessment, and defer the determination of the exact method to the local agency. Even the specification of a range of techniques together with criteria for choosing among these techniques was seen to exclude the use of ideal, unique approaches that might occur to managers "on the scene". Instead, the recommendations suggested the criteria by which a highly qualified manager in the field might determine whether the risk management process was successful. While examples of risk assessment techniques were suggested, it was not mandatory to choose one of the examples. The local manager would be free to innovate in situations where such innovation, in the judgement of that local manager, seemed to be required. The criteria are described in Table III.

The criteria in Table III represent another third-level structural artifact, and illustrates one alternative set of criteria. A more complete set of security criteria at this method-engineering level might offer alternative sets of criteria, perhaps for different levels of security, or different kinds of organizations, (government, manufacturing, retail, financial, *etc.*). The chosen criteria might then be used as a measure of the performance of method engineering in determining the security features (*e.g.* notation) of the second-level method.

4.3 Linking The Imperative Through The Levels

The imperative leads to the addition of notation and criteria to the method. The imperative may take various forms or degrees. Contrast, for example, relatively stronger, highly structured and inflexible security in military situations with relatively weaker, less structured and more flexible security in consumer goods manufacturing situations. The third-level artifacts must support the construction of second-level artifacts that respond to both of these contrasting situations (as well as others). Third-level method engineering must be capable

Table III. Criteria for risk management (adapted from Verrett and Hysert, 1993).

The process should be goal-directed.
The security goals of the government agency must be established at the beginning of the project, must meet applicable policies and standards, must involve the system owner from the start, must define resource constraints up-front, and must be as non-obstructive as possible. These goals should be 'appropriate' for the government group as judged by the managers in charge. The system's nature might take into account the criticality of failures (for example, a police cruiser dispatch system is more critical than a campground firewood management system), or the environment of the system (broad public access or highly restricted access to the system). Examples of such goals include:

- "trouble free operations"
- "minimum events"
- "highly private"

There must be a reasonably exhaustive threat analysis.
The process of risk analysis must include a threat analysis that considers a 'reasonable' range of threats. For a highly critical system, such a 'reasonable' range would necessarily be more exhaustive than non-critical systems. This will typically mean that the process will involve the use of an analytic model (*e.g.*, the US National Institute of Standards and Technology Model) and a reasonable tool or guideline (such as the CCIT Risk Analysis Methodology, CRAMM, a software-based approach).

The process must be updatable and reusable.
The process of risk management must result in the establishment of a permanent maintenance cycle for system security. This typically means that routine security reviews must be held which consider changes in security needs as a result of continued operation of the system. In many situations a security maintenance review plan will be needed that produces a periodic report certifying that the security is still intact. The cognizant manager must know what action is necessary if the report fails to materialize, or appears inadequate.

The process must achieve closure in both certification and accreditation.
The risk management process must conclude with an event of some type that embodies the instance at which the initial risk management project is successfully concluded. That is, such a risk management process must lead to a certifiable result.

The results must be repeatable.
The risk management process must be "logically" repeatable. This does not necessarily mean that anyone actually expects to repeat the process and compare results. Rather, it means that the process must be thoroughly understood as it occurred, and it must be carefully documented. In this way the decision-making process can be reconstructed such that higher management might be able to review whether the decisions about risks were made in a reasonable fashion in a given situation.

of constructing the second-level artifacts (the method) such that they are capable of producing first-level artifacts (information systems) which respond to the human organization. The nature of that response depends of the particular view of the relationship between the information system as a structural artifact and the human organizational structure. Five such views are discussed in the appendix. This illustrates how the ideal set of structural artifacts of method engineering would reflect the intersection of several dimensions: the set of possible imperatives, the forms and degrees of those imperatives, an open set of possible second-level structural artifacts, the set of viewpoints on the relationship between IS artifacts and the organization, and the strength of the harmony among the organization's structural artifacts and between those artifacts and the human organization.

This multi-dimensional nature of third-level structural artifacts introduces some complexity, but this certainly is not imponderable. As an example of how this analysis can be applied to the security imperative, assume the viewpoint (from the appendix) that IT can be used to shape the organization, and strong security is the imperative. Under these conditions, then the ISD method should be characterized by notation and criteria that will lead to prescriptive structural artifacts. Such prescriptive security artifacts within the IS include enforced access controls, which in turn require that the method's notation be characterized by extensiveness in the details in its safeguard categories, safeguard frameworks, design integration and validation routines. In addition, the third-level criteria suggests the need for a detailed goal set, more rigorous forms of threat analysis, such as one that includes automated threat databases (*e.g.,* CRAMM). The criteria under this imperative also indicate artifacts like a formal security maintenance review cycle, initial certification and routine recertification, and closely detailed documentation about the design decisions. Further, the assumed organizational viewpoint pins the achievement of strong security on a fair amount of harmony between the organization's structural artifacts and the structure of the human organization.

As a second, contrasting example of how this analysis can be applied to the security imperative, assume the emancipatory viewpoint (from the appendix), that IT involves ethical decisions about structuring the workplace. This example will also assume the contrasting position that security is fairly weak imperative. Under these conditions, then the ISD method should be characterized by notation and criteria that will lead to the fewest and least constraining, perhaps only implicit, structural artifacts. Such implicit security artifacts within the IS might only include training, simple passwords and data backup routines. These in turn imply that the method's notation be loosely structured, perhaps only free text in a few brief, suggested sections (*e.g,* risk, asset and threat rankings). In addition, the third-level criteria suggests only a few broad security goals will be involved and an informal, participative threat analysis. The certification and routine reviews will probably be internal, informal, and participative. Further, the assumed organizational viewpoint pins the achievement of reasonable security on a fair amount of highly-motivated participation within the organization itself, and that the structural artifacts related to security must be ethical with regard to the workplace.

5. SUMMARY AND FUTURE RESEARCH

The above discussion demonstrates how method engineering introduces a new level of structural artifact into human organizations. By selecting security as the example for the demonstration, this discussion also highlights the potential for method engineering not only to "situationalize" methods, but to correct general oversights in many of the existing published methods. That is, structural artifacts at the third level may respond to a general set of system imperatives which must be adapted to the development situation. This general set of system imperatives may be more complete, and therefore lead to more complete ISD.

Method engineering represents a third level of abstraction in ISD. This higher level of abstraction increases the need to understand the relationship between human organizations, organizational structure, and structural artifacts. Structural artifacts include IT, ISD methods and method engineering. The resolution of conflict between such artifacts and the organization, and between the artifacts themselves, motivates the introduction of the third-level artifacts of method engineering.

Further research is needed to understand the degree to which method engineering artifacts might conflict with organizational structure, or with each other. The human organizations in question not only include the target organization for the IT design, but also the organizations involved in ISD and method engineering itself. Also the impact of this conflict on the success of method engineering remains an open question until the application of method engineering grows. Additional work is also needed to determine what other imperatives should comprise the structural artifacts of method engineering. Examples might include usability, availability, timeliness, *etc.* In addition, the security exemplar also reveals the need for further research to determine the broad set of security criteria, notation, and other third-level structural artifacts necessary to implement the security imperative in method engineering.

APPENDIX A: VIEWPOINTS OF IT AND ORGANIZATION STRUCTURE

At least five separate viewpoints of the relationship between IT and organizational structure can be distinguished in the literature. Admittedly, each of these viewpoints is somewhat abstract, like stereotypes or caricatures. These will not be found in pure form "in the wild" of real organizational management. However, these theoretic viewpoints inhabit, and may even dominate other theories, practical trends and models of IS and IT. The discussion of each viewpoint will consider its central characteristic, the role of IT and IS under this viewpoint and an example of recently published research that relates critically to this viewpoint.

A.1 IT As A Medium for Organizational Communication

This viewpoint is characterized by the idea that information is a commodity in a similar sense to electricity, water and gas. The function of IT and IS is similar to that of an information utility providing an economical and sufficient supply of good quality information necessary to the organization. The IS parts of the organization act similarly to a sort of the utility company that sets up the data repositories and flow lines as needed in the organization.

As an example of where this viewpoint currently holds a strong influence, consider outsourcing. Practical and research publications on outsourcing often presume that the information utility can be contracted out, like the telephone switchboard and housekeeping. For example, Willcocks and Fitzgerald describe common problems discovered by organizations in their attempts to contract out, in varying degrees, their information technological support (Willcocks and Fitzgerald 1994).

A.2 Strategic Use of IT

This viewpoint is characterized by the assumption that information can be a central organizational product, or an essential enabling factor in a central organizational product. The role of IT and IS is tightly connected with the goals, strategies and purpose of the organization itself. Under this viewpoint, the organization could not produce its products competitively without IT.

The primary examples of this viewpoint include the American Airlines Sabre and American Hospital Supply case studies. These are now also iconic representations of cases where a few success stories dominate a management trend, followed by suspicions that a large number of attempted emulations resulted in failure. Publication readership seems intensely interested in the innovative successes and not in the emulation failures. For example, Kettinger *et al.* (1991) survey the long-range impact of a number of strategic IT systems. For a further example of this viewpoint, see Reich and Benbasat's (1990) study of customer-oriented strategic IT.

A.3 IT As A Mechanism for Shaping Organizations

Other parts of the IT and IS literature are characterized by the instrumental idea that the organization itself can be restructured by restructuring its IT. That is, the shape of the organization will follow the form of its IT. If one reorganizes the IT, one thereby reorganizes the human behavior. The role of IT and IS is therefore one of directing the organizational resources, both enabling and constraining the organizations purposeful work to the paths determined by management.

This view is typified by some of the current writings in Business Process Reengineering. The organization is moved into a new form by destroying the old IT (Hammer 1990), which embodied the old economic-specialization Taylorism, and rationally building a new process-centric organization that is effectively enabled by advanced IT (Davenport and Short 1990). Here again one encounters a similar problem to that of strategic IS, in that the literature is dominated by fairly limited set of success stories, while the practical community seems to be encountering serious problems emulating these successes (Manganelli and Klein 1994).

A.4 Matching IT To The Organization

This viewpoint is characterized by the assumption that the organizational structure is determined independently of its IT, and that successful IT will be shaped to match and support the structure of the organization. The role of IT is that of a tool that makes organizational processes easier under its preexisting structural constraints. The organizational processes must occur with or without IT, and if the IT does not help these processes, then the IT will be irrelevant, become ignored and fall into disuse. Successful IS is determined by its ability to shape itself to the needs of the organization.

This viewpoint is typical of the traditional IS development literature, with its focus on requirements elicitation and specification. Such literature will typically argue that lengthy systems analysis and data modelling is justified by the smooth conversion and enhanced lifespan of the new system (*cf.* Lyytinen 1987).

A.5 IT For Emancipation

This viewpoint is characterized by its focus on the human and social implications of the use of IT. It strongly shaped the socio-technical literature in systems development, with its recognition that IT choices carried ethical determinations in structuring the human workplace. IT could make worker's lives better, worse, or unnecessary. IS design and management was both a social and a technical act.

This viewpoint is typical of the socio-technical literature in IS development, and the trade-union influence in North European IS research. These assumptions dominated some systems development methods, like ETHICS (Mumford 1983) and cooperative prototyping (Er 1987), and is currently found in some of the work in systems development that focusses on the worklife of the developer (*cf.* Hirschheim and Klein 1994).

6. REFERENCES

Amoroso, D. and P. Cheney (1992) Quality end user developed applications: some essential ingredients, *Database 23* (1) (Winter) 1-12.

Avison, D. and G. Fitzgerald (1988) *Information Systems Development: Methodologies, Techniques and Tools.* Oxford: Blackwell Scientific.

Bansler, J. and K. Bødker (1993) A reappraisal of structured analysis: Design in an organizational context, *ACM Transactions on Information Systems 11* (2) 165-193.

Baskerville, R. (1988) *Designing Information Systems Security.* Chichester: Wiley.

Baskerville, R. (1992) The developmental duality of information systems security, *Journal of Management Systems 4* (1) 1-12.

Baskerville, R. (1993a) Information systems security design methods: Implications for information systems development, *Computing Surveys 25*, (4) December 375-414.

Baskerville, R. (1993b) Information systems security: Adapting to survive, *Information Systems Security 2* (1), 1993, 40-47. Reprinted, as New approaches to information systems security in Umbaugh, Robert (Ed.) *Handbook of IS Management 1994-95 Yearbook.* New York: Auerbach, 1994, pp S257-S265.

Baskerville, R. (1995) The second order security dilemma, in Orlikowski, W., Walsham, G., Jones, M., and DeGross, J. (Eds.) *Information Technology and Changes in Organizational Work*. London: Chapman & Hall, pp. 239-249.

Baskerville, R., J. Travis, and D. Truex (1992) Systems without method in Kendall, K. Lyytinen, K. and DeGross, J. (Eds.) *IFIP Transactions on The Impact of Computer Supported Technologies on Information Systems Development*. Amsterdam: North-Holland, pp. 241-270.

Berger, P. and T. Luckmann (1967) *The Social Construction of Reality, A Treatise in the Sociology of Knowledge*, Penguin Books.

Bostrom, R. and S. Heinen (1977) MIS problems and failures: A socio-technical perspective, Part I: The causes, *MIS Quarterly*, (September), 17-32, and MIS problems and failures: A socio-technical perspective, Part II: The application of socio-technical theory, *MIS Quarterly*, (December 1977), 11-28.

Browne, P. (1979) *Security: Checklist For Computer Center Self-Audits*. AFIPS, Arlington, Va.

Checkland, P. and J. Scholes (1990) *Soft Systems Methodology in Practice*. Chichester: J. Wiley.

Coad, P. and E. Yourdon (1991) *Object-Oriented Analysis 2nd Ed.*. Englewood Cliffs: Yourdon.

Commission of European Communities (1990) *Information Technology Security Evaluation Criteria (ITSEC), Provisional Harmonized Criteria, Version 1.2*. Brussels, Belgium: Commission of European Communities, Directorate--General XIII (June).

Connell, J. and L. Shafer (1989) *Structured Rapid Prototyping: An Evolutionary Approach to Software Development*. Englewood Cliffs: Yourdon Press.

Davenport, Thomas and James Short (1990) The new industrial engineering: Information technology and business process redesign, *Sloan Management Review* (Summer) 11-27.

Davis, G. (1982) "Strategies for information requirements determination," *IBM Systems Journal 21* (1) 4-30.

Embley, D., B. Kurtz and S. Woodfield (1992) *Object-Oriented Systems Analysis: A Model-Driven Approach*. Englewood Cliffs, N.J.: Yourdon Press.

Er, M. (1987) Prototyping, participative and phenomenological approaches to information systems development, *Journal of Systems Management* (August) 12-15.

Farquhar, B. (1991) One approach to risk assessment, *Computers & Security 10*, 1, 21-23.

Finkelstein, C. (1989) *An Introduction to Information Engineering: From Strategic Planning to Information Systems*. Sydney: Addison-Wesley.

Fisher, R. (1984) *Information Systems Security*. Englewood Cliffs: Prentice-Hall.

Fitzgerald, J. and A. F. Fitzgerald (1990) *Designing Controls Into Computerized Systems*. Jerry Fitzgerald & Associates, Redwood City, Ca.

Forcht, K.A. (1994) *Computer Security Management*, Danvers, Massachusetts: Boyd & Fraser.

Galletta, D. and R. Heckman (1990) A role theory perspective on end-user development, *Information Systems Research 1*, (2) (June) 168-187.

Gause, D. and G. Weinberg (1989) *Exploring Requirements: Quality Before Design* New York: Dorset House.

Giddens, A. (1984) *The Constitution of Society: Outline of the Theory of Structure.* Berkeley, Calif: Univ. of California Press.

Ginzberg, M. J. (1981) Early Diagnosis of MIS Implementation Failure: Promising Results and Unanswered Questions, *Management Science 27*, (4).

Hammer, M. (1990) Reengineering work: Don't automate, obliterate, *Harvard Business Review* (July-August) 104-112.

Hirschheim, R. and H. K. Klein (1992) Paradigmatic influences on information systems development methodologies: Evolution and conceptual advances. *Advances in Computers 34*, 294-381.

Hirschheim, R. and H. K. Klein, (1994) Realizing emancipatory principles in information systems development: The case for ETHICS, *MIS Quarterly 18* (March) 83-95.

Hitchings, J. (1995) Deficiencies of the traditional approach to information security and the requirements for a new methodology. *Computers & Security 14* (5), 377-383.

Hutt, A. E., S. Bosworth and D. B. Hoyt (eds.) (1988) *Computer Security Handbook.* Macmillan Publishing Co., New York, NY.

Jackson, M. C. and P. Keys, (1984) Towards a system of systems methodologies. *Journal of The Operational Research Society 35*, 473-486.

Jayaratna, N. (1988) Guide to methodology understanding in information systems practice. *International Journal of Information Management 8*, 43-53.

Jayaratna, N. (1993) Methodology assistance in practice: A critical evaluation. *Systemist 15*, (1) February, 5-16.

Kettinger, W., V. Grover, S. Guha, and A. Segars (1994) Strategic information systems revisited: A study in sustainability and performance. *MIS Quarterly 18* (1) (March) 31-58.

Krauss, L. I. (1980) *SAFE: Security Audit And Field Evaluation For Computer Facilities And Information.* AMACOM, New York, NY.

Kumar, K. and R. Welke (1992) Methodology engineering: A proposal for situation-specific methodology construction, in W. Cotterman, and J. Senn (Eds.) *Challenges and Strategies for Research in Systems Development.* New York: John Wiley & Sons, pp. 257-268.

Kyng, M. (1991) Designing for cooperation: Cooperating in design, *Communications of the ACM 34* (12) (December) 65-73.

Lane, V.P. (1985) *Security of Computer Based Information Systems.* London: Macmillan.

Lyytinen, K. (1987) Different perspectives on information systems: Problems and solutions, *ACM Computing Surveys* (1) (March) 5-42.

Lyytinen, K. (1988) Expectation failure concept and systems analysts view of information system failures: Results of an exploratory study, *Information & Management 14,* 45-56.

Lyytinen, K. and R. Hirschheim (1987) Information systems failures: A survey and classification of the empirical literature, *Oxford Surveys in Information Technology 4.*

Manganelli, R. and M. Klein (1994) Should you start from scratch? *Management Review 83* (7) (Jul) 45-47.

McLean, E. R. (1979) End users as application developers, *MIS Quarterly 3* (4) (December) 37-46.

Mumford, E. (1983) *Designing Human Systems For New Technology: The ETHICS Method.* Manchester: Manchester Business School.

Naumann, J. and A. Jenkins (1982) Prototyping: The new paradigm for systems development, *MIS Quarterly* (Sept) 29-44.

Naur, P. (1993) Understanding Turing's universal machine: Personal style in program description. *The Computer Journal 36* (4) 351-372.

Neugent, W. (1982) Acceptance criteria for computer security, *NCC Conference Proceedings*. Arlington, Va: AFIPS Press.

Neumann, Peter G. (1995) *Computer Related Risks*. New York: ACM Press.

Oliga, J. (1988) Methodological foundations of systems methodologies. *System Practice, 1* (1) (March), 87-112.

Olle, A., J. Hagelstein, I. Macdonald, C. Rolland, H. Sol, F. Van Assche, and A. Verrijn-Stuart (1988) *Information Systems Methodologies: A Framework for Understanding*. Wokingham: Addison Wesley.

Olle, T. W., H. G. Sol and A. A. Verrijn-Stuart, (1982) (eds) *Information Systems Design Methodologies: A Comparative Review*, Amsterdam: North Holland.

Olle, T. W., H. G. Sol and C. J. Tully, (1983) (eds), *Information Systems Design Methodologies: A Feature Analysis*, Proceedings of the IFIP WG 8.1 Working Conference on Feature Analysis of Information Systems Design Meeting, York, UK, 5-7 July, 1983, Amsterdam: North-Holland.

Orlikowski, W. and D. Robey (1991) Information technology and the structuring of organizations, *Information Systems Research 2* (2) (June) 143-169.

Ozier, W. (1992) Risk Assessment and Management *Data Security Management* Report 85-01-20. New York: Auerbach.

Parnas, D. and P. Clements (1986) A rational design process: How and why to fake it. *IEEE Transactions on Software Engineering SE 12* (2), February, 251-257.

Reich, B. and I. Benbasat (1990) An empirical investigation of factors influencing the success of customer-oriented strategic systems. *Information Systems Research 1* (3) (September) 325-347.

Sandman, P., C. Klompus and B. Yarrison (1985) *Scientific and Technical Writing*. Ft. Worth, Texas: Holt, Rhinehart and Winston.

Schnebeger, S. (1995) Distributed computer system complexity versus component simplicity. Its effects on software maintenance. Georgia State University Manuscript, summarized in J. DeGross, G. Ariav, C. Beath, R. Hoyer and C. Kemerer (eds.), *Proceedings of the Sixteenth International Conference on Information Systems*. New York: ACM Publ. p. 351.

Schneidewind, N. (1987) The state of software maintenance. *IEEE Transactions on Software Engineering SE-13* (3) March 303-310.

Sumner, M. and R. Kleer (1987) Information systems strategy and end-user application development, *Data Base 18* (4) (Summer) 19-30.

Truex, D. and H. K. Klein (1991) A rejection of structure as a basis for information systems development. In R. Stamper, R. Lee, P. Kerola and K. Lyytinen (Eds.), *Collaborative Work, Social Communications and Information Systems*. Amsterdam: North-Holland, pp. 213-236.

Verrett, R. and R. Hysert (1993) Summary of findings, working group 2, managerial and structural issues in the draft risk management framework. in *Proceedings 5th International*

Computer Security Risk Management Workshop. Ottawa: National Institute of Standards and Technology and Communications Security Establishment, 7-9.

Wand, Y., and Ron Weber (1995) On the deep structure of information systems, *Information Systems Journal 5* (3) (July) 203-223.

Willcocks, L. and G. Fitzgerald (1994) Toward the residual is organization? Research on it outsourcing experiences in the united kingdom. in Baskerville *et al.* (eds) *Transforming Organizations with Information Technology*. Amsterdam: North-Holland, pp. 129-152.

Wood, C. C. (1995) Identity token usage at American commercial banks. *Computer Fraud and Security Bulletin* (March) 14-16.

Wynekoop, J. and N. Russo (1993) System development methodologies: Unanswered questions and the research-practice gap, in J. Degross, R. Bostrom, and D. Robey (Eds.), *Proceedings of the 14th International Conference Information Systems*. New York: ACM Publ. pp. 181-190.

Yourdon, E. (1989) *Modern Structured Analysis*. Englewood Cliffs, NJ: Yourdon Press.

7 BIOGRAPHY

Richard Baskerville is an associate professor in the School of Management at Binghamton University. His research focusses on security and methods in information systems, their interaction with organizations and research methods. He is an associate editor of *MIS Quarterly* and *The Information Systems Journal*. Baskerville's practical and consulting experience includes advanced information system designs for the U.S. Defense and Energy Departments. He is vice chair of the IFIP Working Group 8.2, and a Chartered Engineer under the British Engineering Council. Baskerville holds MSc and PhD degrees from the London School of Economics.

3

Characterizing IS Development Projects

Kees van Slooten and Bert Hodes
School of Management Studies, University of Twente
P.O. Box 217, 7500 AE Enschede, The Netherlands
E-mail: cvs@sms.utwente.nl

Abstract

The relationship between project context and project situation is described by defining a number of contingency factors and components of a project approach. The applied contingency model is based on existing literature about situated method engineering. Relationships between contingency factors and the components of the project approach are analyzed for nine non-standard projects of the systems development department of a bank organization. The conclusion is that the choices of project managers concerning the project approach can be related to the project situation. The result of this research is a starting point for a contingency approach of information systems development projects in a bank.

Keywords

Systems development, situated methods, method engineering

1 INTRODUCTION

During a field-study, the organization of the information systems development process of a major bank in the Netherlands was investigated. Up to now, centralization of computer-based data processing was the main approach, including one standard approach to information systems development. However, more specific requests from clients and an increasing dynamic environment require more flexibility and variety from the applied approaches to information systems development. New trends in technology like client/server, relational database, fourth generation tools, end-user computing, object orientation, office automation, groupware and multimedia will influence information systems development. Consequently, one standard approach to information systems development will not suffice and more situation-specific approaches will be necessary. The need for situation-specific approaches has also been emphasized by: Kumar and Welke (1992), Van Slooten and Brinkkemper (1993), Vessey and Glass (1994).

The concept of Methodology Engineering has been an attempt of Kumar and Welke to define the next level of evolution of methodologies. They discuss the need to customize methodologies to meet the requirements of the development context. Van Slooten and Brinkkemper prefer the term Method Engineering instead of Methodology Engineering. Subsequently, we follow the terminology of Van Slooten and Brinkkemper, and especially of Van Slooten (1995).

Method Engineering is performed by configuring a project approach or situated method for systems development, utilizing existing method fragments to serve the project in context. Figure 1 is a simplified representation of situated method engineering. Method fragments are coherent components of existing methods. The project context includes the existing systems development organization, the customer organization, the supplier organization, the area of application, information and computerization policies, etc. Contextual or contingency factors, derived from the project context, are important for the entire method engineering process (arrow 1). However, it may sometimes be desirable to change the project context as a result of the method engineering process (arrow 2).

The configuration process comprises characterizing the project and selecting or constructing a situated method. The most important project contingency factors are determined during project characterization as a result of interviewing, brain storming sessions, questionnaires or other knowledge acquisition techniques. The prevalent contingency factors are utilized for the selection or construction of a situated method (arrow 5). This is supported by a method engineering information system, consisting of formalized rules and a method base. The components of the method base are method fragments and route maps. Route maps are plans associated with development strategies, including the activities to be performed and the products to be delivered. The method engineering information system can be considered as a knowledge-based information system supporting the configuration process. It contains method fragments and route maps for the construction of a situated method (arrow 6).

A systems development project is initially started, using the situated method determined during the configuration process (arrow 3).

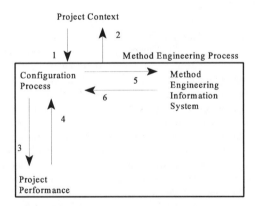

Figure 1. Situated Method Engineering

Unforeseen contingency factors may arise during project performance necessitating im provements and/or clarifications of the project characterization and an adjustment of the situated method (arrow 4). Evaluations during and after project performance may yield new knowledge about situated systems development, which is stored by the method engineering information system (included by arrow 4 and 5).

The bank organization is in the middle of a process of developing a new architecture for information systems development in which the contingency approach takes a central position. This means that various approaches must be available from which the best fitting is chosen depending on the project context. Also Necco (1987) already said that guidelines should be developed within the organization to provide direction for various approaches, which the organization selects for its systems development process. However, before formulating guidelines, it is necessary to know more about possible choice alternatives, prevalent contingency factors, and the relationship between the contingency factors (section 2) and the choice alternatives (section 3). The contingency model (section 2.1) is based on a situated method engineering approach (figure 1, after Van Slooten 1995). The choice alternatives have been made explicit after analyzing the existing practice of information systems development projects within the bank organization. The analysis of actual projects in practice also made some relationships between contingency factors and project approaches available (section 4). Projects selected for this research, are non-standard projects. We avoided standard projects, because standard approaches are linked to standard projects, which will not reveal much information about the relationship between contingency factors and choice alternatives. Furthermore, the research was focused on choices that can be made by project managers, and not on decision making by higher or lower levels of agents in the organization, which is outside the scope of this research.

2   CONTINGENCIES AND CONSTRAINTS

2.1 The contingency model

The contingency model of this research is based on the situated method engineering approach of figure 1. But the focus of this field study is on determining contingency factors as components of the project context, eliciting route maps and method fragments as components of possible project approaches, and relating contingency factors and project approaches (figure 2). The components of approaches may consist of methods, techniques, and tools for information systems development as well as for project management. This means an extension of the definition of method fragments. Contingency factors are variables from the project context with a certain value between Low (L) and High (H) that affect the project approach. Constraints can be considered as a specific kind of contingency factors causing limitations for the approach.

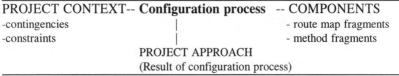

Figure 2   Contingency model

2.2 Contingency factors

The explicitation of contingency factors is based on the work of Van Der Hoef et al. (1995). They composed a list of contingency factors and constraints, which is the product of collecting and integrating existing lists from various sources. However, we removed some inconsistencies from this list and selected the most important factors for the field study according to experts of the bank. Some factors, which have the same value for each project (e.g. the quality of information planning), are outside the scope of the field study. Other factors are a generalization or a specialization of the factors of Van Der Hoef et al. Finally, the list of contingency factors is:

- *Management commitment*. To what extent management supports the project.
- *Importance*. To what extent the project or information system is important for the organization.
- *Impact*. To what extent the information system will change business operation after implementation.
- *Resistance and conflict*. To what extent stakeholders have different or conflicting interests.
- *Time pressure*. To what extent the available time for the project is experienced as insufficient.
- *Shortage of human resources*. To what extent the number of people available for the project is experienced as insufficient.
- *Shortage of means*. To what extent the means available for the project are experienced as insufficient.
- *Formality*. To what extent there are lasting rules, procedures, and standards for the business processes and supporting information.
- *Knowledge and experience*. To what extent the users possess enough knowledge and experience to develop the required information system.
- *Skills*. To what extent the members of the project-team possess enough knowledge and experience to develop the required information system.
- *Size*. The number of people being a member of the project-team.
- *Relationships*. To what extent there are relationships between the new information system and other information systems.
- *Dependency*. To what extent the project depends on activities and conditions outside the project.
- *Clarity*. To what extent the goals, needs, and desires of the users are clear and coherent enabling a sound specification of the functional requirements.
- *Stability*. To what extent the goals, needs, and desires of the users will not change over

time enabling a stable specification of the functional requirements.
- *Complexity.* To what extent the functional components of the information system are complex.
- *Level of innovation.* To what extent the applied technology and/or the applied methods, techniques, and tools are new to the organization.

2.3 Constraints

Constraints are specific contingency factors without a relative value between Low (L) and High (H), but they definitely affect the project approach. Constraints are specific circumstances restricting the number of choice alternatives and affecting the relationships between contingency factors and project approach. The influence of constraints on these relationships is outside the scope of this field study. One may distinguish five kinds of constraints: Contracts, Type of information system, Standards, Technical constraints, and External factors. We do not want to go into detail, because it is not part of this research.

3   CHOICE ALTERNATIVES

3.1 Definitions

The situated method engineering approach contains two kinds of building blocks: route maps and method fragments. To describe the situation of the bank more precisely, we shall define the concepts *route map fragment* and *method fragment* as follows.
A *route map fragment* is a coherent part of the complete route map of a systems development project. A route map fragment may refer to strategies, activities, and products concerning systems development as well as project management.
A *method fragment* is a coherent part of a method(ology) for systems development or project management. Method fragments may be linked to a route map, which may establish a complete project approach or a situated method.

3.2 Route map fragments

Tracing and dividing
One of the first activities of a project manager is to determine the scope of the project in co-operation with the users. We distinguish two possibilities for tracing the business functions for the project: *tight (T)* and *wide (W)*. Tight tracing means that the functionality required will partly be realized outside the project. Wide tracing means that the functionality required will be completely realized during the project. Related to tracing the functionality is dividing the functionality into subsystems, which will be developed separately. We distinguish: *one system (o)* and *subsystems (s)*.

Delivery strategy
The delivery strategy is the way of delivering and introducing the information system in the organization. We distinguish three options: *at once (o)*, *incremental (i)*, and

evolutionary (e).
- (o). Delivery at once means that the entire system is delivered at once.
- (i). Incremental delivery means that the system is delivered by a serial delivery of subsystems, each containing a part of the functionality.
- (e). Evolutionary delivery means that the system is delivered by successive versions of the entire system partly containing the entire functionality. Functional requirements may change between two versions.

The delivery strategy deals with subsystems and not with subprojects. The distinction between subsystems and subprojects is important throughout this paper. Different stages of developing one (sub)system may be realized by different subprojects.

Realization strategy

The realization strategy is the way of realizing the various subsystems with respect to sequence and concurrence. We distinguish four options: *at once (a)*, *concurrent (c)*, *overlapping (o)*, and *incremental (i)*.
- (a). Realization at once means that the entire information system is developed at once.
- (c). Concurrent realization means that all subsystems are concurrently developed.
- (o). Overlapping realization means that some subsystems are concurrently developed and other subsystems consecutively.
- (i). Incremental realization means that all subsystems are developed one after another.

Establishing subprojects

There are several ways to divide information systems development into subprojects. We distinguish four options: *one project (o)*, *process-oriented (p)*, *system-oriented (s)*, and *hybrid (h)*.
- (o). One project means no division into subprojects.
- (p). Process-oriented means division into subprojects based on information system development subprocesses.
- (s). System-oriented means division into subprojects based on subsystems.
- (h). Hybrid means division into subprojects partly based on subprocesses and partly on subsystems.

Project organization

Of course, one needs a project organization to run the project. Decisions have to be taken about who is involved and who is responsible for what takes place. A communication structure is provided describing on which levels communication is necessary and its frequency. The project manager may choose a *standard (s)* or an *adapted (a)* structure for the project organization.

Project management products and activities

Other activities of project management are for example: estimating risks, determining the required means, investigating the consequences of the project. These activities, plans and reports concern the performance of the project. These project management products may be *standard (s)* or *adapted (a)*. In the first case the format and the contents are well defined. In the second case we have to deal with more informal project control.

Development strategy

The development strategy is a generic strategy for the sequence and the selection of activities supporting the development of a system (that is) not further divided into subsystems. Also based on Van Slooten and Schoonhoven (1994) we distinguish five options: *phase-wise (p)*, *tile-wise (t)*, *prototyping (g)*, *iterative (i)*, *outsourcing (o)*.

- (p). Phase-wise is strict linear development without prototyping.
- (t). Tile-wise is linear development with partly overlapping phases.
- (g). Prototyping is linear development including prototyping, so-called throwaway prototyping. During functional design a prototype is built to improve the functional requirements or to show the feasibility of a certain technology.
- (i). Iterative or keep-it prototyping. The cycle of analysis, design, implementation and evaluation is reiterated several times. After each iteration the system may be adapted until there are no additional requirements.
- (o). Outsourcing or software package selection means that the system is not developed by the bank organization. Before outsourcing the functional requirements are determined by the bank organization. Required modifications of a software package are realized by the supplier.

System development products and activities

Project management determines which system development products must be delivered. There is a standard list of products, but the project manager may construct his own list if he has good reasons to do so. The products may describe different aspects of the business system and/or the information system. System development activities must be determined to develop the products. Possible options are *standard (s)* and *adapted (a)*.

- (s). Standard if the standard list is used.
- (a). Adapted if the standard list is not completely used.

3.3 Method fragments

Method fragments may come from methods, techniques, and tools for project management as well as systems development. There is a standard way of working for project management, which is described in a manual. The manual contains descriptions of activities for project management and techniques and tools that should be applied. This means that the project manager has two options: *standard (s)* and *adapted (a)*.

- (s). Standard means that the project manager follows the manual to the letter.
- (a). Adapted means that he changes the standard.

Methods, techniques, and tools for systems development deal with the contents of the information system that must be developed. The standard method for the bank organization is Method/1 and a few other tools for specific tasks. This means that here too there are two options: *standard (s)* and *adapted (a)*.

4   RESEARCH APPROACH AND RESULTS

4.1 Projects

The following nine projects, with deviations from the standard approach to systems development within the bank organization, have been selected for this field study:

- Developing an information system establishing data administration to enter the exchange market of shares for a major telecommunication organization in Holland.
- Realizing some changes in information systems supporting business in stocks, which is necessary for maintaining a certain service-level and realizing some changes.
- Developing a new information system dealing with information supporting questions and complaints concerning foreign promotion activities.
- Developing an information system for processing guaranteed means of payment such as cheques, utilizing imaging technology.
- Enhancing a voice-response application with functionality for transactions by phone.
- Re-designing the back-office for business in stocks by developing an information system based on a software package for storing stock transactions.
- Modifying a number of heavy applications to decrease the workload of the mainframe computers.
- Developing an information system that is capable of collecting, enriching, storing, and distributing data from various central databases, supporting various accounting information systems.
- Developing a pilot information system in a client/server environment, supporting the communication between advisers and clients.

Table 1 represents the contingency factors related to the fragments of approaches to systems development for the nine projects. Deviations from the standard approach are printed in bold type. The contingency factors may have the following values: l (low), n (normal), or h (high). These values are determined by interviewing the project managers and by sending them a questionnaire to respond. Some contingency factors did not cause a deviation from the standard, e.g. the factor 'resistance and conflict'. Sometimes, the standard approach may allow more than one value of a contingency factor or approach fragment. The standard approach is defined as follows: (Tracing = tight, Dividing = one system, Delivery Strategy = at once, Realization Strategy = at once, Establishing Subprojects = one project, Project Organization = standard, Project Management Products and Activities = standard, Development Strategy = phase-wise, Systems development Products and Activities = standard, Project Management Method Fragments = standard, Systems Development Method Fragments = standard).

Table 1   Contingency factors and approaches for the nine projects

Contingency factors	*1*	*2*	*3*	*4*	*5*	*6*	*7*	*8*	*9*
Management commitment	h	h	n	n	n	h	n	n	h
Importance	h	h	h	h	h	h	h	h	h
Impact	n	h	h	h	n	h	n	h	n
Resistance and Conflict	l	n	n	n	n	n	n	n	n
Time pressure	h	h	n	n	n	n	h	n	h
Shortage of human resources	h	h	l	l	l	l	n	n	l
Shortage of means	l	l	n	n	n	n	n	n	l
Formality	h	h	h	h	h	h	h	l	l
Knowledge and experience	h	h	h	h	h	h	h	h	h
Skills	h	h	n	n	n	l	h	n	n
Size	h	h	n	n	h	n	h	h	n
Relationships	n	h	h	h	h	h	h	h	n
Dependency	n	h	l	l	h	h	n	l	l
Clarity	h	n	h	h	h	l	h	l	l
Stability	n	l	n	l	l	l	h	l	l
Complexity	l	h	n	n	h	h	h	h	h
Level of innovation	l	l	h	h	h	h	l	h	h

Approach

	1	*2*	*3*	*4*	*5*	*6*	*7*	*8*	*9*
Tracing (*t=tight, w=wide*)	t	t	t	w	w	w	w	w	t
Dividing (*o=one system, s=subsystems*)	s	s	s	s	s	o	s	s	o
Delivery Strategy (*o=at once, i=incremental, e=evolutionary*)	o	e	i	o	o	o	i	i	o
Realization Strategy (*a=at once, c=concurrent, o=overlapping, i=incremental*)	c	o	o	c	c	a	o	o	a
Establishing Subprojects (*o=one project, p=process-oriented, s=system-oriented, h=hybrid*)	h	h	s	o	o	p	h	h	o
Project Organization (*s=standard, a=adapted*)	a	a	a	s	s	a	a	a	a
Project Management Products and Activities (*s=standard, a=adapted*)	a	s	s	s	s	a	a	s	s
Development Strategy (*p=phase-wise, t=tile-wise, g=prototyping, i=iterative, o=outsourcing*)	to	t	po	po	to	o	t	tgi	i
Systems Development Products and Activities (*s=standard, a=adapted*)	a	s	a	s	s	a	a	s	a
Project Management Method Fragments (*s=standard, a=adapted*)	s	s	s	s	s	a	s	s	s
Systems Development Method Fragments (*s=standard, a=adapted*)	s	a	s	s	s	a	a	a	a

4.2 Discussion of relationships

Management commitment and importance

The factors *management commitment* and *importance* are considered as one factor, because it was difficult to deal with these factors separately. The importance of the project and commitment of management affect the project a lot. Cooperation and flexibility of groups of specialists in the organization will increase considerably if one can rely upon strong interest of management, implying a project of high priority. However, the influence on the actual approach is limited, only the project organization was adapted for three projects that were of great importance.

Project organization. A first consequence was to involve senior employees as a kind of sponsor of the projects, which means decisions will be taken at a higher level. During one project, a board of managers of various business units was available to take important decisions. A second consequence, if we have to deal with high time pressure as well, was including people from the department for computer and network facilities responsible for the technical operation of systems.

Impact

The influence of developing an information system on the users organization depends on to what extent business operation will change because of implementing the system. Important aspects are the number of people for whom work will change and to what extent the work itself will change. The impact of the information system hardly affects the approach to the project. Five of the nine projects had to deal with high impact, one of which had to change the delivery strategy.

Delivery strategy. The delivery strategy for standard projects is delivery of the whole system at once. It was already mentioned that for only one project, impact of the information system was a reason for choosing another delivery strategy, namely an evolutionary strategy. Changing the users organization at once should not be acceptable.

Time pressure

We have to deal with projects that have a deadline. Time pressure increases if the available time becomes much less than the time needed. The high time pressure for four of the nine projects affected a number of approach fragments: tracing, realization strategy, project organization, project management products and activities, development strategy, and systems development products and activities.

Tracing. High time pressure was a reason to limit the functionality of the information system for the time being. A small and simple application with limited functionality can be realized in a shorter time.

Realization Strategy. For three projects, high time pressure was a reason for choosing a concurrent or overlapping realization. Concurrent development of all subsystems should occur as much as possible to decrease the time elapsed for the whole project. Sometimes, a concurrent realization strategy was not possible because of a lack of human resources. In that case, an overlapping realization strategy was chosen.

Project Organization. High time pressure affected the project organization in different ways:

- To tune activities, oral communication was emphasized instead of written documents saving a lot of time.
- Utilizing external workers if nobody else is available. Generally, external workers lack knowledge about the existing systems. Consequently, projects were organized enabling cooperation between internal and external workers.
- Keeping people from specific departments like quality assurance, system management, or computer and network facilities (production management) outside the project organization, if their contribution can be missed.
- Including people from the production management department (computer and network facilities) into the project, if one may expect problems during the transfer of the system, ready for actual operation, to the production management department.

Project Management Products and Activities. Due to time pressure it was decided for one project to deliver only a limited number of project management products like plans for quality assurance, risk management, approach to the project, documentation management, etc.

Development Strategy. Due to time pressure the following development strategies were selected:

- A tile-wise development strategy means that the next phase will start before the current phase is finished. Formal approval of one or more phases was postponed, because this takes time. Sometimes two or more phases were turned into one phase to save time.
- Because of time pressure or shortage of human resources an outsourcing strategy was frequently chosen. The functional requirements were determined by the bank, after which the remaining phases were established by an external organization. However, accepting and introducing the system were again internal activities.

Systems Development Products and Activities. Because of time pressure sometimes only systems development products and connected activities were selected which were absolutely necessary. Sometimes other products were delivered instead of the products, prescribed, if it speeded up the process. It is easier to obtain approval for delivering less or other products if the importance of the project is high.

Shortage of human resources

In only two of the nine projects the shortage of human resources was high. This contingency factor affected the project organization and the delivery strategy.

Project Organization. The shortage of human resources was resolved by hiring external workers if the budget for the project was sufficient.

Delivery Strategy. In one project, shortage of resources was a reason for partly outsourcing systems development. Because of time pressure it was not possible to postpone systems development.

Formality

In seven out of nine projects the formality was high as in standard projects. This contingency factor only affected the systems development products and activities.

Systems Development Products and Activities. In two projects with a high value for formality less products were made, because some products to be made were similar to already existing system documents, e.g. the data model, which means that in such cases it was possible to use existing products.

Size

The size of five projects was high (more than ten persons). The following approach fragments were affected by the size of the project: tracing, dividing, realization strategy, and establishing subprojects.

Tracing. Problems with the management of a project will arise if many people are working for the project at the same time. Therefore, it was tried to trace the project as tight as possible, which means postponing or deleting functionality, if not absolutely necessary. Another way of limiting the size of a project is lengthening the time for the project. However, this was not possible because of a fixed deadline.

Dividing. The size of the project was mentioned most often as the reason to divide the system into subsystems. Therefore, the functionality was divided into coherent subsystems enabling independent development of these subsystems.

Realization Strategy. In a number of projects was chosen for an overlapping strategy instead of realization at once, because of the size of the project. Through realizing the subsystems partly in sequence instead of all subsystems concurrently, it was possible to limit the size of the project. Further decreasing the size of the project by using an incremental realization strategy was often not possible because of high time pressure.

Establishing subprojects. Establishing subprojects was affected for some projects by the size of the project. Generally, subprojects are established for recognized subsystems. However, size was the reason for a number of projects to choose a hybrid approach for establishing subprojects, which means that also for certain phases of the systems development process different subprojects are established.

Dependency

Dependency was high for three projects, but the approach of these projects was hardly affected, only dividing into subsystems.

Dividing. Dividing into subsystems was affected by the dependency of other activities in only one project. There was a strong dependency of a system in the middle of a development process. Therefore, it was decided to consider the functionality that was dependent on another project as a separate subsystem. This subsystem was developed after the other project had been finished.

Clarity and stability

The reason for joining clarity and stability of the functional requirements is that the approach was only affected by instability of the functional requirements if, at the same time, clarity of the functional requirements was low. There was also a relationship between the formality of the business processes, and the clarity and stability of the functional requirements. If the formality was low, then the clarity and stability of the functional requirements were also low. Unclear functional requirements affected the tracing of the functionality and the development strategy. Instability of the functional requirements only affected the development strategy.

Tracing. Unclear requirements of users were the reason for one project to limit initially the functionality of the system. A large number of interest groups put forward their own specific and often conflicting ideas about the application. Consequently, functionality was restricted to common requirements.

Development Strategy. An iterative development strategy was chosen for two projects instead of the usual phase-wise development strategy, because of unclear and unstable user requirements. The requirements were determined and realized during a first development cycle, after which the user could improve his requirements by using the application developed. A precondition for choosing such a strategy is the availability of CASE-tools that facilitate a rapid application development.

Complexity

For six projects complexity was high. The complexity of the functional components of the system affected the way of tracing and dividing functionality, establishing subprojects, project organization, the development strategy, and the systems development method fragments.

Tracing. High complexity of the required functionality was for two projects the reason for limiting functionality with consequently fewer problems during systems development.
Dividing. High complexity of the system was during one project one of the reasons for dividing the functionality into subsystems. The functionality was divided into two subsystems. Different kinds of expertise were required for developing these subsystems.
Establishing Subprojects. In a number of projects the complexity was a reason for choosing a process-oriented or hybrid approach to establish subprojects for certain processes or phases of systems development. In two cases it was decided to test the application in a separate subproject. In another project with many modifications of existing systems the analysis phase of these systems was established in a separate subproject because of the complexity and the different kind of expertise that was needed for the various systems. Finally, in one project complexity was the reason for realizing a data model in a separate subproject, because specific knowledge was necessary, which was not available in the project-team of the systems development department.
Project Organization. In one project, complexity was the reason for involving people with specific expertise from various departments. One dealt with a technical migration project including technical improvements of existing systems. Because of the complexity it was decided to add experts in databases, hard systems software, etc. to the project-team.
Development Strategy. In one project the complexity was the reason for choosing a tile-wise development strategy. A badly documented system had to be modified. It was decided to start a functional and technical design as partly overlapping phases enabling a clear specification of what should be modified. In another project complexity was the reason for choosing an outsourcing strategy, because an existing software package was more appropriate than internal development of a new application.
Systems Development Method Fragments. In two projects, high complexity was the reason for applying other tools than standardly available. In one project monitoring tools supporting the analysis of complex systems were necessary. In another project a tool for testing programs was necessary, because of the complexity of the interaction of many interacting subsystems.

Level of innovation

In principle, the applied technology is part of the approach in correspondence with functionality. However, during the nine projects the technology was mostly supplied by the users organization. Up to now the central mainframe was the standard platform for running the applications, which means that other environments like LAN, WAN, or PC are new. The level of innovation was high in non-mainframe environments (six projects). The level of innovation affected the division of the system, the project organization, the development strategy, the systems development products and activities, and the systems development method fragments.

Dividing. In three projects the level of innovation was a reason to divide the system into subsystems. The functionality was divided into two subsystems. One was realized on the mainframe (communication with central systems and processing of central data) and the other on the decentralized environment (the actual application).

Project Organization. In two projects the level of innovation was the reason to involve external workers in the project organization. They participated in project- and working groups with the intention of knowledge transfer from the external workers to the workers of the bank. In other projects of a high level of innovation outsourcing the innovative part of the application was preferred (see also effect on the development strategy). Mutual adjustment of the functional specifications was necessary in this case, enabling the co-operation between the internal and external parts of the application.

Development Strategy. The high level of innovation did affect the development strategy of various projects. It depends on the question whether the organization likes to acquire more knowledge of the new technology or not. In two projects an innovative system was developed in cooperation with an external supplier. For one of these systems, the high level of innovation was the reason for choosing a prototyping strategy. A prototype was constructed to estimate the feasibility of the new technology. An iterative development strategy was used for the development of the prototype. The final specifications were determined by evaluating and modifying the prototype. In the other project (pilot) the prototype was experimental, which meant in this case that the desirability and feasibility of a new kind of application was investigated. An iterative development strategy was chosen again. In three other projects with no intention of transferring knowledge, an outsourcing strategy was chosen for the development of the innovative part of the application. Outsourcing of the development of a subsystem also affects the project management products and activities. In this case, one has to deal with a contract with the external supplier, but such activities are mostly the responsibility of the user's organization with some assistance of a special department. The systems development department is responsible for the control of the contents of the activities of the external workers.

Systems Development Products and Activities. In one of the projects the high level of innovation was the reason to perform other activities and deliver other products than usual. The alternative environment and the tools available enabled another way of developing information systems. The usual systems development products did not fit here, because these usual products were based on the development of mainframe applications.

Systems Development Method Fragments. In one project the high level of innovation was the reason for not applying the standard methodology Method/1. The systems development activities and their sequence was determined by common sense. In two innovative projects the presence of new technology was the reason for applying new tools like: fourth generation environments, object-oriented programming languages, and tools for developing graphical user interfaces. These kinds of tools have until now not been applied in the mainframe environment of the bank, but only in client/server environments.

5 CONCLUSIONS AND FURTHER RESEARCH

This research shows that the project approach is affected by the project context, in spite of the present standards, procedures, and uniform way of working. Generally, a contingency approach to systems development was not supported by the bank organization. A project manager may construct a project approach by choosing various components of an approach as described by this paper. There are several options available for each component of an approach. In the former section it was described how the choices were affected by the contingency factors of the project situation. Some contingency factors did not affect the project approach at all (table 1). It was possible to explain the choices made by the project manager using the current set of contingency factors. However, this does not mean that the current set is the ultimate set of contingency factors for this organization. It is a starting point for further research. We have already seen that sometimes two contingency factors can be handled as one factor, e.g. *management commitment* and *importance*, *clarity* and *stability*. Of course, this research has some limitations:

- The projects have not been evaluated.
- Too few projects have been analyzed in order to support this research with quantitative results.

This means that the found relationships between contingency factors and project approach do not necessarily guarantee a 'best' approach. The relationships found are based on choices made by senior project managers.

This research aims to contribute to the development of a contingency model for systems development projects. Further research must be focused on the determination of successful relationships between the project context and the project approach by evaluating chosen project approaches depending on the situational factors, i.e. contingency factors including constraints.

6 REFERENCES

Hoef, R. van der, et al. (1995), Situatie, Scenario en Succes (Dutch), Memoranda Informatica, Internal Technical Report, University of Twente.

Kumar, K., R.J.Welke (1992), Methodology Engineering: A Proposal for Situation-Specific Methodology Construction. In: *Challenges and Strategies for Research in Systems Development*, Wiley and Sons Ltd.

Necco, C.R., et al. (1987), Systems Analysis and Design: Current Practices. In: *MIS Quarterly*, 11, 4.

Slooten, C. van, S. Brinkkemper (1993), A Method Engineering Approach to Information Systems Development. In: *Information Systems Development Process*, Proceedings IFIP WG 8.1, Elsevier Science Publishers (North-Holland).

Slooten, C. van (1995), Situated Methods for Systems Development, Thesis, University of Twente.

Slooten, C. van, B. Schoonhoven (1994), Towards Contingent Information Systems Development Approaches, In: *Methods and Tools, Theory and Practice*, Proceedings of ISD'94, Bled.

Vessey, I., R.L. Glass (1994), Application-Based Methodologies: Development by Application Domain. In: *Information Systems Management*, Fall 1994.

4

Towards an integrated environment for method engineering

John C. Grundy and John R. Venable
Department of Computer Science, University of Waikato
Private Bag 3105, Hamilton, New Zealand
email: jgrundy@cs.waikato.ac.nz or jvenable@cs.waikato.ac.nz

Abstract
In order to facilitate better Information Systems Development (ISD), Method Engineering technqiues and tools are needed that support flexible creation, modification, and reuse of ISD methods and tools for use on specific problem domains. A metamodelling notation is needed for specifying and integrating different design notations. MetaCASE support is required for building, reusing and evolving tools for these design notations. Process modelling tools for both the coordination of these design notation tools and the evolution of software processes are also needed. We describe our work on developing an integrated environment which supports metamodelling, metaCASE and flexible software process modelling, and illustrate its use for supporting Method Engineering.

Keywords
Method engineering, metamodelling, metaCASE, software process modelling

1 INTRODUCTION

Information Systems Development (ISD) methodologies are generally assumed to be situation-independent. However, there are a multitude of different development methods and techniques that each have various advantages and disadvantages, some of which relate to the problem domain or the development context. A stream of research has developed investigating the possibility to choose, tailor, or engineer the development method accordingly. Kumar and Welke (Kumar, 1992) coined the term methodology engineering and postulated this new field, i.e. engineering a new ISD methodology by composing it from various techniques in order to address problems in a particular domain. Vessey and Glass (Vessey, 1994) noted that, in any case, system developers adapt and modify the methods that they use to the situation and their preferences. Recently, Harmsen and Brinkkemper (1995) found that due to the increasing complexity of Information Systems, development teams often require methods tailored to a particular system development situation, which they term Situational Method Engineering.

Developers may need to create a new method from scratch, modify (e.g. incrementally improve or tailor) an existing method, or reuse parts of various methods and techniques and recombine them into a new method, or any combination of the above. Developers may even need to modify and adapt the development method while the development process is ongoing. Our goal is to support this flexible sort of situational method engineering. In order to facilitate this, developers need flexible support for:

- Design notation metamodelling and notation integration. This allows developers to specify data models for the design notations they wish to use for development of a system, and in the case of multiple design notations, to specify common information that will be shared between the notations. Developers should be able to reuse all or parts of existing notations, and be able to integrate different notations when one notation best supports modelling part of the problem domain, and another notation is better suited to another.
- Tool construction facilities. These are used to build or modify CASE tools to support the various design notations to be used. This includes the ability to keep information shared by different design notations consistent i.e. to keep different notation repository information consistent under change. Developers also need to specify the editors and rendering of notation data models they desire.
- Software process modelling and work coordination. Process modelling specifies which notations and tools will be used for different aspects of the system under development. Work coordination support is needed to coordinate tool usage. Evolution and reuse of process models allows developers to improve their development processes from one project to another. Modelling the Method Engineering process itself provides a meta-process level which helps to improve Method Engineering on subsequent projects.

Ideally a Method Engineering environment should support all of these activities in an integrated fashion. Developers should be able to define and/or reuse software processes either for developing a new system or for modifying an existing system and its existing descriptions. They should be able to tailor existing design notations in either case. CASE tools supporting the required notations should be built using the notation metamodels as repository specifications, and common information in different tool repositories should be kept consistent. Developers should be able to flexibly define and revise software processes during system development, and be able to reuse these models on new projects.

   Our approach is to combine techniques and tools from three distinct, yet related, areas of our recent research. We have developed the CoCoA meta-modelling notation (Venable 1993, Venable 1995) and have used this for design notation metamodelling and integration (Grundy, 1995a, Grundy, 1995b, Venable, 1995). We have developed the MViews framework for constructing CASE tools and integrated Information Systems Engineering Environments (ISEEs) (Grundy, 1993, Grundy, 1995a) and used this to develop ISEEs which support multiple design notations [Grundy95a, Grundy95b]. Recently we have been developing a tool for the coordination of work in CSCW systems (Grundy, 1995c), which also supports flexible software process modelling. This paper describes our current work developing an integrated environment for the definition, construction and coordination of ISEEs using these techniques.

2   RELATED RESEARCH

Current approaches to notation integration, CASE and metaCASE, and method engineering support tools, go some way to addressing the Method Engineering aims from Section 1, but do not completely satisfy them. Some work has been done on the static integration of notations. Venable (1993) has performed detailed analyses and integrations of both data flow models and conceptual data models. Campbell and Halpin (1994) have analysed levels of abstraction for conceptual schemas. Falkenberg and Oei (1994) have proposed a metamodel hierarchy.

Wieringa (1995) has compared JSD, ER modelling and DFD modelling. Data modelling has been used to compare different notations (Nuseibeh, 1992) and support methodology engineering (Heym, 1992). Process-modelling has also been applied to compare and integrate notations (Song, 1992).

Integrated ISEEs (or Integrated CASE tools and programming environments) allow designers to analyse, design, and implement Information Systems from within one environment, providing a consistent user interace and consistent repository (data dictionary). They help to minimise inconsistencies that can arise when using several separate tools for information systems development (Wasserman, 1987, Reiss, 1990). These ICASE environments allow developers to analyse and design software using a variety of different notations, with limited inter-notation consistency. Such tools do not generally support complex mappings between the design notations, such as propagating an ER relationship addition to a corresponding OOA/D or NIAM diagram. As an example, Software thru Pictures™ (Wasserman, 1987) uses a single metamodel repository for all notation diagrams, although it only supports basic forms of internotation consistency. The implementation of these environments is generally not sufficient to allow different design notations to be effectively integrated, and consistency between design and implementation code is often not maintained (Meyers, 1991). For example, MethodMaker from Mark V Systems (Mark, 1995a) allows new notations and methods to be built, but provides very limited inter-notation consistency management facilities. FIELD (Reiss, 1990) and Dora (Ratcliffe, 1992) provide abstractions for keeping multiple tools and textual and graphical views consistent under change. They do not, however, provide any mechanism for propagating changes between views which can not be directly applied by the environment, such as ER relationship changes to NIAM or OOA/D relationship changes. Thus changes which can not be automatically translated to another notation are not supported.

Process-centred environments utilise information about software processes to enforce or guide development. Examples include Marvel (Barghouti, 1992), CPCE (Lonchamp, 1995), and ConversationBuilder (Kaplan, 1992). These environments usually provide low-level text-based descriptions of work rationale, and often do not effectively handle restructuring of development processes while in use (Swenson, 1993). ProcessMaker (Mark, 1995b) supports the definition and use of multiple process diagrams, but only supports limited integration and no event handling for I-CASE tools. Computer-Aided Method Engineering (CAME) tools, such as Decamerone (Harmsen, 1995) and Method Base (Saeki, 1993), provide support for configuring development processes and tools to a particular application, but often utilise complex textual specifications, and don't facilitate coordination of different notation tools during development.

3 THE COCOA META-MODELLING LANGUAGE

3.1 CoCoA

We have been using the CoCoA conceptual data modeling language (Venable, 1993) as a meta-model for modelling Information System Modelling Languages (ISMLs). CoCoA is designed to support modelling of complex problem domains and extends existing Entity Relationship (ER) models. Figure 1 depicts the seven main CoCoA abstractions. Entities are the things in a problem domain and attributes describe and/or identify them (Figure 1 (a)). Named relationships have the semantics of ER relationships, and are composed of named roles, played by entities. Cardinality constraints are indicated with each role (Figure 1 (b)). CoCoA supports generalization and specialization, and where specialization is based on a partitioning attribute, that attribute is shown (Figure 1 (c)). CoCoA extends other ER models by the implicit use of categories, allowing the entity planing a role in a named elationship to be one of one or more entity types, shown by connecting more than one entity (type) to the same role (Figure 1 (d)). CoCoA derives its name from a fifth data modelling concept, that of <u>Co</u>mplex <u>Co</u>vering

Aggregation. Covering aggregation distinguishes the aggregation of entities into composite entities from the aggregation of attributes into entities. Complex covering aggregation is distinguished from simple covering aggregation in that aggregation of named relationships into the composite entity is allowed (Figure 1 (e)). CoCoA supports aliases, which are useful for model integration, showing old local names together with standardized names for synonyms (Figure 1 (f)). Derived concepts (attributes, entities, named relationships, or covering aggregation relationships) are annotated with a '*' (Figure 1 (g)).

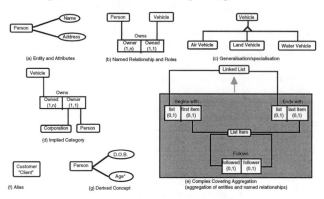

Figure 1   The CoCoA model notation.

3.2   MetaModelling with CoCoA

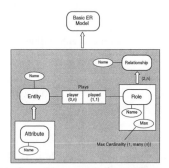

Figure 2   Metamodel of core ER concepts.

We have used CoCoA to derive conceptual data models for the ER, NIAM, DFD, STD and OOA/D design notations. As an example, the data model describing the fundamental abstractions of ER models is shown in Figure 2. Enities are named and have zero or more named attributes. Relationships are named and have two or more named roles. Roles link entities and relationships and may include a maximum cardinality. Extensions to this basic ER schema include provision for entity subtyping, optional and mandatory roles, and distinguished key attributes of entities (Venable, 1993).

Figure 3 shows NIAM's main abstractions. A NIAM entity is named and may have a reference, made by one or more named labels. Fact types are named and have one or more roles. The "derived" attribute of the fact type entity is marked as derived (by the asterisk) because its value is true if it is related to a derivation rule. Roles link entities to facts, and are named. Nested fact types are both entities and facts, i.e. they have roles but also behave as entities, being linked to zero or more facts via further roles. A CoCoA model of other NIAM constraints is omitted for brevity, but can be found in (Venable, 1993). NIAM derivation rules are not specified further because they are not fully specified by Nijssen and Halpin (1989). Other notation meta-models can be found in (Venable, 1993, Grundy, 1995a).

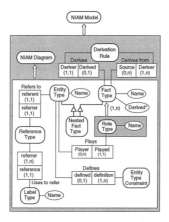

Figure 3   Metamodel of core NIAM concepts.

3.3   Notation MetaModel Integration with CoCoA

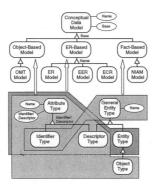

Figure 4   An integrated conceptual data model.

We have developed integrated data models which capture the overlaps between ER, EER, OMT's object model, and NIAM. Figure 4 shows a *partial* metamodel integrating the entity and attribute data modelling aspects of ER, EER, NIAM, and OMT. The ER and OMT models differentiate between entities and attributes, whereas NIAM integrates these concepts into a general entity type. The main difference between the OMT and ER conceptual data models is OMT's support for class methods. The overlaps between the notations are indicated by covering aggregation showing the composition of each data model from the integrated data model entities and relationships. Further discussion of these and of relationship type classifications is in (Venable, 1993).

4   THE MVIEWS FRAMEWORK

4.1   MViews

Our design notation environments are implemented as a collection of Snart classes, specialised from the MViews framework (Grundy, 1993). MViews supports the construction of new ISEEs by providing a general model for defining software system data structures and tool views, with a flexible mechanism for propagating changes between software components, views and distinct software development tools. Figure 5 shows an example of the structure of SPE, an ISEE for object-oriented software development. ISEE data is described as *components* with *attributes*, linked by a variety of *relationships*. Multiple views are supported by representing each view as a graph linked to the base software system graph structure. Each view is rendered and edited in either a graphical or textual form. Distinct environment tools can be interfaced at the view level (as editors), via external view translators, or multiple base layers may be connected via inter-view relationships, as described in (Grundy, 1994).

When a software or view component is updated, a change description is generated. This is of the form UpdateKind(UpdatedComponent, ...UpdateKind-specific Values...). For example, an attribute update on Comp1 of attribute Name is represented as: update(Comp1,Name,OldValue,NewValue). All basic graph editing operations generate change descriptions and pass them to the propagation system. Change descriptions are propagated to all related components that are dependent upon the updated component's state. Dependents interpret these change descriptions and possibly modify their own state, producing further change descriptions. This change description mechanism supports a diverse range of software development environment facilities, including semantic attribute recalculation, multiple views of a component, flexible, bi-directional textual and graphical view consistency management, a generic undo/redo mechanism, and component "modification history" information (Grundy, 1995d). New environments are constructed by reusing abstractions provided by an object-oriented framework, and ISEE developers specialise MViews classes to define software components, views and editing tools. A persistent object store is used to store component and view data.

MViews environments support version control and collaborative facilities via the C-MViews extensions to MViews (Grundy, 1995d). Version revision, alternates and merging are supported by having change descriptions cached in a number of version records for components and views. Merging of alternate versions is carried out by successively reapplying one alternate's change descriptions to the other alternate component. Any merge conflicts (structural or semantic) are presented to the merging user. Semi-synchronous and synchronous editors are provided for views by propagating change descriptions on a view to other users' environments as they occur. With semi-synchronous editing, these change descriptions are presented to collaborating users, who may then choose to incorporate them into their own view alternatives. For synchronous editing, a central server "owns" the shared view, and all edits must be sent to this server for actioning and propagation to other users. Fine-grained view component locking is maintained by the server to ensure no simultaneous component update is permitted by multiple users.

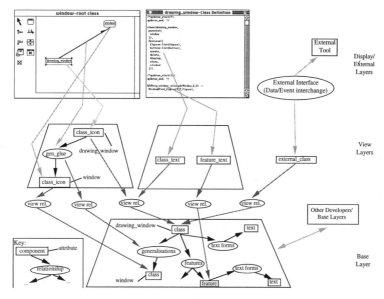

Figure 5   The MViews Architecture.

4.2   Notation Integration with MViews

In addition to SPE, we have developed several other ISEEs using MViews. MViewsER provides integrated Entity-Relationship diagrams and textual relational schema. MViewsER has been integrated with SPE to produce OOEER, an integrated environment for OOA/D and EER modelling (Grundy, 1995a). MViewsNIAM provides NIAM modelling views, and has been inegrated with MViewsER to produce NIAMER (Venable, 1995). MViewsDP provides a graphical drag-and-drop interface builder for dialog boxes, with the dialog interface and validation rules being defined in textual views (Grundy, 1995d). EPE is an environment for constructing EXPRESS specifications and corresponding EXPRESS-G diagrams (Amor, 1995a). C-SPE and C-MViews provide collaborative, integrated software development support via synchronous, semi-synchronous and asynchronous editing (Grundy, 1995e).

Figure 6 shows a screen dump from OOEER. The OOA/D views are kept consistent with **all** changes to the EER views, and vice-versa, even when a direct translation is not possible by the environment. The dialog shown holds change descriptions (the "modification history") for the customer OOA class. The change descriptions highlighted by '→' were actually made to the EER view (diagram) and automatically translated into OOA/D view updates (where possible) by OOEER. Unhighlighted items were made by the designer to the OOA view to fully implement "indirect" translations that could only partially by implemented by OOEER.

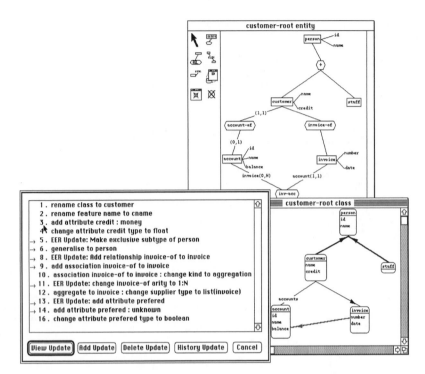

Figure 6   Integrated OOA/D and EER views in OOEER with bi-directional consistency.

The OOEER integration was achieved by adding an additional data dictionary graph level below the data dictionaries of the SPE and MViewsER tools. This layer is responsible for translating, where possible, between the different notations and notifying tools where automatic translations are not possible. Neither SPE nor MViewsER required any significant change to achieve this integration. Figure 7 shows an example of the structure of OOEER. Figure 7 illustrates this integration process. When an SPE view is edited (1), the modification is translated into SPE repository updates (2), generating change descriptions. The inter-repository relationships are sent change descriptions, and respond to these by updating the integrated repository (3). When the integrated repository components change, the inter-repository relationships to MViewsER's repository components translate the integrated repository components change descriptions into updates on MViewsER repository components (4). Indirect mapping changes are defaulted where possible and change descriptions displayed in views. Both SPE and MViewsER keep their multiple views consistent (5 and 6).

5   THE SERENDIPITY PROCESS MODELLING TOOL

ISEEs should support the coordination of cooperative work activities that is inherent within ISD (Krant, 1995). Therefore, CSCW features are needed in ISEEs. An ISEE should support users in collaboratively planning and executing work activities, as well as in being informed about and maintaining their awareness of relevant work by others, the contexts in which those other users' work is carried out, and the rationale for the decisions they have made. In particular, support is needed for defining activities to be done (plans), coordinating the planning activity itself (meta-plans), and restructuring the history of work done to more effectively convey intent ("rewriting history"). Unfortunately most existing workflow systems are inadequate for real-world applications due to many exceptions to the workflows and their inability to adapt to changing work processes (Swenson, 1993). Similarly, must existing process modelling tools utilise either complex, textual specifications which are inaccessible to many end-users, or do not support facilities for integration and event handling with existing tools.

We have developed Serendipity, a process modelling, enactment and work planning environment, which also supports flexible event handling mechanisms, group communication, and group awareness facilities (Grundy, 1996). Fig. 8 shows a Serendipity process model for updating a software system ("m1:modify system-process"). The notation is an adaptation and extension of Swenson's Visual Planning Language (Swenson, 1993), which does not support artefact, tool or role modelling, nor arbitrary event handling mechanisms.

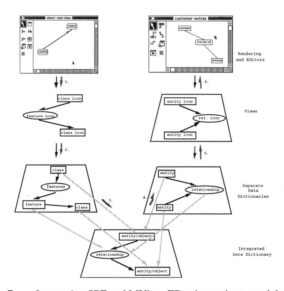

Figure 7   Integrating SPE and MViewsER using an integrated data model.

Stages describe steps in the process of modifying a software system, with each stage containing a *unique id*, the *role* which will carry out the stage, and the *name* of the stage. Enactment *event flows* link stages. If labelled, the label is the *finishing state* of the stage the flow is from (e.g. "finished design"). The shadowing of the "m1.2:implement changes" stage indicates that multiple implementers can work on this stage (i.e. the stage has multiple subprocess enactments). Other items include *start stages, finish stages, AND* stages, and *OR* stages (empty round circle). Underlined stage IDs/roles mark presence of a *subprocess* model, for example "m1.1:plan changes-subprocess" is a subprocess for "m1.1:design changes". The italicised "check out design" stages in this subprocess model indicate stages reused from a *template* process model.

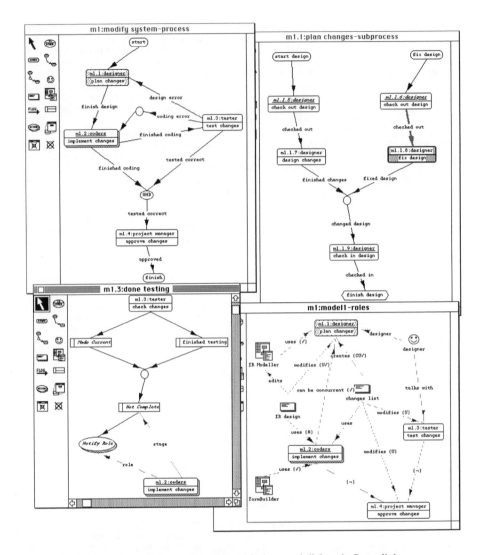

Figure 8   Software process model views and dialogs in Serendipity.

Serendipity supports artefact, tool and role modelling for processes, as in "m1:model1-roles",
which shows a different perspective of "m1:model1-process". *Usage connections* indicate how
stages, artefacts, tools and roles are used. Optional annotations indicate: whether data is created
(C), accessed (A), updated (U), or deleted (D); whether a stage must use only the tools,
artefacts or roles defined (√); and whether a stage cannot use a particular tool, artefact or role
(¬). If a stage is linked to another stage by a usage flow, "√" specifies the stage may be enacted

when the other stage is enacted, while "¬" specifies the stages can not be enacted at the same time.

In addition to specifying the static usages and enactment event flows between process model stages, Serendipity supports *filters* and *actions*, which process arbitrary enactment and work artefact modification events. View "m1.3:done testing" shows an example of enactment event filtering. The filters "Made Current" and "finished testing" determine if "m1.3:check changes" has been made the current enacted stage or has been finished. If so, then if the "m1.2:implement changes" process has not completed (determined by filter "Not Complete"), the role associated with this stage is notified of testing being started or completed.

Stages are *enacted* for a project, highlighted by colour and shading, as shown in Figure 8. The shaded stage with a bold border ("m1.1.8:fix design") is the *current enacted stage* for the user i.e. their current work context. As a stage completes in a given finishing state, event flows with this state name (or no name) activate to enact linked stages. Enactments of stages are recorded, as are process model changes, and all enacted stages for a user can be shown in a "to-do" list dialog.

6 AN INTEGRATED METHOD ENGINEERING APPROACH

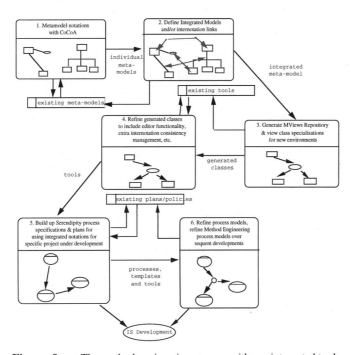

Figure 9   The method engineering process with our integrated tools.

We are currently building an MViews-based environment for CoCoA modelling, which will form the basis of an integrated environment for Method Engineering with our tools. Figure 9 shows how this tool will be used to generate MViews framework classes for specifying new or modified tool repositories and views. Developers will augment these specifications with appropriate editor configurations and notation renderings, and any additional consistency management techniques not generated from the CoCoA metamodels. As our Serendipity work coordination tool can be used with any MViews environments, developers will then be able to specify appropriate plans (i.e. process models) for different systems under construction. This may include enabling usage of certain tools and artefacts for certain parts of the new system development or to particular groups of developers. Once these plans have been created, developers can later abstract these plans to form policies and reuse their policy process models for subsequent systems, and thus incrementally refine these process models. CoCoA models and MViews environments and tools can also be created and/or modified from one project to the next to build up appropriate tools for each system development.

5.1   CoCoA Metamodelling of Notations

The first step (#1 in Figure 9) is to build up CoCoA metamodels of the desired design notations to be used on a new system development. This might include the reuse of previous CoCoA models, the combination of parts of one metamodel with another, or the development of new metamodels which are problem-specific. In previous metamodelling with CoCoA, we have used a drawing editor to produce these metamodels (Grundy, 1995a, Venable, 1995). We are currently implementing an MViews tool for CoCoA modelling which will be used to construct new CoCoA models, and will include multiple views of CoCoA models and libraries of views and models to assist in model reuse.

As an example, we have recently integrated our NIAMER (supporting NIAM and ER views) and OOEER (supporting OOA and EER views) environments with the MViewsDP form/report designer by hand. Using our CoCoA modelling tool instead, integration of these tools would initially begin using our integrated CoCoA/MViews environment to metamodel each notation that is to be used on a development project.

5.2   Conceptual Notation Integration with CoCoA

Integrating different design notations with CoCoA involves either the definition of integrated models or specifying links between components of one model and related components in another model (Grundy, 1995a, Venable, 1995). In addition, dynamic mappings must be specified between these notation components i.e. what happens to related components when a component instance is changed. For example, in OOEER, if an ER relationship is added between two entities, a default association relationship is added between the corresponding two object/classes in the OOA model (Grundy, 1995a). Our MViews editor for CoCoA will support both the static integration and/or linking of notation components, and the specification of dynamic mappings between notation components. Static integration is a straightforward view integration, supported by aspects of the CoCoA data modelling language. We are currently adapting a view mapping language (Amor, 1995b) which will allow us to declaratively specify the dynamic notation mappings in this tool. In previous notation integration we have informally specified these dynamic mappings using English and informal diagrams, but this is not sufficient to generate internotation relationships for MViews tool integration.

In our integrated ISEE, integration of OOEER, NIAMER, and MViewsDP was implemented by adding inter-repository relationships between repositories, in addition to the hierarchial repository relationships used in NIAMER and OOEER. Appropriate links were specified between the components of the CoCoA metamodels for each notation and then dynamic mappings were defined between related components. In future environment integration, this will all be carried our within our CoCoA modelling tool.

5.3   MViews Tool Generation from CoCoA Models

CoCoA models have been used as the specifications for MViews tool repositories in our previous notation integration work (Grundy, 1995a, Grundy, 1995b, Venable, 1995). However, MViews repository and view information has been hand-generated from these models. We are extending our CoCoA modelling tool to generate class interfaces and method code directly from different notation and integrated notation metamodels. Quite a large amount of MViews framework code can be generated in this way: previous development of MViews environments has shown over 60% of the code relates to defining class structures which represent repository and view data, and method code to link these data items in appropriate ways. All of this code can be generated from CoCoA metamodels by our modelling environment. Internotation relationships and a large amount of consistency management code can also be generated in this way, from the static integration and the specification of dynamic mappings in our CoCoA editor, even in some cases the user interface.

For example, if two constructs in two notations are represented by the same entity type in the integrated CoCoA model, a change to one of them in one view results in the same change in the second view/notation. In this case, the user of the second view need only be notified of the change and the repositories updated. Similarly, if the construct changed in one view is a subtype of a construct in another view, changing an instance of the first construct will require the same change on the supertype construct (as long as it has the required attributes). In either of these cases, code for handling the propagation of these changes (including the receiving view's user interface) can be generated automatically. However, the reverse is not true (i.e. we cannot generate the code for propagation of a change to a construct that is the supertype of a construct in another view which needs to be updated).

5.4   MViews Tool Refinement and Integration

While repository and view structures (and some semantic values) can be generated directly from CoCoA metamodels, extra code needs to be written by developers to appropriately configure editors and specify some consistency management code which can not be automaticlly generated. We are allowing developers to further specialise classes generated from our CoCoA modelling tool to define editing mechanisms and internotation consistency management code which can not be specified in a declarative way. For example, developers will specify default techniques for keeping data in different notations consistent declaratively, but may then want to define complex consistency management techniques operationally (i.e. using MViews code). An example from NIAMER is when a NIAM entity is added. Since, in the integrated CoCoA model, a NIAM entity is a supertype of both the EER attribute and entity, it could be mapped to either. NIAMER defaults the automatic translation to adding an entity and allows users of the integrated environment to modify the ER entity to an attribute if desired. This default code could also be generated, but might be incorrect if the default should have been to add an attribute instead. In that case, a developer would need to rewrite a small amount of MViews code. Alternatively, other user interfaces might be desired, such as preseting the user with a menu to add either an entity or an attribute to the EER view, adding reconciliation of the change to a to-do list, or simply suggesting a change. We are currently looking at ways to declaratively specify the desired behaviour with annotations to the CoCoA models. Our approach allowing developers to make these alterations by further specialising the generated classes, which avoids the problem of when the CoCoA models are modified and classes regenerated. The further specialised classes are not lost when this regeneration occurs.

Of course, we also need to code the rendering of the notation on the user's screen. This is currently done by hand, but within the MViews library framework. We are looking at how this might be done declaratively with annotations to the CoCoA metamodel, then generating the rendering code.

5.5   Process Model Specification

After building appropriately integrated tools, developers can then specify how these tools are to be used on the particular system under construction. Serendipity allows developers to specify which tools and work artefacts are used for different plan stages and hence which tools/artefacts can be used for a particular software process. Serendipity process models can guide developers i.e. suggest which tools are appropriate for different development tasks. They can also be used to suggest or to enforce the use of specific tools, so, for example, a project manager may specify one development group uses OOA/D modelling while another uses ER/DFD modelling. As these tools have integrated repositories (via OOEER), the designs produced by each group are still integrated and kept consistent.

In a collaborative, integrated ISEE, users must be informed of changes to work and plan artefacts that are relevant to them and they are currently interested in (Grundy, 1995c). Some changes a developer makes are directly relevant to their collaborators, such as renaming or deleting entities and attributes, and collaborators should be informed of these immediately. Other changes, such as the addition of new entities, relationships, attributes or forms and reports can be sent for later perusal, as they have more limited effects on collaborators' work. Low-level changes, such as the implementation of procedures, forms or reports not affecting a collaborator's work need not be presented. Collaborators can see from plan histories and various active stages the kinds of activities another developer is doing, and may choose to view these changes or modified artefacts on-demand, using any of the informing mechanisms described above.

In most CSCW environments, only artefact-level information about changes is presented to collaborators, either directly updating their work artefact views or using version control facilities to indicate changes made by other users. Serendipity provides collaborating users not only with change descriptions describing actual work (or plan) artefact changes, but also with extra information about the work context in which the changes were carried out. Examples of this work coordination can be found in (Grundy, 1995c, Grundy, 1996).

5.6   Tool/Process Refinement and Reuse

Serendipity views assist in Situational Method Engineering (Harmsen, 1994) by allowing developers to incrementally refine their development methodology, processes and work plans. As process stages record information about the tools to use, artefacts to modify/produce, subsequent stages, and also may be exploded into more detailed plans, they facilitate the engineering of software processes in a manner similar to Method Engineering tools. Our approach has some advantages over comparable notations, such as MEL (Harmsen, 1995), in that its visual nature is more accessible to developers for visualising and modifying plans than the textual notations of other approaches. As Serendipity models were designed for general work process modelling, its high-level nature allows developers to more readily understand and modify process descriptions than text-based process-centred environments or method-engineering tools. It also allows users to modify their process and work plans while a model is in use. Finally, Serendipity allows users to restructure copies of processes and plan histories after completion so that new, improved process model templates can be developed for later reuse.

Our integrated, collaborative ISEE supports collaborative planning via collaborative editors for Serendipity views, and allowing other Serendipity views to act as meta-process views. Collaborating developers share software process views and can collaborate on modifying these models. The use of these shared models for work context capture and presentation, and specifying interest in changes, allows Serendipity to be used for work coordination, collaborative planning, recording development histories, and method engineering. Figure 10 shows an example of process improvement with Serendipity. The process model is extended to include a "m1.5:check design" stage, to be carried out before coding starts. Coder "john"'s work plan is also extended by adding 'm1.2.11:modify branch table'. This handles an exception to the work plan due to the addition of the "address" table. Such changes could be made before, during or after the model and plan are used.

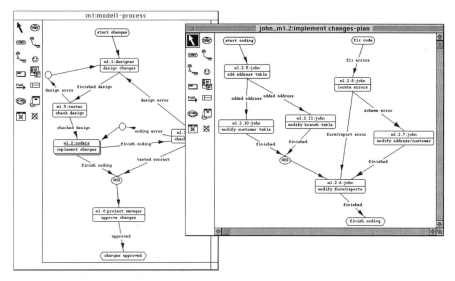

Figure 10   Process and plan improvement example.

Our integrated ISEE allows different tools to be used on the same problem domain, with tool data being kept consistent under change and the tools sharing a consistent user interface. Serendipity allows software processes to be reconfigured during development to better suit a particular development project. Software process models thus evolved can be reused in subsequent development by saving them as reusable templates. The specification of artefacts, roles, CASE tools and interest obligations for plan stages gives our integrated environment similar method engineering capabilities to method engineering tools. In addition, it supports work coordination. Our CoCoA/MViews environment can itself make use of Serendipity views to model, plan and coordinate the Method Engineering process itself. This allows the Method Engineering process to be refined over several projects, in addition to the refinement of the integrated design notation tools.

7   SUMMARY AND FUTURE RESEARCH

We have described our recent work on developing a metamodelling language, CoCoA, notation integration using CoCoA, the construction of integrated Information Systems Engineering Environments based on CoCoA metamodels using MViews, and the development of a work coordination and software process modelling tool, using an extended form of the Visual Planning Language. Used in conjunction, these tools allow system developers to model and integrated different design notations and to construct integrated tools and environments supporting these notations. Developers can plan and coordinate the use of different tools within this environment using our Serendipity tool.

We are currently implementing an MViews environment for CoCoA which will support notation metamodelling and notation integration. MViews classes to implement an integrated environment will be generated from these metamodels, together with internotation relationships and consistency management support. Serendipity will be used to coordinate the use of these integrated environments for different system developments, and will be used by the CoCoA/MViews environment itself to plan, coordinate and refine the Method Engineering process itself. We are also engaged in further research to enhance and add to the CSCW features of our environments and to consider ways to utilise declarative annotations to the CoCoA models to further improve the CoCoA/MViews environment's code generation capabilities.

REFERENCES

Amor, R., Augenbroe, G., Hosking, J.G., Rombouts, W., and Grundy, J.C. (1995) Directions in modelling environments, *Automation in Construction*, **4**, 173–187.

Amor, R.W. and Hosking, J.G. (1995) Mappings: the glue in an integrated system, in *1st European Conference on product and process modelling in the building industryindustry*, A.A. Balkema Publishers, Rotterdam, The Netherlands.

Barghouti, N.S. (1992) Supporting Cooperation in the Marvel Process–Centred SDE, in *Proceedings of the 1992 ACM Symposium on Software Development Environments*, ACM Press, pp. 21–31.

Campbell, L. and Halpin, T. (1994) Abstraction Techniques for Conceptual Schemas, in *Proceedings of the 5th Australasian Database Conference*, Global Publications Services, Christchurch, New Zealand, 17–18 January 1994, pp. 374–388.

Falkenberg, E.D. and Oei, J.L.H. (1994) Meta Model Hierarchies from an Object–Role Modelling Perspective, in *First International Conference on Object–Role Modelling* (ed. Halpin, T. and Meersman, R.), Key Centre for Software Technology, The University of Queensland, Brisbane, Australia, 4–6 July 1994, pp. 310–323.

Grundy, J.C. and Hosking, J.G. (1993) A framework for building visusal programming environments, in *Proceedings of the 1993 IEEE Symposium on Visual Languages*, IEEE Computer Society Press, pp. 220–224.

Grundy, J.C. and Hosking (1994) J.G., *Constructing Integrated Software Development Environments with Dependency Graphs*, Working Paper, Department of Computer Science, University of Waikato.

Grundy, J.C. and Venable, J.R. (1995a) Providing Integrated Support for Multiple Development Notations, in *Proceedings of CAiSE'95*, Finland, June 1995, Lecture Notes in Computer Science 932, Springer–Verlag, pp. 255–268.

Grundy, J.C., and Venable, J.R. (1995b) Developing CASE tools that support integrated design notations, in *Proceedings of the 6th European Workshop on Next Generation of CASE Tools*, pp. 109–116.

Grundy, J.C., Mugridge, W.B., Hosking, J.G., and Apperley, M.D. (1995c) Coordinating, capturing and presenting work contexts in CSCW systems, in *Proceedings of OZCHI'95*, Wollongong, Australia, Nov 28–30 1995, pp. 146–151.

Grundy, J.C., Hosking, J.G., and Mugridge, W.B. (1995d) Supporting flexible consistency management via discrete change description propagation, to appear in *Software – Practice and Experience*.

Grundy, J.C., Mugridge, W.B., Hosking, J.G., and Amor, R. (1995e) Support for Collaborative, Integrated Software Development, in *Proceeding of the 7th Conference on Software Engineering Environments*, IEEE CS Press, Netherlands, April 5–7 1995, pp. 84–94.

Grundy, J.C. (1996) *Serendipity: integrated environment support for process modelling, enactment and improvement*, Working Paper, Department of Computer Science, University of Waikato.

Harmsen, F., Brinkkemper, S., and Oei, H. (1994) Situational Method Engineering for Information System Projects, in *Proceedings of the IFIP WG8.1 Working Conference CRIS'94* (ed. Olle, T.W. and Verrijn, A.A.E.), Maastricht, 1994, North–Holland, Amsterdam, pp. 169–194.

Harmsen, F., and Brinkkemper, S. (1995) Design and Implementation of a Method Base Management System for a Situational CASE Environment, in *Proceedings of the 2nd Asia–Pacific Software Engineering Conference (APSEC'95)*, IEEE CS Press, Brisbane, December 1995, pp. 430–438.

Heym, M. and Osterle, H. (1992) A Semantic Data Model for Methodology Engineering, in *Proceedings of the Fifth International Workshop on Computer–Aided Software Engineering*, IEEE Computer Society Press, Washington, D.C., pp. 142–155.

Kaplan, S.M., Tolone, W.J., Carroll, A.M., Bogia, D.P., and Bignoli, C. (1992) Supporting Collaborative Software Development with ConversationBuilder, in *Proceedings of the 1992 ACM Symposium on Software Development Environments*, ACM Press, pp. 11–20.

Krant, R.E. and Streeter, L.A. (1995) Coordination in Software Development, *CACM*, **38** (3), 69–81.

Kumar, K. and Welke, R.J. (1992) *A proposal for situation–specific methodology construction*, Challenges and Strategies for Research in Systems Development. Wiley, New York.

Lonchamp, J. (1995) CPCE: A Kernel for Building Flexible Collaborative Process–Centred Environments, in *Proceedings of the 7th Conference on Software Engineering Environments*, IEEE CS Press, Netherlands, April 5–7 1995, pp. 95–105.

Mark V Systems Ltd (1995)*MethodMaker*, 16400 Ventura Boulevard, Encino, California 91436.

Mark V Systems Ltd (1995) *ProcessMaker*, 16400 Ventura Boulevard, Encino, California 91436.

Meyers, S. (1991) Difficulties in Integrating Multiview Editing Environments, *IEEE Software*, **8** (1), 49–57.

Nijssen, G.M. and Halpin, T.A. (1989) *Conceptual Schema and Relational Database Design: A Fact Oriented Approach.* Prentice–Hall, Englewood Cliffs, NJ.

Nuseibeh, B. and Finkelstein, A. (1992) ViewPoints: A Vehicle for Method and Tool Integration, in *Proceedings of the Fifth International Workshop on Computer–Aided Software Engineering,* IEEE Computer Society Press, Washington, D.C., pp. 50–61.

Ratcliffe, M., Wang, C., Gautier, R.J., and Whittle, B.R. (1992) Dora – a structure oriented environment generator, *IEE Software Engineering Journal,* **7** (3), 184–190.

Reiss, S.P. (1990) Connecting Tools Using Message Passing in the Field Environment, *IEEE Software,* **7** (7), 57–66.

Saeki, M., Iguchi, K., and Wen–yin, K. (1993) A Meta–model for representing software specification and design methods, in *Proceedings of the IFIP WG8.1 Conference on Information Systems Development* (ed. Prakash, N., Rolland, C., and Pernici, B.), Como, Italy.

Song, X. and Osterweil, L.J. (1992) A Process–Modeling Based Approach to Comparing and Integrating Software Design Methodologies, in *Proceedings of the Fifth International Workshop on Computer–Aided Software Engineering,* IEEE Computer Society Press, Washingon, D.C., pp. 225–229.

Swenson, K.D. (1993) A Visual Language to Describe Collaborative Work, in *Proceedings of the 1993 IEEE Symposium on Visual Languages,* IEEE CS Press, Bergen, Norway, pp. 298–303.

Venable, J.R. (1993) CoCoA: *A Conceptual Data Modelling Approach for Complex Problem Domains*, Ph.D. dissertation, Thomas J. Watson School of Engineering and Applied Science, State University of New York at Binghampton, 1993.

Venable, J.R. and Grundy, J.C. (1995) Integrating and Supporting Entity Relationship and Object Role Models, in *Proceedings of the 14th Object–Oriented and Entity Relationship Modelling Conferece (OO–ER'95)*, , Gold Coast, Australia, Dec 13–16 1995, Lecture Notes in Computer Science 1021, Springer–Verlag.

Vessey, I. and Glass, R.L. (1994) Applications–based Methodologies, *Information Systems Management*, 53–57, Fall 1994.

Wasserman, A.I. and Pircher, P.A. (1987) A Graphical, Extensible, Integrated Environment for Software Development, *SIGPLAN Notices*, vol. 22, no. 1, 131–142.

Wieringa, R.J. (1995) Combining static and dynamic modelling methods: a comparison of four methods, to appear in *Computer Journal*.

BIOGRAPHY

Dr John Grundy has been a Lecturer in Computer Science in the Department of Computer Science, University of Waikato since 1993. He holds the BSc(Hons), MSc and PhD degrees, all in Computer Science from the University of Auckland, New Zealand. His research interests include software engineering environments, software process technology, software engineering methodologies, visual programming, and object–oriented systems. He is currently developing the Serendipity process modelling and enactment environment, and using Serendipity to provide a process modelling and work coordination tool for large CSCW systems, such as collaborative software engineering environments.

Dr John Venable has been a Lecturer in Information Systems in the Department of Computer Science, University of Waikato, Hamilton, New Zealand since 1994. He obtained his PhD in Computer Science and Information Systems in 1994 from Binghamton University in Binghamton, New York, USA. He has lectured since 1983 at Binghamton University, Central Connecticut State University, and Aalborg University, Denmark. Dr Venable's main interests are in information systems development, particularly in its practice, methods, and appropriate tool–based support. Currently, he is researching the incorporation of CSCW features into CASE tools to better support and improve the systems development process.

5

A Functional Framework for Evaluating Method Engineering Environments: the case of Maestro II/ Decamerone and MetaEdit+

P. Marttiin [a], F. Harmsen [b], M. Rossi [a]
[a] Department of Computer Science and Information Systems,
University of Jyväskylä, P.O.Box 35, 40351 Jyväskylä, Finland
E-mail: {ptma, mor}@jyu.fi
[b] Department of Computer Science, University of Twente,
P.O.Box 216, 7500 AE Enschede, The Netherlands,
E-mail: harmsen@cs.utwente.nl

Abstract

CASE environments with method customisation capabilities and Computer Aided Method Engineering (CAME) environments have emerged during the last few years. While many research papers discuss the principles of method engineering and suggest requirements for new environments, we do not have critical evaluations of CAME environments using a wider method engineering framework. The aims of this study are twofold: 1) to build a preliminary framework for comparative studies of CAME environments, and 2) to increase the knowledge of the 'state of the art' in CAME by evaluating two CAME environments. We adapt a functional framework – originally built for CASE technology – to examine the following two research questions: *How well can a method be defined in a CAME environment?*, and *How well is the defined method supported in a customisable CASE environment?* The environments chosen for evaluation are *Maestro II /Decamerone*, and *MetaEdit+*. As an outcome, we will describe what framework aspects these environments support, and discuss the aspects not supported.

Keywords

CASE evaluation, metaCASE, method engineering, systems development, co-ordination

1   BACKGROUND AND MOTIVATION

Despite extensive comparative research on information system development methods[1] during the 1980's (Olle et al., 1982, 1983, 1986), research interest in assessing methods is still strong. According to Norman and Chen (1992), methods have evolved in parallel with changing application domains and to the need to improve method support through tools. Recently, the object-oriented paradigm has yielded numerous new methods and new contexts for applying methods (e.g., business engineering) have emerged. These have given rise to the continuing method evolution. Furthermore, we believe improved mechanisms for method customisation in CASE environments will increase organizations' willingness to adjust and to improve their method practices.

To obtain a better understanding of the study domain and the environments compared, we need first to discuss some basic concepts. Because various definitions and views of CASE abound (e.g., Henderson and Cooprider, 1994), we do not try to suggest clear and exact definitions for CASE and CASE environment. We consider CASE to be a design aid technology for ISs, and a CASE environment a collection of design aid tools for ISs. While traditional CASE environments – based on the fixed repository structure, and containing editors and other tools only for a fixed method – support a few popular methods, a customisable CASE environment – having a flexible repository structure and technique specific editors and tools – is capable to support any method specified into it. We can define a customisable CASE environment more precisely:

> Definition 1. *A customisable CASE environment is a CASE environment having mechanisms to support any method specified into it.*

Brinkkemper (1995) has defined *method engineering* as 'a discipline to design, construct and adapt methods, techniques and tools for the development of information systems'. If the method engineering process is supported by specific computer aided tools, we call the engineering discipline *Computer Aided Method Engineering (CAME)*, and the supporting tools *CAME tools*. According to Harmsen et al. (1994), we define a CAME environment as follows:

> Definition 2. *A CAME environment is a collection of CAME tools for 1) specifying methods to be used in CASE environments, 2) comparing, analysing, and selecting methods, and/or 3) storing the accumulated knowledge of methods and situation factors.*

Bubenko (1988) introduced a term *CASE shell* to denote a tool including mechanisms to define CASE support for an arbitrary method, thus, corresponding to the first part of CAME tool definition. The most common term *metaCASE environment* is used to denote either a CASE shell, or an integrated CASE shell and a customisable CASE environment (Marttiin et

---

[1] Wynekoop and Russo (1993) define a method as 'a systematic approach to conduct at least one complete phase (e.g. design, testing) of IS production, consisting a set of guidelines, activities, techniques and tools, based on a particular philosophy of system development and the target system'.

al., 1993). To avoid misunderstandings, we have selected the terms 'a customisable CASE environment' and 'a CAME environment' to be used later in this study.

Historically, in the late 1970's and in the 1980's, metaCASE environments were studied and designed mainly in academic research laboratories. Such environments include *SEM* (ISDOS, 1981), *RAMATIC* (Bergsten et al., 1989), *MetaPlex* (Chen and Nunamaker, 1989), *MetaEdit* (Smolander et al., 1991), *MetaView* (Sorenson, 1988), and *ConceptBase* (Hahn at al., 1991). During the early 1990's commercial metaCASE environments have appeared in the market. Current metaCASE products include e.g. *Graphical Designer* by ASTI (Advanced Software Technologies, *Toolbuilder* by Lincoln Software/IPSYS, *Paradigm Plus* by Protosoft, *ObjectMaker* by Mark V Systems, *Maestro II* by Softlab, and *MetaEdit+* by MetaCase Consulting.

Each metaCASE environment takes a different view on methods, and they employ different mechanisms for defining the supported method. Furthermore, the supported method aspects vary considerably (see Marttiin et al., 1993; Vessey et al., 1992; Verhoef and ter Hofstede 1995). For example, some environments define integration just for techniques, whereas others tie techniques to the IS development process. This divergence of tools requires analysis and evaluation of metaCASE using a wider method engineering framework.

To construct a framework for new research areas (we can consider method engineering as such one), we need to look at available research and research directions. Brinkkemper (1995) presents some research questions for method engineering: *meta modelling techniques, tool coverage and interoperability, situational methods,* and *comparative review of methods and tools.* We now discuss these questions closely.

1.1 Meta-modelling techniques

Meta-modelling techniques deal with issues related to both meta-modelling language and process.

A meta-modelling language is a language for specifying techniques (e.g., OPRR [Smolander, 1992]), interrelations of techniques (e.g., PSM [Ter Hofstede and van der Weide, 1993]), consistency rules and transformations (e.g., ETL [Boloix et al., 1991]), development tasks (e.g., Task Structures [Wijers, 1991]), decisions (Jarke et al., 1994), and tools (Sorenson et al., 1988), as examples. Comprehensive criteria to evaluate meta-modelling languages, such as those proposed to conceptual modelling languages (see Venable, 1993), are lacking. The open research issues include, e.g., *the richness, simplicity,* or *granularity of a meta-modelling language* to define various aspects of a method, which are discussed by Verhoef and Ter Hofstede (1995).

Second, meta-modelling process deals with the steps and actors needed in modelling method (i.e. method engineering steps). The important questions include how to manage method evolution, how to use the method knowledge, and who are participating the method engineering process. Different scenarios on meta-modelling process are discussed in (Harmsen et al., 1994).

1.2 Tool coverage and interoperability

To provide support for various method aspects, a customisable CASE environment needs to operate with a large set of tools. The art of integrating all the tools – tools for CASE, software engineering, and project management – is called *interoperability* of tools (Brinkkemper, 1995).

Another issue is the *coverage* of the design aid support for specific purposes. For example, matrix techniques require matrix tools, graphical techniques require graphic tools, and some techniques such as *Petri nets* are hardly useful without formal analysis or simulation mechanisms. Moreover, how do we manage techniques that do not focus on modelling, but rather on idea generation, communication or reasoning? The question of tool coverage can be formulated as: What design tasks need to be supported by specific design aid tools, and what tasks can be managed by general purpose tools (such as text editors and electronic mail), or without any tool support?

1.3   Situational methods

Methods are always of a generic nature and dependent on the contextual situations – calling for situational methods. For example, Wijers and van Dort (1990) observed that tools built around fixed handbook techniques and process models hindered projects to use their own dialects. Moreover, finding the *best* or *appropriate* method for a *specific* system may currently put a development project into a trial. For these reasons, approaches for situational method engineering have been introduced (Kumar and Welke, 1992; Harmsen and Brinkkemper, 1995) and related supporting CAME environments designed such as *Decamerone* (Harmsen and Brinkkemper, 1995), and *Method Base* (Saeki et al., 1993).

1.4   Comparative review of methods and tools

Several frameworks for methods have been constructed (e.g., Essink, 1986, Olle et al., 1991). Also, a number of frameworks and models for CASE and method support are available (Lyytinen et al., 1989; Wijers, 1991; Heym and Österle, 1992; Henderson and Cooprider, 1994). However, only few studies tackle issues related to CAME. Comparisons (Vessey, 1992; Crozier et al., 1989) have been made by focusing on CASE tool capabilities. The comparison of three metaCASE environments (Marttiin et al., 1993) examined the functionality to specify a new technique. Also, Verhoef and Ter Hofstede (1995) evaluated the feasibility of the conceptual basis of metaCASE environments. Notable is the lack of empirical evaluation of CAME tools: we found only Cronholm and Goldkuhl (1994), which describes five cases of method modification.

This research issue (1.4.) motivated us to evaluate two environments, while the others guided us to focus on prominent method engineering aspects in the CAME framework. Aims of this study are to build a framework to study *How well can a method be defined in a CAME environment?*, and to increase knowledge of the 'state of the art' in CAME by evaluating two CAME environments. A cornerstone in CAME is its meta-modelling language, which raises another research question: *How well is the defined method supported in a customisable CASE environment?* The environments in comparison are: *Maestro II* (Merbeth, 1991) with *Decamerone* (Harmsen and Brinkkemper, 1995) and *MetaEdit+* (Kelly et al., 1996). Analysis and comparison of these environments are carried out and reported based on the two questions above and a detailed framework presented in Section 2.

The study is structured as follows. In Section 2 we introduce the framework and adapt it into CAME. Section 3 introduces the basic architecture and tools of the environments. Section 4 evaluates the CAME part of these environments, and Section 5 discusses shortly customised

CASE by applying the framework. Finally, in Section 6 we draw conclusions and discuss our future work.

2 FRAMEWORK FOR CUSTOMISABLE CASE AND CAME

A number of CASE technology frameworks have been proposed (Lyytinen et al., 1989; Misra, 1990; Crozier et al., 1989; Wijers, 1991; Heym and Österle, 1992; Fuggetta, 1993; Henderson and Cooprider, 1994). We selected the 'functional model' for CASE (Henderson and Cooprider, 1994) to be applied for CAME technology. The selection is based on the following reasons: First, the framework takes a comprehensive view of CASE technology. Second, it can be easily adapted to any design aid domain including CAME. The rationale for adapting the framework as such into CAME is found in (Auramäki et al., 1988; Nijssen, 1989). According to their architectural principles, CAME technology – a design aid technology for methods and CASE tools – can be similarly treated with CASE technology. Third, the model is based on empirical studies and contains several strictly formulated questions for CASE. This is the main limitation of other framework candidates. Furthermore, our earlier comparison (Marttiin et al., 1993) based on the framework of Lyytinen et al. (1989) did not focus extensively on CAME aspects, and it concentrated on issues not relevant for this study (e.g. portability to use various operating systems, and DBMSs).

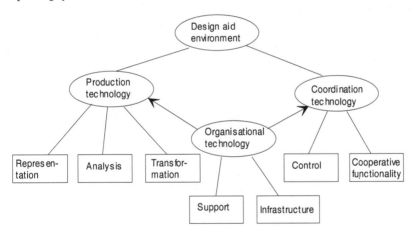

Figure 1   A functional model of CASE technology (Henderson and Cooprider, 1994).

Henderson and Cooprider (1994) conceptualise design aid technology as a combination of *production, co-ordination*, and *organisational* technology (Figure 1). Each of these main functions divides into sub-functions. In the following we present the main issues of each sub-function, discuss shortly the functions for customisable CASE, and try to capture the basic functions a future CAME environment need to supply.

2.1   Production technology

Production technology (as an individual's point of view to analyse, design and generate products) is divided into components of *representation, analysis* and *transformation* (see Figure 1). Representation focuses on abstraction and conceptualisation of phenomena into models. Analysis reflects the problem solving and decision making aspects of development. Transformation calls for rules and mechanisms to transform models into another form.

Customisable CASE
Representation in customisable CASE calls for the possibility to model ISs using various techniques, and to support modelling using various notations (textual, diagram, matrix, tabular) by corresponding editors (Chen and Nunamaker, 1989). As a modelling support, representation function deals with issues on creating, editing, composing, integrating, retrieving, and viewing IS models and components of them.

Analysis requires verification, validation and simulation support for IS models. Verification deals with issues such as consistency checking, rules, equivalencies and redundancies in IS models, change analysis, and querying IS models (Henderson and Cooprider, 1994). Validation can be achieved by using metrics, decision aids, requirements tracing, or supporting versions of models. Simulation is used for testing the completeness and performance of IS model by running it.

Transformation considers, for instance, how to transform a logical model into a physical one. The other issues include reverse engineering, change propagation, generation of reports, documentation, and code, and the generation of screen mock-ups and executable code for prototyping.

CAME
While the representation function for customisable CASE focuses on how to model ISs, the representation function for CAME focuses on how to specify methods, and how to manage their use in CASE. This is related to meta-modelling techniques discussed in Section 1.1. We consider here *meta-modelling languages, abstraction mechanisms* and *notations* used in modelling methods.

- According to earlier studies (Brinkkemper, 1990; Heym and Österle, 1992; Jarke et al., 1994, Marttiin et al., 1995), the suggested method fragments (i.e. a method specification or part of it) contain some features of all the CASE framework functions. Thus, in practice the primary focus has been on the production: defining a method for representing, analysing, and transforming IS models. As noted in our earlier comparison (Marttiin et al., 1993), we need a richer meta-modelling language to be able to capture more details of any method aspect. This will lead to consider both the feasibility and the possible granularity of any supported method aspect (Verhoef and Ter Hofstede, 1995).
- In some cases the method fragments are produced from 'scratch', but the need to store them into a method base, and reuse and recompose them requires the use of abstraction principles. Basic abstraction principles used in conceptual modelling (Brodie, 1984): *generalisation – specialisation* and *aggregation – decomposition* are suitable for method fragments. Further, the research on meta-modelling hierarchies (Oei and Falkenberg, 1994) introduces also *restriction* and *degeneration* principles when discussing changes in the meta-modelling language and its effects on the power of a modelling language.

- CAME representation deals with editing and viewing method fragments in various notations: structured text, forms, matrices and graphics, as examples. CAME tools have basically supported textual notations (see Marttiin et al., 1993), although graphics are used in *MetaEdit* (Smolander et al., 1991), and *GraphicalDesigner*.

Analysis covers *verification, validation* and *simulation* of *method fragments.*

- Verification for methods is mostly situation independent, and thus it can be better formalised and implemented than validation. Verification includes consistency requirements for methods including precedence, input/output, and granularity consistency or the checking of duplicate concepts and uncompleted relationships in methods.
- Kumar and Welke (1992) pointed out that method engineering follows the incremental learning strategy: every time a project starts the experience and 'wisdom' from earlier successful and unsuccessful projects are accumulated and included into the method fragments. Validation of the method fragments can be done by comparing them with a number of project factors such as available domain knowledge, the technology used, the organisational size, and the amount of resources available (Slooten and Brinkkemper, 1993). Some references (e.g., Euromethod, 1994; Harmsen et al., 1995) give high-level heuristics to match situations with suitable method fragments.
- A specific simulation can be accomplished when following the 'method engineering by example' strategy, where method components are modelled in the same form as they will appear in CASE as in 'query-by example'.

Transformations in method base can be divided into *generations between various levels of method fragments, implementation transformations* and *document generation.*

- Transformations between method fragments can be used to partly automate the production of situational methods or to transform a method fragment from the coarse-featured form into the detailed one. Situational methods may require a possibility to combine a set of rules for selecting elementary method fragments and composing them into a rough 'method template'.
- Implementation transformation occurs when we transform a method fragment into an executable form for a customisable CASE environment, or into a form required by another CAME environment. An example of the former is the transformation from *Decamerone* to the *Prolan* language used in *Maestro II* (Harmsen and Brinkkemper, 1995). The bridge between *MetaEdit* and *RAMATIC* (Rossi et al., 1992) serves as an example of the latter case. Transformations between CAME and CASE have mostly been uni-directional. However, to manage IS model updates when changing a method may require more seamless solutions to integrate the two levels.
- Creation of method documentation belongs to CAME representation. However, its generation into a CASE tools' help is a specific transformation issue.

2.2 Co-ordination technology

Co-ordination technology includes functions of *control* and *co-operation*. Henderson and Cooprider discuss control in terms of *resource management* and *access control*. Resource management enables managers to utilise project resources consistently with project goals. Access control implies, e.g., ways to manage access rights to user groups that participate in the development. It is closely related to database technology and its mechanisms.

Alternatively, co-operation enables to exchange information between developers (co-operative modelling) and users (user involvement) for the purpose of influencing the ISD process, or product. Design aid tools and methods themselves can be used for co-operative purposes: the use of graphical models in co-operation is a case in point. On the other hand, using a specific functionality can increase co-operative support for the design aid: both for CASE and CAME.

Customisable CASE

To establish control mechanisms for the customisable CASE environment, we need to deal with, for instance, the concepts of *process*, *project* and *user roles* (Curtis et al., 1992). Development process is both project and method dependent. A process model constructs development tasks into precedence order, integrates techniques and tasks, and allocates users to participate in the tasks. Process models in customisable CASE are discussed in, among others, (Jarke et al., 1994; Marttiin, 1994). The characterisation of project and user roles is discussed in (Hahn et al., 1991, Curtis et al., 1992, Marttiin et al., 1995). Other control issues relate to project management such as schedules, deadlines, project complexity metrics, and quality assurance.

Co-operation for customisable CASE calls for possibility to use co-operative tools, which support messages, notes, anonymous feedback, announcement of changes, and design rationale concerning models or development tasks. We can divide the support into asynchronous communication (electronic mail as an example) and synchronous modelling (several developers editing the same model simultaneously). Other more advanced group interaction mechanisms include brainstorming and other group development techniques that are currently managed using separate tools. The possibility to integrate these into CASE is a challenging future task.

CAME

Method engineering requires the co-ordination and organisational functions, though these do not have such a prominent position as in the production function. The current CAME literature does not tackle the co-ordination issues involving multiple method engineers or stakeholders.

We can discuss, however, control and co-operation aspects of method engineering. Controlling method evolution is critical, in particular when the changes to a method take place during the IS development and create effects on CASE and IS models. Such effects arise for example when one deletes a concept in a technique or an attribute of a concept. Co-operation in CAME can be seen as an exchange of method engineering experiences and a use of the collected expertise (Kumar and Welke, 1992). As a note to user involvement aspects, method users may include system designers, software engineers, and project managers.

2.3 Support and Infrastructure

All production and co-ordination functions can be supported by using organisational technology: the *infrastructure* catching standard operating procedures and quality standards, and the *support* functionality dealing with organisational guidelines, on-line helps, learning aid, 'user friendliness' and 'easiness', which can assist users to understand and use design aid effectively.

Table 1 A functional framework of customisable CASE and CAME

Function	Customisable CASE	CAME
Representation	• Modelling of ISs using various methods: *concepts, notations, and abstraction mechanisms to represent IS models*	• Modelling of methods using a meta-modelling language: *concepts, notations and abstraction mechanisms to represent methods*
Analysis	• Verification of IS models: *consistency checking for IS models* • Validation of IS models: *traceability to requirements, design rationale of IS models* • Simulation of IS models	• Verification of methods: *consistency checking for methods* • Validation of methods: *situational methods, analysis on earlier methods, the use of method base, design rationale of methods* • Simulation of methods: *'method engineering by example'*
Transformation	• Transformations between IS models • Code and report generation from IS models • Generation of screen mock ups and executable code for prototyping	• Transformation from situation factors into methods • Generation of methods into CASE: *generation of method documentation* • Generation of CASE tools & management of repository mappings
Control	• Resource management: *resource capacities, organisational goals, deadlines, priorities, managerial control for CASE* • Access and change control for IS models • ISD process models: *management of ISD tasks and deliverables, automation of CASE*	• Resource management: *resource capacities, organisational goals, deadlines, priorities, managerial control for CAME* • Access and change control for methods: *change effects into CASE* • Method engineering process models: *management of ME tasks and deliverables, automation of CAME*
Co-operation	• CASE as co-operative aid: *notes, design rationale support for IS models* • Technical support for co-operative CASE: *group interaction mechanisms, asynchronous/ synchronous CASE*	• CAME as co-operative aid: *notes, design rationale support for methods* • Technical support for co-operative CAME: *group interaction mechanisms, asynchronous/ synchronous CAME*
Support & infrastructure	• Help, learning aid and organisational policies for the areas of customisable CASE representation, analysis, transformation, control, and co-operation	• Help, learning aid and organisational policies for the areas of CAME representation, analysis, transformation, control, and co-operation

Customisable CASE and CAME

Organisational support for CASE involves help, learning aid and organisational policies for any CASE framework functions: representation, analysis, transformation, control, and co-operation. As we discussed earlier, method guidance can be modelled during the method engineering process and generated into customisable CASE. In this manner the maintenance of method guidance will be easier when methods evolve.

Similarly to customisable CASE, organisational support for CAME means help, learning aid and organisational policies for the areas of CAME representation, analysis, transformation, control, and co-operation.

The main issues (a bullet for each) and some illustrative examples (italics after colon) discussed in this Section are summarised into Table 1.

3 OVERVIEW OF THE ANALYSED ENVIRONMENTS: MAESTRO II/ DECAMERONE AND METAEDIT+

In this section we take an overview to the architecture and tools of *Maestro II/ Decamerone* and *MetaEdit+* environments.

3.1 Maestro II and Decamerone

The analysis in respect to the tools and functions of environment is based on *Maestro II* product (Merbeth, 1991) and the design of *Decamerone* (Harmsen and Brinkkemper, 1995).

Maestro II is a metaCASE environment offering experienced developers all possibilities to develop diagram editors, repository structures, process enactment mechanisms, etc. It is a multi-user environment based on a client/server architecture. It includes the following tools:

- Repository tools: *Object Management System (OMS)*,
- Model editing tools: *Text Developers System* and *Graphics Editor*
- Project and process management system: *Project and Configuration Management System (PCMS)*
- Method management tools: *Data Model Declaration Table (DMDT)*, *Tool Customisation Interface (TCI)* including *Symbol Editor*

Figure 2 depicts the architecture of *Decamerone*, which is implemented in Maestro II, and consists of a CAME and a CASE component.

The CAME component is built upon a *method base management system (MBMS)*, and provides facilities for specifying, storing, and selecting method fragments, and for assembling method fragments into a situation method. The selected method fragments are stored in a *Selected Method Fragments Repository (SMFR)*, from which they are retrieved by the assembly functions.

CASE component uses the situational method as a definition for its repository structure, its editors and report generators, and its process engine. Method fragments are specified and manipulated both by entering specifications and issuing commands in a textual method engineering language called *MEL*, and by a tool called *MEL editor*. Both of these translate commands to a *MEL interpreter*, which makes use of the MBMS facilities. Decamerone offers also graphic tools. *The Concept Structure Diagram (CSD) editor* acts as a graphical user interface to the Maestro II's Data Model Declaration Table. The *Process Structure Diagram (PSD) editor* enables definition of task classes, deliverable classes and their relationships, yielding a task structure that is input to the Maestro II's PCMS. The CSD/PSD/MEL editors are currently being implemented.

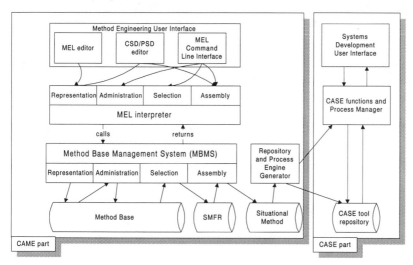

Figure 2 Architecture of Decamerone.

3.2 MetaEdit+

The analysis is based on *MetaEdit+* product (MetaEdit+, 1995; Kelly et al., 1996), and two prototypes: hypertext sub-system (Oinas-Kukkonen, 1995a, 1995b), and process sub-system (Marttiin, 1994; Koskinen, 1996).

MetaEdit+ is a multi-user and multi-tool environment developed in the MetaPHOR-project. It consists of tools for both CAME and CASE. MetaEdit+ can run either as a single-user workstation or simultaneously on many workstation clients connected by a network to a server. Each client contains a running instance of MetaEdit+, including *MetaEngine* and a set of tools. MetaEngine manages all operations on the underlying conceptual data model. Tools communicate with each other only through the MetaEngine, and thereby through the shared data in the repository. MetaEdit+ includes the following tools:

- Environment management tools: tools for managing features of the environment, its main components, and for launching it.
- Model editing tools: tools for creating, modifying, viewing and deleting models or their parts, and deriving new information from existing design information including *Diagram Editor*, *Matrix Editor*, and *Table Editor*.

- Model retrieval tools: tools for retrieving design objects and their instances from the repository for reuse and review including *Repository Browsers*, *Report Tool,* and *Query Editor*.
- Method management tools: a set of form based tools for defining methods and their components (see Figure 3).
- Hypertext subsystem, which gives, for instance, the ability to link design objects for traceability, annotating model instances, and maintain conversations about design issues (*Debate Browser*).
- Process subsystem containing a set of form based tools for defining a process modelling language and *Process Editor* for modelling ISD process and using it for guidance and co-ordination purposes.

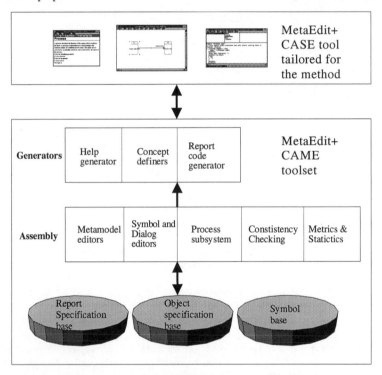

Figure 3   Method management tools in *MetaEdit+*.

Assembly in Figure 3 includes a set of editors for defining method fragments (method's conceptual structure including basic consistency rules, and method's process structure), method symbols, dialogues, and helps, and tools for producing method specific reports and code. These editors contain mechanisms to generate a method to be automatically used in CASE.

The MetaEdit+ server forms the repository holding all the data contained in models, and also in the method fragments. The MetaEdit+ repository includes *object specification base* containing all the method fragments; *symbol base* containing all symbols needed to represent method concepts; and *report specification base* containing all report and other output specifications. The repository holds also tool related information including spatial co-ordinates in a diagram, and user information including passwords, access rights, and current locks.

4 DEFINING A METHOD BY USING THE CAME ENVIRONMENTS

In this section we analyse the CAME functions in both of the environments. Table 2 presents the supported CAME functions.

Table 2 Supported CAME functions

CAME support	in Maestro II/Decamerone	in MetaEdit+
Representation	• *CSD/PSD editor* • *MEL editor*	• Form based meta-modelling tools: *Graph tool, Object tool, Property tool, Relationship tool, Role tool, Binding tool, Symbol Editor* • Other meta-modelling tools: *Table Editor, Matrix Editor and Diagram Editor* • Form based process meta-modelling tools & *Process Editor*
Analysis	• *MEL editor:* consistency checking	• Meta-modelling tools: consistency checking • *Process Editor:* task precedence
Transformation	• Transformations from CSD/PSD to MEL, and from MEL to MBMS • *Repository generator* • *Process engine generator*	• Form based meta-modelling tools: method generation into customisable CASE, method help generation • *Report Generator, Process Editor*
Control	•	• Access control for methods
Co-operation	• The use of various notations of method fragments • Co-operative information in MEL	• The use of various notations of method fragments
Support & infrastructure	•	• Help for meta-modelling language and tools

4.1 Representation

We evaluate here the meta-modelling language, abstraction mechanisms and notations used in CAME.

Meta-modelling language

Decamerone uses MEL (see Harmsen and Saeki, 1996) as a meta-modelling language. MEL is based on the basic type *method fragment*, the instances of which varies by attaching pre-defined or user-definable *property types* and *property values*. MEL allows for an integrated view on both the conceptual view of a method by providing *process fragments* and *product fragments* and the technical view (CASE tool part) by allowing to define *technical method fragments*. Process fragments can denote iteration, parallelism, non-determinism and decisions, whereas product fragments describe both 'high-level' method products (such as Functional Specification) and diagrams, concepts, and associations. Further, MEL offers facilities to anchor method descriptions in an ontology, and contains operations to administrate method fragments in the method base, to query them, and to assemble method fragments into a situational method.

MetaEdit+ uses GOPRR (Kelly et al., 1996) as a meta-modelling language. GOPRR contains a set of elementary types (*object, role,* and *relationship*), a concept for collecting the elementary types into model (*graph*), and mechanisms to decompose and structure elementary concepts (*binding*). GOPRR focuses on the modelling of the conceptual structure of techniques and various relations between these (explosions, polymorphic modelling concepts). A process modelling language can be defined using an extended GOPRR model called *GOPRR-p* (see Koskinen, 1996). The extensions contain information about the behavioural aspects of a process, e.g., states, precedence and parallelism of process elements. Moreover, related product (models or reports) and tool information can be attached to process elements.

Abstraction mechanisms

Decamerone supports aggregation and decomposition mechanisms: method fragments defined by MEL can be decomposed to detailed granularity level, and the detailed method fragments can be composed into various method fragments in general granularity level. Specialisation is supported by the IS_A keyword in MEL.

MetaEdit+ supports aggregation and decomposition of methods by collecting reusable elementary method types using the concept *Graph*. Further, a set of graphs is collected into a project. Instances of each GOPRR element are modelled using specialisation hierarchies. Therefore, *MetaEdit+* supports different ways of technique development: creation from scratch, where all the parts of the technique are defined as new concepts, component oriented, where techniques are constructed by using prefabricated parts, and reuse oriented, where the goal of technique development is to allow maximal generality of the concepts and then to specialise these general components for different techniques.

Notations

Decamerone provides two ways to represent method fragments: graphically, by using the CSD/PSD editor, and textually, by using the MEL editor. The graphical representation format is intended for initial and global specification, whereas the MEL specification contains all details of the method fragment. Process Structure Diagrams support the notions of process, trigger, and product, of which the latter provides the link with the Concept Structure Diagram editor.

In *MetaEdit+* product the primary support for technique component definition and retrieval is available as a set of form based tools, where the attributes of the component are filled and checked for their internal validity. Also, tabular, graphics and matrix support have been designed. Process structure is defined graphically.

4.2 Analysis

Validation and simulation of method fragments are not currently supported in either of the CAME environments. Therefore, we only consider the verification capabilities.

The design of *Decamerone* currently does not include a verification component. However, MEL is designed to attach information for checking consistency into its property types. Also, formalised consistency rules are available, and can be transferred to Prolan rules (Hoef and Harmsen, 1995).

The method consistency is ensured in *MetaEdit+* by implementing a GOPRR technique, which prevents the definition of syntactically incorrect methods. *MetaEdit+* approach aims to give the method engineers a maximum degree of freedom, so the tools do not try to do any semantic checking for the models. Anything that can be defined with the meta-modelling tools, is a valid technique specification in this approach. Nevertheless, a number of checks and quality reports have been defined to inform the method engineer about the possible problems in his model. Analysis according to development process, e.g. task precedence, will be supported by using a process model.

4.3 Transformation

In the following we discuss both transformations between various forms of method fragments, and transformations into CASE including documentation generation.

Transformations between method fragments

In *Decamerone* graphics (CSD/PSD) are used to define method fragments in earlier phases of CAME. These forms are transferred into MEL specifications, in the form of which the detailed method fragment is constructed.

MetaEdit+ can use table, matrix and graphics notation in the CAME process. Yet, form based meta-modelling tools can only attach symbols into method concepts and generate a method into CASE.

Transformations into CASE

MEL specifications in *Decamerone* are transformed into MBMS calls in *Maestro II*, enabling storage in the database. The finest granularity product fragments (concepts, their properties and associations) in the situational method are input to the repository generator. The process fragments in the situational method, along with the coarser granularity product fragments (e.g., a functional specification report) are transferred to the process engine generator, which creates an instance of *Maestro II's* PCMS.

Diagram editors are specified in *Maestro II*. The method data model and the representational aspects of the technique to be supported are specified separately. The method data model and conceptual definitions of all diagram editors are specified in a Data Model Declaration Table (DMDT). The notational elements are specified by using the Tool Customising Interface (TCI). The DMDT defines the repository structure managed by the Object Management System (OMS).

MetaEdit+ directly translates the method fragments into parts of its design object repository. Thus, when the user has defined the techniques: concepts and their representations, the method can be tested immediately. The form based tools have a two-way connection to the repository, but the tools using other representation form can only define components, but not retrieve them from the repository. *MetaEdit+* will test the use of pre-defined process templates to be copied and specified for projects' use.

Document creation

In *MetaEdit+*, method specific helps can be generated as a by-product of a method, and method specific reports can be created by using a Report Generator. Learning material and examples of *MetaEdit+* are separated, but implementable as external documents using hypertext subsystem.

4.4 Co-ordination: control and co-operation

The CAME environments in comparison are focused on production. However, some support for control and co-operation is found.

Control mechanism of *MetaEdit+* multi-user environment is designed also for CAME level. Co-operative aid is supported by the use of various representations of a method in each CAME environment. Also, *Decamerone's* MEL language is designed to attach situation information not generated into CASE, but usable in co-ordination of method fragments. Anyway, specific CSCW tools are not integrated.

4.5 Support

MetaEdit+ contains on-line help including descriptions of GOPRR concepts and guidelines how to use them. Since the environments are still at the early stages, the ways of supporting will improve.

5 SUPPORTING A METHOD BY USING THE CUSTOMISABLE CASE ENVIRONMENTS

In this section we shortly discuss the differences of the customisable CASE environments in their method support. Table 3 represents the functions and tools (*italics*) of the customisable CASE environments.

5.1 Representation

In contrast to drawing tools, both *Maestro II* and *MetaEdit+* are concept-oriented environments. Concepts are implemented as classes, which store information into their properties. In *Maestro II* the integration between techniques is achieved by using the DMDT, which contains references to object classes, relationships and attributes. Attributes can be shared by referring to the defining template. The following integration mechanisms are used in *MetaEdit+*: concept reuse between models, property sharing between concepts (e.g., object appears as a relationship in another technique), and explosions from an element to a model of different type.

Both CASE environments separate the conceptual and representational (notations) information. Representation forms for *MetaEdit+* are structured graphics, matrices and tables and for *Maestro II* structured graphics and text. Both of the CASE environments handle the basic graphical semantics. However, they are limited to deal with, for instance, layered complex models in the same diagram, and specific graphical rules and constraints.

Table 3 Supported CASE functions

CASE support	in Maestro II	in MetaEdit+
Representation	• *Tool Customisation Interface (TCI)* including *Diagram Editor* • *OMS Interface*	• Model editing tools: *Diagram Editor, Matrix Editor, Table Editor* • *Repository Browser*
Analysis	• *Prolan* language: user defined rules • Query mechanism	• Model editing tools: consistency checking • *Report Editor*: reports for checking • *Query Editor* • *Linking Ability*: requirement tracing
Transformation	• Report generation • Code generation • Links to other CASE tools	• *Report Editor*: generation of reports and code
Control	• *Project Configuration and Management System (PCMS)* • *Function Point Analysis* -tool	• *Project tool* • *Process Editor*
Co-operation	• *PCMS* • E-mail facilities	• Hypertext tools: *Linking Ability, Debate Browser* • *Process Editor*
Support & infrastructure	• On-line help	• Hypertext tools: *Debate Browser* • Tool guidance • Context specific method guidance

5.2 Analysis

Maestro II allows to define a wide spectrum of method specific rules by using a Prolan rule language. In *MetaEdit+* GOPRR manages a set of general rules (cardinality, connectivity and composition rules) and offers possibilities to define checking reports.

Validation of IS models in *MetaEdit+* means traceability to requirement documents. This functionality is provided by the Linking Ability. *Maestro II* offers no support for validation.

Simulation is not used in conceptual modelling domains, but essential, if we want to support process and behaviour modelling by using, for instance, State Transition Diagrams or Petri nets. Both environments do not offer simulation mechanisms.

5.3 Transformation

Maestro II provides transformation facilities such as advanced report generation, code generation, screen mock-ups, and reverse engineering. It has facilities to generate reports of the database (OMS) and project (PCMS) contents. Besides, there exist tools that provide links with other CASE tools such as Knowledgeware's ADW (Bosua and Brinkkemper, 1995).

MetaEdit+ contains a *Report Tool* to define report models and programming language structures. Therefore, transformations from a higher level model to a detailed one or a data structure of programming language can be specified.

5.4 Control

As noted before, *Maestro II* contains a Project Configuration and Management System (PCMS), which guides the user in applying a method by offering references to required tasks and deliverables. In addition, the state automaton of PCMS defines the dynamics of a project by keeping track of the various states of deliverables as well as their state transitions. Freeze and unfreeze of artefacts, and configuration and version management can be achieved. A project manager can keep track of the current state of all the activities performed by project members and compare their activities with the project plan by using the project scheduling tool incorporated in the PCMS. For estimating, a Function Point Analysis tool is developed as an extension to PCMS.

MetaEdit+'s repository is an object base, which stores the objects as such. Repository provides the locking mechanism to avoid simultaneous editing of the same diagram. However, current implementation does not provide versioning of models. GOPRR provides the automatical change propagation between the model elements that share properties. Further, the Process Editor for the guidance and co-ordination of the project specific development process is currently being implemented.

5.5 Co-operation

The CASE environments contain minor differences in their co-operative support. Both are multi-user environments having locking mechanisms for asynchronous development (one developer at a time). *Maestro II* supports communication by its e-mail facility. *MetaEdit+* co-operative functionality is found in its hypertext subsystem containing, e.g., annotations and debates attached to either modelling concepts or their representations. Moreover, by using a *DebateBrowser*, structured conversations can be managed. Still, specific group interaction mechanisms and functionality for synchronous modelling are lacking in these CASE environments.

5.6 Support

Dependent on the method or the tool used, *Maestro II* provides on-line help screens in various levels of detail. Help screens are laid out as hypertexts, enabling the user to cross-reference other topics.

MetaEdit+ offers on-line help to its general CASE tool functions. Context specific aid, descriptions of concepts, techniques and tasks, are generated as a by-product of their creation in method engineering tools. Explanations and discussions according to project tasks, models, model elements, model versions can be attached by using the hypertext support discussed above. Furthermore, the joint menus and functions of various CASE tools are designed similarly.

6 CONCLUSIONS AND FUTURE WORK

In this study we developed a framework for evaluating CAME and customisable CASE properties of current 'state of the art' environments. We selected the framework for CASE functionality presented by Henderson and Cooprider (1994) and tailored it for customisable CASE and CAME. We used the comparison framework to evaluate the properties of two environments *Maestro II* with *Decamerone*, and *MetaEdit+*.

The aim of this study was to answer the questions: *How well can a method be defined in a CAME environment?*, and *How well is a defined method supported in a customisable CASE environment?* As a result we presented the functionality and tools that are available in two environments, and functionality required after the framework.

If we consider the framework used, we can conclude that current CAME technology focuses on production, but does not deal adequately with co-ordination and support. Further, in production technology there exists several issues that have not been sufficiently examined, such as specifying the methods in detailed granularity, reuse of method fragments, and change propagation to customisable CASE.

If we look at the second question, we can conclude that in the evaluated environments method support can be achieved by representing and storing models and by checking their consistency. Also, the development process is either supported or under construction. Validation support is limited and behavioural semantics of modelling elements for, e.g., simulation of Petri-net diagrams is not available. Moreover, both environments are limited in their integration of tools for specific tasks, including co-operation, project management, and learning issues.

The main purpose of the environments examined is to improve IS development support by tailoring a method specific CASE for project needs. The quality of such a tailorable environment means the support for the methods required by customers, the methods without any hard-coded CASE support, and the freedom to modify methods. Further, this study explained the framework functions supported. It did not focus on usability or integrity of the tools supporting these functions. Therefore, one should not draw a straightforward conclusion that an environment supporting all framework aspects is a good one.

In the future we would need to use a more comprehensive approach to evaluate these environments. First, we will generate a set of exact questions for each CAME function. Second, we will select an example method to be modelled for the CASE environments. By using this comprehensive approach for evaluating the environments we will obtain a detailed view of the environments. The evaluation of other environments should also be performed.

7 ACKNOWLEDGEMENTS

We would like to thank the other members of the projects MetaPHOR (University of Jyväskylä) and Method Engineering Group (University of Twente), and in particular Sjaak Brinkkemper for his assistance and co-operation, and Steven Kelly, Kalle Lyytinen, and Tuuli Rossi for the improvements on this paper.

8 REFERENCES

Auramäki, E., Leppänen, M. and Savolainen, V. (1988) Universal framework for information systems. *Data base*, **19**, 1, pp. 11-20.

Bergsten, P., Bubenko, J., Dahl, R., Gustafsson, M. and Johansson, L.-Å. (1989) RAMATIC - a CASE shell for implementation of specific CASE tools. TEMPORA T6.1 report, SISU, Stockholm, Sweden.

Boloix, G., Sorenson, P.G. and Tremblay, J.P. (1991) On Transformations Using A Metasystem Approach To Software Development. Technical report, The University of Alberta, Edmonton, Alberta, Canada.

Bosua, R. and Brinkkemper, S. (1995) Realisation of an Integrated Software Engineering Environment through Heterogeneous CASE-Tool Integration. *Software Engineering Environments* (Ed. M.S. Verrall), IEEE Computer Science Press, pp. 152-159.

Brinkkemper, S. (1990) Formalisation of Information Systems Modelling. Ph.D. Dissertation, University of Nijmegen, Thesis Publishers, Amsterdam.

Brinkkemper, S. (1995) Method engineering: engineering of information systems development methods and tools. *Information and Software Technology*, **37**, 11, pp. 1-6.

Brodie, M. (1984) On the developments of data models. *Perspectives from Artificial Intelligence, Databases and Programming Languages* (Eds. M. Brodie, J. Mylopoulos and J. Schmidt), Springer-Verlag, pp. 19-47.

Bubenko, J.A. jr. (1988) Selecting a strategy for computer-aided software engineering (CASE). SYSLAB Report No 59, SYSLAB, University of Stockholm, Sweden.

Chen, M., Nunamaker, J.F. jr. (1989) MetaPlex: an integrated environment for organization and information systems development. *Proceedings of the 10th ICIS* (Eds. J.I. DeGross, J.C. Henderson and B.R. Konsynski), ACM Press, New York, NY, pp. 141-151.

Cronholm, S. and Goldkuhl, G. (1994) Meanings and Motives of Method Customizations in CASE Environments. *5th Workshop on Next Generation of CASE Tools*, June 6-7. Utrecht, The Netherlands.

Crozier, M., Glass, D., Hughes, J., Johnston, W. and McChesney, I. (1989) Critical analysis of tools for computer-aided software engineering. *Information and Software Technology*. **31**, 9, pp. 486-496.

Curtis, B., Kellner, M.I. and Over, J. (1992) Process modeling. *Communications of the ACM*, **35**, 9, pp. 75-90.

Essink, L. (1986) A modelling approach to information system development. *Information Systems Design Methodologies: Improving the practise* (Eds. T.W. Olle, H.G. Sol and A.A. Verrijn-Stuart), North-Holland, Amsterdam, pp. 55-86.

Euromethod (1994) Euromethod Architecture. Euromethod project deliverable Work Package 3, 1994.

Fuggetta, A. (1993) A classification of CASE Technology. *IEEE Computer*, **26**, 12, pp. 25-38.

Hahn, U., Jarke, M. and Rose, T. (1991) Teamwork Support in a Knowledge-Based Information Systems Environment. *IEEE Transactions on Software Engineering*, **17**, May, pp. 467-481.

Harmsen, F. and Brinkkemper S. (1995) Design and Implementation of a Method Base Management System for a Situational CASE Environment. *Proceedings of the 2nd Asian-Pacific Software Engineering Conference (APSEC'95)*, IEEE Computer Society Press, Los Alamitos, CA, pp. 430-438.

Harmsen, F., Brinkkemper S. and Oei H. (1994) Situational Method Engineering for Information System Projects. *Proceedings of the IFIP WG8.1 Working Conference CRIS'94* (Eds. T.W. Olle and A.A. Verrijn-Stuart), North-Holland Publishers, Amsterdam, pp. 169-194.

Harmsen, F., Lubbers I. and Wijers G. (1995) Success-driven selection of Fragments for Situational Methods - The S cube model. *Proceedings REFSQ'95 Workshop* (Eds. P. Peters and K. Pohl), Aachener Berichte zur Informatik, pp. 104-115.

Harmsen, F., and Saeki, M. (1996) Comparison of Four Method Engineering Languages. *Proceedings IFIP WG8.1/8.2 Working Conference on Principles of Method Construction and Tool Support (ME'96)*, Atlanta, Georgia, USA.

Henderson, J.C. and Cooprider, J.G. (1994) Dimensions of IS Planning and Design Aids: A Functional Model of CASE Technology. *IT and the Corporation of the 1990's: Research studies* (Eds. T. Allen and M. Scott-Morton), Oxford University Press, pp. 221-248.

Heym, M. and Österle, H. (1992) A reference model of information systems development. *The Impact of Computer Supported Technologies on Information Systems Development* (Eds. K.E. Kendall, K. Lyytinen and J.I. DeGross), Amsterdam, North-Holland, pp. 215-240.

Hoef, R. van de and Harmsen F. (1995) Quality requirements for situational methods. *Proceedings of the NGCT'95 Workshop*, Jyväskylä, Finland.

ISDOS (1981) An introdution to the System Encyclopedia Manager, ISDOS Ref #81 SEM-0338-1, ISDOS Project, Department of Industrial and Operations Engineering, The University of Michigan, Ann Arbor, Michigan.

Jarke, M., Pohl, K., Rolland, C. and Schmitt, J.-R. (1994) Experience-Based Method Evaluation and Improvement: A process modeling approach. *Proceedings of the IFIP WG8.1 Working Conference CRIS'94* (Eds. T.W. Olle and A.A. Verrijn-Stuart), North-Holland Publishers, Amsterdam, pp. 1-27.

Kelly S., Lyytinen, K. and Rossi, M. (1996) MetaEdit+ A Fully Configurable Multi-User and multi-Tool CASE and CAME Environment. *Proceedings of the CAiSE'96 conference*, 20-24 May, Heraklion, Crete, Greece.

Koskinen, M. (1996) Designing Multiple Process Modelling Languages for Flexible, Enactable Process Models in a MetaCASE Environment, *Proceedings of the 7th European Workshop on Next Generation CASE Tools (NGCT'96)*, Heraklion, Crete, Greece.

Kumar, K. and Welke, R.J. (1992) Methodology Engineering: A proposal for Situation-specific Methodology Engineering. *Challenges and Strategies for Research in Systems Development* (Eds. W.W. Cotterman and J.A Senn), John Wiley and Sons Ltd., pp. 257-269.

Lyytinen, K., Smolander, K. and Tahvanainen, V.-P. (1989) Modelling CASE Environments in Systems Work. *CASE' 89 conference papers*, Kista, Sweden.

Marttiin, P. (1994) Towards Flexible Process Support with a CASE Shell. *Advanced Information Systems Engineering* (Eds. G. Wijers, S. Brinkkemper and T. Wasserman), LNCS#811, Springer-Verlag, pp. 14-27.

Marttiin, P., Lyytinen, K., Rossi, M., Tahvanainen, V.-P., Smolander, K. and Tolvanen, J.-P. (1995) Modeling Requirements for Future CASE: modeling issues and architectural considerations. *Information Resource Management Journal*, **8**, 1, pp. 15-25.

Marttiin, P., Rossi, M., Tahvanainen, V.-P. and Lyytinen, K. (1993) A Comparative Review of CASE Shells: a preliminary framework and research outcomes. *Information and Management*, **25**, pp. 11-31.

Merbeth, G. (1991) Maestro II - das integrierte CASE-System von Softlab. *CASE Systeme und Werkzeuge* (Ed. H. Balzert), BI Wissenschaftsverlag, pp. 319-336.

MetaEdit+ (1995) MetaEdit+: Method Workbench User's Guide (version 2.0). MetaCase Consulting, MicroWorks Finland.

Misra, S.K. (1990) Analysing CASE system characteristics: evaluative framework. *Information and Software Technology*, **32**, 6, pp. 415-422.

Nijssen, G.M. (1989) An Axiom and Architecture for Information Systems. *Information System as an In-Depth Analysis* (Ed. E.D. Falkenberg), Elsevier Science Publishers B.V. (North-Holland), IFIP, pp. 157-175.

Norman, R.J. and Chen, M. (1992) Working together to integrated CASE. *IEEE Software*, March, pp. 13-16.

Oei, J.L.H. and E.D. Falkenberg (1994) Harmonisation of Information System Modelling and Specification Techniques. *Proceedings of the IFIP WG8.1 Working Conference CRIS'94* (Eds. T.W. Olle and A.A. Verrijn-Stuart), North-Holland Publishers, Amsterdam, pp. 151-168.

Oinas-Kukkonen, H. (1995a) Linking Ability - a Model Linking Tool for MetaEdit+ Environment. Working paper series B39, Department of Information Processing Science, University of Oulu, Finland.

Oinas-Kukkonen, H. (1995b) Debate Browser - a Design Rationale Tool for MetaEdit+ Environment. Working paper series B40, Department of Information Processing Science, University of Oulu, Finland.

Olle, T.W., Hagelstein, J., MacDonald, I.G., Rolland, C., Sol, H.G., Van Assche, F.J.M. and Verrijn-Stuart, A.A (1991) *Information Systems Methodologies: A framework for understanding*. Addison-Wesley Publishing Company, Wokingham, England.

Olle, T.W., Sol, H.G. and Tully, C.J. (Eds.) (1983) *Information Systems Design Methodologies: A Feature Analysis*. Elsevier Science Publishers, North-Holland, Amsterdam.

Olle, T.W., Sol, H.G. and Verrjin-Stuart, A.A. (Eds.) (1982) *Information Systems Design Methodologies: A comparative review*. Elsevier Science Publishers, North-Holland, Amsterdam.

Olle, T.W., Sol, H.G. and Verrijn-Stuart, A.A. (Eds.) (1986) *Information Systems Design Methodologies: Improving the practise.* Elsevier Science Publishers, North-Holland, Amsterdam.

Rossi, M., Gustafsson, M., Smolander, K., Johansson, L.-Å. and Lyytinen, K. (1992) Metamodeling Editor as a Front End Tool for a CASE Shell. *Advanced Information Systems Engineering* (Ed. P. Loucopoulos), LNCS#593, Springer-Verlag, Berlin, Germany, pp. 546-567.

Saeki, M., Iguchi, K., Wen-yin, K. and Shinohara, M. (1993) A meta-model for representing software specification & design methods. *Proceedings of the IFIP WG8.1 Conference on Information Systems Development Process* (Eds. N. Prakash, C. Rolland and P. Pernici), Como, pp. 149-166.

Slooten, K. van, and Brinkkemper S. (1993) A Method Engineering Approach to Information Systems Development. *Proceedings of the IFIP WG8.1 Conference on Information Systems Development Process* (Eds. N. Prakash, C. Rolland and P. Pernici), Como, pp. 167-186.

Smolander, K., Lyytinen, K., Tahvanainen, V.-P. and Marttiin P. (1991) MetaEdit - A flexible graphical environment for methodology modelling. *Advanced Information Systems Engineering,* (Eds. R. Andersen, J. Bubenko and A. Sølvberg), LNCS #498, Springer-Verlag, pp. 168-193.

Smolander, K. (1992) OPRR - A Model for Methodology Modeling. *Next Generation of CASE Tools* (Eds. K. Lyytinen and V.-P. Tahvanainen), Studies in Computer and Communication Systems, IOS press, pp. 224-239.

Sorenson, P.G., Tremblay, J-P. and McAllister, A.J. (1988) The Metaview system for many specification environments. *IEEE Software*, **30**, 3, March, pp. 30-38.

Ter Hofstede, A. H. M. and Weide, Th. P. van der (1993) Expressiveness in data modeling. *Data & Knowledge Engineering*, **10**, pp. 65-100.

Venable, J. (1993) CoCoA: A Conceptual Data Modelling Approach for Complex Problem Domains. Ph.D. dissertation, State University of New York, Binghampton.

Verhoef, T.F. and Ter Hofstede, A.H.M. (1995) Feasibility of Flexible Information Modelling Support. *Advanced Information Systems Engineering* (Eds. J. Iivari, K. Lyytinen and M. Rossi), LNCS #932, Springer-Verlag, pp. 168-185.

Vessey, I., Jarvenpaa, S. and Tractinsky, N., Evaluation of Vendor Product: CASE Tools as Methodology Companions. *Communications of the ACM*, **35**, 4, pp. 90-105.

Wijers, G. and Dort, H. van (1990) Experiences with the use of CASE tools in the Netherlands. *Advanced Information Systems Engineering* (Eds. B. Steinholz, A. Sølvberg and L. Bergman), LNCS#436, Springer-Verlag, pp. 5-20.

Wijers, G. (1991) Modelling Support in Information Systems Development. Ph.D. dissertation, Thesis publishers, Amsterdam.

Wynekoop, J.D. and Russo, N.L. (1993) System development methodologies: unanswered questions and the research-practice gap. *Proceedings of 14th ICIS* (Eds. J.I DeGross, R.P Bostrom and D. Robey), Orlando, USA, pp. 181-190.

9 BIOGRAPHY

Pentti Marttiin is a researcher in the MetaPHOR project funded by the Academy of Finland. He received his M.Sc. (1991) and Econ.Lic. (1994) at the Department of Computer Science and Information Systems, University of Jyväskylä, Finland. He has written articles on method engineering and metaCASE environments published in Information and Management, Information Resource Management Journal, and several conferences. He has participated ICIS'92 doctoral consortium, served as a program committee member in CAiSE'95, and involved in the development of metaCASE tools for Meta Case Conculting. His current research interest focuses on process and agent modelling aspects in metaCASE.

Frank Harmsen is a researcher in the Information Systems Design Methodology Research Group at the Computer Science Department of the University of Twente in the Netherlands. He holds a B.Sc and M.Sc in Mathematics and Computer Science from the University of Nijmegen. His research interests are information system methodology, meta-modelling, method engineering, and CASE tools, about which he has published several papers. Current research activities focus on defining formalisms and tools for representation and assembly of method fragments for Situational Method Engineering. He was co-editor of the 1993 edition of the Workshop on Next Generation of CASE Tools (NGCT), and served on the organisation committee of CAiSE'94 (Conference on Advanced Information Systems Engineering). He is a member of the Netherlands Society for Informatics.

Matti Rossi is a researcher in the MetaPHOR project funded by the Academy of Finland. He received his M.Sc. (1994) and Econ.Lic. (1996) at the Department of Computer Science and Information Systems, University of Jyväskylä, Finland. He has published in Information and Management, Information Systems, and Information Resource Management Journal, and participated CAiSE, ECOOP, WITS and SERF conferences. He has served on the Workshop, Poster and Exhibition Chair of the CAISE'95 conference. He is also a member of the board in Meta Case Conculting, and has involved in implementing the report generation facility of MetaEdit and CAME tools of MetaEdit+. His research interests include database management, object-oriented data representation, metamodelling, transformations in metamodelling, and the applications of the previous items to software engineering.

6

Method rationale in method engineering and use

H. Oinas-Kukkonen
Department of Information Processing Science
P.O. Box 400, FIN-90571 Oulu, Finland
Tel. (358) 81 553 1900, Fax. (358) 81 553 1890
Email: hok@rieska.oulu.fi

Abstract
While the major aspect in method engineering is method assembly, a second aspect is the argumentation behind the methods. This paper introduces the concept of method rationale in method engineering and use as a communication vehicle between method and software engineers, and describes tools that support the capture and management of method rationale in a computer-aided method engineering environment.

Keywords
Information systems development, method engineering, CASE, metaCASE, CAME, design rationale, method rationale, hypertext

1 INTRODUCTION

The emergence of metaCASE and Computer-Aided Method Engineering (CAME) technology has provided the field information system development (ISD) with new promises. One of them is the utilization of the same computerized environment to develop both ISD methods and target information systems. Still, even when methods can be assembled in a CAME environment, part of the important method-related knowledge normally remains implicit, e.g. experience accumulated about the methods in use (Jarke et al., 1994). Computerized support for capturing this kind of semi-structured information is also needed.

A simple means for modelling experience information in conjunction with metaCASE is to maintain a textual note for each method (Heym and Österle 1993). The solution in this paper, however, provides a method and metamodelling independent, and a more sophisticated and effective means for recording semi-structured information. This paper considers information systems development and method engineering as a special case of design, and bases its solution on the concept of **design rationale** (Fischer et al., 1991, Ramesh and Dhar, 1992). Design rationale means basically the understanding of **why an artifact has been designed the way it has**, which may include information on e.g. requirements, assumptions, decisions, and alternative solutions. The benefits of design rationale capture include the achievement of increased rigor and clarity of thinking, augmentation of the designer's memory, better communication among team members and stakeholders, and improved meetings (Conklin and Yakemovic, 1991). The concept of design rationale in conjunction with method engineering and ISD (i.e. method use) is leveraged here in the following manner. **Method rationale means method design and usage rationales and their linkages to design artifacts across various phases of method engineering and use.**

This paper introduces tools which can be utilized to support method rationale in a full-blown CAME environment, and describes an approach by which method rationale can be used as a communication vehicle between the stakeholders in this kind of environment.

2   RESEARCH ENVIRONMENT

MetaEdit+ is a fully configurable multiuser, multitool Computer-Aided Software and Method Engineering environment (Kelly et al., 1996). In addition to basic model editing and retrieval tools, MetaEdit+ also includes tools which enable the creation, modification and deletion of annotations and navigational hyperlinks between models or their parts. The model annotation and linking tools (Debate Browser and Linking Ability) are seamlessly integrated with the model editing tools (Diagram Editor, Matrix Editor and Table Editor), and they are used for commenting model instances, maintaining conversations about design issues, linking design objects for traceability and as a reminder, or finding specific locations in the design space.

Debate Browser

The Debate Browser is a hypertext-based toolset for supporting the capture and use of design rationale knowledge. It utilizes an argumentation method similar to IBIS (Conklin and Begeman, 1988), known as QAR (Question-Answer-aRgument). QAR has been abstracted from various design rationale methods for our purposes in MetaEdit+ environment, simplifying the explicit rhetorical structure of design rationale (Oinas-Kukkonen, 1996). The discussion is expressed using three kinds of nodes, questions, answers, and arguments. There is also a particular way of registering that a question has been resolved by agreement upon some answer by selecting and presenting one of the suggested answers as a decision. A node always belongs to a **hyperdocument**, a collection of discussions, consisting of **nodes and links** between the nodes. There can be various design rationale hyperdocuments for debates on different kinds of subjects, for example different organizational, research, product and other problem domains, as well as within a project for analysis, design, implementation and review concerns.

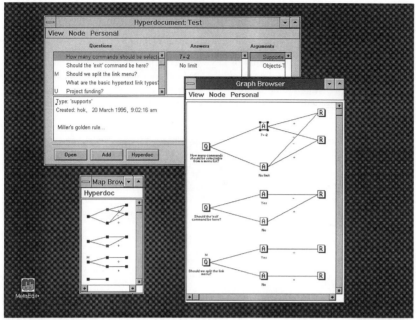

Figure 1   Graphical and textual views in Debate Browser toolset.

Debate Browser enables the investigation of design rationale hyperdocuments and their nodes and links with two browsers, a document browser and a graph browser. (See Figure 1.) The document browser gives text lists of all the question nodes of a hyperdocument, the answer nodes of an activated question, and the argument nodes of an activated answer, with the active node always visible at the bottom of the browser. The graph browser presents a graphical web view of the design rationale hyperdocument, supporting the investigation of a full hyperdocument as well as a single question and its associated answers and arguments. The zoom capability enables the investigation of the hyperdocument through map views (see lower left corner in Figure 1). The investigation of questions and their relationships is enabled from different perspectives in all views, i.e. as a plain collection of questions or from generalization-specialization, replacement-replacer, or parent-child perspectives. Nodes which have not yet been investigated by an individual reader can be highlighted, node marking is enabled, and summary reports of the design rationale hyperdocuments can be given among other features.

Linking Ability

Design rationale has to be integrated with construction environment to contextualize the rationale, and with the issues to concentrate more on design than merely philosophical discussions (Fischer et al., 1991). This can be achieved via attaching associative

hyperlinks to design diagrams and design rationale nodes (which are different from the responds, supports etc. links within design rationale hyperdocuments) through the Linking Ability tool. All hyperlinks are created by hand at will, and they can lead to any other design rationale node or diagram. More semantics can be stored into a link through link attributes, e.g. type information or keywords. The hyperlink attribute query facility helps to find specific linkages. Other sophisticated hypertext browsing features include an interaction history, filtering mechanism, and landmark and bookmark lists. This kind of hypermedia functionality also gives good modelling transparency (Brinkkemper, 1993).

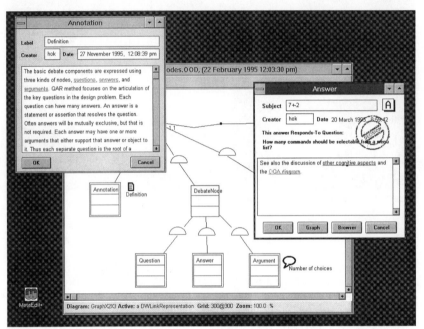

Figure 2   Linkages between a diagram, a design rationale node and an annotation.

Linking Ability also enables the attachment of annotations to diagrams or design rationale nodes. (See Figure 2.) There are two hyperlinks in an object-oriented diagram, represented by graphical symbols. The traversal of the hyperlinks takes the reader to corresponding nodes. The 'Definition' hyperlink leads to an annotation node 'Definition' commenting on the relationships between design rationale nodes. The annotation node includes three hyperlinks to other annotations. The 'Number of choices' hyperlink leads to a design rationale node (answer) '7+-2', which has been selected as a decision for a certain question. The design rationale node includes hyperlinks to another node and a diagram as well. Relationship representation and navigation and requirements tracing can be supported through this kind of linking capability.

3 APPLICATION OF THE MODEL ANNOTATION AND LINKING TOOLS

Let us now imagine a software project, consisting of a group of software designers and a smaller group of method engineers. Methods for business processes, information system planning, analysis and design, e.g. value chain, work flow models, and OMT (all adapted to the situation at hand), have been defined by **method engineers** using the metamodelling language and its rationale. Both the method-specific and general design rationale behind this method assembly has been captured using the Debate Browser. Figure 3 describes the role of method rationale in ISD and ME activities (it is modified from the software process support of Jarke et al. (1994)).

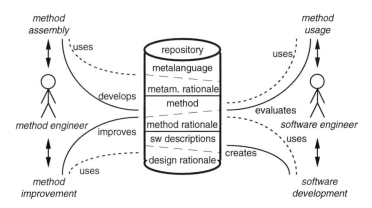

Figure 3   Method rationale in ISD and ME activities.

The methods and their design rationale guide **software designers** in their work. When software engineers use the methods to develop software artifacts they parallelly evaluate the methods in a realistic context and capture debates on them into the corresponding hyperdocuments. Software engineers are also encouraged to record software design rationale. All this takes place through the Debate Browser. When design problems or method evaluation are not mature enough for explicating debates, software engineers can attach annotations to design diagrams instead of structured discussions. Software engineers may also represent dependencies between artifacts and rationale through hyperlinks in Linking Ability, in which they may also attach specific keywords, e.g. 'method' to represent its perceived potential for method improvement.

Method engineers are interested in investigating the debates, annotations and linkages, which relate to methods and have been recorded by software engineers during their normal working process. First, they investigate the method evaluation documents, consisting of debates between software engineers regarding various aspects of method usage. Second, method engineers investigate method-related annotations through Linking Ability. Third, they are able to find and traverse the dependencies between argumentation and the design artifacts. Method engineers especially benefit from link attribute queries, such as obtaining all hyperlinks, where keyword 'method' is attached, then backtracking or traversing to either of the link end-points.

To summarize, the model annotation and linking tools can be utilized in method engineering and use in the following ways.

• Method engineers use Debate Browser to capture the design rationale behind the method assembly, which then guides software engineers in their work. Later, during development projects software engineers and reviewers capture debates behind software design, relating this kind of project performance either directly or indirectly to methods used.

• Software engineers use Linking Ability to represent the dependencies between models, rationale, and annotations through hyperlinks. A descriptive traceability process model or process trace (Jarke et al., 1994) is established among the design diagrams through linkages. When the design problems are not mature enough for explicit design rationale, software engineers can built annotations instead. This helps in avoiding premature segmentation of knowledge.

In the MetaEdit+ environment the process models and meta-models help to specify the occasions and events when method and design rationale is to be captured, e.g. phases, steps, decisions, milestones or reviews (Marttiin, 1994). Overall, the captured method rationale can be applied to method evaluation and improvement, to raise the level of consciousness and communication among the stakeholders, and to provide a help or learning system. Method rationale may play an especially important role in very large projects or in method engineering which takes place over time.

4   DISCUSSION AND CONCLUSIONS

This paper has described tools and principles for collecting and sharing experience and other information on the applicability of methods used. The proposed solution consists of capturing the method rationale in a CAME environment. Method rationale means method design and usage rationales and their linkages to design artifacts across various phases of method engineering and use. The tools described in this paper already exist in the MetaEdit+ environment, and even if they have been used so far to capture only software design rationale, we believe that they can be utilized in a similar manner to capture and share knowledge about methods.

The computerized method rationale capture takes place as an active and integral part of the ISD and ME processes, lessening the need for e.g. after-project interviews or other manual tasks. In this manner method rationale and its support tools help to achieve an advanced CAME environment. Capturing method rationale also provides a means for analysing and comparing different methods through their existing or non-existing features, e.g. requirements and assumptions. The original design rationale concept also becomes especially interesting when it is enlarged to method, process, project and business knowledge, supporting the creation and use of organizational memory.

Method rationale embeds a new conceptual structure and description language to a CAME environment, and it can be utilized on any level of abstraction or in any phase of the ISD or ME activities. In general, model annotation and linking tools in computer-aided design environments may enhance both target system quality and the quality of the process through which they are developed. One of the most important steps in future research is the development of principles for utilizing method rationale for method refinements, e.g. defining the connection between software process models and method rationale capture.

5 ACKOWLEDGEMENTS

I want to express my thanks to the other members of the MetaPHOR project, in particular Juha-Pekka Tolvanen, Steven Kelly, and Pentti Marttiin for our discussions on method engineering.

6 REFERENCES

Brinkkemper, S. (1993) Integrating Diagrams in CASE Tools Through Modelling Transparency. *Information and Software Technology*, **35**, 2, 101-105.

Conklin, J. and Begeman, M.L. (1988) gIBIS: A Hypertext Tool for Exploratory Policy Discussion. *ACM Transactions on Office Information Systems*, **6**, 4, 303-331.

Conklin, E.J. and Yakemovic, KC Burgess (1991) A Process-Oriented Approach to Design Rationale. *Human-Computer Interaction*, **6**, 3&4, 357-319.

Fischer, G., Lemke, A.G., McCall, R. and Morch, A.I. (1991) Making Argumentation Serve Design. *Human-Computer Interaction*, **6**, 3&4, 393-419.

Heym, M. and Österle, H. (1993) Computer-Aided Methodology Engineering. *Information & Software Technology*, **35**, 6&7, 345-354.

Jarke, M., Pohl, K., Rolland, C. and Schmitt, J.-R. (1994) Experience-Based Method Evaluation and Improvement: A Process Modeling Approach, in *Methods and Associated Tools for the Information Systems Life Cycle* (eds. A.A. Verrijn-Stuart and T.W. Olle), IFIP Transactions A-55, North-Holland, Amsterdam, 1-27.

Kelly, S., Lyytinen, K., and Rossi, M. (1996) MetaEdit+: A Fully Configurable Multiuser and Multitool CASE Environment, in *Proceedings of the Eigth International Conference on Advanced Information Systems Engineering (CAiSE '96)*, Crete, Greece, May 1996.

Marttiin, P. (1994) Towards Flexible Process Support with a CASE Shell, in *Advanced Information Systems Engineering* (eds. G. Wijers, S. Brinkkemper and T. Wasserman), LGNS#811, Springer-Verlag, 1994, 14-27.

Oinas-Kukkonen, H. (1996) Debate Browser - An Argumentation Tool for MetaEdit+ Environment, in *Proceedings of the Seventh European Workshop on Next Generation of CASE Tools (NGCT '96)*, Crete, Greece, May 1996.

Ramesh, B. and Dhar, V. (1992) Supporting Systems Development by Capturing Deliberations During Requirements Engineering. *IEEE Transactions on Software Engineering*, **18**, 6, June, 498-510.

7

How to compose an Object-Oriented Business Process Model?

P. Kueng[1], P. Bichler[2], P. Kawalek[1] and M. Schrefl[2]

[1] *IPG, Computer Science Department, University of Manchester, Oxford Road, Manchester M13 9PL, UK. Tel: +44 161 275 6183 Fax: +44 161 275 6236 Email: {kueng, kawalek}@cs.man.ac.uk*

[2] *DKE, Department of Information Systems, University of Linz, Austria. Tel: +43 732 2468 9479 Fax +43 732 2468 9471 Email: {bichler, schrefl}@uni-linz.ac.at*

Abstract

Faced with the intensive business process reengineering activities in many companies, it is not surprising that the issue of process modelling has become a central concern. This paper shows that object-oriented system development methods can be applied to the field of business process modelling, but that certain steps are needed in advance. For example, it is necessary to compose a goal-means hierarchy, to establish necessary activities and roles, and to determine the input and output for each activity. In this paper, we examine step by step how business processes can be modelled, which data are needed for each step and which result would be produced during each step.

Keywords

Business process modelling, goal-means hierarchy, object-orientation

1 INTRODUCTION

Today, many organizations undertake fundamental change programmes with the aim of improving their market competitiveness. Typically, the main challenges they confront are the reduction of cycle time, decreasing overall costs, and the improvement of customer satisfaction. In pursuit of such benefits the organization may seek to adapt or design processes with the aim of simplification, better control or the ready availability of information relating to the state of extant business cases. These changes are often accompanied by increased dependency on complex and heterogeneous software systems. Against this background it is not surprising that more and more enterprises establish new workflow systems for which they aim to prove coherent support of their business processes. Whilst the demand concerning business process related software and development methodologies has already reached a notable level, commercially available workflow management systems are only now evolving beyond a rather overly simple, Taylorist, production-line metaphor. Furthermore empirically proven methodologies for modelling and implementing business processes do not exist, cf. [Swenson/Irwin 95].

The rest of the paper is concerned with the presentation of a modelling approach. It focuses upon the notion of a goal. The hypothesis is that the modelling of behaviour (e.g. a business process) is best understood as purposeful, and can be described through goals. This work has been developed at the University of Linz and shall be progressed in collaboration with the University of Manchester. The paper is organized as follows: Section 2 gives an overview to today's business process modelling approaches. Section 3 gives a short introduction to a business process, showing how a system development life cycle could look like and how our goal-based modelling process is embedded. Section 4 shows how both enterprise-wide and business process-related goals can be modelled. In section 5, we use a case study to transfer goals into activities and explain how logical dependencies between activities can be visualised. Section 6 presents and applies the concept of roles. In section 7, our example will be transformed into an object-oriented model. Section 8 concludes with a summary and an outlook on additional issues to be addressed in our research. Overall, we believe the contribution to be the innovation of a methodological framework rather than the creation of new notations.

The case study considers an insurance company with offices throughout Europe. The investigators spoke to commercial underwriters and administrators in the London headquarters and local office. Compared to other insurance sectors (e.g. motor policies, home insurance), the commercial sector is low volume and highly labour intensive. Underwriters receive submissions from brokers which describe major risk proposals (e.g. all the factories of a multi-national manufacturer). To process a single submission can be time-consuming. It is likely to involve many interactions with the broker and within the insurance company itself (e.g. between underwriters and administrators). The case study took place with the company in a phase of expansion.

2 THE STATE OF THE ART

To date several methodologies have been proposed. They can be grouped into four broad categories:

Activity-oriented approaches: As the name implies, activity-oriented approaches focus primarily upon activities (sometimes referred to as tasks). The flow of information, the involved organizational units, and data are either not considered or are understood in the context of the description of activities. Activity-oriented approaches are well suited to high level process description. At a lower level they are used for simulation, e.g. estimating of cycle time. There are many activity-oriented approaches, e.g. Information Control Nets [Ellis/Nutt 80], Trigger Modelling [Joosten 94], Event-driven Process Chains [Scheer 94]. Taking into account that the mentioned methods differ from each other, criticism can be only fragmentary:

- Activity-oriented approaches generally offer good support to the process of refinement. However this may encourage too much attention to be paid to the detailed process structure and too little to the main structure of the business process.

- Activity-oriented approaches tend to define a business process as a specific ordering of activities. This mechanistic view may fail to represent the true complexity of work, and may lead to the failure of the implementation of a new business process.

Object-oriented approaches: The principles which we associate with object orientation, for example encapsulation and specialization, may in various ways be a part of other approaches (e.g. activity-oriented approaches, role-oriented approaches). The well known object-oriented methods (e.g. [Booch 94], [Embley et al. 92]) are widely used for designing and implementing software systems. It seems obvious that the principles of object orientation be applied to business process modelling. Are the techniques, in their current form, adequate for business process modelling? Not fully, because:

- If the focus is only upon objects – describing structures and methods – the objectives of the business process may not be considered. Starting with our hypothesis about the value of understanding business through purpose, it can be implied that whilst object orientation offers well understood benefits, it does not follow that a business needs to be considered as a set of objects at all levels of abstraction. An alternative is to recognise other semantic concepts such as purpose and to map them to an object structure at an appropriate level. In this way the approach differs from some others which also give a high level view of the business, e.g. [Graham 95].

- Business processes are not designed by information systems specialists but primarily by process owners or their team members. Empirical evidence of case studies suggests that if you ask these people how a certain business process operates, they will give a description of activities, e.g. [Kawalek 95]. In other words: process owners and team members describe their work through activities rather than objects.

- Most object-oriented methodologies apply object interaction diagrams. In these diagrams we can identify the concept of roles. The weakness of this approach is that the assignment of roles is done normally as a minor matter. If roles are important to us then we need to give more attention to their assignment.

Role-oriented approaches: Probably the best known role-oriented technique is the Role Activity Diagram (often called just RADs) [Ould 95]. The origin of the technique lies with the modelling of coordination by [Holt et al. 83]. The concept of 'role' is obviously central and yet is rather loosely defined. Ould suggests that a role "... involves a set of activities which, taken together, carry out a particular responsibility or responsibilities" [Ould 95, p. 29]. To Halé a role is "The position played in a process by an individual, team or unit" [Halé 95, p. 237]. Given these broad definitions we can describe many things as roles, whether they be whole job descriptions (e.g. administrator), parts of work activity (e.g. make expense claim) or sub-parts of that activity (e.g. calculate expenses). It follows that roles are conceptually similar to modules. They allow a grouping of primitive activities which can then be assigned to a particular person or agent. [Kawalek 95] argues that the strengths of RADs lie with their ability to express this modularity of work through roles and the synchronisation between these roles. Essentially this means that through a role-oriented approach we are able to describe process behaviour at different levels. We can describe the co-ordination between roles and demarcate this from our concern for the co-ordination within roles. RADs are increasingly popular, especially within the UK. They seem to have many strengths but also some weaknesses, for example:

- RADs are not very suitable if it is important to express an intricate sequencing logic. For example, it can be difficult to express behaviours where two activities can be carried out alternatively. It is still more difficult a behaviour where the sequence of two or more activities is undefined except for the fact that they cannot be carried out concurrently.

Speech-act oriented approaches: Speech act theory was mainly created by Austin and his student Searle, cf. [Winograd/Flores 86, p. 58]. Further development, under the label "Language/Action Perspective" were made by Winograd, Flores and Medina-Mora, cf. [Medina-Mora et al. 92]. The underlying concept behind Language/Action Perspective is the so called "ActionWorkflow Loop": In each communication process (workflow) we can distinguish between a customer and a performer. The communication process itself consists of a four-phased loop: proposal, agreement, performance, and satisfaction. The speech-act approach is novel, interesting and potentially very significant. From various sources (e.g. [Agostini et al. 94]) empirical examples of its use are being assembled. What are the current limitations of speech-act oriented approaches?

- Carrying out business cases is always seen as a communication between a customer and a performer. The model doesn't take into account several parties. Furthermore it is not always obvious which part is customer and which is performer. In different business cases they can have a different behaviour.

- It is not clear whether speech-act oriented approaches are primarily dedicated for analysing existing processes or for creating new processes. In the former case, a speech-act oriented approach could help to analyse communication flow between process participants. In the case of creating new processes, this approach doesn't provide much help: neither does it help to find adequate roles nor does it help to identify activities for supporting given goals.

As a broad conclusion concerning the aforementioned approaches, it seems that today's business process modelling approaches are still immature. There could well be a viable synthesis of approaches in the future. Such a synthesis would have to address three things: First, it would have to look broadly at business processes and appreciate the relationship between the operational behaviour and managerial co-ordination, control, development and policy [Beer 79]. Secondly, it would need to describe the process of modelling. Thirdly, developing the previous point, they need to describe what kind of information has to be input to a methodology and is output from its application. In this way we would be able to select methods in an contingent way according to the circumstances of our modelling project.

3 KEY ELEMENTS CONCERNING BUSINESS PROCESS MODELLING

Generally speaking, a model highlights certain aspects of the real world and omits others. What does this mean with regard to the subject of business processes? According to [Davenport 93] and [Hammer/Champy 93] a *business process* can be characterised by five elements: (1) a business process has customers; (2) a business process consists of activities; (3) these activities create value for the customer; (4) activities within a business process are carried out by humans or machines; (5) business processes often involve several organizational units; that means more than one organizational units are responsible for a whole business process.

How are these aspects interrelated? As a core element of a business process model we have *business cases*, which are instances of a business process. Business cases have to be carried out. That means fulfilling *business goals* and satisfying *stakeholders*. Business cases are composed of *activities* (sometimes referred to as functions or working steps or tasks) which can be further decomposed into subactivities. Activities within an office environment need information as *input*. That input has to be provided by an *information producer*. Activities also produce an *output* which will be delivered to the *customer*, probably the most important player within a business process. Activities have to be carried out by *roles*.

Creating and implementing new business processes is a highly complex task. There are still few empirically established examples. Furthermore it is difficult to appreciate the most important requirements at the beginning of a project. It is effectively impossible to estimate if the proposed process model would lead to the desired state.

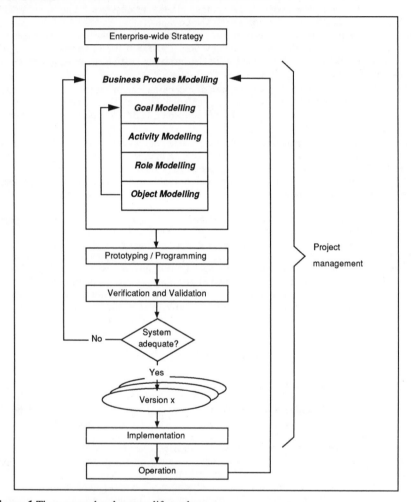

Figure 1 The system development life cycle.

In order to reduce these problems we propose to apply a cyclic stage model. Figure 1, which includes ideas from [Floyd et al. 89] and [Hammer/Champy 93], shows that the development and implementation of a business process is made up of several activities: First of all, an enterprise-wide strategy – which describes the enterprise-wide as well as the future product and service portfolio – has to be developed. After that, the business process(es) have to be modelled; an activity we describe in detail later. Subsequently the modelled business process has to be verified and validated. Whereas verification is usually done by formal methods, validation may efficiently be carried out by prototypes. Prototyping allows potential users to judge if the system is adequate or not. After several iterations the business process model has to be transformed into an executable system. This might be done using either a workflow management system or in a traditional way, e.g. coding a C++ application. If an executable program has been created it has to be implemented in a designated environment. Generally speaking, implementation means developing a plan that addresses the organization of change. On the organizational side this may include transformations concerning hierarchy of management, incentives, performance measurement, job description, job changes, skills, and training. After successful implementation the system goes into the operation. After an unknown duration in operation, process goals are likely to change and this eventually leads to a new development cycle. Furthermore customer needs, overall policies or profitability of certain activities may also change – and as a result, business processes or part of them may be outsourced.

Figure 1 shows that the mentioned steps of a system development life cycle are surrounded by project management. It is a ongoing activity and defines some key elements which affects the success of a project much more than technical aspects. Project management includes, but is not limited to the following aspects: organizational structure of the project team, staff (quantity and qualification), maximum project duration, maximum project cost, methods and standards concerning each development step, monitoring and measurement of progress and risks, facilities and technical equipment.

Before proceeding, three preliminary remarks have to be made: (1) During the modelling process (analysis and design), we do not look at a possible implementation strategy. That means, the subsequently modelled business processes would be technology-independent. (2) Business processes discussed in this paper concern the area of office systems, e.g. informational processes. In other words, at present, manufacturing processes which have the objective to produce physical materials (tables, printers, cars, ...) are beyond our discussion. (3) We do not take into account existing IT components. In contrast to the fountain life cycle model (cf. [Graham 95, p. 350]), aspects of reuse are beyond the scope of this paper.

4 MODELLING OF GOALS

In traditional system development life cycles, the first step is typically described as "requirements analysis". Experience of several projects has showed that the process of eliciting requirements cannot be seen as an isolated step, cf. [Floyd et al. 89]. Furthermore, traditional requirements analysis may produce lists with a vast number of items. For this reason, we propose to model not traditional requirements, but the more abstract notion of goals which have to be fulfilled. Goal modelling can be applied on an enterprise-wide level as well as on business process level. After starting the first business process modelling project, we have to create a model on the enterprise-wide level. That means, the goals on the top-level has to be captured and subsequently broken down into subgoals until they can be assigned to business processes.

Our work leads us to believe, that the following approach would be fruitful. To achieve a clear structure of our goal model, we divide goals into the following three categories:

- **Business process-related goals**: If business processes have to be modified – and this should happen in every process modelling project – this kind of goals are of primary importance. In the case study that follows, business process-related goals include: "making profit by selling insurances" and "increasing turnover", cf. figure 2. How should process-related goals be modelled? The objective is to reduce or decompose process-related goals until they can be transformed into activities which have to be carried out within a business process. If a certain activity is a component of several business processes, this activity has to be placed – for reduction of redundancy – as part of a *support process*. It should be noted, that goals may not only be defined in the positive sense of "ensure that something happens" but also in the negative sense of "ensure that something does not happen".

- **Information system-related goals**: This kind of goals are sometimes referred to as *requirements concerning the product*. The product would be, in our area of application, an information system, such as a workflow system. IS-related goals are usually not very process-specific and for this reason it would not be efficient to define them for each project. For the purpose of reuse, we can distinguish between enterprise-internal and enterprise-external IS-related goals; furthermore we can divide the two categories into enterprise-specific and process-specific goals. This means that IS-related goals can be defined for the whole company and then just have to be specialized (by refinement or extension) for a certain business process. Furthermore, IS-related goals cannot often be translated into business process activities during the first stages of process modelling. Nevertheless, it is important to make clear at the beginning of a project, which IS-related goals have to be considered whilst a new business process is being created and probably implemented in several information system components. Examples of IS-related goals are availability, conformity with user expectations, confidentiality, consistency, controlability, error tolerance, modifiability, reliability, response time, self-descriptiviness, and suitability for learning.

- **Project management-related goals**: These goals deal with the process of "information system development". As we can infer from figure 1, these goals cannot be addressed to a certain development step. In other words, it is not possible to generally define on which modelling step what type of project management-related goal has to be used. What do we mean by project management-related goals? Some examples may make it clearer: standards and guidelines concerning modelling methods and implementation aspects, organizational structure of the project team, project duration, costs, monitoring and measurements of progress and risks, quantity and qualification of project staff, facilities and technical equipment.

5 MODELLING OF ACTIVITIES

As mentioned in section 2, many modelling approaches are activity-based. That means the first step would normally be "defining activities which have to be carried out whilst a business case progresses". These approaches raise the question "How can we identify the appropriate activities?". This question is very important but until now relatively little attention has been paid on it. How do we identify activities of a business process? There are four sources:

- **Goals and subgoals**: As [Hammer/Champy 93] mention, business processes should only include such activities which create value for the customer. In other words, activities have to make a contribution to the business process goals. Referring to our example, figure 2 shows that the subgoal "minimum of losses" leads to the activity "refuse risky submissions".

- **Measurement of goal achievement**: As we have seen above, activities should make a contribution to the fulfilment of goals. This raises the question "How can we measure the extent to which a business goal is fulfilled?". The degree of fulfilment of goals has to be measured by activities. In other words, for each business process goal we not only have to define the criteria by which the achievement can be measured, we additionally have to define activities for measuring the degree of fulfilment. This is shown in the example. Figure 2 shows for example that the goal "making profit" leads to the activity "record cost and return for each business case".

- **Restrictions**: The definition of business processes is not a fully boundless task. It is to be expected that we have to take into consideration certain restrictions. They may come from the enterprise itself or from third parties. Restrictions can be divided into three categories: legal restrictions, technical restrictions, and social restrictions. For example, in the case study we only consider commercial insurance, because it is perceived to be technically different from other kinds of insurance (e.g. life insurance, motor insurance).

- **Input delivery**: Business processes may subsume activities, which do not produce value for the customer, which are not used for measuring goal fulfilment, and which are not derived from restrictions. What are they good for? Activities need – if they have to be carried out – input. This input has to be delivered by an activity which is either located within or outside of the business process. As we will see in table 1, concerning our example, we have several activities whose "goal" is to deliver input for already identified (possibly value generating) activities. For example, the activity "record customer request" delivers the input for the subsequent activities.

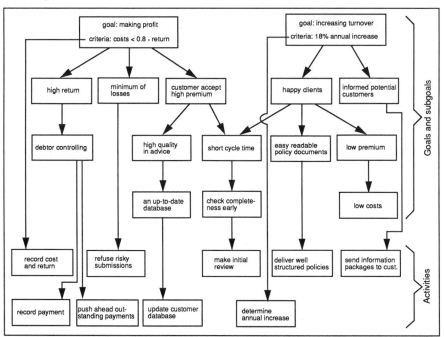

Figure 2 Goal/Activity Model for the business process "Insure customer objects".

As we have seen above, in order to identify necessary activities of a business process, we have to define not only business goals, business restrictions, and general requirements, but also the input and output for each activity. It should be mentioned that we use input and output not only for identifying activities but also for describing the activities more precisely. In other words, we have to define what data must be available for activities to be carried out. Similarly we have to describe which data (output) has to be delivered to the process customer, to a third party, or to another business activity.

With reference to the definition of Input/Output Models (cf. table 1), it is useful to note that activities are regarded as isolated modules. For this reason any input, which is needed for carrying out an activity has to be listed. In other words, an activity cannot make any reference to a data pool, even certain data has been defined as input for another activity. The advantage of this concept is threefold: (1) activities may be placed freely, because we do not take into account the dataflow between activities; (2) if we analyse the inputs concerning their frequency and volume, we get some indications of which data are candidates for an efficient management, e.g. by database management systems; (3) the concept of isolated modules does not pre-determine any technical realisation.

What level of abstraction would be appropriate to define Input/Output Models? We take a very pragmatic position on this issue and raise the question "What kind of information can we get from people who are participating in the modelling project"? If they are thinking in categories of attributes, we would use them. If they prefer to speak about types of documents, we would record them. Much more important than the level of abstraction is the consistency. We have to guarantee that each data item (attribute or document) which is used as an input of an activity, is produced by another activity. In other words, Input/Output Models may "generate" new activities. If we compare figure 2 with table 1, we may discern that the activity "record customer request" in table 1 does not take feature in figure 2. This is because this activity has not been derived from the goal hierarchy, but for carrying out the activity "make initial review" we would use the customer request as input. Another example shows that the input of certain activity must not be produced in the discussed business process: the activity "assess risk" needs a "risk/usage matrix" as input, but as we can recognize, this "risk/usage matrix" would not be produced within our business process.

Table 1 Input/Output Model for the business process "Insure customer objects".

Activity	Input	Output
record customer request	customer request (i.e. customer name, uninsured objects and their usage)	recorded customer request (i.e. a new business case)
make initial review	a) recorded customer request; b) different information about customer and his objects	submission
assess risk	a) submission; b) risk/usage matrix	risk score for the submission
accept submission	a) submission; b) risk score for the submission	acceptance letter at the customer
refuse submission	a) submission; b) risk score for the submission	refusal letter at the customer
update database	a) submission; b) risk score for the submission	updated database
compose policy document	a) submission; b) risk score for the submission; c) terms&condition list	policy document
send policy document to customer	policy document	policy document at the customer

Furthermore, looking at figure 2, it can be seen that there are some activities which are not taken into account; for example "record cost and return", or "send information packages to customer". Why is this the case? In order to achieve a compact business process model, activities which are either components of several business processes, or activities which are of a support character should be part of support processes. Furthermore, during the defining of the essential activities it is sometimes useful to break up an activity into two or more activities. An example is the activity "deliver well structured policy documents" which has been broken down into "compose policy document" and "send policy document to customer". To summarize, the Input/Output Models helps to find the essential activities.

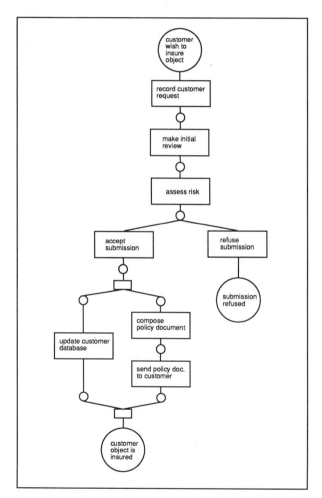

Figure 3 Dynamic Activity Model for the business process "Insure customer objects".

Although the essential activities are defined (cf. figure 2 and table 1), we have not yet defined the logical dependencies between activities. In other words it is not yet clear which activities can be carried out sequentially, alternatively, or concurrently. To consider this aspect we apply Petri-nets; and within this category we use condition/event nets, cf. [Jensen 92]. Condition/event nets possess three strengths: (1) they facilitate a compact and precise description of the dynamic process aspects; (2) they support the concept of specialization, cf. [Kueng/Schrefl 95]; (3) they support process simulation as well.

Figure 3 shows the Dynamic Activity Model for the business process "Insure customer objects". It should be recognized that the usage of symbols in condition/event nets may vary. In these diagrams, states are shown as circles, transitions as rectangles. To make the net more compact, states are shown as very small circles and a textual description is omitted. Furthermore, transitions which have only support character (e.g. AND forks) are drawn as small rectangles. We can see that the activities "record customer request" and "make initial review" proceed sequentially whereas the activities "accept submission" and "refuse submission" are carried out alternatively. The activities "update customer database" on one side, and "compose policy document" and "send policy document to customer" on the other hand are carried out concurrently.

6 MODELLING OF ROLES

What do we mean by the term role? The Workflow Management Coalition [WfMC 94] distinguish between two kind of roles: Process Roles and Organizational Roles. The first term refers to a collection of activities. The second one refers to the functional requirements of an organizational or technical unit. Following Ellis and Wainer we use the term role in the following way: "A role is named a designator for an actor, or grouping of actors which conveniently acts as the basis for the partitioning of work skills, access control, execution control, and authority/responsibility. (...) A role may be associated with a group of actors rather than a single actor. (...) An actor is a person, program, or entity than can fulfil roles to execute, to be responsible for, or to be associated in some way with activities and procedures" [Ellis/Wainer 94, pp. 78].

The strengths of the role-concept is twofold: (1) during the modelling stage we do not have to discuss skills, functionalities, competences, and responsibilities for each activity within our business process; (2) during the operational stage people and machines (programs) with the same role are potentially interchangeable.

In some traditional approaches (e.g. Porter's value chain), activities have sometimes been misinterpreted as functions – in an organizational sense. "Experience from development and analyzes in the Norwegian TOPP study in mechanical and electrotechnical industries shows that activities are easily interpreted as functions. Misinterpretation of the term activities as functions will bring you back to the outdated organizational structure model" [Rolstadas 95, p. 153]. Without careful role assignment we may unintentionally develop hierarchical departmentalized structures and have a negative impact on the motivation of the staff. This in turn may lengthen cycle time and may decrease customer satisfaction. In other words, the assignment of activities to roles is important and has to be done very carefully – and separately from activity modelling.

Before activities can be allocated to roles it is necessary to decide which activities should be carried out by humans and which by machines. According to [Bailey 89, pp. 189] we can distinguish between five allocation strategies:

- *comparison allocation*: each activity has to be analysed and then compared with established human and machine performance criteria;
- *leftover allocation*: as many activities as possible are allocated to a machine and the activities left over are done by humans. Bailey remarks, that this strategy would probably be the most popular;
- *economic strategy*: the decision, man versus machine, based completely on financial assessment;
- *humanized task approach*: the main goal of this approach is to design meaningful human jobs/ human roles;
- *flexible allocation*: humans allocate activities in the system based on their values, needs, and interests.

Due to space limitation we resist a further discussion of these allocation strategies. Nevertheless, it seems reasonable to propose that the humanized task approach and the flexible allocation would be the two most appropriate strategies.

How should activities be assigned to roles? Although this question has been considered by many researchers, it has not been answered properly. Here we make just a general remark: instead of many particular specialized workplaces we should create "self-contained units". We achieve this by adherence to the principles of decoupling and cohesion which govern good modular design. This helps to reduce the need for coordination and scheduling work. Furthermore, it would possibly improve lateral relations crossing the divisions' borders, cf. [Rolstadas 95, p. 156].

After this short theoretical background we turn to the roles in our case study. We show how we graphically assign them to activities. The roles we are dealing with are the following: "administrator", "assistant", "customer" (policy holder), and "underwriter", cf. figure 4. In our small example, every activity is assigned to humans. Of course, this does not always happen, but during modelling on a relatively high level this is the normal case. In other words: although we do not have any assignments to machines this doesn't imply humans wouldn't be supported by machines; it indicates that activities have to be split up into subactivities for their further assignment to machines.

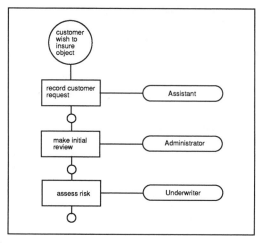

Figure 4 Role Activity Model (partly) for the business process "Insure customer objects".

7 OBJECT MODELLING

In the previous part of the paper we showed how to model business processes on a conceptual level. This section explains how a conceptual model can be transformed into a pre-implementation, object-oriented model. Object-oriented models are constructed out of – as the name makes clear – objects. The two core elements of objects are: (1) they have a structure, and (2) they have a behaviour. While the structure is normally described by attributes and relationships to other objects, the behaviour of objects is defined by the methods objects can carry out. In other words, objects can be described by Object Relationship Models and Object Behaviour Models. Furthermore, in our universe of discourse, we have to take into account that certain objects can interact (in a certain state) with other objects. To depict this information, we need a third type of model: an Object Interaction Model.

In the phase Object Modelling (cf. figure 1) we have to answer the question "Which object classes should our model subsume and how do these objects interact?". To answer this we distinguish three object classes:

- **Business case classes**: Objects of these class describe and control the sequence of events. Their attributes describe the actual states of the running business cases, and they define the relationships between a certain business case and the associated input-output classes. In other words, business case classes define the characteristics of business processes.[1] How do we identify business case classes? It is simple: each business process has one business case class. The name of this business case class would be identical to the name of the business process itself. In our case study, the business class would be called "Insuring objects", cf. figure 5. As instances we have business cases, e.g. "business case 29".

- **Input/output classes**: Objects of these classes are passive, i.e. they can not initiate an action or a communication to other objects. Objects of input/output classes are identified by looking at the Input/Output Model, cf. table 1. It gives relevant information concerning data (objects) which has to be available for carrying out activities within the business process. Furthermore, the Input/Output Model shows which data has to be produced – for the process customer or a subsequent activity. In our case study, we can identify as input/output classes e.g. "Customer", "Customer Request", "Customer Objects", and "Submission", cf. figure 5. An instance of the class "Submission" could be "submission 84371".

- **Role classes**: Objects of these classes are roles (cf. figure 4) – which carry out activities. These objects can send messages to every other object (to passive objects as well as to active objects). Therefore objects of role classes are referred to as active objects.[2] In our example, we have four role classes: "Customer", "Administrator", "Assistant", and "Underwriter". For having a compact example of an Object Relationship Model (figure 5) we consider only the first two mentioned roles. An instance of the role-class "Administrator" is e.g. "Mrs. Smithfield".

To show the interaction between the captured objects (figure 5) we use Object Interaction Models, cf. figure 6. Reading this diagram, in natural language, we would say: if a customer places a request for insuring his objects at the insurance company, the request has to be

---

1. It has to be remarked, that the main characteristics of a business process could also be defined – as attributes and methods – in the "normal" classes. The advantage of creating a separate object class is twofold: (1) the structure of a business process would be easier to understand, and (2) the concept of inheritance would be applicable in a more extensive way, cf. [Müller-Luschnat et al. 93].

2. The concept of roles – in the context of Office Systems – has been introduced by [Lyngbaek/McLeod 84].

recorded. As an object-oriented expression, we would say: the object Customer sends a message to the object Customer Request.

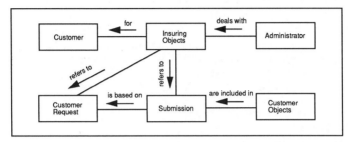

Figure 5 Object Relationship Model (partly); notation according to [Embley et al. 92].

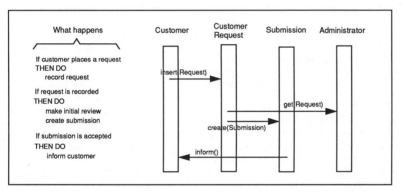

Figure 6 Object Interaction Model (partly); notation following to [Jacobson et al. 94].

It would be possible to develop this model further. For this example we have refrained from doing so as the reader will, in any case, be able to reference the huge volume of literature about object-oriented systems development.

8 SUMMARY AND FUTURE WORK

In an influential paper [Curtis et al. 92] suggested there are four important perspectives to process models. These are the functional, the behavioural, the organizational, and the informational perspective. They provide a useful framework for considering the coverage of the approach presented in this paper. The functional perspective of a business process is given by Object Interaction Models, cf. figure 6. The behavioural perspective of a business process (e.g. activity sequencing) is represented on two levels: at the pre-object-oriented level it is represented by Dynamic Activity Models (Petri-nets, cf. figure 3) whilst at the object-oriented level it is represented by Object Behaviour Diagrams. The organizational perspective of a business process (which shows by whom are activities carried out) is represented by Role Activity Models, cf. figure 4. The informational perspective of a business process (e.g. the entities produced) is represented by Object Relationship Models, cf. figure 5.

What are the strengths of the goal-based modelling approach which is presented here?
- The methods of the objects (activities) are derived from business goals. In other words, if business goals change, we can easily establish which methods have to be updated.
- Activities are used as modules because all of them have their own input-output interfaces. The advantage of this is twofold. First, we can arrange our activities (at least in the first development cycle) within a business process in a way that is relatively free from restriction. Secondly, for every activity we can decide to perform it in-house or to buy it from a third party.

Where are the limits of our approach?
- The goal-oriented approach does not provide any help for appraising design alternatives.
- In order to realise successful business processes, we not only have to have a mature business process model, we also have to implement it successfully. In other words, following the proposed steps cannot guarantee efficient business processes.

This paper has given an overview of an approach to modelling business processes. We have showed which steps would be needed to create an object-oriented business process model, how these steps can be carried out, and how the main ideas are applied in a case study. Some answers have been given, others need further research investigation.

A prominent issue is the development of the goal model. It is intended to extend the goal model in order to support the description of richer goal structures. It is intended to do this with more enhanced features, such as conjunctive, disjunctive, and conflicting subgoals. These will not only allow to identify the activities needed to achieve them, but will also allow to infer restrictions on their logical order. For example, if a goal is decomposed into two conjunctive subgoals, the activities associated with these subgoals must be either executed in sequence or in parallel, but may not be executed alternatively.

To conclude, it is useful to list other questions which need further research. These include the following: What organizational and technical means do we have to depict individual/ social/personal/organizational goals? How could user participation, during business process modelling, be augmented? How can we support the process of finding the appropriate activities? How can we establish the appropriate role for each activity? How would business process modelling be influenced by implementation aspects (WFMS versus conventional programming)? How can we measure the quality of a business process model in each modelling step?

Acknowledgement

The work of Peter Kueng has been supported by the Swiss National Science Foundation.

9 BIBLIOGRAPHY

[Agostini et al. 94] Agostini, A.; De Michelis, G.; Grasso, M.; Patriarca, S.: Re-engineering a business process with an innovative workflow management system – a case study. In: Collaborative Computing, Vol. 1, No. 3 (September 1994), pp. 163-190.

[Bailey 89] Bailey, Robert: Human Performance Engineering – Using Human Factors/Ergonomics to Achieve Computer System Usabiliy. Prentice-Hall, 2nd ed., London 1989.

[Beer 79] Beer, Stafford: The Heart of Enterprise. John Wiley & Sons, Chichester 1979.

[Booch 94] Booch, Grady: Object-Oriented Analysis and Design with Applications. Benjamin/ Cummings, 2nd ed., Redwood City CA 1994.

[Curtis et al. 92] Curtis, Bill; Kellner, Marc; Over, Jim: Process Modelling. In: Communication of the ACM, Vol. 35, No. 9 (September 1992), pp. 75-90.

[Davenport 93] Davenport, Thomas: Process Innovation – Reengineering Work through Information Technology. Harvard Business School Press, Boston 1993.

[Ellis/Nutt 80] Ellis, Clarence; Nutt, Gary: Office Information Systems and Computer Science. In: ACM Computing Surveys, Vol. 12, No. 1 (March 1980), pp. 27-60.

[Ellis/Wainer 94] Ellis, Clarence; Wainer, Jacques: Goal-based models of collaboration. In: Collaborative Computing, Vol. 1, No. 1 (March 1994), pp. 61-86.

[Embley et al. 92] Embley, Davis; Kurtz, Barry; Woodfield, Scott: Object-Oriented Analysis – A Model-Driven Approach. Yourdon Press, Prentice Hall, Englewood Cliffs 1992.

[Floyd et al. 89] Floyd, Christiane; Reisin, Fanny; Schmidt, Gerhard: STEPS to Software Development with Users. In: Ghezzi, C.; McDermid, J. (Eds.): Proceedings, 2nd European Software Engineering Conference, ESEC '89. LNCS 387, Springer-Verlag, Berlin 1989, pp. 48-64.

[Graham 95] Graham, Ian: Migrating to Object Technology. Addison-Wesley, Wokingham, England 1995.

[Halé 95] Halé, Jacques: From Concepts to Capabilities – Understanding and Exploiting Change as a Competitive Advantage. John Wiley & Sons, Chichester 1995.

[Hammer/Champy 93] Hammer, Michael; Champy, James: Reengineering the Corporation – A Manifesto for Business Revolution. Harper Business, New York 1993.

[Holt et al. 83] Holt, Anatol; Ramsey, Rudy; Grimes, Jack: Coordinating System Technology as the Basis for a Programming Environment. In: Electrical Communication, Vol. 57, No. 4 (1983), pp. 307-314.

[Jacobson et al. 94] Jacobson, Ivar; Christerson, Magnus; Constantine, Larry: The OOSE Method – A Use-Case-Driven Approach. In: Carmichael, Andy (Ed.): Object Development Methods. SIGS Books, New York 1994, pp. 247-270.

[Jensen 92] Jensen, Kurt: Coloured Petri Nets – Basic Concepts, Analysis Methods and Practical Use; Volume 1. Springer-Verlag, Berlin 1992.

[Joosten 94] Joosten, Stef: Trigger Modelling for Workflow Analysis. In: Chroust, Gerhard; Benczur, Andras (Eds.): Workflow Management – Challenges, Paradigms and Products; Conference Proceedings of CONnectivity '94, Linz, Oct. 19-21. Oldenburg Verlag, München 1994, pp. 236-247.

[Kawalek 95] Kawalek, Peter: An introduction to a process engineering approach and a case study illustration if its utility. In: Browne, J.; O'Sullivan, D. (Eds.): Re-engineering the Enterprise; Proceedings of the IFIP TC5/WG5.7 Working Conference, Galway, April 1995. Chapman & Hall, London 1995, pp. 248-272.

[Kueng/Schrefl 95] Kueng, Peter; Schrefl, Michael: Spezialisierung von Geschäftsprozessen am Beispiel der Bearbeitung von Kreditanträgen. In: HMD – Theorie und Praxis der Wirtschaftsinformatik, Jg. 32, Heft 185 (September 1995), S. 78-94.

[Lyngbaek/McLeod 84] Lyngbaek, P.; McLeod, D.: Object Management in Distributed Office Information Systems. In: ACM Transactions on Office Information Systems, Vol. 2, No. 2 (1984), pp. 96-122.

[Medina-Mora et al. 92] Medina-Mora, Raul; Winograd, Terry; Flores, Rodrigo; Flores, Fernando: The Action Workflow Approach to Workflow Management Technology. In: Proceedings of the Conference on Computer-Supported Cooperative Work, CSCW '92, Toronto, Oct. 31-Nov. 4, pp. 281-288.

[Müller-Luschnat et al. 93] Müller-Luschnat, Günther; Hesse, Wolfgang; Heydenreich, Norman: Objektorientierte Analyse und Geschäftsvorfallsmodellierung. In: Mayr, H.; Wagner, R. (Hrsg.): Objektorientierte Methoden für Informationssysteme; Proceedings der der GI-Fachgruppe EMISA, Klagenfurt, 7.-9. Juni 1993. Springer-Verlag, Berlin 1993, S. 78-94.

[Ould 95] Ould, Martyn: Business Processes – Modelling and Analysis for Re-engineering and Improvement. John Wiley & Sons, Chichester 1995.

[Rolstadas 95] Rolstadas, Asbjorn (Ed.): Performance Management – A business process benchmarking approach. Chapman & Hall, London 1995.

[Scheer 94] Scheer, August: Business Process Engineering: Reference Models for Industrial Enterprises. Springer-Verlag, 2nd ed., Berlin 1994.

[Swenson/Irwin 95] Swenson, Keith; Irwin, Kent: Workflow Technology – Tradeoffs for Business Process Re-engineering. In: Conference on Organizational Computing Systems, COOCS '95, Aug. 13-16, Milpitas, USA. ACM Press, New York 1995, pp. 22-29.

[WfMC 94] Glossary: A Workflow Management Coalition Specification. Authored by Workflow Management Coalition Members, Brussels 1994. (Updated information may be found on http://www.aiai.ed.ac.uk/WfMC/).

[Winograd/Flores 86] Winograd, Terry; Flores, Fernando: Understandig Computers and Cognition – A New Foundation for Design. Addison-Wesley, Readings 1986.

10 BIOGRAPHY

Peter Bichler received his Dipl.-Ing. degree in computer science from Johannes Kepler University of Linz, Austria, in 1993, where he currently works on his PhD thesis. His research interests are authorization in workflow systems and active object-oriented database systems.

Peter Kawalek is a Research Associate of the University of Manchester. His research considers the use of process models as integrating frameworks. He also works as a consultant for Manchester Informatics Limited and has undertaken many process modelling projects with industrial collaborators.

Peter Kueng received his Doctorate from Fribourg University, Switzerland, in 1994. After finishing his studies in business-oriented computer science he worked at Fribourg University as well as for IBM Berne in the field of database systems. In 1995 he worked as Visiting Researcher within the Data & Knowledge Engineering research group at Linz University. Currently, he is Visiting Researcher at Manchester University.

Michael Schrefl received his Dipl.-Ing. degree and his Doctorate from Vienna University of Technology, Vienna, Austria, in 1983 and 1988 respectively. Presently, he is Professor of Information Systems at Johannes Kepler University, Linz, Austria. His research interests are in the fields of object-oriented systems and workflow management.

8

Human work as context for development of object oriented modelling techniques

J. J. Kaasbøll and O. Smørdal
Department of informatics, University of Oslo
P.O. Box 1080, Blindern, N-0316 OSLO, Norway
Phone: + 47 22 85 24 29, Fax: + 47 22 85 24 01
E-mail: {Jens.Kaasboll, Ole.Smordal}@ifi.uio.no

Abstract

Computer systems are increasingly being used for communication and coordination of work, while object-oriented modelling techniques aim at modelling the problem domain of the computer system. Current techniques have been developed with respect to easy implementation, while we argue that further development of the modelling techniques should also be based on knowledge about human work in organisations.

We outline a learning cycle of modelling technique and point to where such knowledge should be included.

We have carried out two alternative approaches to development of object oriented techniques based on these ideas, and we outline these development processes. One approach is based on semiotic concepts, the other is based on activity theory.

Keywords

Research Method, Method Engineering, Learning Cycle, Activity Theory, Semiotics, Evaluation

1   INTRODUCTION

Object oriented modelling techniques should be developed according to knowledge about human work within organisations. This paper argues why and points to ways to change current development practice.

The basic ingredients of object-oriented techniques for modelling are the mechanisms provided by object-oriented programming languages. In short, these mechanisms consist of encapsulated objects with properties and behaviour, and specialisation of classes by means of inheritance. It is often claimed that object-oriented modelling of the domain of an information system is easy, because object-orientation corresponds to our natural conception of the world.

Considering that the core concepts of object-oriented techniques consist of implementation restrictions, we doubt the correctness of this claim.

Object oriented techniques are used within application areas that include human work within some organisation. Lately, the techniques have also been used to capture aspects beyond the domain of work, e.g., aspects relating to actors, communication, coordination of work, task flow, and work procedures. This is due to a shift of perspectives regarding the role of the computer in work settings; from a focus on the computer as means of control and administration of a problem domain, to a focus that also include the computer as a mediator in the work setting, e.g., as in CSCW applications. Carstensen et al (1995) point to inadequacies of object-oriented modelling in these respects. Others have reported problems related to modelling of different roles of actors (Richardson and Schwarz, 1991; Coad, 1992). These findings underpin our disbelief in the claim of the easiness of modelling. Research on the difficulties of learning object-oriented modelling (Vessey and Conger, 1994) also indicate that the claim is incorrect.

We interpret these observations as symptoms of an underlying problem: that the development of object-oriented techniques for modelling has been too restrained by implementation considerations. The inadequacies that have been detected have been explained within the frame of the mechanisms of object-oriented programming languages, the theoretical contributions have been restricted to formal arguments within this frame and, consequently, the suggestions for improvements of the techniques have not extended these mechanisms. This paper aims at arguing that the way of developing techniques should open for a wider range of explanations, theories, and suggestions. In particular, we will show how we have included knowledge concerning actors in the process of developing object-oriented techniques for modelling.

1.1   Suggestions in the literature

A way to improve methods called "method engineering" has been defined as "the disciplined process of building, improving or modifying a method by means of specifying the method's components and their relations" (Heym and Österle, 1993; Rossi and Brinkkemper, 1995). The concept is used to capture the development of a method and the adaptation of a method in a specific situation (Kumar and Welke, 1992; Harmsen et al, 1994), and method engineering is compared with the development and modification of an information system in an organisation.

Since the problems referred above concern object-oriented techniques for modelling in general, method engineering, which only deals with individual methods and compilation of methods from techniques, will fall short with respect to the generality of the problem. In addition, method engineering does not enrich the concepts and mechanisms for modelling, such that actors, roles, task flow, etc., are more easily modelled.

1.2   Seamlessness in modelling

An argument for object-oriented development is the seamlessness from analysis to design and implementation: the same concepts are used in all phases, such that no magic transition is needed. When arguing for richer concepts for modelling, we may put the seamlessness principle in danger.

To be precise in the further discussion, we first define areas that can be modelled during system development, based on similar concepts in Mathiassen et al (1993).

The **problem domain** of a computer system is what the computer system is about; the part of the world that the computer system is supposed to handle, control or monitor. Examples (with basic components): a flight booking system (flights, seats, reservations, customers), a banking system (customers, transactions, accounts, loans, interests).

The **application domain** of a computer system consist of the users, the organisational context, and the work in which the computer system is used, e.g., a travel agency, a bank. Elements of the application domain are employees, the coordination of work, communication, power structures, ad-hoc organised work, interruptions in work, etc.

The **computer system** including its application program, data/object base, user interface module, and communication modules.

When analysing functionality requirements of a system, one could make a model of the application domain. Since it is assumed that the problem domain is more stable than the functional requirement, making an object-oriented model of the application domain is often not considered worthwhile.

Many object-oriented methods suggest that one should model the problem domain, because this is what the computer system shall represent. The model is supposed to describe how the system developers and users conceive the problem domain. For now we regard this model as based on consensus among users and developers. An advantage of a model of the problem domain is that the model is independent of the technology for implementing the system. The model can be used as a part of a specification, such that computer systems conforming to the specification can be implemented on several platforms or with different languages.

A model of the future computer system will often be an extension of a model of the problem domain in order to include software modules and objects needed for implementation. Because the same concepts are used in all models and in the implementation, the model of the future computer system can be aligned with the model of the problem domain. This is referred to as the seamlessness of object-oriented system development.

However, iterations are carried out during development, and implemented systems are changed during long periods of further development. Experience shows that changes are often carried out directly on the code, without updating the models. To keep the seamlessness, it must be possible to keep the models in alignment with the code. If other concepts are introduced in the model of the problem domain, more effort may be required to keep the models updated.

We want to include in our models issues of work organisation, and this suggests an extension of the problem domain to include aspects of the application domain. The domain definitions given above represent useful distinctions. Hence we want to introduce an another concept, the model domain, which denotes the area of concern when modelling. As we identify in the next section, the most usual model domain for object-oriented modelling techniques is the problem domain, but we also identifies some approaches that have the future computer system as the model domain.

In our work we define the **modelling domain** to be the problem domain plus the aspects of the application domain that is mediated by the computer system. We discuss the domain for object oriented modelling techniques in Section 2.3.

1.3 Overview of the paper

The paper is organised as follows: Section 2.2 presents a learning cycle for development of object-oriented techniques, based on the interplay between modelling in practice and theoretical contributions. We identify contributions from some current object-oriented techniques in respect to 1) their notions and concepts, 2) their embedded theory, and 3) the reported technique development.

We conclude that most techniques have had a technology driven development. In Section 2.3 an extension of the domain of object-oriented techniques is suggested, also including issues of work organisation, roles, and communication between the users. Section 2.4 and 2.5 presents two development cycles that address this extended domain, one using semiotic concepts, the other using activity theory.

2   THE DEVELOPMENT OF TECHNIQUES

In order to discuss different approaches to development of techniques for modelling, we outline a learning cycle for identifying the stages and components of the development.

Gaining new scientific knowledge can be regarded as a continuous cycle of formulation of hypotheses, evaluation in practice, explanation of results, contributions to theories, reformulation of hypotheses, etc. The learning cycle of development of techniques consists of four phases and transformations from one phase to the next, see Figure 1.

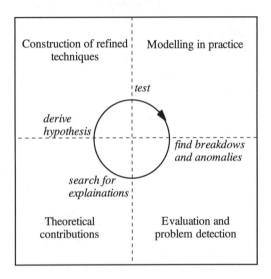

Figure 1 A model of technique development.

Modelling in practice is the area we learn from, and also the area we want to improve.

Evaluation and problem detection is triggered by experiences when modelling is not straightforward. The main concern in this phase is to identify problems that stem from the use of this technique in a practical system development context. The problems may be identified due to 1) breakdown in the use of a technique, e.g., some property of the application domain could not be captured in the model, or the appearance of inconsistencies in the model, or 2) anomalies in the model or in the use of a technique, e.g. the resulting model seems strange compared to the application domain.

Theoretical contributions. When explaining problems in a scientific way and considering ways to avoid them, one has to consult other scientific results and theories. One may try to explain the problems within the frame of the research or search for other theories.

Construction of refined techniques. When the appropriate theoretical considerations have been made, one may have to adjust the technique and possibly include new mechanisms, metaphors and notation. Hypotheses concerning the techniques and the approach to evaluate the hypotheses are worked out.

Modelling in practice. The cycle restarts with using the technique in modelling. Any kind of practice which contributes to learning about the technique and its place in system development is feasible.

Galliers (1992) separates research goals into theory building, theory testing, and theory extension. He argues that case study, survey, forecasting, simulation, argumentation, interpretation, and action research are possible research approaches for theory building. According to his categorisation, these research methods are appropriate in the phases of evaluation and theoretical contribution. The theories are tested in the phases construction of refined techniques and modelling in practice. Theorem proof, laboratory experiment and field experiment are suited for theory testing, according to Galliers. In our learning cycle, theorem proving may take place in the theoretical contribution and during construction of techniques.

Braa and Vidgen (1995) outline three types of knowledge interests in system development research: intervention, science, and interpretation. Intervention aims at change in the organisations where computer systems are used and developed, science aims at general knowledge that is useful for prediction, and interpretation aims at explaining and understanding information systems development in organisations from different viewpoints. Inspired by these three types of knowledge interests, we construct a taxonomy of three ways of developing techniques for modelling. We will use this taxonomy to discuss how the phases of the learning cycle are covered in the way techniques are developed.

The consultant approach. A consultant is involved in development of systems, and gathers experience of her/his ways of working, and expresses this experience in general terms as techniques and methods. In this approach, the evaluation is carried out in an unscientific manner, and theoretical explanations and contributions are not included. The main goal of this approach is improvement of system development practice.

Method engineering. Scientists measure use of methods in system development. After identifying problems, they calculate improved principles, formalise vague parts of the methods, and improve tools to support implementation. In this approach, all aspects of the cycle are included, but the theoretical considerations are limited to formal theories. The main goal of methods engineering is improved predictability of system development when it is carried out according to the method.

System development research. Scientists study system development and the role of methods in practical projects. Problematic areas are identified. Relevant theories are called upon to understand and explain the problems. Improved knowledge of system development constitutes the basis for possibly suggesting improved guidelines and techniques. The main goal of the research is improved knowledge of system development from different viewpoints, and the role of techniques therein.

Method engineering addresses methods and techniques in particular. System development research has a wider scope, and improvements of techniques is one of many possible outcomes. We nevertheless argue that development of methods and techniques should also be carried out in the perspective of system development research, because it opens for a richer variety of research methods and theories. When problems that lend themselves to formal methods are encountered, there is nothing that prevents an engineering approach to deal with these problems. However, if working within a method engineering perspective as outlined here, the perspective does not open for alternative interpretations or research methods.

Main differences between method engineering and system development research are found in the theoretical and the constructive phases of the learning cycle. They are summarised in Table 1.

Table 1 Differences between Method engineering and System development research

	Method engineering	*System development research*
Viewpoint	Unified	Diverse
Explanation	Within the frame of object-orientation	Within any scientific frame
Theoretical contribution	Formal	Any kind
Suggestions for improvements of techniques	Constrained by straightforward implementation in object-oriented language	May require extensive implementation efforts or changes in the object-oriented languages

In the following, we will see that development of object-oriented techniques for modelling so far has been mainly carried out according to the methods engineering approach.

2.1   Explanations

In order to illustrate how problems in modelling often are explained, we consider modelling of actors.

When an actor can have roles that change over time, one encounters a problem in object-oriented modelling. The problem has been explained within the common concepts of object-orientation to be that the actor object has to change its class (e.g., Richardson and Schwartz, 1991; Nerson, 1992; Gottlob et al, 1996). The suggestions for solutions have been minor extensions of the object concept along with guidelines for implementation.

Coad (1992) refers to another discipline when diagnosing problems in object-oriented modelling. Inspired by the concept 'pattern' in architecture, he explains that some of the problems in modelling appear because the basic object-oriented concepts are too fine-grained to capture some frequently occurring structures in domains. This explanation is grounded outside the area of object-orientation, and Coad therefore transcends the method engineering approach. The conclusion he draws is to suggest patterns of objects connected by well-known relations. This suggestion is well inside current object oriented concepts.

2.2   Theoretical contributions

Essink and Erhart (1991) have suggested a theoretical framework for conceptual modelling during analysis. Their framework departs from an ontology that is close to the core of object-orientation. The only extension is that they claim that "objects are bound by (natural) laws" (p.91), and this claim does not penetrate the formalistic assumption of object-orientation.

From their framework, they generate four kinds of abstraction relations: specialisation, containment (aggregation with parts depending on the whole), assembly (aggregation with independent parts), and grouping (set inclusion). These four relation types are specialised according to whether they are permanent or temporary, e.g., "roletype" is a temporary specialisation that may meet the need for modelling roles, which is an important aspect of actor concepts. The suggestions of Essink and Erhart have neither been used in recent methods for modelling (Henderson-Sellers and Edwards, 1994; Reenskaug et al, 1996) nor been quoted in the solution presented in (Gottlob et al, 1996), even if their roletype relation is similar to the solution that is elaborated by Gottlob et al. One reason may be that it may be hard to decide when and how to use the different types of relations suggested, based on the brief discussion in the conference paper.

van de Weg and Engmann (1992) suggest another framework where they distinguish between interobject and intraobject structures, and static and dynamic properties. They also suggest a "role-of" relationship. Their framework does not support their suggestion of this relationship, instead they refer to an earlier suggestion by Pernici (1990), while ignoring Essink and Erhart (1991). van de Weg and Engmann's role-of relation is also ignored in recent methods (Henderson-Sellers and Edwards, 1994; Reenskaug et al, 1996), even though roles are considered in these methods and other research is cited.

The ignorance of these research suggestions shows that they have not succeeded in adding new issues to the core of object-orientation. In addition, the suggestions have been limited to formal theories.

We have not been able to collect much information about development of modelling techniques from the literature, and we have not carried out a survey on our own. Nevertheless, the available information from the method designers support the observation that the theoretical contributions have not entered the methods properly.

Rumbaugh tells how he collects knowledge for updating his Object Modelling Technique (OMT):

> Any method must grow or die, so I have used three drivers in guiding the evolutions of OMT: user experience and feedback, good ideas from other authors, and new insights of my own. (Rumbaugh, 1995, p.21)

While his reference to user experience indicates a consultant approach, he also gets good ideas from others. The material he outlines includes research discussions, e.g., concerning constraints, so he is carrying out method engineering. His considerations do not go beyond the formal and implementation issues, however. E.g., a discussion about objects that are part of several aggregates does not go beyond defining relations.

Other authors of modelling methods may draw upon a richer background of literature. However, since they to a limited extent refer to the research of formal or implementation character, it seems unlikely that they have brought wider focused theories into their considerations.

The OOram method (Reenskaug et al, 1996) is one exception, in which Weber's bureaucratic theory is used as a template for how to provide structure to a system. This structure concerns design of the relations between objects and roles in the computer system, and it is not indicated that Weber's theory can be effective in modelling of the problem.

2.3   Suggestions for change of techniques

Based on a literature survey of object-orientation, Bjornestad (1994) summarises the core of object-orientation to consist of the following:
- encapsulated objects with properties and behaviour,
- classes of objects, and
- inheritance of general properties and behaviour to specialised classes.

Monarchi and Puhr (1992) have surveyed object-oriented methods, and the methods seem to conform to the general core of object-orientation, with one exception: communication between objects is found in a majority of the methods in the survey. Somewhat surprisingly is aggregation only found in 5 of 19 methods, and 7 of the methods include constraints on structure, e.g., cardinalities.

Recently, the methods have adapted a larger number of concepts for modelling (e.g., Embley et al, 1992; Martin and Odell, 1992; Henderson-Sellers and Edwards, 1994), and aggregation and constraints are included. However, no standard definition of aggregation has emerged (Motschnig-Pitrik, 1994), so even this minor extension of object-orientation has not yet succeeded, nearly twenty years after it was suggested in data modelling (Smith and Smith, 1977).

It is commonly assumed that the object-oriented model should represent the domain to be modelled. A step towards a more radical extension is found in the methods by Wirfs-Brock et al (1990), Jacobson et al (1992) and Reenskaug et al (1996). These methods suggest that the interaction between the user and the computer system should be the starting point for selection of objects rather than first achieving a model of the problem domain. Designing a system according to a desired human-computer interaction opens for modelling domains from different user viewpoints. However, the methods go for a unified model that is supposed to serve all interests, without separating between different viewpoints in the model.

2.4   Current trend: Method engineering

Conclusively, we have seen some explanations of modelling problems that extend object-oriented theories. However, neither these nor other theoretical contributions have extended the basis for deriving concepts for modelling. Consequently, the suggestions for improvements of techniques have been constrained by the implementation considerations. In addition, neither the theoretical considerations nor the techniques captures multiple perspectives on domains in the models. Taken together with Rumbaugh's story, this indicates that the way second generation object-oriented methods are developed conforms to method engineering rather than the system development research approach.

3   THE DOMAIN OF TECHNIQUES

As we mentioned in the introduction, we have noticed a shift in the perspective in respect to the roles the computer systems may play in human work within organisations. Earlier, a common view of the computer was that it was used for handling or controlling the problem domain, hence the models did not address elements in the application domain explicitly. Lately there has been an increasing attention in both system development practice and in the research community toward using the computer as a medium in the work organisation, thus enabling the use of computers as means of coordinating work and communication in and about work. (Simone and Schmidt, 1993; Carstensen et al., 1995).

We have in the previous section identified that the modelling domain of object oriented modelling techniques usually is the problem domain, and in some approaches the future computer system. Apart from the use-case technique (Jacobson, 1992), we have not identified any object oriented modelling technique that explicitly address the application domain. However, Carstensen et al (1995) have applied an object oriented analysis technique to capture aspects of the application domain, and have reported problems with modelling interactions between actors involved in coordinating their activities. Other have reported problems related to modelling of different roles of actors in respect to the computer system (Richardson and Schwarz, 1991; Coad, 1992).

We want to apply oo modelling techniques in a human work context, where the computer has a role in interhuman communication, coordination of work and cooperation. With the problems mentioned above in mind we claim:

- that the notation and concepts for modelling either fails to or makes it difficult to model issues of work context, and
- that the theoretical foundations for oo techniques do not give clues as to what properties of the work context that should be modelled, and how this should be done.

According to our learning cycle, the problems are both on a theoretical and on a modelling technique level. We argue that the perspective on human work is fundamental to the selection and development of theoretical foundations for modelling.

3.1   Human work and modelling domains

We have reached a position to not model human work itself, but rather model the roles the computer have in the work. There are both political and theoretical arguments for this position. One the political side, we fear a de-skill of workers if the computer systems control the execution of work, in terms of what activities should be done, and in what sequence. On the theoretical side, we regard work to be to complex to model. Several schools of theories of work exist, and we use some of their findings to support this claim:

- Strauss (1988) reports that tasks and lines of work do not automatically arrange themselves in proper sequences or with proper scheduling, hence further work must be done in order to get the work done. This work, denoted articulation work, is driven by the situation at hand, and is often a result of contingencies. We regard it difficult to be explicit about articulation work itself, as would be necessary when trying to model it.
- Suchman (1987) reports that work is not strictly governed by plans, rather it is driven by the possibilities and limitations of the situation at hand. We regard a model of e.g. a work task or a routine a plan in this respect, hence problems related to ad-hoc arrangements in a practical setting are expected.
- Several persons are often involved in work, because several areas of competence are needed. This requires that they integrate and coordinate their individual activities in order to get the work done. When modelling the different actors of the application domain, and their roles should be made explicit in the model, to ease this coordination.

To summarise, we have identified a need for representing the different actors in the application domain, and a need to model the role of the computer in a work context. The issue of actors and roles is covered by a theoretical approach based on semiotic concepts, presented in the next section. The role of the computer is covered by an approach based on activity theory, presented in Section 2.5.

4   A LEARNING CYCLE BRINGING IN A SEMIOTIC RELATION

Problems of object oriented modelling of actors with roles (Kvisli, 1993; Ressem, 1995) and entities that have both form and content (Fog, 1992) have been reported. Others have explained the problems of roles within the object-oriented perspective (e.g., Richardson and Schwartz, 1991; Nerson, 1992; Gottlob et al, 1996). In order to explain both types of problems, we have searched for new ways to interpret the phenomena to be modelled. One approach has been to study the referential aspects of information systems.

Information systems are referential systems, because the data in information systems is perceived by their users to refer to things and events that are separated from the information system. Roles also exists in information systems e.g., persons playing the roles of users, and computer hardware playing roles of data processing units. We have therefore regarded the referential aspects of information systems as a domain for modelling, and we have seen how theories relevant to this area can contribute to the learning cycle of development of modelling techniques.

The data of information systems are expressions that refer to extensions, e.g., the object 'Diana Smith' in the airline reservation system refers to a specific passenger. In order to explain how the hardware of computers can play the role of data processing, one identifies layers of implementation, e.g., saying that an object is implemented in ASCII code, which is implemented in binary code, which is implemented in electronic circuits. During system design, one often has to construct programs at different layers. A similar separation into layers is also found in semiotics (Andersen, 1990), where the form of expressions is realised in substance. E.g., letters are realised in black curves on white background. In order to explain roles in a broader framework than object-orientation, we have therefore adopted this semiotic form-substance relation.

In order to deal with other issues as well, e.g., entities that have both form and content, we have defined a more general relation. Since the substance has to exist for the form to exist, the relation is defined to capture this property, and it is called the "lifetime dependency" relation (Kaasbøll and Motschnig-Pitrik, 1996). We have demonstrated that this relation is more general than previous solutions to role modelling, including those of Essink and Erhart (1991) and van de Weg and Engmann (1992), because it allows an object to be a role of several objects. This is not possible in previous approaches.

We have also started evaluating the lifetime dependency relation (Kaasbøll, 1996). The hypotheses were that the relation occurred in most domain models, and that the models became less complex when using the relation. In the initial evaluation that we have carried out, we departed from object-oriented models of domains, and remodelled them using the lifetime dependency relation. This test showed a higher frequency of the relation than expected. We also achieved some reduction of complexity in the models through a decrease in the number of relations (Kaasbøll, 1996).

The planned further evaluation includes modelling of systems that are going to be replaced. Also working out guidelines for implementation and suggestions for changes of programming tools and languages remain.

Although this learning cycle is not fully completed, it illustrates that problems of modelling can be explained in another context than object-orientation, and that such a widening of scope can contribute to new suggestions for changes in techniques. This may require more extensive implementation efforts than previous suggestions, which is the problematic side of trying to carry out system development research instead of method engineering.

5   A LEARNING CYCLE BRINGING IN ACTIVITY THEORY

As we have mentioned, Carstensen et al (1995) have reported problems in modelling interaction between actors involved in coordinating their activities. We have not identified any theoretical foundation of object oriented modelling techniques that include issues of work coordination, communication or interaction among actors in the application domain. Therefore we have started the learning cycle with a search for a theory that address issues of work context and how computers are used in order to mediate communication, coordination and interaction. Activity theory was selected, and extended to explain the role of computers in human work. This work was done in a case study, in an organisation using Lotus Notes to communicate, share documents and coordinate work.

Activity theory address human work within a social context (Engeström, 1987). The theory accounts for the individuals' relations to the object of work, and to the fellow workers. The relationships are not dual, but mediated through instruments, e.g. computers. We use the relationships as a basis for understanding the role of computers in an activity.

Production denotes the relationship between subject (a human) and object. The relationship is mediated through tools. The computer may be regarded a tool in this relation. See example in figure 2.

Distribution denotes the relationship between community (e.g. the workgroup or the employees in the organisation) and object. This relation is mediated through the division of labour. The computer may be regarded a mediator of this division of labour, in the sense that coordination of work may be done by means of the computer.

Exchange denotes the relationship between the a subject and the community. This relation is mediated through rules of social behaviour and communication. The computer may be regarded a communication channel in this relation. E-mail and conferencing software are examples of this role in the work context.

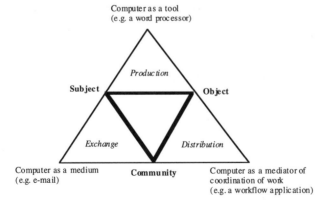

Figure 2 The aspects of a human activity, and the corresponding roles of a computer system.

According to Engeström, the three relations constitutes an organic whole. Issues of integration of the roles of the computer in a human activity is an issue (Fjuk et al, 1995), and therefore the interdependencies of the various roles should be made explicit in the model.

The next step in this work is to do a systems development project, in order to derive hypothesis regarding how metaphors and notation in a object oriented modelling technique should be developed. This work will be carried out in a large Norwegian municipal organisation, see Smørdal (1996). The learning cycle is restarted by testing the modelling technique in a practical setting.

6   CONCLUSION

New computer applications address issues of work context, in addition to representing the object of work. Object-oriented models of such systems therefore have to capture some aspects of work, e.g., actors and roles. Since human work is complex and governed by rules to a much lesser extent than computer processing is, the modelling techniques have to avoid making assumptions about regularities in work. Therefore object oriented modelling techniques should be developed according to knowledge about human work within organisations.

In order to point to how to bring such knowledge into the process of developing techniques, we have outlined a learning cycle consisting of practice, evaluation, theoretical contribution, and suggestion of improved techniques.

We have defined method engineering to be a way to develop methods, where formal theories and implementation considerations are used in evaluation, theoretical contribution, and as the basis for suggesting improvements in techniques. The literature indicates that most development of techniques for modelling has been carried out according to a method engineering approach.

In order to develop the techniques such that they can model issues related to work properly, knowledge of work has to be included in the ways modelling problems are explained and new modelling mechanisms are suggested. Therefore, we have argued to widen the theoretical scope of development of techniques from the focus on formal and implementation considerations in method engineering to a system development research learning cycle that is open for any contribution to understanding the domain that is to be modelled. We have illustrated the system development research approach with two cases of our own research, and shown that new concepts for modelling may emerge.

To develop these concepts into practical techniques, guidelines for implementation have to be worked out. For this part of the research, an engineering approach is probably well suited.

Even if we argue for widening the scope during development of techniques, we are aware that widely focused research into the techniques may lead to new knowledge that provides no clues as to how to improve the techniques. Instead, the research may, e.g., point to needs for better training or project organisation. We have introduced our contributions with an eye to the possibility for also using the wider focus for constructive suggestions to solve modelling problems. This points to the fact that choosing research approach is only one condition for setting the direction for development of techniques. The background of the researchers and their knowledge may be more decisive. Being aware of where to place ones development effort in method engineering or system development research may help to see the limits and possibilities of the effort.

7 ACKNOWLEDGEMENTS

This article has benefited from discussions with Frieder Nake and Markku Nurminen.

8 REFERENCES

Andersen, P.B. (1990) A Theory of Computer Semiotics: Semiotic Approaches to Construction and Assessment of Computer Systems, Cambridge University Press.

Bjornestad, S. (1994) A research programme for object-orientation *European Journal of Information Systems* 3, 1, 13–27

Braa, K.; Vidgen, R. (1995) Action Case: Exploring The Middle Kingdom in IS Research Methods, to be published in *Proceedings of Computers in Context: Joining Forces in Design,* Aarhus, Denmark.

Carstensen, P. H.; Krogh, B.; Sørensen, C. (1995) Object oriented Modelling of Coordination Mechanisms, in Dahlbom, B.; Kämmerer, F; Ljungberg, F; Stage, J.; Sørensen, C. (Eds.) *Proceedings of IRIS 18,* Gothenburg Studies in Informatics, Report 7.

Coad, P. (1992) Object-Oriented Patterns *Communications of the ACM* 35, 9, 152–159.

Embley, D.W.; Kurtz, B.D.; Woodfield, S.C. (1992) *Object-Oriented Systems Analysis: A Model-Driven Approach* Prentice-Hall, NJ

Engeström, Y (1987) Learning by Expanding. An activity-theoretical approach to developmental research. Orienta-Konsultit Oy, Helsinki.

Essink, L.J.B.; Erhart, W.J. (1991) Object Modeling and System Dynamics in the Conceptualization Stages of Information Systems Development. In van Assche, Moulin, and Rolland (eds.) *Object Oriented Approaches to Information systems* North-Holland, Amsterdam, 89–116

Fjuk, A; Sandahl, T.; Smørdal, O. (1995) Toward Incorporating Computer Applications in Cooperative Work Arrangements –An activity theoretical approach, in Dahlbom, B.; Kämmerer, F; Ljungberg, F; Stage, J.; Sørensen, C. (Eds.) *Proceedings of IRIS 18,* Gothenburg Studies in Informatics, Report 7.

Fog, C. (1992) A comparison of flow- and object-oriented analysis of information processing: Iterations and intuition in interpretation of large quantities of information Master thesis in Norwegian, Department of Informatics, University of Oslo.

Galliers R.D. (1992) Choosing Appropriate Information Systems Research Approaches: A Revised Taxonomy, in Galliers, R. (Ed.) *Information Systems Research: issues, methods and practical guidelines.* Blackwell Scientific, Oxford.

Gottlob, G.; M. Schrefl; and B. Rock (1996) "Extending Object-Oriented Systems with Roles" *ACM Transactions on Information Systems* Volume 14, Number 3, July.

Harmsen, F.; Brinkkemper, S.; Oei, H. (1994) A language and tool for the engineering of situational methods for information systems development. In Zupancic and Wrycza (eds.) *Proceedings of The Fourth International Conference Information Systems Development — ISD'94 Methods & Tools. Theory & Practice* Moderna Organizacija, Kranj, 206–214

Henderson-Sellers, B. and Edwards, J. (1994) BOOKTWO of Object-Oriented Knowledge: The Working Object. Object-Oriented Software Engineering: Methods and Management. Prentice-Hall, Sydney

Heym, M. and Österle, H. (1993) Computer-aided methodology engineering. *Information and Software Technology* 35, 6/7, 345–354

Jacobson, I.; Christerson, M.; Johnson, P.; Övergaard, G. (1992) Object oriented Software Engeneering. A Use Case Driven Approach. Addison-Wesley.

Kaasbøll, J. J. (1996) Between controlled irrelevance and unrepeatable complexity: Initial evaluation of the concepts of domain modelling techniques. Accepted for publication at the Workshop on Evaluation of Modeling Methods in Systems Analysis and Design, The 8th Conference on Advanced Information Systems Engineering. Software engineering challenges in modern information systems. (CAiSE*96) (Heraklion, Greece, 20-24 May, 1996)

Kaasbøll, J. J. and Motschnig-Pitrik, R. (1996) Lifetime dependency relationships and their application to modelling roles and relationship objects. In A.G. Sutcliffe, F. van Assche, and D. Benyon (eds.) *Domain Knowledge for Interactive System Design*. Chapman & Hall, London

Kumar, K. and Welke, R. J. (1992) Methodology engineering: A proposal for situation-specific methodology construction. In Cotterman and Senn (eds.) *Challenges and Strategies for Research in Systems Development*. John Wiley and Sons, Chichester, 257–269

Kvisli, J. (1993) *Object-oriented analysis and design of adminstrative computer applications* Master thesis in Norwegian, Department of Informatics, University of Oslo

Martin, J. and Odell, J.J. (1992) *Object-Oriented Analysis and Design* Prentice-Hall.

Mathiassen, L.; Munk-Madsen, A.; Nielsen, P. A.; and Stage, J. (1993)Object Oriented Analysis (In Danish) Forlaget Marko, Aalborg

Monarchi, D. E. and Puhr, G. I. (1992) A Research Typology for Object-Oriented Analysis and Design *Communications of the ACM* 35, 9, 35–47

Motschnig-Pitrik, R. (1994) Analyzing the notions of attribute, aggregate, part, and member in data/knowledge modelling. In Zupancic and Wrycza (eds.) *Proceedings of The Fourth International Conference Information Systems Development — ISD'94 Methods & Tools. Theory & Practice* Moderna Organizacija, Kranj, pp.31–42

Nerson, J.-M. (1992) Applying Object-Oriented Analysis and Design. *Communications of the ACM* 35, 9, 63–74

Pernici, B. (1990) Objects with Roles, SIGOIS Bulletin 11, 2/3, 205–215.

Reenskaug, T., with Wold P.; Lehne O. A. (1996) *Working With Objects: the OOram Software Engineering Method.* Manning, Greenwich

Ressem, J. E. (1995) Where do all the objects come from? A study of the approach of three object-oriented methods to the identification of objects Master thesis in Norwegian, Department of Informatics, University of Oslo

Richardson, J. and Schwarz, P. (1991) Aspects: Extending objects to support multiple, independent roles, *SIGMOD Record*, 20, No.2, 298–307

Rossi, M. and Brinkkemper, S. (1995) Metrics in Method Engineering. In Iivari, Lyytinen, and Rossi (eds.) *Advanced Information Systems Engineering. CAiSE '95*, LNCS 932, Springer

Rumbaugh, J. (1995) "OMT: The object model" *Journal of object-oriented programming* January, 21–27

Simone, C.; Schmidt, K. (eds.) (1993) *Computational Mechanisms of Interaction for CSCW*, COMIC, Esprit Basic Research Project 6225, Lancaster University, Lancaster.

Smith, J.M. and Smith, D.C.P. (1977) Database Abstractions: Aggregation and Generalization *ACM Transactions on Database Systems* 2, 2, 105–133.

Smørdal, O. (1996) Soft Objects Analysis – A modelling approach for analysis of interdependent work practices. Forthcomming.

Strauss, A. (1988) The Articulation of Project Work: An Organizational Process, in *The Sociological Quarterly,* Vol. 29, (2), pp 163-178.

Suchman, L. A. (1987) *Plans and Situated Actions,* Cambridge University Press.

van de Weg, R. L.W. and Engmann, R. (1992) A framework and Method for Object-Oriented Information Systems Analysis and Design. In E.D. Falkenberg, C. Rolland, and E.N. El-Sayed (eds.) *Information System Concepts: Improving the Understanding* ISCO 2, IFIP Transactions A-4, North-Holland, 123–146.

Vessey, I. and Conger, S. A. (1994) Requirements Specification: Learning Object, Process, and Data Methodologies. *Communications of the ACM* 37, 5, 102–113

Wirfs-Brock, R.; Wilkerson, B.; Wiener, L.(1990) *Designing Object-Oriented Software* Prentice-Hall, NJ

9   BIOGRAPHY

Jens Kaasbøll i assistent professor at the Department of Informatics, University of Oslo. He has published in Information Systems Journal, Journal of Object-Oriented Programming and in international conferences. He has served as a co-editor of Scandinavian Journal of Information Systems. His research interests are in object-oriented modelling and in ways of providing computer support in organizations such that the systems fit user tasks and seem integrated from users' points of view.

Ole Smørdal is a research associate in the Department of Informatics, University of Oslo. Current research interests include theoretical foundations for object oriented modelling in relation to information systems.

9

Translating OMT* to SDL, Coupling Object-Oriented Analysis and Design with Formal Description Techniques

K. Verschaeve, B. Wydaeghe, V. Jonckers, L. Cuypers
Vrije Universiteit Brussel
Laboratory for System and Software Engineering, Vrije Universiteit Brussel,
Pleinlaan 2, 1050 Brussel, Belgium. Telephone: +32-2-6292974.
Fax: +32-2-6292870. email: kaversch@info.vub.ac.be

Abstract

This paper presents an automated transition from OMT* (a formal variant of OMT) towards SDL. This work is a partial result from a larger research effort proposing an integrated methodology and toolset based on the combination of Object-Orientation and Formal-Description Techniques. In this project OMT is used as the systems requirements analysis technique and OMT* for for System Design, while SDL (Specification Description Language) is targeted for the design phase. The transition from OMT to OMT* is manual process described by a set of guidelines (Holz et al. 1995) We developed a transformational semantic for OMT*, i.e. a set of transformation rules mapping OMT* constructs to SDL constructs. The translation from OMT* to SDL preserves the logical structure of the specification. This way it is possible to preserve the efforts done in the analysis phase and to make a smooth transition towards design.

Keywords

OMT*, SDL, Analysis, Design, Transformational Semantics, Software Engineering

1 INTRODUCTION

1.1 The INSYDE Project

The INSYDE (INtegrated methods for evolving SYstem DEsign, INSYDE 1994) methodology is a set of techniques and tools to enable the evolving co-design of hybrid systems. A hybrid system is one which contains significant hardware and software components. As the complexity of such systems is constantly increasing, the development of large systems requires a consistent and integrated methodology for proceeding from analysis to implementation. The INSYDE project will produce a prototype methodology and toolset based on the combination of Object-Orientation and Formal-Description Techniques and covers the development lifecycle from Systems Requirements Analysis over System Design to Detailed Design and Validation in an integrated way.

The INSYDE project is an EU ESPRIT III funded project. The consortium consists of Alcatel Bell Telephone (Belgium), Dublin City University (Ireland), Humboldt Universität zu Berlin (Germany), Intracom S.A. (Greece), Verilog S.A. (France) and Vrije Universiteit Brussel (Belgium).

The INSYDE methodology integrates the object-oriented analysis methodology OMT (Object Modeling Technique, Rumbaugh 1991) with two domain specific formal description techniques, namely SDL '88 (CCITT, 1988) and VHDL (Navabi, 1993). OMT is used as the system requirements analysis technique and also as the technique for the initial design stages. This allows the methodology to provide mechanisms for combining the individual design techniques (OMT, SDL, VHDL), maintaining the consistency of partial models at the detailed design stage and co-simulating the formal description to validate the hybrid system against the system specification. The relative strengths of each design technique (SDL for asynchronous communication systems, VHDL for synchronous reactive systems) can thus be exploited in an optimal way.

Our Lab for System and Software Engineering (LaSSE) does research in the field of telecommunication systems. Therefor we focus on the use of SDL in the INSYDE methodology, SDL being a widely used specification standard and very well suited for our purpose.

In this paper we limit the scope to the translation of OMT to SDL. This transition happens partially manually and partially automatically as explained below. This translation is important and interesting because there is a strong need for an automatic reuse of analysis information into software specification languages like SDL. An automatic translation encourages the developer to make a more thorough system design model. Moreover, the structure of the resulting SDL model will be like the structure of the OMT model, resulting in system that is easier to maintain.

1.2 OMT*

In our methodology the analysis is done in OMT, using the full richness of OMT as defined by Rumbaugh et al. (1991). Constructs such as classes or associations can have different semantics depending on their context, which is useful during the requirement analysis phase.

While OMT is a good analysis methodology, the informal nature of OMT makes an automatic translation to SDL infeasible. In our methodology the analysis document is manually prepared for translation during system design. During this phase subsystems are identified, communication is formalized and information is ordered. To describe these aspects we developed a new language OMT* (formal definition in Wasowski, 1995), aimed to meet the requirements of system design. In our methodology OMT* is close to both OMT and SDL.

- OMT* is close to OMT because they use the same syntactic structures and because the semantics of OMT* are compatible with Rumbaugh, i.e. the semantics of OMT* do not conflict with OMT. OMT* differs from OMT in that it contains a number of syntactical constraints and in that the possible interpretations of an OMT construct are reduced and clearly described. Detailed guidelines of how to make the transition from OMT to OMT* can be found in the INSYDE application guidelines (Holz et al. 1996). Also a brief overview of the methodology is available in (Sinclair et al., 1995).
- OMT* is close to SDL because there is automatic translation and because OMT* and SDL have corresponding structure and semantics. The generated SDL is readable and contains enough detail to be a good framework as a starting point for detailed design.

1.3   Quick Preview of the Translation from OMT* to SDL

In this paper, we describe the transformation of OMT* to SDL by defining a *transformational semantics* for OMT*. These semantics consists of a set of translation rules for the object model and the dynamic model. We do not use the functional model of OMT, because this model does not give much additional information over the object and dynamic models to generate SDL.

The translation rules for OMT* are based on the availability and the semantics of constructs in both OMT and SDL. Figure 1 shows how some of the OMT constructs are mapped on SDL constructs. For example the basic building blocks in OMT are classes while in SDL they are the system, blocks and processes. So it is a natural choice to map a class on either a system, block and/or process. In the same way the structuring mechanism of OMT is aggregation while in SDL this is done by nesting of blocks. Finally the expression of relationships between classes is done by associations in OMT and with communication paths in SDL.

Semantics	OMT*	SDL
Basic Building Block	Class	System, Block, Process
Structuring (Subsystems)	Aggregation	Nested Blocks
Relationship between classes	Association	Communication

Figure 1 Mapping of object model of OMT* constructs on SDL

We have a similar table for the translation of the dynamic model of OMT*, see figure 2. In OMT* the behaviour of a class is expressed by a state diagram. This state diagram is translated as a SDL process specification. It is straightforward to translate state and state transitions to the equivalent constructs in SDL. Entry and exit actions are translated as actions on the transition to and from that state respectively. Internal transitions are translated as transition with itself as destination.

OMT*	SDL
Activity	Process or Part of Process
State	State
State transition	State Transition
Entry/Exit Actions	Actions on State Transition
Internal Transitions	State Transition to Self

Figure 2 Mapping of dynamic model of OMT* on SDL

As some OMT constructs can take several possible translations, local translation of each construct in the OMT model by a corresponding construct in SDL is not possible. We need global information of the model to make the correct translation. In an extra phase before the translation (sections 3 and 5) we gather this information.

1.4 Structure of the paper

In the next section we will start with a short overview of OMT* to introduce the concepts used in the translation. In section three we will describe how we prepare the translation of the object model followed in section four by the translation rules for the object model. Section five describes the preparation of the translation for the dynamic model and section six gives the translation rules for the dynamic model.

Within this paper we use only tiny OMT and SDL examples to clarify some concepts. The INSYDE methodology and the translation of OMT* to SDL has been successfully tested is an industrial case studies of a Video-on-Demand server system (Peeters et al. 1995).

We assume that the reader is acquainted with both OMT and SDL.

2 OVERVIEW OF OMT*

This section gives a short overview of OMT*. This language is used as a system design language between the analysis in OMT and the detailed design in SDL. OMT* has a syntax which is very similar to OMT but it has well defined semantics defined by its translation towards SDL.

2.1 Object model

An OMT* specification is entered through the object model. The dynamic model is accessed through the object diagram. The classes in the object diagram contain pointers to the different state diagrams in the dynamic model.

The syntax of OMT* contains a number of restrictions as opposed to OMT, because some constructs in OMT have an ambiguous semantics or are very difficult to translate into SDL. More specifically, the object model is restricted to object diagrams that

- do not contain multiple inheritance
- contain only binary associations,
- do not contain general constraint expressions,
- do not contain discriminator or restrictor rules.

These restrictions are only valid during system design. The analysis is done in full OMT, without these constraints. There are detailed guidelines available how to manually translate OMT into OMT* in (Holz et al. 1996), available at the World Wide Web at "http://www.compapp.dcu.ie/ gclynch/papers.html". In general we could say that most changes needed to get OMT* are rather intuitive for somebody that is acquainted with the translation rules to SDL.

Model definition. An OMT* model contains a list of classes and a list of associations. Figure 3 shows the model of a Movie-Box containing three classes. The classes *Control* and *Motor* do have pointers to a state diagrams shown below.

Class definition. An OMT* class is a six-tuple (id,V,O,sn,G,d) where *id* denotes the name of the class, V denotes the set of attributes, O denotes the possible input events and functions defined, *sn* is the name of the superclass, G is the set of components and d is the state diagram, describing the dynamic behavior of this class. In our example (figure 3) the six-tuple describing class *motor* is

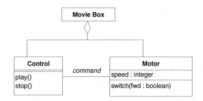

Figure 3 Simplified Model of a Movie-Box in OMT*

$(motor, \{speed\}, \{switch\}, \epsilon, \emptyset, \epsilon)$, where *speed* and *switch* are references to the specific attribute and operation respectively.

Attributes and operations. An attribute has a name, a type and, optionally, a default value. In OMT* types are only names. It is thus impossible to check whether a value is of a certain type or not.

An operation either is an input event or a function. Apart from the fact that an operation can have a result type, input events and functions differ in the following:

- An input event is used to initiate a state transition within the state diagram of its class. It cannot be used to change or retrieve the contents of an attribute. It is our intention that an input event can be described within the dynamic model. The parameters passed to an input event can then be used by passing them to a function activation.
- A function is used to do some calculations on the given parameters and on the attributes of an object. As a result, a value can be returned to the "caller" and the values of some attributes of the function's object can be changed.

Aggregations and associations. Unlike in OMT, aggregations and associations in OMT* are described differently. This is because the semantic differences are strong enough to separate those two concepts. Aggregations are used to model the "part-whole" relationships within the real world or to model subsystem relations. Associations denote communication between objects.

In OMT* an association is a unbounded construct, described as a seven-tuple (id,lc,rc,lm,rm,lr,rr) where id denotes the name of the association, lc and rc are the names of the classes that are connected by this association, lm and rm denote the multiplicities and lr and rr denote the roles. In our example (figure 3) the seven-tuple of the association *command* could be described as $(command, Control, Motor, 1, 1, \epsilon, \epsilon)$.

In OMT* an aggregation is part of the specification of a class. An aggregate tuple contains a component id, the aggregate multiplicity and the component multiplicity. We limit the aggregate multiplicity to the values 1 and $\{0,1\}$, mainly because in SDL is strictly hierarchical, i.e., a process can never be in two disjunct blocks at the same time. The set of aggregates (G) of the MovieBox class is $\{(Control, 1, 1), (Motor, 1, 1)\}$.

2.2 Dynamic Model

States Diagram. A state diagram in OMT* describes the control aspects of *one specific* class. It contains the possible states of an object, describes how input events are used to initiate state transitions and describes when and how functions are activated.

A state diagram consists of a number of state definitions (in figure 4, the states *idle* and *play*) and exactly one initial lambda transition (in figure 4, the transition going from • to *idle*). This initial lambda transition is fired on creation of the object. The state diagrams of OMT* are currently restricted to state diagrams that

1. do not contain concurrent sub-state diagrams,
2. do not contain any splitting/synchronization of control,
3. contain exactly one initial lambda transition.

Each of these restriction can be worked around: restriction 1 by using two classes, restriction 2 by using extra synchronization events and restriction 3 by introducing an extra state. All other features of OMT state diagrams, like nested state-diagrams, activities and entry and exit actions, are fully supported in OMT*.

States. A state is defined by its state name, which must be unique within the state diagram. It optionally contains a number of entry actions, exit actions and an activity.

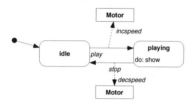

Figure 4 Dynamic Model of the *Control* class of figure 3.

Actions in the states and on the transitions are used to compute values, assign values to attributes and generate output events. Entry and exit actions, like in OMT, are executed on entering and leaving the state respectively.

While in OMT activities are poorly defined, in OMT* three kinds of activities are defined: substate-diagrams, continuous activities and time consuming activities. An activity of a state always starts when the state is entered and ends when the activity is finished or when a state is left.

- A substate-diagram is a complete state diagram, with states and transitions, embedded in a state. There is no limitation in the nesting of substate-diagrams. During the translation to SDL, substate-diagrams are flattened.
- A continuous activity is a simple activity that is automatically terminated when leaving the state. A continuous activity consists of a name from which a placeholder for an entry and exit action is generated. The entry action should start up the activity as a side effect, while the exit action should stop the activity. In figure 4, *show* is an continuous activity because *show* is not defined as an operation in the *Control* class. The translation of *show* is shown in figure 9.
- A time consuming ending activity calls a function. Executing this function may take time and cannot be interrupted. After the activity has finished, the state is left by firing a lambda transition.

State Transitions. State transitions allow performing actions or activities reacting on incoming events. Three kinds of transitions exists: external transitions, external lambda transitions and internal transitions.

An external transition consists of the name of the destination state, a list of input events, a condition and an action list.

An external lambda transition is exactly like a normal external transition except that the former does not have an input event nor a condition associated with it. If combined with an ending activity, the lambda transition is fired when the activity is finished.

An internal transition differs from an external transition in that it has no destination state name, since both the source and destination state are the state in which the transition is defined. Firing an internal transition does not cause the state to be left, as a consequence, the entry and exit actions are not executed.

Within the abstract syntax a terminal state is denoted by defining an empty destination state name in an external (lambda) transition. As a consequence the terminal state (graphically a dot within a circle) cannot have a name.

Actions list.   An action list consists of several actions. An action list may contain any combination of assignments, output events and function calls.

A function is called or an event is sent by specifying the function name or the input event name and giving expressions for every formal parameter in the definition of the function or event. An output event optionally takes a receiver, with specifies to which class the event is sent.

3   PREPARING THE OBJECT MODEL TRANSLATION

A primary requirement for the transformation of the OMT* object model to SDL, is that the resulting SDL specifications should match the logical structure of the OMT* specification as much as possible. This is mainly because the generated specifications will be further refined by human developers. Therefore, they must be able to recognize the logical structure defined within the original OMT* specification. Concretely, this implies that in case of a trade off between completeness and readability, readability should be favored as much as possible.

Before translating an OMT* object model we will first remove inheritance using some flattening functions. This is necessary because SDL'88 does not contain the notion of inheritance. Afterwards we build a kind of an annotated aggregation tree. This step facilitates the translation process considerably, because the aggregation structure is not available as such in the OMT* abstract syntax, where all classes are defined on the same level. As a last step before the translation all associations have to be rerouted because of the translation of aggregation into subblocks.

3.1   Removing inheritance

To flatten the inheritance structure we first have to introduce an auxiliary function *Subtree*. This function returns the set of classes that are in the aggregation tree for a given class.

Definition 31 *(Subtree(c))* *Let* $c = (id, V, O, S, G, d) \in <class>$.
Then $Subtree(c) = \{c\} \cup \bigcup_{g \in Aggregates(c)} Subtree(g)$

Using this function we can flatten every OMT* class with the following flattening functions.

Definition 32 *(Flattening-functions)* *Let* $m = (id, C, A) \in <model>, where C \subset <class>$. *Let* $c = (id, V, O, s, G, d) \in C$, *and let* $E \in <inputevent\ dcl>$ *and* $F \in <function\ dcl>$ *such that* $O = E \cup F$
Define then

- $Attributes(c) = V \cup \{v \in Attributes(s) \mid v \notin V\}$
- $Events(c) = E \cup \{e \in Events(s) \mid e \notin E\}$
- $Functions(c) = F \cup \{f \in Functions(s) \mid f \notin F\}$
- $Operations(c) = Events(c) \cup Functions(c)$
- $Components(c) = G \cup \{g \in Components(s) \mid g \notin G\}$
- $Associations(c) = \{a \in A \mid lc \in Subtree(c) \text{ or } rc \in Subtree(c)\}$

3.2   Building the aggregation tree

The aggregation tree is built by adding a path to every class. This path consists of an ordered list with the names of all classes which connect the given class with a top node. Therefore we will first introduce the function TopClasses. This function returns the set of all classes in a given model m that are on top of the aggregation trees (they are no part of the set of aggregations of any class in the model).

Definition 33 $(TopClasses(m))$ Let $m = (id, C, A) \in\ <model>$ be an OMT* model such that $C = \{c_1, \ldots, c_k\}$, $A = \{a_1, \ldots, a_l\}$, then
$TopClasses(m) = C \setminus \bigcup_{x \in C} Aggregates(x)$

If the model contains only one topclass, this class is translated into SDL as the *system*. Otherwise a new *system class* is added to the model, see figure 5. The *system class* for a model m is constructed by taking all *TopClasses* as components, but no attributes, operations or state diagram. Because of this definition there will always be only one topclass.

Definition 34 $(Paths)$ A path is a n-tuple $(p_1, \ldots, p_n)$ such that $p_1 \in TopClasses$ and $\forall i, 1 < i \leq n : p_{i+1} \in Aggregates(p_i)$. The set of all paths is called "Paths".

Because of the construction of a system class, the paths of all classes in a model will start with the system class, since it is the only TopClass in the model. For example, in figure 5 Class C has as path (System, A, C).

Definition 35 $(ExpandedClasses(m))$ Let $m = (id, C, A) \in\ <model>$ be an OMT* model then $ExpandedClasses(m) = \{\ (id, Attributes(c), Operations(c), superclass, Aggregations(c),Path)$ $\mid Path = (p_1, \ldots, p_n) \in Paths$ such that $p_n = c \in C\}$

In other words expanded classes is the set of all classes after flattening inheritance and extended with path information. This path is then used to reroute associations, see below.

3.3   Annotate the associations

Since we translate aggregation into subblocks we have to reroute an association to the environment of the enclosing block before we are able to connect it. Therefore we define functions to split the associations into partial-associations and complete-associations, see figure 5. A partial-association denotes a connection between a block and its environment and a complete-association is a connection at the lowest level were we can connect the two parts of an association.

The following rules define the partial associations and the complete associations.

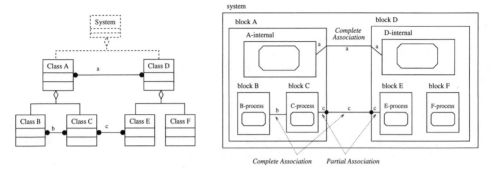

Figure 5 Translation of the OMT* structure and the associations towards SDL

Definition 36 (*Partial–association(c)*)
  Let $a = (id, lc, rc, lm, rm, lr, rr) \in Associations(c)$,
let $plc = (plc_1, \ldots, plc_m) = path(lc), prc = (prc_1, \ldots, prc_n) = path(rc)$, and
let $commonp = (c_1, \ldots, c_p)$, such that $\forall i \leq p : c_i = plc_i = prc_i$.
  Then
$Partial–associations(c) =$
        $\{a \in Associations(c) \mid c \in (plc_{p+1}, \ldots, plc_m)$ or
          $c \in (prc_{p+1}, \ldots, prc_n)\}$

A complete associations is added when a class is the "deepest" class in the common part of the paths of the left and right class of an association. In order to store which components must be connected, the functions return a set of 3-tuples. For example, in figure 5 the *System* gets two complete association because the paths for A and D and for C and E come together in System. The classes to be connected are A and D in both cases.

Definition 37 (*Complete–association(c)*)
  Let $a = (id, lc, rc, lm, rm, lr, rr) \in Associations(c)$,
let $plc = (plc_1, \ldots, plc_m) = path(lc), prc = (prc_1, \ldots, prc_n) = path(rc)$, and
let $commonp = (c_1, \ldots, c_p)$, such that $\forall i(i \leq p)c_i = plc_i = prc_i$
    Then
  $Complete–associations(c) =$
        $\{(a, tlc, trc) \mid a \in Associations(c)$ and $c = plc_p = prc_p$ and
          $tlc = plc_{p+1}$ and $trc = prc_{p+1}\}$

In addition we use a function *Local–Signals(c)* to gather the necessary signal declarations in a given class. The gathering of declarations are defined by three rules. A signal is declared in a given class if

- The class itself uses the signal.
- Or two components of the class use the same signal.
- And signal is *not* already declared in one of its aggregates (recursive definition).

4 TRANSLATION RULES FOR THE OBJECT MODEL

An OMT* model is translated into an SDL system containing the SDL translations for the classes and associations defined within the model.

Translation rule 41 (*sdl–module*) *Let* $m = (id, C, A) \in <model>$ *be an OMT* model. Let system* $= (id, V, O, sc, G, sd, path)$ *be the expanded-system-class of* m *as defined in section 3.2, and* $\{top\_ec_1, \ldots, top\_ec_k\}$ *the expanded classes of Components(system), and* $\{ec_1, \ldots, ec_k\} = ExpandedClasses(m) \setminus Components(system), and\{sa_1, \ldots, sa_n\}$ =Complete-Associations(m), and$\{ev_1, \ldots, ev_m\} = Local$–Signals(system)

Then sdl–module(m) is constructed by

> **system** $<id>$;
>> **signal** *sdl–event-declaration(ev_1), \ldots, sdl–event-declaration(ev_m)*;
>> $<sdl$–*class (top_ec_1)$>$; /* *system blocks**/
>> $\vdots$
>> $<sdl$–*class (top_ec_k)$>$;
>> $<sdl$–*CompleteAssociation (sa_1)$>$; /* *channels* */
>> $\vdots$
>> $<sdl$–*CompleteAssociation (sa_n)$>$;
> **endsystem** $<id>$;
> $<sdl$–*class (ec_1)$>$; /* *referenced blocks**/
> $\vdots$
> $<sdl$–*class (ec_k)$>$;

Classes An OMT class definition c is translated to SDL as a block containing:

- A subblock containing the behaviour and data of c. This includes the attributes, operations and state diagram of c. This is a leaf block. If c does not have any components, the surrounding subblock is skipped.
- A subblock for every component class p in the aggregation tree of c, generated by calling *sdl–class(p)* recursively.

Translation rule 42 (*sdl–class(c)*)
    Let $c = (id, V, O, sc, G, sd)$ *be an OMT* class, such that* $attributes(c) = \{v_1, \ldots, v_k\}$, $operations(c) = \{o_1, \ldots, o_l\}$, $PartialAssociations(c) = \{pa_1, \ldots, pa_m\}$, $CompleteAssociations(c) = \{ca_1, \ldots, ca_n\}$, *and* $Components(c) = \{g_1, \ldots, g_q\}$. $Local$–Signals(c) = \{ev_1, \ldots, ev_p\}$

Then sdl–class(c) is constructed by

> **block** $<id>$;
>> **substructure**
>>> /* *Signals Definitions**/
>>> **signal** *sdl–event-declaration(ev_1, \ldots, ev_p)*;
>>> /* *Components* */

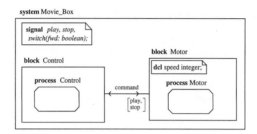

Figure 6 Translation of the Object Model of the Movie-Box

> **block** $<g_1>$ **referenced**;
> ⋮
> **block** $<g_q>$ **referenced** ;
>
> **block** $<id>$-*intern* ; /* skipped if q=0 (no components) */
>   **process** $<id>$-*process* ;
>   **dcl** $<sdl-attribute(v_1, \dots, v_k)>$
> $<sdl-operation(o_1, \dots, o_l)>$
>   /* no signal routes */
> $<sdl-state-diagram(sd, attributes(c))>$; /* optional */
>   **endprocess** $<id>$-*process* ;
>   **endblock** $<id>$-*intern* /* skipped if q=0 */
>
> $<sdl-PartialAssociations\ (c, pa_1, \dots, pa_m)>$; /* channels */
> $<sdl-CompleteAssociations\ (ca_1, \dots, ca_n)>$; /* channels */
> **endsubstructure**
> **endblock** $<id>$;

Associations.   Associations are translated to channels connecting the blocks associated with its left and right classes. To calculate the events sent between two classes we use the function *between*. This is the intersection between the events sent by its first argument and the events declared within its second argument.

Translation rule 43 (*sdl-CompleteAssociation*)
If $ca = (a, tlc, trc)$ where $a = (id, lc, rc, lm, rm, lr, rr) \in <Associations>$ and $tlc, trc \in <class>$. Then sdl-CompleteAssociation(ca) is constructed by

channel $<id>$
    from $<lc>$ **to** $<rc>$
      with $<between(lc, rc)>$;
    from $<rc>$ **to** $<lc>$
      with $<between(rc, lc)>$;
endchannel $<id>$

PartialAssociations are translated in a similar way, it differs only in that a partial association goes to the environment (**ENV**) instead of to a class.

Attributes and operations. An attribute is translated into an SDL declaration of the correct type and initial value, e.g. *Speed* in figure 6. A function is translated into a skeleton of an SDL procedure. Th return type of the function is translated as an in/out parameter of the procedure.

5 PREPARING THE TRANSLATION FOR THE DYNAMIC MODEL

An OMT* state diagram will be translated into an SDL state diagram. For each state within the OMT* state diagram one state within the SDL state diagram is introduced. As SDL, however, does not distinguish between internal and standard transitions, caution is needed in the translation of entry and exit actions. This is solved by executing an entry action only on external transitions, before the SDL state is entered.

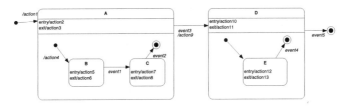

Figure 7 Example of a Nested Statediagram.

The most difficult part is however the translation of substate diagrams. The substates need a copy of the transitions of their superstates, but these transitions need to be expanded with additional exit actions for the substate. Also, the destination of a transition should be changed to the initial state of the substate diagram of the destination state. Therefore we expand the states with path information which allows us to build all transitions.

5.1 Building the Substate Tree.

As with expanded classes, we expand all states with path information, so that each state exactly knows in which substates it is defined. In following definitions we use two functions: *Substates(state)* returns the substates of a given state and *TreeSubStates(state)* which is like *Substates* but include the substate of the substates and so on.

Definition 51 (*StatePaths*) *A statepath is an n-tuple* $(s_1, \ldots, s_n)$, *such that for each* $i \in \{1, \ldots, n-1\}$ *holds* $s_{i+1} \in Substates(s_i)$.

Definition 52 (*ExpandedState(sd)*) *Let* $sd = (i, S) \in$ <*state-diagram*>, *where* i *ist the initial state and* S *is the set of states of sd. Then* $ExpandedStates(sd)$ *is the set of all tuples* $(id, entry, exit, activity, transitions, Path)$ *where exists a* $Path = (s_1, \ldots, s_n) \in StatePaths$, *such that*

- $s_1 \in S$
- $s_n = (id, entry, exit, activity, transitions) \in TreeSubStates(S)$}

In other words, *ExpandedStates* gathers all the states in a statediagram, including substates, and appends path information to each state. In the example in figure 7, state A has path (A), state B has path (A,B), state C has path (A,C), etc. So B and C inherit all transitions from A.

5.2   Copying and Rerouting Transitions.

The function ExpandedTransitions calculates all the transitions for a specific (sub)state, given its path. The algorithm is based on the fact that the base-state is the last element in the path and the state from which the transitions are copied is the first element. In each recursive step all transitions from the top state are copied and extended with the exit actions of all states on the path and the initial actions for entering the destination state. The set of transitions is then extended by a recursive call with a shorter path, i.e. the first element is removed. In this way the target state gets the transitions of all its superstates.

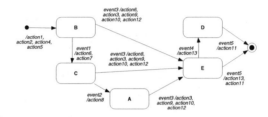

Figure 8 Flattening in OMT* of the Nested Statediagram Example.

The function *ExpandedTransitions* calculates all transisitions of a state, given its path. But because of the complexity and size of the function definition, we only show here the result after applying the flattening functions to the example in figure 7. The flattened statediagram is shown in figure 8.

Notice that the state transition with event3, previously going to state D, is now going to state E immediately because state E is the initial substate of D. For the same reason, state B is now the initial state of the statediagram.

Notice also that event3 is now present in states A, B and C, but that the transition starting in state A calls less exit actions than the transition starting from B and C. Therefor it is not possible, in general, to assign the same transition to a state and its substates.

6   TRANSLATION RULES FOR THE DYNAMIC MODEL

Given the expanded states and expanded transitions, the translation is straightforward. No environment information is needed, because each OMT* construct can be translated in the same order as it appears in the syntax tree. Notice that the state-diagram is flattened, so all states are on the same level. Figure 9 shows the translation of the state diagram of the *control* class (figure 4).

Translation rule 61 (*sdl–state–diagram(sd)*) Let $sd = (i, S) \in$ *<state diagram>*, where $i = (dest, \epsilon, actions) \in$ *<u>initial</u> lambda transition>*, let $d \in S : name(dest) = d$, d is then the initial state of sd $(a_1, \ldots, a_k) = initial - actions(sd)$ $\{s_1, \ldots, s_k\} = expanded - states(TreeSubStates(S))$.

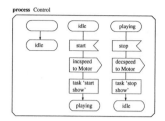

Figure 9 Translation of the Dynamic Model of the Control

Then sdl–state–diagram(sd) is constructed by

> **start** ;
> $\quad$ *sdl–action–list(a_1) ... sdl–action–list(a_k)*
> $\quad$ **nextstate** *<name(sub − dest(d))>* /* **stop** *if d = ε* */
> *<sdl–state(s_1)>*
> $\quad$ ⋮
> *<sdl–state(s_k)>*

6.1 States

An OMT* state is simply translated as an SDL state containing all Expanded-Transition on the path of the state and all internal transitions of the state, see figure 8 and figure 9.

Translation rule 62 (*sdl–state(s)*)
$\quad$ *Let $s = (id, e, x, activity, T, path) \in <expanded\text{-}state>$, where $id \in <name>$, $e \in <entry$ action list$>$, $x \in <\underline{exit}$ action list$>$, activity $\in <activity>$, $(t_1, \dots, t_m) = \overline{Expanded Transitions}(path)$, $(i_1, \dots, i_n) = InternalTransitions(path − states(path))$, and path is a statepath.*

Then sdl–state(s) is constructed by

> **state** *<id>* ;
> $\quad$ *<sdl–external–transition(t_1)> ... <sdl–external–transition(t_m)>*
> $\quad$ *<sdl–internal–transition(i_1)> ... <sdl–internal–transition(i_n)>*
> **endstate** *<id>* ;

6.2 Transitions

When performing an external transitions, all the entry actions and exit actions that were calculated in the expanded transitions should be executed. The following rule also applies to lambda transitions.

Translation rule 63 (*sdl–external–transition(t)*) *Let $t = (dest, event, cond, exit, action, entry) \in <expanded\text{-}transition>$, where $dest \in \epsilon(<\underline{destination\ state}$ name$>)$ event $\in \epsilon(<input\ event>)$, cond $\in \epsilon(<\underline{boolean}$ expression$>)$, and action $= (a_1, \dots, a_k), a_{1 \dots k} \in <action\text{-}list>$.*

Then sdl–external–transition(t) is constructed by

> **input** $<sdl$–$input$–$event(event)>$; /* *Skipped if event* $= \epsilon$ */
> **provided** $<sdl$–$expression(cond)>$; /* *Skipped if cond* $= \epsilon$ *and event* $\neq \epsilon$ */
> /* **provided** *true   if event* $= cond = \epsilon$ *
>
> $<sdl$–$action$–$list(a_1)>$;
> $\vdots$
> $<sdl$–$action$–$list(a_k)>$;
> **nextstate** *dest;*

Internal transitions are translated like external transitions, except that an internal transition only contains one action list and that nextstate is set to "-" to return to the same state at the end of the transition. Note also that for internal transitions there must always be an event, i.e. an empty event is not allowed, so the "input" line is never skipped.

6.3   Actions

An action-list is of course translated as a list of actions. There are three kind of actions: function-call, output event and assignment. For each kind there is a different translation rule, described below.

- function–call, let $f = (func, arg) \in$ <function call>
  call <func> $(<sdl$–$expression(arg_1)>$, ..., $<sdl$–$expression(arg_k)>$);
- output–event, let $e = (event, arg) \in$ <output event>
  output <event> $(<sdl$–$expression(arg_1)>$, ..., $<sdl$–$expression(arg_k)>$);
- assignment, let $a = (attr, expr) \in$ <assignment>
  $attr := sdl$–$expression(expr)$;

7   CONCLUSION

We present an automated transition from OMT* to SDL. OMT has been chosen for its wide spread use in system engineering and for its integration of static and dynamic information. SDL on the other hand, is very well suited for the design of highly interactive systems in a formal way. In the development of large complex systems which involves many people, it is important to have a smooth transition from analysis to design while preserving as much information as possible. In order to allow such a transition we developed OMT*.

OMT* is used as a system design language. The transition from an OMT requirement analysis to an OMT* system design model requires manual design decisions. Detailed guidelines about this transition are available in (Holz et al. 1996). OMT* is a subset of OMT, but OMT* contains as many constructs of OMT as possible. The semantics of OMT* are well defined with a transformational semantics to SDL'88.

OMT*, and the translation to SDL, should not be seen as a way to design and implement an arbitrary system modeled in OMT. Instead, OMT and OMT* should be seen as a front-end to the design of a system that is being designed in SDL anyway. We state that OMT provides the right abstraction level for requirements analysis and that OMT* successfully couples the object-oriented modeling technique (OMT) with the software description language (SDL). We do know of some companies (Alcatel Mobile and IskratTEL) that already use both OMT for analysis and SDL for design in the development of very large telecommunication systems. Of course, those companies could get immediate benefit from our methodology.

Future plans on OMT* include a translation towards SDL'92. This version of SDL has object capabilities and allows probably a better translation in that it preserves more information expressed by the system design model such as aggregation and inheritance.

Apart from SDL, other languages can be generated starting from OMT. In the INSYDE project (INSYDE, 1994) SDL and VHDL are generated for hybrid systems co-design. A translation for the object model into Z is given in (Abowd, 1993). A formal semantics in terms of algebras has been defined for the object model in (Bourdeau, 1995). The programming techniques group at CERN (Aimar et al., 1993) describe a configurable code generator for OO methodologies. However, most of these proposals support only the translation of the object model of OMT, while we also integrated a thorough translation for the dynamic model. This aspect is very important in the domain of telecommunication.

REFERENCES

G. Abowd, R. Allen, and D. Garlan. Using style to understand descriptions of software architecture. *Procs of the 1. ACM SIGSOFT, Symposium on the Foundations of Software Engineering*, December 1993.

A. Aimar, A. Khodabandeh, P. Palazzi, and B. Rousseau. A configurable code generator for OO methodologies. Technical report, Programming Techniques Group, 1993.

R. Bourdeau and B. Cheng. A formal semantics for object model diagrams. *IEEE Transactions on Software Engineering*, October 1995.

CCITT, Geneva. *ITU Specification and Description Language SDL, Recommendation Z.100 Blue Book.*, november 1988.

E. Holz, M. Wasowski, D. Witaszek, S. Lau, J. Fischer, P. Roques, K. Verschaeve, E. Mariatos, and J.-P. Delpiroux. The insyde methodology. Deliverable INSYDE/WP1/HUB/400/v2, ESPRIT Ref: P8641, January 1996.

INSYDE. *Technical Annex: "Integrated Methods for Evolving System Design"*, ESPRIT-III Project P8641, restricted report edition, December 1994.

Z. Navabi. *VHDL Analysis and Modeling of Digital Systems.* McGraw-Hill, Inc., 1993.

J. Peeters, M. Jadoul, E. Holz, M. Wasowski, D. Witaszek, and J.P. Delpiroux. Hw/sw co-design and the simulation of a multimedia application. In *7th European Simulation Symposium*, October 1995.

J. Rumbaugh, M. Blaha, W. Premerlani, F. Eddy, and W. Lorensen. *Object-Oriented Modeling and Design.* Prentice Hall, 1991.

D. Sinclair, G. Clynch, and B. Stone. An object-oriented methodology from requirements to validation. In *2nd International Conference on Object Oriented Systems*, December 1995.

M. Wasowski, D. Witaszek, K. Verschaeve, B. Wydaeghe, E. Holz, and V. Jonckers. The complete omt*. Deliverable INSYDE/WP1/HUB/300/v3, ESPRIT Ref: P8641, December 1995.

10

Lazy Functional Meta-CASE Programming

S. Joosten
Computer Information Systems department
Georgia State University
P.O. Box 4015, Atlanta, GA 30302-4015, USA
tel. +1(404)651 4392, fax +1(404)651 3842
e-mail sjoosten@gsu.edu

Abstract

This paper proposes the use of a lazy functional programming language, such as Miranda or Haskell, as embedded language in meta-CASE tools. Functional programming saves time and effort, because method engineers write programs on the appropriate level of abstraction, without any concern about the order of computations. As a consequence, method engineers build more reliable tools for application engineers to work with. The argument is exemplified by a meta-CASE program, which defines the well known Entity-Relationship modeling technique. Two different semantics are presented to demonstrate typical use: one is the transformation to a relational model and the other is SQL code generation. The full Haskell program to do this is presented, showing the conciseness and the simplicity of that program. This illustrates the type of programming that is done by a method engineer to specify customized modeling techniques.

This paper is written for designers of CASE and meta-CASE tools. The work is also interesting for functional programmers who wish to see an appropriate application of lazy evaluation.

1 INTRODUCTION

This paper proposes the use of a lazy functional programming language, such as Miranda [Turner, 1985], or Haskell [Hudak et al., 1992, Hudak and Fasel, 1992] as an embedded programming language in meta-CASE tools.

A *meta-CASE tool* is a software tool in which modeling techniques are specified in order to generate a CASE tool to support that technique. A *modeling technique* is a graphical notation (i.e. a picture containing nodes and arcs) with semantics attributed to it. Specifying a modeling technique means to define a class of graphs, to specify the visual appearance of each graph, to delimit the modeling technique by imposing restrictions on the class of graphs, to define operations that change the graph (edit operations) and to define operations that interpret the graph (e.g. produce views, transform to other graphs, generate code, perform syntactic and semantic checking)

A *method engineer* uses a meta-CASE tool, such as MAESTRO [Merberth, 1991] or Meta-Edit [Smolander et al., 1991], for the purpose of creating new modeling techniques, adapting existing techniques to specific requirements, or integrating method fragments into a CASE tool that supports a larger part of a given method [Harmsen et al., 1994, Kumar and Welke, 1992]. Method engineers write programs in order to generate a CASE tool for a particular, user defined modeling technique. Their users are *application engineers*, who construct application models using a CASE tool generated by a method engineer. An *application model* is any model used (by application engineers) to build end-user applications.

The *method model* is the object which is manipulated by a method engineer using a meta-CASE tool. A meta-CASE tool contains a method base and CASE tool generators. The method base contains ready-to-use method fragments, from which the method engineer construct (assembles) a method model. These fragments represent modeling techniques (such as ER [Elmasri and Navathe, 1989] or data flow [Yourdon, 1989] modeling), project management techniques (e.g. PERT or GANTT charts), process modeling techniques, configuration management techniques, etc. The method base is enriched by a method engineer, in defining new method fragments. A CASE tool generator is used to generate a CASE tool once the method has been constructed. This generator performs a function similar to a code generator in a compiler.

A meta-CASE programming language is the language embedded in a meta-CASE tool. Method engineers therefore have no choice but to use the language provided with the meta-CASE tool. The particular setting of method engineering yields a unique set of requirements for meta-CASE programming languages. Simplicity and correctness of code are important, because the application engineer does not accept a CASE-tool with errors in it. Although execution performance is important, application engineers do not typically engage in large scale computations. They do require, however that the code generated for their applications is efficient. An important requirement is that a method engineer spends little time programming. A method engineer is supposed to spend time supporting application engineers instead of programming his meta-CASE tool. A complete overview of meta-CASE tool requirements is given in [Harmsen et al., 1994].

This paper starts with the motivation to choose a lazy functional programming language for meta-CASE programming. Next, the Entity-Relationship modeling technique is defined in a functional language (section 3), to exemplify defining a method model. Semantics (meaning) is attributed to the method model in the following section, using the same functional language. This is achieved by defining functions that operate on method fragments. So, form (syntax) and meaning (semantics) can be defined in the same formalism. The next section demonstrates these manipulations on an actual ER diagram (an application model). This model is an instance of the method model defined in section 3. It shows how transformations on models can be combined to achieve larger transformations. It also brings the reader back to the "real world" of actual information systems models. The last part, starting with section 6, contains a discussion, focusing on the role of the programming language in which method models are expressed. The functional language notation is explained in the appendix.

I want to thank Sjaak Brinkkemper, Frank Harmsen, Rolf Engmann Maarten Fokkinga, and four anonymous reviewers for their comments on this text. Thanks are also due to Bob Rockwell, who inspired me to write this paper.

2 Motivation

Two reasons motivate the choice for having a lazy functional meta-CASE programming language. First, it allows programmers to think on the graph level instead of the node level. Second, it annihilates the issue of control flow, i.e. thinking about a computational order to traverse a graph. Both reasons lead to time savings for the method engineer, and an improved quality of the generated CASE tools. This section explains why.

Programming and thinking in entire graphs produces better code than working on the conceptual level of nodes and arcs does. The functional programming literature at large (e.g. [Harrison, 1993, Joosten, 1989]) shows concise and understandable examples of code which are intricate in terms of nodes and arcs. Kashiwagi and Wise study a general way for implementing graph algorithms in a lazy functional language [Kashiwagi and Wise, 1991]. King and Launchbury demonstrate the usefulness of lazy functional languages for graph algorithms with polynomial complexity [King and Launchbury, 1993]. Meta-CASE tools operate on graphs, which represent modeling techniques. Meta-CASE programming involves graph algorithms that edit graphs, define transformations on graphs, and provide interpretations of graphs. Typical algorithms transform one type of graph into another, which corresponds to deriving one method model from another. This is done on the basis of values, contained in both the nodes and arcs of a graph. Besides, modeling techniques have hierarchical decomposition, making the graph algorithms even more complicated. The structure of data type definitions leads directly to the computational structure of operations on those data types [Gibbons, 1995]. This is helpful to meta-CASE programmers, because it allows them to think beyond the level of nodes and arcs, and work in the realm of graphs as a unit. So, it makes sense to try working in a programming language that supports mathematical abstractions [Harrison, 1993]. Following sections of this paper demonstrate how this works out in one particular example.

Lazy evaluation obliterates the need to think about the order of computations when a graph is traversed. This is caused by the proven fact that a lazy evaluator minimizes the number of evaluation steps for any program. The proof [Abramsky, 1990] consists of showing that a lazy evaluator (i.e. normal order with sharing) executes only essential steps in the computation. A consequence is that all non-essential steps are omitted, producing the minimal number of computation steps for the entire evaluation. This has important consequences for programmers. For example, an nonterminating computation means that no alternative computational order produces a result. This excludes a fair amount of possibilities in searching for errors. It equally well reduces the number of opportunities to make errors in the first place, which reduces programming effort. Graph algorithms are reknown for their intricacies, because graph traversal is often difficult to visualize and imagine. Some errors show up in rare circumstances, adding to the overall perception that graph algorithms are difficult. For this reason, researchers tend to accept only those algorithms that are proven to be correct. In view of this difficulty, a lazy evaluator offers important help to method engineers. If execution fails, the method engineer does not spend time to find an execution path that works, as is the case in procedural languages such as Prolan [Merberth, 1991], or even in non-lazy functional languages such as ML [Milner et al., 1989] or Scheme [Rees and Clinger (editors.), 86].

The two reasons mentioned support the argument that meta-CASE programming in a lazy functional language is less time consuming and less error prone. In order to answer how much better it works, comparative research needs to be done using tools that differ only with respect to their embedded programming language. A meta-CASE tool in which the language is a variable and in which a lazy functional language is built, is (to the best of my knowledge) not available. Therefore, the argument has to be settled (for the time being) with the next best thing: examples of typical use.

The choice of an example is guided by "typical use" and by the desire to cover appropriate aspects of meta-CASE programming. In order to cover "typical use" within the limits of a paper, we decided to build a (partial) method model of the Entity-Relationship modeling technique [Elmasri and Navathe, 1989]. This choice was guided solely by the familiarity of the subject matter in the reader community. This choice is meant to keep the reader (as much as possible) on familiar ground with respect to the subject matter. In this way, attention is maximally focused to notation rather than to understanding the subject of ER-modeling. The following aspects were identified to be in the demonstration:

1. representing a graph
   Since a model is a graph in all modeling techniques, yet one of a different kind in each different technique, the representation of a graph is an issue. The example given in the following section defines a data structure which represents ER diagrams.

2. representing properties
   Properties, both of nodes and of arcs, need to be represented to demonstrate that graph semantics can be represented. The example contains entities and relationships that have attributes and links that have a name and cardinalities associated with them.

3. representing semantics
   Semantics are represented by functions that operate on the entire graph, so this needs to be included. The demonstration shows a function which generates SQL code, by way of defining the semantics of the graph.

4. representing transformations
   A transformation from the ER diagram to a relational model is defined in our example, to illustrate a transformation from one modeling technique to another, and to illustrate the transformation from a modeling technique to a realization in code.

5. composition of operations
   A requirement for meta-CASE tools is that primitive operations on models can be combined in order to define more powerful interpretations and transformations.

6. size of code
   The full Haskell code is presented to illustrate the amount of code needed and how it is understood.

Since method models are essentially graphs that describe other graphs, programming in a meta-case tool consists mainly of graph transformations. The choice for modeling the Entity-Relationship modeling technique [Elmasri and Navathe, 1989] is arbitrary in that any modeling technique which is represented as a graph will illustrate the idea. Readers who prefer to see an example of a process modeling technique, rather than a (static) data modeling technique, are referred to [Joosten, 1994], which contains an example of transforming a business process model into Petri-Nets.

3 A METHOD MODEL FOR ER DIAGRAMS

In order to demonstrate the use of a functional programming language, it is inevitable to show some code. Since program code makes notoriously difficult reading, some supplemental documentation is provided in three different ways. First, code is explained elaborately where appropriate. Second, many small examples of the effect of using code have been added. Third, appendix A gives a brief introduction to functional programming. The intention is that readers with no knowledge of functional programming can still appreciate the observations and conclusions (sections 6 and 7).

The method model of Entity-Relationship diagrams [Elmasri and Navathe, 1989] is built up by first introducing entities and relationships. Then, *links* are introduced and these definitions are assembled into ER diagrams. Operations on ER diagrams are not introduced until section 4.

3.1   Entities and Relationships

Entities and relationships are the main objects in an ER diagram. In Elmasri & Navathe's notation, they are the nodes in the graph. Each entity and every relationship carries a scheme with the name, attribute and key information in it. The following type is introduced:

```
data ER = ENT Scheme | REL Scheme
```

This definition introduces a type ER, together with the two alternative representations it has. An object with value ENT s is an entity with scheme s, and an object with value REL s is a relationship with scheme s. ENT and REL serve as labels to distinguish the two.

The data declaration introduces a new type that is distinct from any other type in the language. The introduction of a new type, as opposed to using an already defined type, has the advantage that programming errors due to mixing representations are signalled by the type checker.

A *scheme* is a data structure that contains information about the attributes and keys and also the name of the entity or relationship. The following lines are type synonym definitions, which are recognized by the reserved word type.

```
type Scheme    = (Name, [(Attribute, Bool)])
type Name      = [Char]
type Attribute = Name
```

`Name` is used as a synonym for a list of characters, which is a string. Square brackets mean "list of", so `[Char]` means a list of characters. `Name` is used for strings that represent names. `Attribute` is introduced as a synonym for `Name`, for the sake of readability.

The `type` declaration introduces synonyms. Introducing a synonym provides a name for a (possibly more complex) construction of types, and retaining the option of using all the operations that are already defined on that type. The definitions of schemes is not very different from the type definition in procedural languages, where constructs like records and/or arrays would be used. Some languages require upper bounds for the number of characters in a name or the number of attributes in a scheme.

The definition of `Scheme` involves a tuple (to be recognized by parentheses) that consists of a name (type `Name`) and a list of attribute/boolean pairs. Here is an example of an object (called `testScheme`) of the type \verbScheme":

```
testScheme :: Scheme
testScheme = ( "test scheme"
             , [("NAME",True), ("ADDRESS",False), ("AGE",False)]
             )
```

This definition introduces the object `testScheme`. The double-colon in the first line says that `testScheme` has type `Scheme`. The equals-symbol in the second line defines the value of `testScheme`. As expected, this value consists of a tuple, being a name and a list of attribute-boolean pairs. The boolean that comes with every attribute indicates whether the attribute is a key.

The definition of `testScheme` uses the property that every object has a direct denotation. If this function were implemented by means of a pointer chain, which is done in languages like Pascal or C, the definition of this example would involve some procedure calls as well, making the code larger and less accessible.

The following auxiliary functions on schemes are defined:

```
schemeName              :: Scheme -> Name
schemeName (name, as)   = name

schemeKeys              :: Scheme -> [Attribute]
schemeKeys (name, as)   = [att| (att,key)<-as, key==True]
```

The function `schemeName` reproduces the name of a scheme, and `schemeKeys` gives a list of the key attributes. The code of `schemeKeys` reads: the list of elements called `att`, in which the pair `(att,key)` is an element of `as` and field `key` equals `True`.

These definitions illustrate two useful language issues: hiding representations and list comprehensions. Hiding of representations is known as encapsulation in the object-oriented world, and as abstract data types in programming language theory. The functions `schemeName` and `schemeKeys` are defined to make the type `Scheme` independent of its representation. When a programmer decides to change representations, only a few definitions change. It is especially useful for meta-CASE programming, because data structure representations tend to become intricate once a number of different modeling techniques are involved. The list comprehension, used in the definition of `schemeKeys`, appears frequently in places where imperative languages have iteration. Especially termination conditions and loop invariants are a source of errors, which are mostly avoided in the list comprehension.

The following function, `showScheme`, prints a scheme in ASCII. We use it to demonstrate the dialogue between the user and the computer. The function `showScheme` shows the previously defined scheme `testScheme` in a pretty layout.

```
? showScheme testScheme
test scheme(NAME*, ADDRESS, AGE)
```

The question mark is the prompt. It is followed (on the same line) by the expression typed in by the user. The result is printed directly underneath.

The code of the function `showScheme` is presented only for the sake of making a complete presentation.

```
showScheme :: Scheme -> [Char]
showScheme (name, as)
  = name                                              ++
    "("                                               ++
    chain ", " [att++cond key "*" ""|(att,key)<-as] ++
    ")"
```

This function prints the name and attributes on one line, Each attribute has affix * if it is a key. The attributes are separated by a comma and a space (", ", by using the function `chain`) and enclosed in parentheses.

This completes the definition of entities and relationships (i.e. the nodes) in the ER modeling technique.

3.2 Link

Now let us observe links, which are represented by lines connecting relationships with entities. A link is the line in an ER diagram that is drawn between an entity and a relationship. Links have a name and a cardinality ratio. The name identifies the role of the link, which is left empty if the role is obvious. The cardinality ratio is also stored in the link.

```
type Link    = (Name, CardRat)
data CardRat = R01 | R0n | R11 | R1n
```

The cardinality ratio of a link is represented by a type `CardRat`, that can have only four different values: Each value represents a different meaning. Suppose c is the cardinality ratio (type `CardRat`) of a link between entity X and relationship Y. The meaning is given by this table:

R01   Each x in X occurs only once or not at all in Y.
R0n   There are no restrictions.
R11   Each x in X occurs precisely once in Y.
R1n   Each x in X occurs at least once in Y.

The default value is R0n, which means that there are no restrictions.

The definition of `CardRat` is an enumerated type, a feature available in many programming languages. Here, the notation is a special case of the data definition encountered in the previous section, so enumerated types do not require a special notation. As opposed to encoding the information (for example as integers) the use of enumerated types results in fewer mistakes, because the compiler signals errors that would otherwise show up at runtime.

A link is shown as an English sentence which states the cardinality restriction imposed by the cardinality ratio. For that purpose the function `showCR` is defined.

```
showCR (lName,R01) eName rName
  = "Each " ++ eName ++  " occurs at most once in " ++
    rName ++ role lName ++ "."
showCR (lName,R0n) eName rName
  = ""
showCR (lName,R11) eName rName
  = "Each " ++ eName ++  " occurs once in " ++
    rName ++ role lName ++ "."
showCR (lName,R1n) eName rName
  = "Each " ++ eName ++  " must occur in " ++
    rName ++ role lName ++ "."

role "" = ""
role cs = " as "++cs
```

The function `role` is an auxiliary function, with the sole the purpose of defining `showCR`. Here is an example of how `showCR` works.

```
? showCR ("supervisor", R01) "EMPLOYEE" "SUPERVISION"
Each EMPLOYEE occurs at most once in SUPERVISION as supervisor.
```

This function withdraws knowledge from links in a readable form.

This completes the definition of links. The following definitions combine entities, relationships and links to form ER diagrams.

3.3   ER diagram

An ER diagram is represented by a graph, with nodes of type `ER` and links of type `Link`. Graphically, an `ENT` node is represented by a rectangle and a `REL` node by a diamond. Links are represented by lines, connecting an entity and a relationship.

In order to define the ER diagram, an existing type `Graph` is used. ER diagrams are represented by the type `ERdiagram`:

```
type ERdiagram = Graph ER Link
```

An ER diagram is defined as a graph, with objects of type `ER` as nodes and objects of type `link` as arcs (arrows). For ER diagrams, there is nothing else to define. The definition of `Graph` is given in a prelude, so it is not part of the code. Without that, some code defining graphs and operations on graphs would have to be developed.

The definition of `ERdiagram` is an example of using a data structure (graph), the representation of which is hidden. This type of abstraction is necessary in meta-CASE programming, because graph structures in practice are intricate and therefore error-prone. If a language is used where graphs are defined in terms of pointers to cells, as is the case with a number of procedural programming languages, the definitions are more complicated. Pointer algorithms are notoriously error prone, so it makes sense to avoid their use in meta-CASE programming.

So far, we have discussed new types, synonyms, direct denotation of data objects, absence of pointers, hiding of representations, use of enumerated types, and data abstraction over graphs. The pieces of code presented are tiny illustrations of how these issues help programmers to keep the amount of code low, the level of abstraction high, and the number of mistakes small.

We have introduced the data structure that represents the method model of ER diagrams. Next, operations on ER diagrams are defined to define the meaning of the method model. This is the topic of the next section.

4   MEANING

Any method model is useful only if it has meaning, which is achieved by defining operations. These operations provide interpretations of application models, changes to application models, and of course an algebra to create application models. In this section, we illustrate graph transformations that are typical of meta-CASE programming by defining an interpretation of ER diagrams, which is a relational database scheme with integrity constraints. Apart from being an interpretation of ER diagrams, this also demonstrates a transformation from one (well known, prototypical) modeling technique to another. This is an important aspect of meta-CASE programming.

4.1   Generating attribute vectors

A relational database scheme consists of a set of attribute vectors and a set of integrity constraints. Generation of the attribute vectors is treated in the first subsection. The next subsection shows how integrity constraints are derived and the third subsection integrates these into relational database schemes.

Every entity or relationship carries its own attributes in a scheme. Semantically, all entities and relationships are mapped on relations in the relational model. Throughout this paper the word 'relation' refers to the relational model, while the word 'relationship' has its meaning within the Entity-Relationship modeling technique.

The choice to map entities and relationships to schemes is typically made by the method engineer. Each entity and every relationship is associated with a scheme that contains all attributes relevant to its meaning. For this purpose the function `schemeER` is defined, whose effect is illustrated by this example:

```
? showScheme (schemeER company employee)
EMPLOYEE(Name, Sex, Address, Ssn*, Salary, Bdate)
```

The expression "schemeER company employee" yields the scheme that belongs to the node employee within the ER diagram company. Both employee and company are defined in in section 5, which represent a particular ER diagram. This example showed the scheme associated with an entity (employee). Here is another example that shows the scheme associated with a relationship (controls):

```
? showScheme(schemeER company controls)
CONTROLS(DName*, PName*, DNumber*, PNumber*)
```

The function showScheme was used to generate pretty output. Without the use of that function, the data structure is printed in full detail (layout added):

```
? schemeER company controls
("CONTROLS",[ ("DName",    True)
            , ("DNumber", True)
            , ("PName",   True)
            , ("PNumber", True)])
```

The function schemeER copes with ambiguous attribute names by means of prefixes. Depending on the situation, the attribute name is prefixed with an entity name or a role name. Therefore, an attribute can be renamed if (for every attribute) its name, the entity to which it belongs, and its link name (i.e. role) is known. Due to the disambiguation of names, the code of schemER is more complex than previous examples.

```
schemeER :: ERdiagram -> ER -> Scheme
schemeER dia (ENT scheme) = scheme
schemeER (ers,links) (REL scheme)
 = ( schemeName scheme
   , snd scheme ++
     renameAtts [ (att,name,lname)
                | l<-linksGraph diagram
                , (lname,cr)=lbl(l), ENT (name,atts)=src(l)
                , REL scheme==dst(l)
                , (att,key)<-atts, key]
 )
```

In brief, the function schemeER interprets the graphical elements of ER diagrams and generates a list of attributes (the attribute vector) to be used in a relational database scheme. Entity schemes are copied, whereas the scheme of a relation object is "expanded" by the key-attributes of the adjacent entities.

This is one example which benefits from the fact that control flow is not an issue in a lazily evaluating language implementation. The complexity of the disambiguation problem leads to a complex list comprehension. If the code is written in terms of (imperative) statements, using iteration, selection, and sequence, it becomes even more complicated, because the control flow is no longer as obvious as in simple situations. The opportunities for making mistakes are therefore higher too. Definitions such as schemeER, which are not trivial, are common in meta-CASE programming.

4.2   Integrity constraints

Properties of the ER diagram affect the integrity constraints of the derived database. These constraints limit the possible database instances. The information in the ER diagram makes it possible to derive integrity constraints. A data structure is defined for this purpose.

```
data IntegrityConstraint
   = KEY      Scheme            |
     CARDINALITY Link ER ER
```

Two types of constraints are introduced. Key constraints specify the candidate keys of each relationship scheme. The cardinality constraint is derived from the cardinality ratio. Referential integrity constraint are not treated here, to keep the volume of the text limited.

In order to print an integrity constraint, the function `showIntegrityConstraint` is defined. This function is designed to give more or less understandable english sentences for each constraint. For example, the key-constraint associated with the entity `employee` is printed as:

```
? showIntegrityConstraint (KEY (schemeER company employee))
["Ssn"] is the key of relation "EMPLOYEE"
```

This is how the function `showIntegrityConstraint` is defined:

```
showIntegrityConstraint (KEY rel)
  = "Err: "++show(schemeName rel)++" has no key attributes!",
                                      if schemeKeys rel==[]
  = show (schemeKeys rel)++" is the key of relation "++
    show (schemeName rel),                 otherwise
showIntegrityConstraint (CARDINALITY l e r)
  = showCR l (nameER e) (nameER r)
```

This code uses only language concepts that we used before. Adding concepts to the method model, whether integrity constraints or anything else, leads to a similar use of the language for every new concept introduced. This is the "routine" in which a meta-CASE programmer needs to be trained.

Having introduced the concepts of attribute vectors and integrity constraints, we are set to define Relational Database Schemes.

4.3   Relational Database Scheme

The ER diagram can be used to derive a Relational Database Scheme (RDS), following the choices made by Elmasri & Navathe [Elmasri and Navathe, 1989]. A relational database scheme is represented by the type `RelDBScheme`. It consists of two components: a list of schemes (one for each entity and one for each relationship) and a list of integrity constraints.

```
type RelDBScheme = ([Scheme], [IntegrityConstraint])
```

A relational database scheme can be derived from the ER diagram by means of the function rScheme, which is defined by:

```
rScheme :: ERdiagram -> RelDBScheme
rScheme erDia = (rs, ics)
  where
    nodes = setToList (domGraph erDia)
    links = setToList (linksGraph erDia)
    rs    = [schemeER erDia node |node<-nodes]
    ics   = [KEY scheme| ENT scheme<-nodes]      ++
            [CARDINALITY (lname,cr) e r|
                     ((lname,cr),e,r)<-links, cr/=R0n]
```

This definition introduces some auxiliaries. The nodes and links of the ER diagram are called nodes and links respectively. The list rs contains the database schemes that correspond to the nodes in the ER diagram. The list ics contains the restrictions. There is a key-restriction for every scheme in the ER diagram and a cardinality restriction for every link. A key restriction that corresponds to an entity contains the same information as the scheme of that entity, so each key restriction is represented by copying the corresponding entity scheme. A similar argument holds for links: the information in the link is used to represent the cardinality restriction of that link. However, links with cardinality R0n have no restriction, so they are filtered out. The database scheme implied by the entire ER diagram is the list of schemes rs together with the restrictions in list ics.

A relational database scheme is a nontrivial interpretation of ER diagrams, especially since cardinalities and integrity constraints are included. Yet, the actual code of rScheme consists of 9 lines only. It is of roughly the same complexity as the code of schemeER, and also roughly as long. Although rScheme is on a higher level of abstraction (mentally) than schemeER, the former is still equally complex for a programmer to understand. The reason is that intelligent use has been made of data abstraction (i.e., hiding representations), and list comprehensions. This is made possible because control flow issues are absent. In an imperative language, or even in a non-lazy functional language, data abstractions can sometimes not be combined freely due to control flow problems, which means that these issues absorb time and energy.

In this section we have seen more complex uses of language constructs and discussed how they help a programmer. We have also introduced the operations that constitute an interpretation of Entity-Relationship diagrams, yielding relational database schemes. This can be seen as the result of a method modeling activity, performed by a method engineer. To generate code, to compute metrics, and to define different views are all uses of a method model that are typically supported by meta-CASE tools. To make transformations from one application model to another and then transform onwards down to a realization requires the ability to cascade computations. A typical example is to transform an ER diagram to a relational database scheme first, and then to generate SQL code from the relational database scheme. The following section demonstrates this as an example of using the method model.

5   USING THE METHOD MODEL

This section shows the transformation to SQL code, as an example to illustrate two
points. The first point is that the transformation of an application model to realization
is done in a way which resembles the transformation between two application models,
by making use of high level abstractions, avoiding control flow issues, and defining a
functional transformation concisely. The second point is to illustrate how functional
transformations are composed to describe cascaded computations. This composition will
in the end be responsible for the practical use and the power of meta-CASE tools, because
cascaded transformations create complicated operations that can be used "by pushing one
button" in a meta-CASE tool.

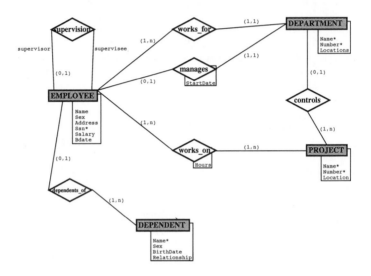

Figure 1 An ER diagram (example, from Elmasri & Navathe)

To make the demonstration concrete, we show an instance of an ER diagram which is
transformed in two subsequent steps. The ER diagram in figure 1 (from fig. 3.13, page 55
in [Elmasri and Navathe, 1989]) is described in terms of the method model in section 3.

Figure 1 has a represention inside the CASE tool (figure 2). This (or similar) code
is generated by the CASE tool, derived from the diagram produced by an application
engineer. It consists of tabular information representing graphs with attributes on the
nodes and arcs. Constraints on the form of the diagram are enforced by the CASE tool.
Therefore, syntactical constraints are not needed in the internal representation.

In figure 2, the first definition (company) represents the actual graph. The graph is
specified by giving each link together with the two nodes that connect the link. Each link
contains a cardinality ratio, which gives restrictions to the number of times an entity may
occur in a relation. The (optional) name of the link identifies the role of the entity in the

relation. The nodes in the graph are either entities or relations, to be distinguished by the labels ENT or REL. Each one of them is defined separately.

For the purpose of this paper the internal representation is written as source code, using the property that even complicated data objects such as an entity-relationship diagram can be denoted directly in the language. The operations defined in section 4 can be used to manipulate the application models. For example, the operation rScheme was defined to transform an entire ER diagram into a relational database scheme. It was used to generate the relational database scheme in figure 3 from the code in figure 2. We demonstrate how to generate SQL code by giving some definitions (figure 4). We make two assumptions in the code. First, since most SQL implementations have non-standard explicit integrity constraint definitions, or none at all, the code for constraints is omitted (leaving some information unused). Integrity constraints from the ER diagram are enforced in the SQL code by procedural constraints. If the ER diagram is adapted to contain attribute types, better SQL code can of course be generated. The second assumption is that every attribute has the type VARCHAR(20), because attribute type information is not available in the relational database scheme.

The SQL code in figure 5 was generated by applying the function sqlDBScheme to the relational database scheme of company.

So far, we have seen two transformations. The transformation from entity-relationship diagram to relational database scheme was done by the function rScheme. The transformation from relational database scheme to SQL was done by the function sqlDBScheme. The composition of these functions is defined using the compose operator (the period symbol):

```
er2sql :: ERdiagram -> [Char]
er2sql = sqlDBScheme . rScheme
```

This new function combines both transformations into one new transformations. Composition is an associative operator, which means that an arbitrary number of functions can be cascaded.

6 OBSERVATIONS

The elaborated example of the ER modeling technique leads to the following observations:

- Defining a method model of the Entity-Relationship modeling technique is a typical example of method engineering, to be supported by a meta-CASE tool.

- Not treated in this article is the link with the graphics of the meta-CASE tool. Naturally, the embedded programming language contains the graphical primitives needed for the CASE tool.

- The method model of the Entity-Relationship modeling technique is concise. Although ER modeling is not the simplest among modeling techniques, it is modeled within the scope of this single paper.

- Both the application model (figure 2) and the method model (section 3) and the computations to generate database schemes are described in the same language. All aspects of method modeling can be defined in the same language.

- In the example, data structures are treated 'as a whole'. For example, graphs are used without knowledge of their implementation. This eliminates the need for programming with pointers. As a result, definitions of complicated operations such as rScheme (fewer than 10 lines of code) remain understandable.

- Transformations from one application model to another are within the scope of the language. The operation rScheme is an example of such a transformation. Since all is described in the same language, it is easy to imagine a cascade of transformations. This is useful: the RDB-scheme can be translated further to SQL or any other formalism for that matter. Or, one could decide to insert a normalization algorithm in the cascade of actions.

- Strong typing, which is part of the language, catches type errors at an early stage. This is economical towards a programmer, because new errors that are a consequence of type errors cannot occur. Fundamental errors directly concerning the modeling activity remain. Of course, such errors cannot be detected by any programming system.

7   CONCLUSIONS

The observations made in the previous section are related to the requirements identified in the introduction. Let us walk through the list of requirements.

- The level of abstraction in the method model is the level of graphs, schemes, attributes, links, entities and relationships. This is the proper level of abstraction for the method engineer. Since modeling concepts translate directly to types, the effort to reach the proper level of abstraction is minimal.

- Opportunities for mistakes are minimized by:

  - defining a data structure as irredundantly as possible; Redundance in data structures is a potential source of errors, because it has consequences for every operator that makes use of the data structure.

  - treating a data structure as a whole; For example, a graph is treated as a single object rather than an intricate network of pointers. This eliminates a large source of potential mistakes (with pointers)

  - strong typing; A host of trivial checks are unneccessary, because the system is under a strong typing regime.

  - absence of side-effects; A program consists of equations, which can safely be interpreted as mathematical equations.

- The tool supports graphs as an abstract data type.

- Overspecification is avoided mainly because control flow is a non-issue in a (lazy) functional programming language. A program has the same meaning, irrespective of the control flow. This contributes to the conciseness and understandability, and eliminates another source of potential errors.

Considering the use of a method model and the role of a method engineer, the requirements of a programming language for meta-CASE tools match the properties of functional programming. That is: correctness, programmer performance, conciseness and expressiveness are more important whereas requirments on computer performance and access to the hardware are less important. So I conclude that the language is suitable for use in a meta-CASE tool.

The use of one language for the internal representation of both application models and method models offers opportunities for sophisticated functionality, such as the cascading of model transformations.

The following appendix is a superficial introduction to functional programming, intended to assist the reader in understanding the presented code. It is not a short course in functional programming. For that purpose I recommend [Bird and Wadler, 1988]

A   A READER'S INTRODUCTION TO FUNCTIONAL PROGRAMMING

Functional programming is mainly used for the purpose of specification and prototyping, because it has a high level of abstraction. It is rarely used in cases where efficiency prevails, because low-level features (hardware access) are not available to the programmer.

A.1   Evaluation

A functional program consists of definitions, which can safely be interpreted as mathematical equations. For example, the definition

```
f(x) = x*x - 2*x + 4
```

introduces a function f, that maps an argument x to the number x*x - 2*x + 4. So, f(3) equals 3*3 - 2*3 + 4, which evaluates to 7. A definition (also called value definition) is recognized by the equals-symbol (=).

The computer serves as a machine, that evaluates expressions. This corresponds to the idea of an ordinary pocket calculator, although the latter works with simpler expressions. The facility to write definitions makes the calculator programmable.

A.2   Types and Values

All objects in a functional programming language have two components: a type and a value. For example, a variable x may have type Int and value "3". Consequently, a definition consists of two parts: the type definition and the value definition. The type definition is denoted with a double colon (::) Example:

```
f   :: Int -> Int
f(x) = x*x - 2*x + 4
```

The first line says that f is an object of type `Int -> Int`, that is, a function that maps an `Int` to an `Int`. The second line defines the value of object f, which means that f is the function that maps any x to $x^2 - 2x + 4$. The computer can often derive the type of an object. In that case it is not necessary to specify the type. If the type is specified anyway, the computer uses that information as a check on the derived type. Normal practice is to specify the type to make code more understandable.

There are three forms of type definition. The double colon (::) defines the type of an object in the language. The reserved word **type** introduces a type synonym, which is used for readability purposes. The reserved word **data** introduces a 'home-made' type. This is used to create data structures suited to particular needs.

A value is given by an expression. A trivial expression, such as 3, obviously denotes the value 3. More complicated expressions, such as `3*3 - 2*3 + 4`, require computation to determine the value.

A.3   Notations

The application of a function to its arguments deserves special attention. The principle is that superfluous parentheses are omitted. So, `f(x)` is conventionally written as `f x` by functional programmers. Both have the same meaning.

When more than one argument is involved, the meaning is no longer equivalent. The expression `f(x,y)` represents the application of a function f to one argument `(x,y)`, which is a tuple containing x and y. This is different from `f x y` which means the application of a function f to two arguments, x and y.

Lists are an important data structure. Square brackets are used to denote lists. Examples:

```
[36,49,64,81]
[361]
[]
[("Jack",0), ("and",332), ("Jill",-18)]
```

The following notation is frequently used to traverse lists. Here are some examples:

expression	result
`[x*x| x<-[6..9]]`	`[36,49,64,81]`
`[y*y| y<-[6..9]]`	`[36,49,64,81]`
`[elem| elem<-[0..100], odd(elem)]`	`[1,3,5,...99]`
`[a+b| a<-[3,30,300], b<-[0,1]]`	`[3,4,30,31,300,301]`
`[a| a<-[3,30,300], a<3]`	`[]`

The notation is best understood by pronouncing the square brackets as "the list of", the vertical bar as "in which", and the symbol <- as "traverses" or "is taken from".

Lists can be concatenated by means of the operator `++`.

expression	result
`[2,0]++[4,2,4]`	`[2,0,4,2,4]`
`"Jack"++"ie"`	`"Jackie"`
`[]++[4,2,4]`	`[4,2,4]`

References

[Abramsky, 1990] Abramsky, S. (1990). *The Lazy lambda-calculus*, pages 65–117. Addison Wesley.

[Bird and Wadler, 1988] Bird, R. and Wadler, P. (1988). *Introduction to Functional Programming*. International Series in Computer Science. Prentice Hall, New York.

[Elmasri and Navathe, 1989] Elmasri, R. and Navathe, S. B. (1989). *Fundamentals of Database Systems*. Addison-Wesley World Student Series. Benjamin/Cummings, Redwood City, CA 94065.

[Gibbons, 1995] Gibbons, J. (1995). An initial-algebra approach to directed acyclic graphs. In Möller, B., editor, *Mathematics of Program Construction*, number 947 in Lecture Notes in Computer Science, pages 122–138, Berlin. Springer-Verlag.

[Harmsen et al., 1994] Harmsen, F., Brinkkemper, S., and Oei, H. (1994). Situational method engineering for information system projects. In Olle, T. and Stuart, A. V., editors, *Proceedings of the IFIP WG8.1 Working Conference CRIS'94*, pages 169–194, Amsterdam. North-Holland.

[Harrison, 1993] Harrison, R. (1993). *Abstract data types in Standard ML*. John Wiley & Sons, Chichester, England.

[Hudak and Fasel, 1992] Hudak, P. and Fasel, J. H. (1992). A gentle introduction to haskell. *ACM SIGPLAN Notices*, 27(5).

[Hudak et al., 1992] Hudak, P., Peyton Jones, S. L., and Wadler (editors), P. (1992). Report on the programming language haskell, a non-strict purely functional language (version 1.2). *SIGPLAN Notices*, 27(3).

[Joosten, 1989] Joosten, S. (1989). *The use of functional programming in software development*. PhD thesis, University of Twente, dept. of Comp. Sc.

[Joosten, 1994] Joosten, S. (1994) *Trigger modelling for workflow analysis*. In Proceedings CON '94: Workflow Management, Challenges, Paradigms and Products (Oct. 1994), G. Chroust and A. Benczúr, Eds., Oldenbourg, Wien, München, pp. 236–247.

[Kashiwagi and Wise, 1991] Kashiwagi, Y. and Wise, D. S. (1991). Graph algorithms in a lazy functional programming language. Technical Report 330, Comp. Sci. Dept, Indiana Univ., Bloomington, Indiana.

[King and Launchbury, 1993] King, D. J. and Launchbury, J. (1993). Functional graph algorithms with depth first searc. In Hammond, K. and O'Donnell, J. T., editors, *Functional programming*, volume II, pages II.1–II.12. Springer-Verlag, Berlin.

[Kumar and Welke, 1992] Kumar, K. and Welke, R. J. (1992). *Methodology Engineering: A Proposal for Situation-Specific Methodology Construction*, chapter 15, pages 257–269. Series in Information Systems. John Wiley, Chichester.

[Merberth, 1991] Merberth, G. (1991). *Maestro II - das integrierte CASE-System von Softlab*. BI Wissenschafsverlag, 3 edition.

[Milner et al., 1989] Milner, R., Tofte, M., and Harper, R. (1989). *The Definition of Standard ML*. MIT Press, Cambridge, MA.

[Rees and Clinger (editors.), 86] Rees, J. and Clinger (editors.), W. (86). The revised report on the algorithmic language scheme. *SIGPLAN Notices*, 21(12):37–79.

[Smolander et al., 1991] Smolander, K., Lyytinen, K., Tahvanainen, V.-P., and Marttiin, P. (1991). Metaedit – a flexible graphical environment for methodology modelling. In Andersen, R., Bubenko, J., and Solvberg, A., editors, *Proc. Third International Conference on Advanced Information Systems Engineering (CAiSE'91)*, number 498 in Lecture Notes in Computer Science, Berlin. Springer-Verlag.

[Turner, 1985] Turner, D. A. (1985). Miranda: A non-strict functional language with polymorphic types. In Jouannaud, J.-P., editor, *2nd Functional programming languages and computer architecture*, number 201 in Lecture Notes in Computer Science, pages 1–16, Berlin. Springer-Verlag.

[Yourdon, 1989] Yourdon, E. (1989). *Modern Structured Analysis*. Yourdon Press Computing Series. Yourdon Press, New Jersey.

```
company :: ERdiagram
company
 = listToGraph
   [ (("supervisor", R01), employee,   supervision )
   , (("supervisee", R0n), employee,   supervision )
   , (("",          R11), department, worksFor    )
   , (("",          R1n), employee,   worksFor    )
   , (("",          R11), department, manages     )
   , (("",          R01), employee,   manages     )
   , (("",          R1n), employee,   worksOn     )
   , (("",          R1n), project,    worksOn     )
   , (("",          R01), employee,   dependentsOf)
   , (("",          R1n), dependent,  dependentsOf)
   , (("",          R01), department, controls    )
   , (("",          R1n), project,    controls    )
   ]

employee     = ENT ("EMPLOYEE",    [ ("Name",         False)
                                   , ("Sex",          False)
                                   , ("Address",      False)
                                   , ("Ssn",          True)
                                   , ("Salary",       False)
                                   , ("Bdate",        False)
                                   ])
dependent    = ENT ("DEPENDENT",   [ ("Name",         True)
                                   , ("Sex",          False)
                                   , ("BirthDate",    False)
                                   , ("Relationship", False)
                                   ])
supervision  = REL ("SUPERVISION", [])
manages      = REL ("MANAGES",     [ ("StartDate",    False)])
worksFor     = REL ("WORKS_FOR",   [])
controls     = REL ("CONTROLS",    [])
dependentsOf = REL ("DEPENDENTS_OF",[])
worksOn      = REL ("WORKS_ON",    [ ("Hours",        False)])
department   = ENT ("DEPARTMENT",  [ ("Name",         True)
                                   , ("Number",       True)
                                   , ("Locations",    False)
                                   ])
project      = ENT ("PROJECT",     [ ("Name",         True)
                                   , ("Number",       True)
                                   , ("Location",     False)
                                   ])
```

Figure 2 internal representation of ER diagram

```
Relations
  DEPARTMENT(Name*, Number*, Locations)    ·
  DEPENDENT(Name*, Sex, BirthDate, Relationship)
  EMPLOYEE(Name, Sex, Address, Ssn*, Salary, Bdate)
  PROJECT(Name*, Number*, Location)
  CONTROLS(DName*, PName*, DNumber*, PNumber*)
  DEPENDENTS_OF(Ssn*, Name*)
  MANAGES(StartDate, Ssn*, Name*, Number*)
  SUPERVISION(supervisee_Ssn*, supervisor_Ssn*)
  WORKS_FOR(Name*, Number*, Ssn*)
  WORKS_ON(Hours, Ssn*, Name*, Number*)
Constraints
  ["Name", "Number"] is the key of relation "DEPARTMENT"
  ["Name"] is the key of relation "DEPENDENT"
  ["Ssn"] is the key of relation "EMPLOYEE"
  ["Name", "Number"] is the key of relation "PROJECT"
  Each DEPARTMENT occurs at most once in CONTROLS.
  Each EMPLOYEE occurs at most once in DEPENDENTS_OF.
  Each EMPLOYEE occurs at most once in MANAGES.
  Each DEPARTMENT occurs once in MANAGES.
  Each DEPARTMENT occurs once in WORKS_FOR.
  Each DEPENDENT must occur in DEPENDENTS_OF.
  Each EMPLOYEE must occur in WORKS_FOR.
  Each EMPLOYEE must occur in WORKS_ON.
  Each PROJECT must occur in CONTROLS.
  Each PROJECT must occur in WORKS_ON.
  Each EMPLOYEE occurs at most once in SUPERVISION as supervisor.
End Relation
```

Figure 3 result of operation rScheme

```
sqlDBScheme :: RelDBScheme -> [Char]
sqlDBScheme(rs,ics)
 = chain ";\n\n" [sqlScheme r| r<-rs] ++ ";\n"

sqlScheme :: Scheme -> [Char]
sqlScheme(name,as)
 = "CREATE TABLE "++name++
   "("++chain indent [sqlAttr a| a<-as]++")"
   where indent = ",\n"++[' '| c<-"CREATE TABLE "++name++"("]

sqlAttr :: (Attribute,Bool)->[Char]
sqlAttr(att,key)
 = att++" VARCHAR(20) NOT NULL", if key
 = att++" VARCHAR(20)",          otherwise
```

Figure 4 SQL generator

```
? sqlDBScheme(rScheme company)
CREATE TABLE DEPARTMENT(Name VARCHAR(20) NOT NULL,
                        Number VARCHAR(20) NOT NULL,
                        Locations VARCHAR(20));

CREATE TABLE DEPENDENT(Name VARCHAR(20) NOT NULL,
                        Sex VARCHAR(20),
                        BirthDate VARCHAR(20),
                        Relationship VARCHAR(20));

CREATE TABLE EMPLOYEE(Name VARCHAR(20),
                        Sex VARCHAR(20),
                        Address VARCHAR(20),
                        Ssn VARCHAR(20) NOT NULL,
                        Salary VARCHAR(20),
                        Bdate VARCHAR(20));

CREATE TABLE PROJECT(Name VARCHAR(20) NOT NULL,
                        Number VARCHAR(20) NOT NULL,
                        Location VARCHAR(20));

CREATE TABLE CONTROLS(DName VARCHAR(20) NOT NULL,
                        PName VARCHAR(20) NOT NULL,
                        DNumber VARCHAR(20) NOT NULL,
                        PNumber VARCHAR(20) NOT NULL);

CREATE TABLE DEPENDENTS_OF(Ssn VARCHAR(20) NOT NULL,
                            Name VARCHAR(20) NOT NULL);

CREATE TABLE MANAGES(StartDate VARCHAR(20),
                        Ssn VARCHAR(20) NOT NULL,
                        Name VARCHAR(20) NOT NULL,
                        Number VARCHAR(20) NOT NULL);

CREATE TABLE SUPERVISION(supervisee_Ssn VARCHAR(20) NOT NULL,
                            supervisor_Ssn VARCHAR(20) NOT NULL);

CREATE TABLE WORKS_FOR(Name VARCHAR(20) NOT NULL,
                        Number VARCHAR(20) NOT NULL,
                        Ssn VARCHAR(20) NOT NULL);

CREATE TABLE WORKS_ON(Hours VARCHAR(20),
                        Ssn VARCHAR(20) NOT NULL,
                        Name VARCHAR(20) NOT NULL,
                        Number VARCHAR(20) NOT NULL);
```

Figure 5 generated SQL code

11

A practical strategy for the evaluation of software tools

Antony Powell, Andrew Vickers
Department of Computer Science, University of York
Heslington, York, UK.
Phone:+44 1904 432722, fax: +44 1904 432708
Email: [alp\andyv]@minster.york.ac.uk

Eddie Williams, Brian Cooke
Rolls-Royce plc
PO Box 31, Derby, UK.
Phone: +44 1332 771700, fax: +44 1332 770921

Abstract

This paper describes a working strategy for software tool evaluations that has resulted from work within Rolls-Royce plc in response to the difficulty, and mixed successes, we have experienced in the selection of software tools. The lack of an acceptable methodology has meant that industrial evaluations are commonly time-consuming, fail to capture both tool and problem *knowledge* in a form suitable to aid future evaluations, and frequently give inconclusive results. Even where rigorous selection methods are used we raise the concern that tool evaluators are failing to address perhaps the most important factors in determining final success namely the non-technical or '*soft*' factors.

In an attempt to overcome some of these problems the proposed strategy provides a qualitative list of important *issues* distilled from many years experience of making tool selection decisions. This generic issue checklist is used to form *domain specific criteria* against which tools can be compared in a more quantitative manner. This process ensures traceability between issues, tool requirements criteria and supporting evidence in order to document decisions and provide assurance that all issues have been addressed. It also helps us to capture valuable corporate knowledge for future evaluations in order to become more efficient at evaluating tools, provide more consistent criteria and to limit the risk of expensive mistakes.

This industrial perspective on tool selection will be of interest to managers and evaluators of organisations who purchase software tools. To a lesser degree the issue guidelines cover method evaluation and tool *emplacement* but further refinement and practical application is recognised. The strategy may also form the basis of a process for tool evaluations as required by higher levels of the SEI Capability Maturity Model (Humphrey, 1988; Humphrey, 1990). Finally, we hope that tool vendors will use it to provide better support for eliciting and meeting customer requirements during the evaluation process.

Keywords
Software tools, industrial practice, evaluation, experience

1   INTRODUCTION

For many years the software engineering community has argued (and vendors have claimed) that significant increases in software productivity can be achieved through the effective use of software tools. Unfortunately, the process of tool selection and emplacement is inherently difficult and expected tool benefits have often failed to materialise. Most organisations who employ software tools can testify to bad experiences of tools that did not meet expectations and legends of more 'spectacular' tool disasters are commonplace. Yet software tools are a necessary and integral part of the modern software development process and are key drivers of productivity and ultimately profitability. It is therefore quite surprising that few companies appear to have a rigorous process in place for the evaluation of software tools.

This paper describes an attempt to address some of the difficulties we have experienced in tool evaluation. This experience comes from many years of selecting and introducing software tools and methods for the development of aeronautical control and monitoring systems. Despite long and very expensive evaluations for major tool purchases we still have, with the luxury of hindsight, made regrettable tool selection decisions. Here we have attempted to distill what distinguishes good from bad tool evaluations and form a more structured method to learn from these experiences and avoid costly mistakes.

We start by explaining our experience of the reasons for the difficulty of the evaluation process, give practical advice in overcoming these problems and describe limitations in the 'state of the art' in the evaluation domain (Section 2). Firstly, we address the problems of the tool selection *decision* itself including the problem of multiple and often conflicting criteria, the environment and nature of the decision, and the flawed decision making process. Secondly, we highlight the problem that evaluators tend to focus on technical capabilities of the tool at the expense of non-technical or '*soft*' factors such as human and business issues. We also acknowledge the problems of successfully introducing the tool into the project domain - a process that we term '*tool emplacement*' (as opposed to 'implementation' in order to distinguish from actual tool usage). Tool emplacement can fail because of poor documentation, lack of compatibility with existing tools, and lack of flexibility. The interesting conclusion is that, despite basic reasons for mistakes in tool selections, decisions are still made with irrational neglect for even elementary issues.

In response to these problems, a joint working party set out to form a strategy for tool evaluation based on the strong belief that we can capture and exploit past experience to improve the quality of decision making in tool selection and emplacement. Section 3 describes the basic strategy that arose from this collaboration. It consists of a method to place 'sanity' checks on decisions and a structured process to aid organisational learning. The result is a strategy that is simple to apply and generic across different problem domains but robust enough to help improve the quality of decision making. We illustrate our approach with a simple example and also contrast our approach with those of others with whom we are aware.

We conclude by describing the more unexpected benefits of the strategy (such as the ability to develop repositories of criteria for different tool domains) and further work required (to address in more detail the problems of method evaluation and tool emplacement). The strategy is currently in use as a practical and evolving set of evaluation guidelines. Whilst the strategy may not necessarily reduce the cost and duration of evaluations (although benefits have been experienced) we believe it will help to avoid costly mistakes.

The paper expresses our concerns about current practice in tool evaluation in particular that bad decisions are made on basic but recurrent mistakes, and hence a need for a more rigorous process. We hope it will act as a prompt for evaluators and decision makers to be introspective and as a result demand higher standards from, and add learning to, a critical corporate process.

2. BACKGROUND

2.1 The problem with tool evaluations

From our practical experience we summarise the key problems of tool evaluation as follows:

Decision criteria - The complexity of evaluating tools appears to rise exponentially with their functionality. Evaluators face the difficulty of weighting many nebulous product criteria (such as 'features', 'usability', 'robustness' and 'quality') often without reference points or benchmarks. This is made worse by limited understanding of the problem which the tool has to solve, imperfect tool information and also, due to cost, the need to evaluate tools outside of their operational environment.

Decision risk and uncertainty - To add to this problem managers need quantification of the benefits of a new system against the risks of change. However, the difficulty of quantifying and comparing criteria leaves a high degree of uncertainty on the likelihood of success.

Consequently an inherently complex multi-criteria decision (even with sound understanding of the problem environment and tool capability) can degrade into a best guess supported by a weak set of figures manipulated to meet the required decision outcome.

Decision pressures - The search for a tool can be triggered by both internal and external stimuli. *Internal* stimuli occur as current systems (gracefully) degrade under the greater demands of a changing operational environment. Tools outlive their cost-effective lifespan by surviving on patches, unofficial procedures or 'skunk-works' with users pushed to, and beyond, their patience threshold. Alternatively a decision can be forced by *external* stimuli such as advances in technology, contractual pressure, changing standards or an irrational need to keep up with competitors tool decisions. The cost and risk of introducing the new tools means the decision to search for a tool is typically made when the existing application is on the verge of collapse. The resulting urgency means that evaluation decision gets pressured and a difficult decision becomes even more risky.

Decision horizon - Decision pressures can also influence the horizon on which a decision is based. Immediate budgetary demands may mean an unwillingness to pay the *prima facie* high price of a tool with disregard to the high through-life costs of apparently 'cheaper' alternatives. The result is a short term fix rather than a long term 'solution'.

Decision making process and responsibility - A key problem is that due to the significant risk of tool failure responsibility for the change is naturally avoided (why risk a promising career?). As a result decisions go underground, are left undocumented or are dissipated by committee dissonance. Lack of documentation leads to loss of both accountability and valuable corporate knowledge.

Post-decision myopia - There is a tendency for the process to end once the purchase decision is made. The tool is thrown 'over the wall' into the user area for them to cope the best they can; by which time the decision makers, evaluators (precisely those people who should understand the tool best) and any potential product 'champions' have long gone. Many tools which are technically sound fail because of inadequate consideration of this emplacement process. Inadequate management of the change process (such as lack of management support, cultural problems, poor training) can destroy any remaining chance of success.

Inevitable or premature tool decline - The volatile environment of tools, tool markets, vendors, standards, upgrades etc. means there is a high likelihood of a premature and somewhat abrupt end to the tool's useful lifespan. Even in the best case scenario; despite the most thorough review of a tool's capabilities, a good decision, and well managed emplacement cannot stop the eventual changing environment that renders the current tool obsolete.

These problems are considerable even when evaluating '*small-scale*' tools that apply to well defined functional problems (such as Statemate for the behavioural specification of systems) but they are exacerbated when considering 'womb to tomb' tools such as Cradle-SEE, Teamwork, RDD-100, etc. Under these circumstances the beaten and downtrodden evaluators are left in a lose-lose situation. Little progress is made, much money is wasted and little is learnt.

2.2   Conventional wisdom and 'state of the art'

The deliberately cynical account described above is intended to highlight the inherent difficulties of the evaluation process. Few are surprising, all are basic, and certainly none are new but readers may nevertheless recognise some or all of the symptoms within their own organisations. Of course, it is not difficult to proclaim sound advice based on the above observations, both our experience and conventional wisdom (Heller, 1991; Kitchenham et al., 1995; Mosley, 1992) reminds us of the importance of:

- **Managing the decision process** - It is critical to document the decision and make people involved responsible and accountable for the decision outcome. Add checks on the decision process to recognise and reduce pressures on decision makers to help avoid foolish decisions.

- **Managing tool emplacement** - Preferably the tool should be evaluated by the people who are going to use it or at the very least ensure their active participation. Careful change management should foster champions, fund appropriate training, and respond to problems as they arise.

- **Managing tool decline** - Try to recognise earlier the degradation of current tools due to internal and external triggers. Planned tool lifecycle management will allow more time for successful tool replacement.

- **Trying before buying** - Experience suggests - and we maintain - that case studies are of greater benefit than stand-alone evaluations particularly for large and important evaluations.

- **Identifying when and what to change** - At some point we need to recognise the hard truth that the tool is good and it is our process that needs change.

How come bad decisions are still made? They are all simple common-sense points but all to frequently missed. What we need to know is *how* to do them effectively, or more importantly from our point of view, what issues should be considered when devising procedures to implement these policies. Hence our reasoning for a more formal and consistent approach to evaluation of both technical and non-technical issues in tool selection.

There are polished accounts (Kitchenham et al., 1995; Shin and Lee, 1996) of mechanisms for the evaluation of tools which address many of the concerns outlined in Section 2.1 and espouse much of the wisdom listed in Section 2.2; however, from a 'functional' or technical point of view. It is our experience that the software issues concerned with *how* the tool may/will be used are the issues that are crucial to a successful evaluation, emplacement and use. It is these issues which we have concentrated on.

3. AN INDUSTRIAL STRATEGY

3.1   Strategy overview

Clearly we need to pay more respect to the intricacies of both the selection decision and the *emplacement* process. To aid this we need more structured evaluation methods to give insight into the factors of tool assessment. Here we describe the approach adopted to improve the evaluation process based on the problems highlighted in Section 2. The strategy has two main characteristics:

Defined process - We view evaluation process as consisting of two main activities: understanding the problem environment (which the tool is to address) and understanding the tool. It is important that we capture knowledge of both these activities for use in future evaluations. The mechanism we use is a defined basic process model with three phases: pre-evaluation (Section 3.2) evaluation (Section 3.3) and post-evaluation (Section 3.4). The phases help ensure consideration of decision impacts and allows decision checkpoints to be monitored. The chosen high level of abstraction allows us to introduce element of standardisation without loss of local flexibility. Throughout we stress the importance of having a managed and documented approach to the process.

Issue checklist - Within the process model we introduce the technique of *criteria generation* from an *issue checklist* (Section 3.3.2). The benefits are two-fold; firstly it prompts consideration of non-technical factors and secondly it helps us to deduce our requirements more appropriately.

The focus of this paper will be the evaluation process itself but we hope the reader will recognise how, by the use of a structured evaluation process the quality of, both pre- and post-evaluation phases can be strengthened. In Section 3.4 we conclude our description of the process with the current status of this strategy and results to date of its operation.

3.2   The pre-evaluation process

The pre-evaluation process is based on a first-pass through of the evaluation process described in Section 3.3. It should consist of the following events:

1. **Trigger recognition** - Recognition of the need for the tool and documentation of the trigger stimulus (i.e. the perceived problems with old tools).
2. **Problem statement** - Formation and documentation of a preliminary statement of the problem which the new tool is intended to address.
3. **Criteria assessment**. Generation of a list of the most important criteria against which tool(s) will be evaluated (based on the problem statement and issue checklist or past evaluation template).

4. **Tool search and shortlist** - Conducting tool search (including finding if anyone within the organisation has prior experience of the tool) and shortlisting of tools against the initial criteria list. Of course this selection may be based on the 'lesser of evils'.

5. **Sourcing decisions** - At some point a decision is made whether to buy a tool or develop an in-house solution. This may be a high-level policy decision.

6. **Evaluation proposal** - A proposal is produced to describe and justify the selected evaluation strategy against a first pass at the evaluation process.

7. **Decision to evaluate** - A formal decision to proceed with (or cease) evaluation of the tool(s) and trigger for full evaluation process.

The relative importance of the tool decision will determine the need for, and extent of, each of these activities.

3.3   The tool evaluation process

3.3.1 Process and Mechanisms

Figure 1 shows the basic process by which an evaluation takes place. The pre-evaluation process is likely to have already made one high-level pass at the evaluation phase in order to shortlist tools and produce the evaluation plan. The full evaluation process is based on the concept of phased evaluations to address the need for an evaluation process which is efficient and economical for the nature and risk of the tool selection decision. We describe the stages of our process as follows:

Demonstration - Used as part of the initial search for tools but should only be used as a basis for the most minor tool purchases (where cost of mistakes is minimal in comparison to evaluation overhead) or where adequate information exists by which to make an informed purchase (evaluators must be confident that this meets all criteria).

Assessment against criteria - Evaluation of tool against the list of issues described in Section 3.3.2 (in full in Appendices A1-A8) and preferably in comparison with another tool for benchmarking purposes. This should be the minimum evaluation level against which tool selection decision made.

Pilot study - Significant tool selection decisions should not be made without recourse to some form of pilot study - either shadowing part of a project or applying it to a low risk part of a live project.

On completion of each technique a decision is made whether to proceed to the next level. Each evaluation process decision is recorded with its reasoning and a final report is produced to record reasons for the tool selection or rejection decision. This process guides evaluators, aids resource allocation and can be used by other parties (managers, quality departments, other evaluators) to confirm reasoning and issue coverage.

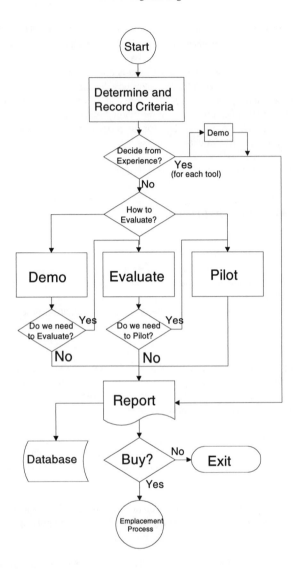

Figure 1: Basic evaluation process.

3.3.2 Issues in the selection of software tools

At the core of our strategy is the issue checklist shown in Figure 2 (presented in full in Appendix A1-A8) is used to form an initial set of more quantitative criteria against which a tool is evaluated. It is suggested that each tool should be assessed against a particular requirement prepared for that tool linked to a particular issue category. The requirement itself should ensure that issues are addressed and indeed provide traceability to them. When forming a business case for tool purchase, evaluators should provide evidence that all relevant issues from the list have been addressed.

The issues are listed in no particular order and may be addressed in sequence of perceived importance.

Business issues reflect the top level business constraints against which the business case for the tool will be made. They represent the environment for the decision and may constrain the tool evaluation process such as limiting the cost of new tools, policies of sourcing and risk to current projects. It is important to accept that sometimes it is impossible to calculate quantitative indices such as return on investment with confidence, in which case qualitative alternatives should be made explicit.

Evaluation issues are those which impact upon the evaluation process itself and represent the method by which evaluation must be justified. These issues form a self-check on evaluators including preconceptions, structuring to capture evaluation knowledge and selection of benchmarks.

External reference issues concern how the tool evaluation and emplacement relates beyond the boundaries of the organisation. The intention is to ensure that evaluators take advantage of information repositories pertaining to the tool (including past evaluations). These can significantly reduce the amount of time and therefore cost needed to evaluate a tool.

Vendor support issues represent concerns about futures in the uncertain tool market. These are frequently overlooked but critical particularly in high integrity and/or defence applications.

Financial issues represent the importance that all the costs incurred in selecting a tool be taken into account and assessed as accurately as possible. Where figures are problematic the level of uncertainty should be emphasised and bounded.

Tool issues represent the critical fitness for purpose of the tool and its method. These are the focus for traditional tool evaluation methods (including things assessment of how a tool affects the process and product integrity, compatibility, acceptability). It is recognised that the need to act to solve a technical problem may outweigh other problems such as vendor . And, once again we must recognise when the tool is good but our process needs changing.

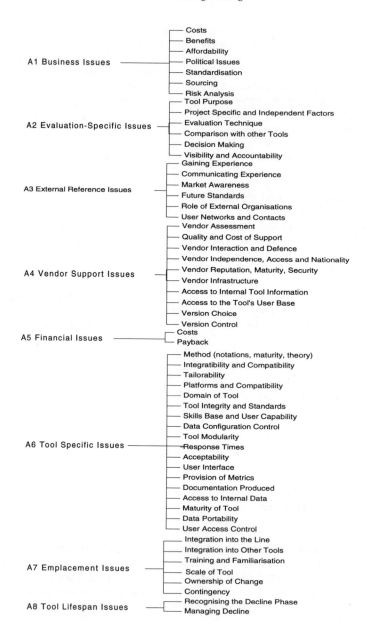

A1 Business Issues
- Costs
- Benefits
- Affordability
- Political Issues
- Standardisation
- Sourcing
- Risk Analysis

A2 Evaluation-Specific Issues
- Tool Purpose
- Project Specific and Independent Factors
- Evaluation Technique
- Comparison with other Tools
- Decision Making
- Visibility and Accountability

A3 External Reference Issues
- Gaining Experience
- Communicating Experience
- Market Awareness
- Future Standards
- Role of External Organisations
- User Networks and Contacts

A4 Vendor Support Issues
- Vendor Assessment
- Quality and Cost of Support
- Vendor Interaction and Defence
- Vendor Independence, Access and Nationality
- Vendor Reputation, Maturity, Security
- Vendor Infrastructure
- Access to Internal Tool Information
- Access to the Tool's User Base
- Version Choice
- Version Control

A5 Financial Issues
- Costs
- Payback

A6 Tool Specific Issues
- Method (notations, maturity, theory)
- Integratibility and Compatibility
- Tailorability
- Platforms and Compatibility
- Domain of Tool
- Tool Integrity and Standards
- Skills Base and User Capability
- Data Configuration Control
- Tool Modularity
- Response Times
- Acceptability
- User Interface
- Provision of Metrics
- Documentation Produced
- Access to Internal Data
- Maturity of Tool
- Data Portability
- User Access Control

A7 Emplacement Issues
- Integration into the Line
- Integration into Other Tools
- Training and Familiarisation
- Scale of Tool
- Ownership of Change
- Contingency

A8 Tool Lifespan Issues
- Recognising the Decline Phase
- Managing Decline

Figure 2: Issues in tool evaluation (Appendices A1-A8).

Emplacement issues reflect the difficulty of successfully integrating a tool into the line and achieving business benefits. They should be addressed by evaluators *before* a tool selection decision is made.

Tool lifespan issues reflect the need to recognise and manage the inevitable decline of a tool against the introduction of its replacement. This is frequently neglected but can impact highly on the quality of the next evaluation decision.

The list may not be 100 percent complete but we have found it to be a useful starting point for addressing the key issues that affect success in tool selection and emplacement in our organisations. It is not very qualitative, but we are not alone in making use of subjective measures, see (Dick and Hunter, 1994) for example. By structuring and documenting tool selection criteria in relation to these issues we stand more chance of ensuring completeness and sensible decisions. In addition, we can construct templates for evaluation and comparison of certain types of tools (Section 3.3.4).

3.3.3 Post-evaluation (emplacement and decline) process
Development of the process for the emplacement and decline of tools has been identified as an issue for further enhancement of the evaluation process. Some of the issues of emplacement and decline have been discussed elsewhere in this document. We believe that more empirical research is necessary into the factors that affect successful emplacement of software tools. We also believe that there is a requirement for more advanced monitoring changes in the internal and external operating environment of a tool and to make replacement decisions earlier. These issues will be the subject of future work.

3.3.4 Operation and results
The described strategy has been incorporated into local quality guidelines for tool evaluations since mid-1995. Feedback forms have been used to communicate results of strategy application within operational areas. We have already observed considerable benefit in compiling knowledge from tool evaluation activities on two levels:

Collection of domain criteria checklists - Different tool domains have varying criteria and weightings, which are capable of being recorded and reused. Such tool domains include general design, requirements management, systems engineering and requirements capture, configuration, testing, document managers, and control specification. There are also academic examples of domain criteria; for instance, Schamp (1995) records the criteria for configuration management tools. These internal (company generated) and external criteria are forming the basis of a tool requirement repository which will be of use in future evaluations.

Collection and publication of tool evaluation results - Through use of organisation-wide process improvement teams we have stimulated cross-organisation communication about tools, toolsets, and tool experience. Tool evaluation intentions and results are published to all relevant parties - allowing us to make best use of organisational knowledge, track weaknesses in particular tools and ensure a proactive attitude in tool policy.

Time will allow us to evaluate and refine the strategy whilst improving our knowledge repository. Initial feedback has indicated strong potential for cost savings and considerable support for valuable cooperation.

4.   AN EXAMPLE

A real demonstration of the usefulness for our approach would require a number of experiments, involving the assessment of a number of different tools, using a variety of evaluation processes (e.g. (Misra, 1990)). Such a presentation would be a paper in itself, but it is useful to provide a sketched example of how our technique could be used to evaluate a software tool. We consider a mythical tool called the Requirements Management Tool (hereafter referred to as RMT) and its evaluation by company XYZ. The scenario is not derived from practices within Rolls-Royce.

1. Members of XYZ have a need for some form of requirements management tool.
2. Members of XYZ receive some technical literature on the RMT tool from the tool manufacturer.
3. The tool looks promising and the XYZ members review their existing evaluation library and discover a review of a requirements specification tool (RST) that offers some similar features. The review for RST is retrieved and previous experience shows that it is the integration of such tools that is often the critical success factor. An RMT review check list is drawn up which includes the following issues:

   ● Business issues - Is the RMT seat price less than £2000?

   ● External reference - Is there an RMT user group?

   ● Vendor assessment - Is the vendor a known supplier to XYZ?

   ● Tool specific - Does the tool link to the existing DMT tool?

4. A demonstration is arranged and the tool looks sufficiently appropriate that an evaluation copy is ordered.
5. During evaluation the RMT tool scores well technically, but it cannot integrate with the DMT tool. As the DMT tool has been used successfully for many years it is decided not to pilot the RMT tool and the evaluation process is terminated.
6. The RMT tool is rejected and the process and supporting arguments are logged in XYZ's tool evaluation library.
7. XYZ management are pleased that an inappropriate tool has not been purchased and that the evidence for such a decision has been formally recorded.

This is a deliberately artificial example but shows how a simple procedure can act as a means of protecting a company from an isolated evaluation performed purely on performance criteria. The process encouraged an orderly evaluation based on a variety of issues, making use of previous knowledge where appropriate. Most importantly, the reasons for the rejection are recorded and placed within the corporate memory.

5. RELATED WORK

Whilst the process presented in this paper is primarily a description of our current practice, it is still appropriate to take some time to place our work in the context of that of others of which we are aware. The significance of software tools to the quality of an overall engineering capability has been documented (Polvia, 1992) and many have written of the importance of software tool evaluation (Heller, 1991; Kitchenham et al., 1995; Mosley, 1992). Our ideas on creating a process for this evaluation (and subsequent emplacement) of tools is not uncommon to that of Rowley's (Rowley, 1993) goal of treating tool evaluation as a project in its own right. Such a view aids repeatability and encourages the recording of decisions and rationale, as well as introducing group accountability. This is a good thing and is not dissimilar to the work of Mosley for instance (Mosley, 1992).

The inclusion of evaluation issues other than just functionality and performance is recognised elsewhere, in particular with regard to the role of different types of tool (Anderson, 1989; Cheng and Pane, 1991; DeSantis, 1994; Miller and Jeffries, 1992). Other organisations have recognised the wider scope of tool evaluations than just performance and functionality and have instigated their own corporate advice centres, see (Scheffler and Marshall, 1991).

Other tool evaluation checklists do exist (Jeanrenaud and Romanazzi, 1994; Klopping and Bolgiano, 1994) but can be criticised (as indeed can ours) for being overly procedural and beaurocratic. McDougal (McDougal and Squires, 1995) discusses the problems of checklists, but we can only really draw on our own experiences. Checklists are laborious to fill in, but they do provide a focus or thought, and do draw the evaluators away from a technocentric approach to evaluation.

6. FINAL COMMENTS

This paper has presented a brief overview of a more detailed tool evaluation process currently in use within Rolls-Royce plc. It is intended to be simple, generic and a working strategy that will evolve with use in order to capture and exploit valuable organisational knowledge generated during tool evaluations. The strategy addresses the weaknesses of the existing evaluation process by attempting to ensure that all issues are structured and addressed particularly *soft* factors overlooked by many formal evaluation techniques. The result is a quality evaluation process that we believe is more effective, more efficient, and less risky.

We believe that the strategy improves our chances of ensuring that conventional wisdom about tool evaluation (Section 2.2) is addressed and against these goals it performs well (and considerably better than no process whatsoever!) However we emphasise the need for exposure of the strategy to generations of tool evaluations and its necessary evolution to capture more detailed evaluator knowledge. Further work on the strategy is required to capture experiences of tool emplacement (which is critical in determining the success of a tool) and enhance it to provide greater support for the more difficult area of method evaluation. These experiences will help us to define precisely how business cases for tool acquisition should be constructed, though we will need more qualitative measures, see Williams (Williams, 1992) for example. We hope to define a business case template which would use the results of our process to format a standard business case for tool selection. We see this as a significant step forward. Finally, we are in the process of assembling a knowledge repository on tool capabilities and application domain criteria. Taking this to the logical conclusion we could lay a foundation for a repository of this kind on the World Wide Web (WWW) thereby making a global tool information knowledge-base (clearly this has problems of regulation, evidence, objectivity, copyright etc. despite the attraction for tool purchasers).

We have made (and perhaps laboured) the point that there are many issues in the use of tools of which only one is the technical capability. Experience has taught us that the subtleties of tool evaluation, selection and emplacement must not be underestimated. A more successful process will come from greater attention to the organisational and behavioural issues. Tools can provide business benefits but all too easily they can be eroded by unsuccessful introduction. In reality it is even harder than this as the introduction of a tool to an organisation will itself change the nature of the organisation. A tool may therefore contribute to its own lack of success because of the changes it introduces! Selecting tools is difficult (good from bad) and whilst we have not addressed all the issues, we believe the techniques presented in this paper are a step towards ameliorating the problems of tool selection.

Finally, we believe that our experience is of benefit both to the users of tools, the developers, and vendors as a means of bringing the parties together for mutual benefit. We encourage use of checklist in Appendix A1-A8 to appraise the reader's organisation's process (if they have one) and we would welcome feedback. Whilst strategy may not necessarily prevent disasters occurring we at least have an opportunity to learn from them.

7.   ACKNOWLEDGMENTS

Peter Jeffery and John Anderson for contributions to the ideas presented in earlier drafts of this paper. Peter Summers of Rolls-Royce who contributed to early versions of the evaluation strategy. Mike Burke at the British Aerospace Dependable Systems Computing Centre at the University of York. Rolls-Royce plc for permission to publish. The anonymous reviewers for providing sharply focused observations on improving the paper.

Please note: This document represents the opinions of the authors and in no capacity does it indicate official policy for Rolls-Royce plc.

8. REFERENCES

Anderson, E. E. (1989) A Heuristic for Software Evaluation and Selection. *Software: Practice and Experience*, 19(8), 707-717.

Cheng, D. Y., and Pane, D. M. "An Evaluation of Automatic and Interactive Parallel Programming Tools." *Supercomputing '91*, Albuquerque, USA, 412-423.

DeSantis, J. (1994) Evaluating Multi-Platform Development Tools. *Object Magazine*, 4(4), 41-44.

Dick, R., and Hunter, R. "Subjective Software Evaluation." *Software Quality Management II: Building Quality into Software*, Edinburgh, UK, 321-334.

Heller, R. S. (1991) Evaluating Software: A Review of the Options. *Computers and Education*, 17(4), 285-291.

Humphrey, W. A. (1988) Characterising the Software Process: A Maturity Framework. *IEEE Software*.

Humphrey, W. S. (1990). *Managing the Software Process*, Addison-Wesley.

Jeanrenaud, J., and Romanazzi, P. "Software Product Evaluation: A Methodological Approach." *Software Quality Management II: Building Quality into Software*, Edinburgh, UK, 59-69.

Kitchenham, B., Pickard, L., and Pfleeger, S. L. (1995) Case Studies for Method and Tool Evaluation. *IEEE Software*, 12(4), 55-62.

Klopping, I. M., and Bolgiano, C. F. (1994) Effective Evaluation of off-the-shelf Microcomputer Software. *Office Systems Research Journal*, 9(1), 46-40.

McDougal, A., and Squires, D. (1995) A Critical Examination of the Checklist Approach to Software Selection. *Journal of Educational Computing Research*, 12(3), 263-274.

Miller, J. R., and Jeffries, R. (1992) Interface-Usability Evaluation: Science of Trade-Offs. *IEEE Software*, 9(5), 97-102.

Misra, S. K. (1990) Analysing CASE System Characteristics: Evaluative Framework. *Information and Software Technology*, 32(6), 415-422.

Mosley, V. (1992) How to Assess Tools Efficiently and Quantitatively. *IEEE Software*, 9(3), 29-32.

Polvia, P. (1992). "A Comprehensive Model and Evaluation of the Software Engineering Environment." *Information Resources Management Association International Conference*, Harrisburg, USA, 302-307.

Rowley, J. E. (1993) Selection and Evaluation of Software. *ASLIB Proceedings*, 45(3), 77-81.

Schamp, A. (1995) CM-Tool Evaluation and Selection. *IEEE Software*, 12(4), 114-118.

Scheffler, F. L., and Marshall, R. R. "The Software Technology Support Centre: Help for Acquiring Sofware Tools." *National Aerospace and Electronics Conference*, Dayton, OH, USA, 647-653.

Shin, H., and Lee, J. (1996) A Process Model of Application Software Package Acquisition and Implementation. *Journal of Systems and Software*, 32, 57-64.

Williams, F. (1992) Appraisal and Evaluation of Software Products. *Journal of Information Science, Principles and Practice*, 18(2), 121-125.

APPENDICES A1-A8

A1 - Business issues

These strategic issues reflect the top level business constraints against which the business case for the tool will be made. It is important to accept that sometimes it is impossible to calculate quantitative indices such as return on investment with confidence, in which case qualitative alternatives should be made explicit.

- **Costs** - The total cost, from licences to attaining necessary competencies, should be calculated and depending on the level of confidence an upper bound be determined.

- **Benefits** - The benefits should be estimated in as quantitative way as possible but where qualitative arguments from considerations such as those in the rest of this section are used they must be made explicit.

- **Affordability** - There should be adequate resources - human, financial and material to perform the assessment. Adequate evaluation time should be budgeted.

- **Political issues** - The constraints arising from contractual commitment or the need to visibly conform to an industrial consensus should be addressed.

- **Standardisation** - Evaluators should recognise policy decisions on preferred methods, notations, or platforms to which tools should conform. They should also try to be aware of any likely future directions for relevant standards.

- **Sourcing** - The policy as to the selection of third party, in-house or commissioned tools should be identified and agreed.

- **Risk analysis** - Risk analysis should be performed before any significant purchase decision is made.

A2   Evaluation-specific issues

Evaluation issues are those which impact upon the evaluation process itself. Evaluators should address these issues when planning an evaluation. These include:

- **Analysis of the purpose of the tool** - The evaluator should have a clear understanding of the process and technical activity which the tool is intended to support. The evaluator should also understand the role which the tool is intended to fulfil and ensure that the means to meet this are addressed by the evaluation process.

- **Project specific and project independent factors** - Evaluators should address both project specific (e.g. specific platform and network requirement) and non-project specific factors (e.g. quality of the method), which may require evaluation by different personnel.

- **Evaluation technique** - Evaluators should consider the comparative value and cost of different evaluation mechanisms:

- demonstrations (by the supplier);

- structured assessments using criteria checklists;

- pilot studies.

- **Comparison with other tools** - The evaluator should form a strategy for comparison of one tool against another including the baselining and use of scoring systems for prioritisation.

- **Decision making** - Evaluators should clarify the basis upon which decisions will be made including who is responsible for the tool selection decision.

- **Visibility and accountability** - Evaluators should provide visibility of the evaluation to all interested parties and ensure accountability and documentation of all decisions.

A3   External reference issues

External organisation issues concern how the tool evaluation and emplacement relates beyond the boundaries of the organisation. These include:

- **Gaining experience** - The experience of other users, projects and/or companies should be identified and exploited where possible.

- **Communicating experience** - The sharing of experience with other users, projects and/or companies should be an integral part of the evaluation process.

- **Market awareness** - Line departments should keep abreast of the tool market to ensure that all potential solutions are considered and that the timing of tool evaluations and purchase is appropriate.

- **Future standards** - Line departments should keep abreast of potential changes to methods and standards which may affect the lifespan of the tool.

- **Role of external organisations** - Line departments should make active use of external organisations who can provide consultancy, tool information and contacts.

- **User networks and contacts** - Line departments should establish and maintain links with other users to ensure that experience continues to shape the use of the tool once it is in operation in the line.

A4   Vendor support issues

Vendor support issues represent concerns about futures in the uncertain tool market. These include:

- **Vendor assessment** - Evaluators should consider undertaking a formal vendor assessment exercise.

- **Quality and cost of support** - Evaluators should balance the level and quality of technical/product support provided and the cost of alternative support options against emplacement needs.

- **Vendor interaction and defence** - Evaluators should appraise and define the nature of the relationship between the vendor and the organisation including quality and style of interaction (sales driven, technically capable and responsive) and form barriers as a defence from unnecessary interruption.

- **Vendor independence, access and nationality** - Evaluators should establish the acceptability of the vendor in terms of their independence, ease of access and problems of nationality.

- **Vendor reputation, maturity and security** - As far as possible evaluators should ensure the vendor's long-term commitment to the product, the standards to which they operate and their likely survival as a supplier.

- **Vendor infrastructure** - Evaluators should ensure that the infrastructure of the vendor is suitable to effectively support such a product.

- **Access to internal tool information** - Evaluators should test vendor openness about the tool's construction, quality of supporting documentation and tool certification evidence to ensure sufficient contingency.

- **Access to the tool's user base** - Evaluators should seek to consult reference sites and attend user groups for mutual benefit and co-operation and to gain a feel for the vendor.

- **Version choice** - Evaluators should ensure that they evaluate the right version of tool to used. Avoid evaluating beta versions.

- **Version control** - Evaluators should establish the consequential risks of changes in the version of the tool on support software and interfaces with other tools.

A5 Financial issues

It is important that all the costs incurred in selecting a tool be taken into account and assessed as accurately as possible. Where figures are problematic the level of uncertainty should be emphasised and bounded.

- **Costs** - Evaluators should calculate the costs arising from (at least) tool licences and maintenance, hardware support, achieving and holding the necessary competence level of personnel, migrating from or integrating with the current toolset and administration.

- **Payback** - Evaluators should estimate the amount potentially saved by automating process and/or lower cost of quality.

A6   Tool specific issues

Tool issues represent the critical fitness for purpose of the tool and its method. These include:

- **Method (notations, maturity, theory)** - The underlying method should preferably be proven and accepted in the field and within the intended user community. The risk of method obsolescence should be minimised.

- **Integratibility and compatibility** - The tool should be demonstrably compatible with existing and prospective tools and techniques.

- **Tailorability** - Evaluators should consider the level of need and provision for tailorability and customisation, but this should be contrasted with potential lack of standardisation.

- **Platforms and compatibility** - Evaluators should address the risks of platform dependence and version incompatibility.

- **Domain of tool** - Evaluators must understand the purpose, functions and applicability of the tool against the problem domain.

- **Tool integrity and standards** - Evaluators should consider tool integrity and standards and should ensure that the integrity of the tool meets its intended use.

- **Skills base and user capability** - Evaluators should consider the level of skills required against currently available skills.

- **Data configuration control** - The tools should allow the user to manage the input and output data in a configurable way.

- **Tool modularity** - Evaluators should consider the benefits of buying tools in discrete functional units and should cost unused features.

- **Response times** - Evaluators should ensure that the tool can withstand realistic usage and demand.

- **Acceptability** - Evaluators should consider the tool's acceptability internally and externally, prejudices should be surfaced.

- **User interface** - Evaluators should be sure that the user interface will be acceptable to the users (by understanding the tool and the user) .

- **Provision of metrics** - The ability of the tool to support any required metrics programme should be considered e.g. such that the effectiveness of the data management (and other) facilities can be judged.

- **Documentation produced** - The tool should enable documentation to be produced of sufficient quality to be easily introduced into existing company standards. This includes the ability to produce sections intended to merge with other documentation sources.

- **Access to internal data** - The need for, and provision of, access to internal data structures should be examined.

- **Maturity of tool** - Evaluators should be aware of the maturity of the tool in the market place, e.g. by examining the level of problems being solved by patches, upgrades etc.

- **Data portability** - Evaluators should ensure that data from the new tools should be machine portable to other tools already in use (or planned to be brought into use).

- **User access control** - Evaluators should consider if the tool has appropriate internal security mechanisms to ensure control of user access at appropriate levels.

A7   Emplacement issues

Emplacement issues reflect the difficulty of successfully integrating a tool into the line and achieving business benefits. They should be addressed by evaluators before a tool selection decision is made. These include:

- **Integration into the line** - The steps for introducing the tool including organisation of human resources, transfer of work and overcoming problems should be made explicit.

- **Integration into other tools** - The practical aspects and cost of getting tools to communicate and operate effectively should be reviewed.

- **Training and familiarisation** - Evaluators should explain and cost a strategy for training and familiarisation to support tool introduction including level and type required, internal or externally sourced, and provision of resources. The assumed pre-requisite skill of the trainee should be established.

- **Scale of tool** - The introduction strategy should reflect the scaleability of the tool in terms of full-scale introduction on a project or selected (gradual) introduction.

- **Ownership of change** - Change owners and tool owners must be identified, consulted and given responsibility to ensure success of the change process.

- **Contingency** - Change owners should minimise the risk of introducing a tool via the use of contingency plans.

A8   Tool lifespan issues

Tool lifespan issues reflect the need to recognise and manage the inevitable decline of a tool against the introduction of its replacement.

- **Recognising the decline phase** - Tool owners and users should monitor tool usage to identify and make contingency for tool decline.

- **Managing decline** - Phase-out and replacement of tools should be managed as part of the tool evaluation and emplacement process.

BIOGRAPHY

Antony Powell is a researcher at the Rolls-Royce University Technology Centre at the University of York. Before this Antony worked for Rolls-Royce and Associates helping to introduce a number of measurement and process improvement activities across the Rolls-Royce group. His research interests include software measurement, process improvement, tool evaluation and software change.

Dr Andrew Vickers is a Lecturer in the Department of Computer Science at the University of York. His research interests include Requirements Engineering, Software Architecture, Technology Transfer, and Safety-Critical Systems. Dr Vickers is a member of the High-Integrity Systems Engineering group at York. As part of this group, he is Assistant Director of the Rolls-Royce Systems and Software University Technology Centre, and Cotechnical Leader of the associated ASSET process improvement programme. He is a member of INCOSE, and the Industrial Liaison Officer for the British Computer Society's Requirements Engineering Specialist Group.

Dr Eddie Williams works for Rolls-Royce and Associates in Derby leading the High Integrity Systems and Software Centre within Rolls-Royce plc.

Dr Brian Cooke works for Rolls-Royce and Associates in Derby leading a Systems and Software Metrics initiative throughout Rolls-Royce plc.

12

Core objects required for a generic CASE repository

Gordon Manson, Siobhán North and Abdullah Alghamdi
Department of Computer Science, University of Sheffield, Regent Court,
211 Portobello Street, Sheffield, UK.   Tel. 0044-114-2825597
EMail: A.Alghamdi@dcs.shef.ac.uk

Abstract

An extendible CASE tools environment is currently being researched at the Department of Computer Science, University of Sheffield. This environment is designed primarily for developing parallel system software but is configurable for other applications. It requires an underlying generic data repository to represent information about the system under development in a consistent and complete form. The representation must be independent of the source, and intended use, of its data.

The paper starts by explaining the importance of a CASE data repository and the overall hierarchical structure of our repository data model. Then, it goes on to suggest a meta-meta data model for a generic CASE repository.

Keywords

CASE tools, MetaCASE Environment, Data Repository

1. INTRODUCTION

The software developer now expects a full CASE tools environment; not just a collection of unrelated CASE tools to support software development, but rather an assembly of integrated CASE tools that link together and provide automated support for all phases of the software life cycle . The data repository is a core technology in reaching high levels of software integration and automation because it provides the underlying framework upon which all the other structures depend (Chen, 1991) (Forte, 1989).

The software engineering environments are perceived, in our system, as a collection of methodologies, each methodology consists of a number of tools (or techniques) and each tool comprises a number of graphical and non-graphical objects used for constructing part of the real life application. In view of this perspective, the overall structure of our CASE repository contents has been divided into a number of different layers of abstraction.

The first and most important step in developing a central CASE repository is to design its meta-meta data model. The abstract entities representing the real diagrammatic objects must be chosen very carefully if the repository is intended to be a generic one because whatever is chosen must be able to support all the currently popular methodologies and, hopefully a few that have not yet been invented (Alderson, 1991). To this end a number of methodologies, representing different paradigms and approaches to software engineering, as well as a number of configurable CASE tools have been reviewed. This allowed the development of an abstract meta-meta data model which could represent all of the diverse structures used in the different methodologies.

2. REPOSITORY META DATA LAYERS

To achieve the integration of various CASE tools and to make the environment open to multiple software engineering approaches, the repository data has been divided into a number of different levels of abstraction.

The "Meta-Meta Data Model" is a highly conceptual layer describing what components and capabilities are available for creating meta models. It provides a sufficient degree of abstraction to deal effectively with many CASE environments. This layer provides another degree of freedom for extending the meta model and also simplifies the definition of design rules and integrity checking.

The next level down is the "Methodology Generic Meta Data Model" layer. In our system a software engineering methodology is perceived as a process for the organised production of software using a collection of predefined tools and notational conventions. This layer is concerned with describing the rules required for building a new methodology, its tools and graphical objects.

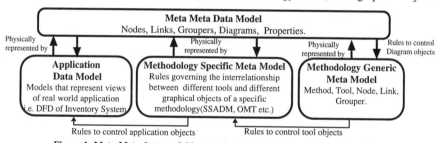

Figure 1: Meta-Meta data model interaction to other meta models in the system

The next layer down is the "Methodology Specific Meta Data Model" layer which describes the interrelationship between the tools and graphical objects of a specific. It contains descriptions of object types such as "process", "data flow" and "control flow", the types of modelling notations and the connectivity rules available to the developer in specifying an application.

The lowest layer is the "Application Data Model" layer which contains the specific models of an application. This layer defines the data flow diagrams, Entity Relationship diagrams, action diagrams, state transition diagrams, etc. that describe the system of interest.

3. THE REPOSITORY META-META DATA MODEL

The meta-meta data model is the collection of primitives used to represent everything stored in a repository because it provides the overall conceptual view of the entire repository contents.

The conceptual objects that have been defined as common to most methodologies are nodes, links and groupers.   A *node* represents any diagrammatic concept which can exist independently from any other objects in the diagram, a *link* represents a connection between two (and only two) nodes and cannot exist without both of these two nodes and a *grouper* represents a grouping of interrelated objects (nodes and links).

A real diagram contains a number of diagrammatic objects connected together.   These objects are not the basic CASE objects mentioned above but are rather, instances of them.   The CASE instance objects store information about the shapes appearing in a diagram.   That means that one instance object will be stored in the CASE data repository for each shape in the diagram. Therefore in one diagram there may be many instances of a basic CASE object and other instances of this object may occur in other diagrams.

Sometimes the basic information stored about a CASE object is not sufficient, additional information is needed for a particular application (say code generation).   This can be represented by what is called an "Object Property".   It allows the analyst to add multi-level structured information to the object, thus making its definition extensible.

Our repository meta-meta data model is represented using Entity-Relationship-Attribute (ERA) model. All the objects outlined above are defined in terms of entities participating in relationships.

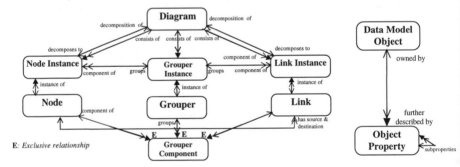

Figure 2: The Repository Meta-Meta Data Model

Two main types of relationships are defined; mandatory and optional.   Diagrammatically a mandatory relationship is represented by an arrow with solid triangular arrow head and an optional one is represented by ordinary arrow head.   A mandatory relationship implies that the destination entity is dependant on the relationship for its existence.

As can be seen from figure 2, the model consists of a diagram entity, which is a collection of graphical instances, a number of basic objects (node, link and grouper) and their instances. Each one of these entities is known as a data model object. Each data model object can be further described by a number of multi-level properties as shown in the same figure (right).

The model does not show all the entities represented in the repository. A number of entities were omitted for simplicity. Some of these entities support reusability, some of them are to support object versioning and configuration management and some are for query optimisation, object-symbol mapping and object security.

Basic CASE objects

Any concept used during the analysis and design stages and represented in a diagram will be stored as a CASE basic object in the CASE repository. The advantages gained from applying such an approach include data persistency, reusability and reduction of data redundancy.

Data persistency is an important concept and, in the context of CASE systems, has two different, but related, aspects. Firstly, it allows information stored in the repository to outlive the process that created it, and secondly, it provides for the possibility of basic information surviving in the repository after the deletion of its instances.

If an object is to be reused by another diagram it must not have any visual or relationship information tying it to a specific diagram and the only objects which have these characteristics are the basic ones. So we also need basic objects to achieve re-usability.

In some applications, more than one instance of the same object might share a number of similar properties. If those properties are duplicated with a copy in each of the instances then the usual problems of data redundancy will occur. This difficulty can be overcome by having a central basic object containing properties common to all instances and allowing each instance to have its own extra properties.

Object Instances

Each basic object may have more than one instance object which represents it visually in a diagram; that means one instance object will be stored in the CASE data repository for each shape in a diagram. The idea behind this approach is to enable the CASE tools to perform consistency checking between diagrams, retrieve graphical information about the CASE objects and optimise the reusability of the basic objects.

Object Property

The object property provides additional, multi-level, explanatory information about an object in the repository data model. By applying this new technique, we have come up with a highly flexible hierarchy of properties. In this hierarchy, a property (or even a group of properties) can be moved around, copied, added to or deleted from any position in any level in the hierarchy without affecting the whole structure.

These characteristics are not offered by most of the available commercial meta-CASE tools environments.   The absence of these characteristics in a similar project (Manson, 1994) made automatic code generation very difficult because of the lack of detailed information about the data and programming constructs.   It is for this reason we have adopted such a flexible structure.

During the very early stages of designing our repository, the properties were exclusive to the basic objects, but after going through a number of real case studies (Alghamdi, 1994) we discovered that the instances need some extra visual and non-visual information which could only be stored as properties.   For that reason we have decided that the instances should have their own properties in addition to those stored in their original basic objects.

4. CONCLUSION

The meta-meta data model described here is the overall conceptual view of the entire repository contents where the CASE objects are defined in terms of entities participating in binary relationships.   The conceptual basic objects that have been defined as common in most methodologies are nodes, links and groupers. A diagram consists of a number of interrelated diagrammatic objects connected together.   These objects are not the basic CASE objects but are rather instances of them.   The CASE instances store information about the shapes appearing in a diagram.

Sometimes the basic information stored about a CASE object is not enough,   additional information is needed to further describe the object in order to be sufficient for some application purposes.   In fact this can be done through what is called an "Object Property".   The multi-level object property allows the analyst (or designer) to add more than one level of structured information to the object.   This makes the object definition extensible.

The fundamental advantage of this approach to CASE system design is that it permits reusable basic data objects to be defined and instances of these objects to inherit their properties and methods.   Moreover, it allows a flexible hierarchy of properties to be constructed for each data model object in the system. It is this flexibility that gives our approach an advantage over more traditional approaches.

5. REFERENCES

Alderson, A. Meta-CASE. (1991)Lecture notes in computer sciences 509, Springer-Verlag
Alghamdi, A. (1994) An extendible MetaCASE repository. Transfer Report, Department of
            Computer Science, University of Sheffield
Chen, Minder and Edgar Sibley, (1991)Using CASE Based Repository for Systems Integration.
            Proceedings of The Hawaii International Conference on Systems Sciences,.
Forte, Gene, (1989) Inside the CASE Repository. CASE Outlook, No 4 Dec.
Manson, G. A. Sahib, S. and Elamvazauthi, C.(1994) "Design and code derivation in the PCSC
            methodology" Information and Software Technology journal, July.

13

A Proposal For Context-Specific Method Engineering

Colette Rolland
Université Paris 1-Sorbonne
17, rue de la Sorbonne
75231 Paris Cedex 5
rolland@masi.ibp.fr

Naveen Prakash
Delhi Institute of Technology
Kashmere Gate
110006 Delhi, India
np@dit.ernet.in

Abstract

The new emerging method engineering discipline acknowledges the need for the construction of methods tuned to specific situations of development projects. This raises at least three problems (1) the representation of method fragments in a method base, (2) the formalization of the notion of project situation and, (3) the retrieval of relevant fragments for the project situation at hand. Our contribution to the first two of these problems lies in the definition of a contextual approach which enables us to represent both method knowledge (i.e. the method base contents) and method meta-knowledge (i.e. knowledge about the potential use of method fragments) as pairs of the form <situation, decision>. This emphasizes both engineering decisions and method engineering decisions, their rationale and situations of applicability. We contribute to the third problem by proposing a tight coupling of method knowledge and method meta-knowledge in the method base. This enables the formal description of the context of use of every method fragment and shall facilitate the retrieval of relevant fragments according to the situation of the project under development. The paper presents and exemplifies the method knowledge and method meta-knowledge levels.

1   INTRODUCTION

The area of method engineering has emerged in response to an increasing feeling that methods are not well-suited (Lyytinen , 1987) to the needs of their users, the application engineers. In particular, it is necessary to change methods from one business situation (Hidding, 1994) to another. Situational method engineering (Welke, 1991) is the construction of methods which are tuned to specific situations of development projects. The Situational Method Spectrum (Harmsen, 1994) organises approaches to situational method engineering according to the degree of flexibility in meeting situational needs and places them on a scale ranging from 'low' flexibility to 'high'. At the 'low' end of this spectrum are rigid methods whereas at the 'high' end is modular method construction (Harmsen, 1994). Rigid methods are completely pre-defined and leave little scope for adapting them to the situation at hand. On the other hand, modular methods can be modified and augmented to fit a given situation.

One proposal (Harmsen, 1994) to situational method engineering looks at the situation of the project to engineer a project-specific method. A method is viewed as a collection of method fragments. A fragment can be either a product fragment or a process fragment. In the former case, it captures product related knowledge of methods whereas in the latter case, it captures activity related knowledge. Method fragments are available in a method base to be assembled together to form a method.

In this approach, the project situation is at a very global level. We believe that even after discovering the project situation, the detailed engineering of a method shall still require knowledge of which fragment can be used in which method engineering situation to achieve which objective. We view the retrieval process of method fragments as being *contextual :* a method engineer is faced to *situations* at which he looks with some *decision* in mind. Supporting the retrieval process requires that knowledge should be provided about *decisional contexts* in which fragments can be used.

Further, in this approach, the project situation is discovered during a separate step in the method engineering process and the method engineer has, thereafter, to find the applicable method fragments. The method base does not carry information about the situation in which method fragments are useful and so no support can be provided in this search task. Our view is that knowledge about the *context of use* of method fragments *shall be formalized* and *stored in the method base* together with the method fragments themselves.

Our approach to method engineering proposes a shift from global and situation based method engineering to modular and context based method engineering. It has three salient features :
- We recognise that method knowledge exists at different granularity levels and different levels of abstraction. Our approach explicitly captures both kinds of method knowledge.
- Since many decisions can be made in a given situation, our approach explicitly recognises the importance of decisions, the value of decision rationale and, additionally, tightly couples situations, decisions and rationales together into the notion of context.
- In order to provide support for retrieval from the method base, the situations and decisions for which a method fragment is applicable are explicitly available in the method base.

We propose to organise the method base at two levels, the *method knowledge level* and the *method meta-knowledge level* respectively. *Method knowledge* is represented in the method base in the form of *method chunks.* These chunks are available at different levels of granularity and at different levels of abstraction. Different granularity levels are made possible by using the NATURE contextual approach (Rolland, 1994), (Rolland, 1995) which organises method knowledge as contexts, trees, and forests of trees. Chunks can be considered to be at different levels of abstraction, the component, method construction pattern, and framework levels. It is possible for a chunk at any level of abstraction to display different granularity.

The application of the contextual approach to the representation of method knowledge has the important effect of making chunks modular. A context is defined as a pair, <situation, decision>. In other words, a method chunk is cohesive because it tells us the situation in which it is relevant and the decision that can be made in this situation. It is loosely coupled to other chunks because it can be used by the method engineer in the appropriate situation (created as a result of another method module) to satisfy his/her intention. Thus, the linear arrangement of method modules is replaced by a more dynamic one.

The *method meta-knowledge* level seeks to capture, in the method base, the situational and intentional knowledge associated with a method chunk. The contextual model of NATURE is an elegant model for representing this meta-knowledge. Since a context is defined as a pair, <situation, decision>, the contextual representation of meta-knowledge naturally captures these two kinds of meta-knowledge. Thus, modularity is extended to the meta-knowledge representation and meta-knowledge modules are tightly coupled to their peer method modules.

In the rest of this paper, we develop in detail the method knowledge and method meta-knowledge levels. Section 2 which deals with the former, presents and exemplifies the different levels of granularity and different abstraction levels which we believe, are relevant for method knowledge representation. Section 3 covers the meta-knowledge representation and illustrates through examples of queries, how method chunks can be retrieved from the method base. In section 4 we draw some conclusions and perspectives of work.

2 THE METHOD KNOWLEDGE LEVEL

Method knowledge is contained in *method chunks* represented in a uniform way but related to different methods and expressed with different granularity, at various levels of abstraction. Examples of such method chunks are (1) the OMT methodology, (2) the ER modelling approach, (3) the rules to define the key of an Entity-Type, (4) a generic outline providing a stepwise organisation of system analysis and (5) a generic set of guidelines for any concept description. The granularity is larger in (1) and (2) than in (3) above. Further, the first three are expressed at a less abstract level than the fourth and fifth examples above.

Notice that depending on its level of abstraction the method chunk will be reused as such (perhaps after some customisation) or will be instantiated before being assembled in the method under construction. Chunks of examples (1) to (3) above are directly reusable whereas each generic activity of the outline (example (4)) has to be instantiated according to the specific product of the method in hand before being used. Similarly the generic guidelines for concept description (example (5)) requires instantiation for each particular concept of the method under construction.

The examples also show that method chunks come from various methods which can have different purposes. The guidelines for an ER approach and of the OMT methodology are system engineering methods whereas the generic guidelines for concept description are part of a meta-method, i.e. a method to support the construction of methods. Our current method base which is implemented in the MENTOR environment (SiSaid, 1996) includes six traditional requirements engineering methods, namely OMT, E/R, OOA, SA/SD, O* and OOD (Plihon , 1994), the From Fuzzy to Formal method developed within the large ESPRIT project F3 (Bubenko, 1994), one meta-method, the NATURE meta-method (Plihon , 1995) and one method for method improvement, namely the learning based way-of-working to support NATURE method improvement (Prat, 1995). In short, we are concerned with engineering and re-engineering methods whose products are either computer based applications or methods themselves.

Therefore, there are two key aspects :
    - a uniform representation of all types of chunks of the method base. For this, we use the NATURE modelling formalism which is based on the notions of *context, tree* and *forest*. All chunks are represented following this formalism as hierarchies of contexts called *trees*. A method is represented as a collection of trees that we refer to as a *forest*.
    - a chunk classification. Chunks are classified into *component, pattern* and *framework* depending on their level of abstraction. We deal with these two aspects in the following.

2.1 Overview of method knowledge organisation

Figure 1 shows the structure of method knowledge in the method base using some binary ER-like notations. A large box represents an Entity-Type (ET) and a small box represents a binary Relationship-Type (RT) between two entity-types. The arrow head indicates the direction in which the label of the relationship-type holds. Cardinalities are also shown. For example, "Tree" and "Forest" are entity-types and are related through the "composed of" relationship-type. The direction of the RT says, "Forest composed of trees".
The notations also include the notion of an "objectified relationship-type" (Tempora, 1994). This notion is an abstraction mechanism which allows a relationship-type to be viewed, at a higher level of abstraction, as an entity-type. This applies for example, to the RT between a "Situation" and a "Decision" which is viewed as the entity-type "Context" to enable it to enter into a RT with the ET "Tree".

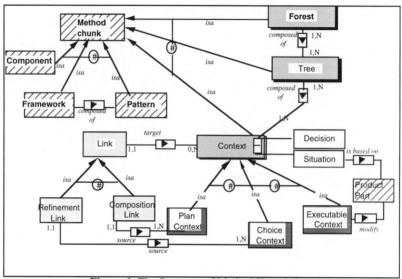

Figure 1 The Structure of Method Knowledge.

According to their type, method chunks are classified into *component, pattern* or *framework*. The entire OMT method description is an example of component, a set of generic guidelines for concept identification is an example of pattern, the NATURE meta-method (the method to guide the construction of any NATURE way-of-working) is an example of framework. This classification is borrowed from the Object Oriented area and shall be made precise in the next section.

According to their granularity, method chunks are classified into *forests, trees* or *contexts*. Within the OMT method, a single piece of knowledge such as the description of a Class in the Dictionary is modelled as a context. This context couples the decision Describe_Class_into_Dictionary to the situation a Class_has_ been_created. The set of guidelines to Identify_ a_Class is a more complex chunk of knowledge which can be modelled as a tree to compose the context for Identifying_the_Class and the one for Validating_The_Class. The OMT methodology itself can be represented as a forest of trees, with a tree for each model, namely the Object Model, the Dynamic Model and the Functional Model.

Figure 1 shows that these two classifications of method chunks are orthogonal. They constitute two ways of clustering the method base elements, each method chunk being represented in each of the two clusters. Besides, each cluster is a partition. Thus, a component is neither a pattern nor a framework; a forest is neither a tree nor a context. In the following, we consider the two orthogonal classifications in detail. We first consider the issue of uniform representation of chunks and thereafter their typology.

2.2   Chunk representation

The modelling formalism used to represent method knowledge has been designed with a certain view of engineering process support in mind. We believe that methods which aim at supporting engineering processes must be *contextual*. At any moment, each application or method engineer is in a subjectively perceived *situation* which is looked upon with some specific *intention of decision* in mind. The NATURE modelling formalism (Rolland, 1994), (Rolland, 1995) makes the notions of situation, decision, as well as *context* explicit.

As shown in Figure 1 the notion of *context* constitutes the basic building block of our method modelling approach. Contexts can be linked repeatedly in a hierarchical manner to define *trees*. A tree is composed of *contexts* and *links*. As shown in Figure 1, links are of two kinds : *refinement links* which allow the refinement of a large-grained context into finer ones and *composition links* for the decomposition of a context into component contexts.

A *method* is represented as a collection of hierarchies of contexts that we refer to as a *forest*. This reflects our view of methodological support being based on disconnected prescriptions, i.e. context trees which are not linearly sequenced but which can be dynamically combined according to the situation at hand.

Contexts, trees and forests are the three kinds of method chunks stored in the method base. They might be looked upon as structured modules of knowledge for supporting decision making in engineering processes. Figure 2 presents a partial method for defining an ER diagram made of a forest composed of four trees. Each tree is related to a specific issue : Entity-Type (ET) description (tree 1), Relationship-Type (RT) construction (tree 2), ET checking (tree 3) and ET mapping (tree 4). They will be progressively explained in the remaining of this section.

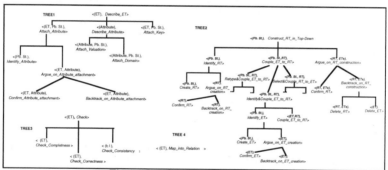

Figure 2 Excerpt of an ER method.

Contexts are defined as couples <situation, decision>, where the *decision* part represents the choice an engineer can make at a moment in the engineering process and the *situation* is defined as the part of the product it makes sense to make a decision on. Notice that our notion of method chunk strongly couples the process part to the product part. Details about this coupling and the product meta-model can be found in (Schmitt, 1993) and (Schmitt, 1995). A decision corresponds to an intention, a goal that the engineer wants to fulfil. Finally contexts can be of three *types*, namely executable, choice or plan. Each type of context plays a specific role in a tree. We now consider each of these types of contexts in turn.

Executable Context

An *executable context* corresponds to a decision which is directly applicable through actions which induce a transformation of the product under development. In tree2 of Figure 2, the context<*(Pb. St.), Create-RT*> is an executable context, (Pb. St. is the abbreviation of Problem Statement). The intention to *Create a Relationship-Type* is immediately applicable through the performance of an action for creating a new Relationship-Type (RT) in the specification under development. Executable contexts are the atomic blocks of our methods. They are often the leaves of trees. Non atomic contexts are built over contexts using refinement or composition links.

Choice Context

When building a product, an engineer may have several alternative ways to solve an issue. For this purpose we introduce the second type of context, namely the *choice context*. The execution of such a context consists of choosing one of its alternatives, i.e. selecting a context representing a particular strategy for the resolution of the issue raised by the context. For example in Figure 2, the context *<(RT, ETs); Argue-on-RT-construction>* is a Choice context introducing two alternatives to a Relationship-Type construction, namely to confirm its creation (*<(RT, ETs); Confirm-RT>*) or to withdraw it (*<(RT, ETs); Backtrack-on-RT-construction>*). Arguments are defined to support or object to the various alternatives of a choice context. For example, the *backtracking-on-RT-construction* is the right decision to make either when the relationship between entities is not sensible or when it is not relevant. Description arguments play an important role in the process model. They help in capturing heuristics followed by the application engineer in choosing the appropriate problem solving strategy.

Finally, it is important to notice that the alternatives of a choice context are contexts too. In the previous example, the first alternative is an executable context and the second one is a plan context. But they could be choice contexts introducing what is referred to as a refinement link between contexts.

As illustrated in Figure 2, we use a graphical notation for contexts and trees. For the sake of conciseness, we will also use a textual notation which, in the case of choice contexts, is based on the OR logical connector (denoted ") between alternatives (denoted alt_i). Thus, the textual notation for a choice context (CC) is : $CC = alt_1 \ "alt_2 \ "... \ " \ alt_n$. For instance, the textual notation for the *<(RT, ETs), Argue-on-RT-construction>* context is *<(RT, ETs), Confirm-RT>* " *<(RT, ETs), Backtrack-on-RT-construction>*.

Plan Context

In order to represent situations requiring a set of decisions to be made for fulfilling a certain intention (for instance to *Construct a RT* in the ER methodology) the modelling formalism includes a third type of context called the plan context. A plan context can be looked upon as a macro issue which is decomposed into sub-issues, each of which corresponds to a sub decision associated to a component situation of the macro one. Components of a plan context are also contexts but related through a *composition link*.

In Figure 2, the context *<(Pb. St.), Construct-RT>* is a plan context composed of three component contexts, namely *<(Pb. St.), Identify-RT>*, *<(Pb. St., RT), Couple-ET-to-RT>*, *<(RT, ETs), Argue-on-RT-construction>*. This means that, when constructing an RT, the method engineer has first to identify the RT, then couple it to all the ETs participating in it, and finally, argue on the construction of the RT. Component contexts of a plan context can be organised in a sequential, iterative and/or parallel manner.

In the textual notation of plan contexts, the sequence is represented by a "•", iteration is denoted by "*" and parallelism by the shuffle symbol "⋀". Therefore, the textual representation of the plan depicted in Figure 3 is *<(Pb. St.), Construct-RT>* = *<(Pb. St.), Identify-RT>* • *<(Pb. St., RT), Couple-ET-To-RT>** • *<(RT, ETs), Argue-on-RT-construction>*.

It can be seen that the uniform representation looks upon chunks as modules. These modules are cohesive : they are contextual and can be used in specific situations to carry out specific intentions. This ensures a tight coupling between the product and process aspects of methods and a chunk represents both these aspects in a unified way. Besides being cohesive, the uniform representation provides loose coupling through the graft (Schwer, 1995) operation. By a use of this operation it is possible to break away from the strict, artificial linearity of methods and couple chunks together more dynamically.

2.3 Chunk typology

Looking to method chunks as reusable elements leads us to classify them into three categories namely, *components, patterns* and *frameworks*.

Early method engineering approaches (Welke, 1991), (Harmsen, 1994) assume that method construction is an assembly process of methods fragments. These method fragments are method specific and can be product or process parts of existing methodologies. One can draw an analogy between such method fragments and reusable classes in object oriented approaches. We refer to these as *method components* or simply *components*.

However, our belief is in the existence of a corpus of both, generic *method knowledge* and generic *method construction knowledge* which has not been looked after, identified and described yet. Our proposal is to develop a *domain analysis* approach to identify objects, rules and constraints which are

  (a) common among different (but similar) methods
  (b) common among different (but similar) ways of method construction
and to formalize them as method chunks.

In this way, method engineering can use the results of method domain analysis and save a significant amount of time as demonstrated in other domains (Arango, 1989). If we assume that the degree of similarity which exists in the construction of methods which belong to the same area is similar to the equivalent degree in system requirements engineering, then method domain analysis can result in significant overall productivity improvement in method construction. Indeed, Jones (Jones, 1984) indicates that only 15% of the requirements for a new system are unique to the system; the remaining 85% comes from the requirements of existing similar ones.

We introduce the notion of *framework* to model commonalties among methods and the notion of a *method construction pattern, pattern* for short, to capture generic laws governing the construction of different but similar methods. A framework is a method chunk which formalizes, in a more abstract way than a component does, knowledge which is common among several methods. A pattern models a common behaviour in method construction. It is generic in the sense that it is used by a typical method engineer in every method construction process. It is more abstract than a component or a framework. Both terms have been chosen by analogy to reuse approaches in the object oriented area. Patterns are there defined as solutions to generic problems which arise in many applications (Gamma, 1993), (Pree, 1995) whereas a framework is application domain dependent (Wirfs-Brock, 1990), (Johnson, 1988).

All examples provided in the previous paragraph belong to the class of method components. In the following, we exemplify the notions of framework and pattern within the NATURE meta-method.

Method Construction Pattern

There can be many different kinds of construction patterns, like the *Identify, Describe, Construct* and *Define patterns*. A more detailed presentation of these patterns can be found in (Rolland, 1996). These patterns already form a part of our method base. In addition, we are in the process of defining additional patterns for *checking* and *refinement*. In this section, we illustrate the notion of a pattern through the *Describe* pattern. Its genericity is brought out by applying it to OMT and ER approaches.

We carried out a domain analysis and tried to identify common patterns of behaviour that method engineers shall exhibit when instantiating the concepts of the NATURE modelling formalism in order to construct methods. This leads us to two major conclusions :

- there exist generic laws underlying method construction; these laws are generic in the sense that they can be applied to the construction of many methods. Using these laws, we generate for instance, six of the traditional analysis methodologies, OMT, OOA, SA/SD, ER, O* and OOD. These laws can be encapsulated in method construction patterns and made available in a library, the method base. Patterns are method chunks and therefore, like any other method chunk, can be expressed using the NATURE modelling formalism : patterns are trees of contexts.

- the structure of the product generated by the method is a key constructional factor and, therefore, the main parameter of the generic laws. We have calculated, for example, that varying the typology of concepts used to represent the OM product structure of OMT can lead to 13000 different ways of engineering it. This demonstrates, in some way, the genericity of the patterns and partly provides a measure of their effectiveness.

Let us take for instance, the example of any description of a concept in a schema - whatever the product under construction is (e.g. ER, OMT, etc.) - such a description follows the pattern shown Figure 3. The pattern identifies discriminant criteria which are, in this case, types of concepts. For instance, we make the distinction between *constructional concepts* - which participate to the structuration of the product - and *definitional concepts* - which only contribute to the definition of the constructional concepts (Prakash , 1994). For instance, in an ER model, an Entity-Type (ET) is an example of a constructional concept whereas a Domain is a definitional concept. Definitional concepts are further refined into *Properties, Prop, Constraint,* Const, or *Cd-Concept,* Cd (concept for the definition of another concept). In an ER model, the Valuation of an Attribute is a Property, the Key of an Entity-Type is a Constraint and the Attribute could be regarded as a definitional concept participating in the description of the constructional concept Entity-Type. Besides, from the point of view of their granularity, concepts are classified into *atomic concepts* - they are stand-alone concepts and *compound concepts* - they are built upon other concepts. In an ER model, a Relationship-Type will be a compound concept while a Domain is an atomic concept.

It is important to notice that the classification of concepts of a given model (let say the ER model) is not unique but specific to each method based on this model. For instance, a particular ER based method can consider the concept Attribute as a Cd-concept participating in the definition of Entity-types whereas it could be a constructional concept in another method. Therefore, different topologies of concepts can be derived for the same model from the above classification.

$<(C)$, *Describe_C>* = ⋀ $(<(C, Pb.St.)$, *Attach_Cd>** • $<(Cd)$, *Describe_Cd>** , $<(C, Pb.St.)$, *Attach_Prop>**) • $<(C, Pb.St.)$, *Attach_Const>**) $<(C, Pb.St.)$, *Attach_Cd>* = $<(Pb.St.)$, *Identify_Cd>* • $<(C, Cd)$, *Argue_on_Cd_attachment>*   ∪ $<(Pb.St.)$, *Identify_Cd>* $<(C, Cd)$, *Argue_on_Cd_attachment>* = $<(C, Cd)$, *Confirm_Cd_attachment>* ∪ $<(C, Cd)$, *Backtrack_on_Cd_attachment>*   ⋀ : shuffle   • : sequence   ∪ : alternative

Figure 3 The Pattern for concept description.

The pattern in Figure 3 is a plan-context stating that the description of a concept C requires the attachment of all its definitional concepts ($<(C, Pb.St.)$, *Attach_Cd>**) followed by their description ($<(Cd)$, *Describe_Cd>**), the attachment of its properties ($<(C, Pb.St.)$, *Attach_Prop>**), and constraints ($<(C, Pb.St.)$, *Attach_Const>**). The shuffle symbol indicates that the attachment of properties and definitional concepts can be made in any order.

The generic method construction pattern is based on the recursive description of a concept (since Cd "is-a" C, Describe_Cd "is_a" Describe_C). This allows us to deal with compound definitional concepts which have themselves to be described. Attachment may be with

(<(Pb.St.), *Identify_Cd*> • <(C, Cd), *Argue_on_ Cd_ attachment*>) or without argumentation (<(Pb.St.), *Identify_Cd*>).

When applying the pattern to each concept of the model in use, the method engineer has first, to instantiate Cd, Prop and Const for this concept and secondly to choose an order for the various attachments or to leave open the option of their intertwining. This results in a plan-context which is the methodological guideline for describing a concept. The previous actions must be repeated for each component context of the plan referring to a compound definitional concept . This will result in a tree structure as a methodological guideline. Figure 4 gives the tree generated by the application of this pattern to the concept of Entity-Type.

<(ET), *Describe_ET*> = (<(ET, Pb.St.), *Attach_Attribute*>* • <(Attribute),
Describe_Attribute>*) • <(ET, Pb.St.), *Attach_Key*>
<(ET, Pb.St.), *Attach_Attribute*> = <(Pb. St.), *Identify_Attribute*> • <(ET, Attribute),
Argue_on_ Attribute_attachment>
<(ET, Attribute), *Argue_on_Attribute_attachment*> = <(ET, Attribute), *Confirm_Attribute
_attachment*> ∪ <(ET, Attribute), *Backtrack_on_Attribute_attachment*>
<(Attribute), *Describe_Attribute*> = <(Attribute, Pb.St.), *Attach_Valuation*> • <(Attribute,
Pb.St.), *Attach_Domain*>

Figure 4 Instantiating the *Describe* pattern on the concept of Entity-Type.

The corresponding graphical representation is shown in Figure 5. It corresponds also to tree 1 in Figure2. The method engineer has chosen to sequentially order the attachment of Attributes to Entity-types, their description and the Key constraint definition. This corresponds to the first instantiation of the *Describe* pattern. He/she chose to argue on the attachment of Attributes to Entity-Types but not on the one of the Key. Finally, since Attribute is a compound definitional concept, the *Describe* pattern has to be applied a second time to decide in which way attributes will be described. Assume, there are two properties describing the Attribute concept namely, Valuation and Domain and no constraint. The <(Attribute), *Describe_Attribute*> context is then a plan-context with two executable component contexts, <(Attribute, Pb. St.), *Attach_ Valuation*> and <(Attribute, Pb.St.), *Attach_Domain*> .

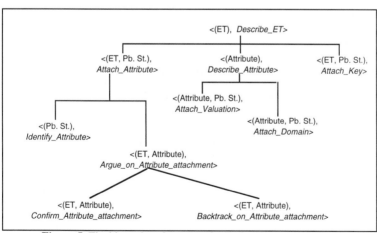

Figure 5 The hierarchy of contexts for Entity-Type description.

For constructing an ER method, the *Describe* pattern will be applied to every constructional concept of the model e.g. Entity-Type and Relationship-Type. But it can be applied in a similar way to generate description guidelines for any other concept in any other method. As an illustration, Figure 6 shows, in a textual form, the tree generated for the description of the concept Association of the OMT methodology.

```
<(Association), Describe_Association> =
        <(Association, Pb.St, Attach_Attribute_to-Association>* • <(Attribute),
Describe_Attribute>*,
        • <(Association, Pb.St), Attach_Multiplicity_to_Association>*

<(Association, Pb.St), Attach_Attribute_to_Association> =
        (<(Pb.St), Identifiy_Attribute>
            • <(Association, Attribute),
Argue_on_Attachment_of_Attribute_to_Association>)

<(Attribute), Describe_Attribute> =
        (<(Attribute, Pb.St), Attach_Domain_to_Attribute>
        • <(Attribute, Pb.St), Attach_Valuation_to_Attribute>

<(Association, Attribute), Argue_on_Attachment_of_Attribute_to_Association> =
        <(Association, Attribute), Confim_Attachment_of_Attribute_to_Association>
        " <(Association, Attribute), Backtrack_on_Attribute_Attachment>
```

Figure 6 Instantiating the *Describe* pattern on the concept of Association.

An association is a constructional concept with two definitional concepts: its attributes and its multiplicity. Therefore, the description of an association is guided by a plan consisting of the attachment of attributes to the association (<(Association, Pb.St, Attach_Attribute_to_Association>*), their description (<(Attribute), Describe_ Attribute>*) followed by the attachment of the multiplicity constraint related to each of its roles (<(Association, Pb.St), Attach_Multiplicity_to_Association>*). Notice that the shuffle has no influence since an association does not have properties and has only one Cd-concept, attribute. Consequently there is only one possible ordering of contexts in the plan.

The importance of patterns lies in their genericity, in their ability to be used systematically in constructing a large number of methods. Chunks which are patterns make available this genericity to method engineers.

Method framework

Frameworks have already proved their efficiency in software design (Johnson, 1991), (Johnson, 1988), (Wirfs-Brock, 1990) and particularly in interface development (Krasner, 1988), (Wilson, 1991), (Weinand, 1989). The design and improvement of frameworks (Wirfs-Brock, 1990), (Johnson, 1991) have been studied and approaches developed. In information systems design, a number of conceptual frameworks have been proposed (Olle , 1988), (Pohl , 1993), (Krogstie , 1995a) and even merged (Krogstie , 1995b). We believe that method frameworks can play a role in method construction and should be integrated in method bases. The way we understand the concept of framework is close to the notion of outline in (Harmsen, 1994) and road map. Let us take, as an example, the NATURE meta-method.

In the NATURE project we initially addressed the problem of constructing methods by providing a process meta-model (the NATURE formalism presented in the previous section), under which methods can be generated by instantiating the meta-model. This provides a way by which method engineers can define, in a systematic manner, the desired methods. However, this does not obviate the need for a prescribed method for the method engineer, the meta-method, which could be followed for method construction.

When developing the meta-method, it was possible to develop yet another formalism for representing it. However, by extending the NATURE contextual approach to the meta-method, it was possible to represent it in contextual terms, apply the modelling formalism to the meta-method, and treat it as just any other method. The NATURE method, once prescribed, can be used within the MENTOR environment which provides guidance to any process which is in accordance with it. Therefore, since the meta-method is just another process, we can extend the full guidance capability to it.

The meta-method is encapsulated in a framework depicted in Figure 7. We organise the construction of a specific method as a plan composed of three components to respectively, find the basic blocks of the method under construction (<(Method Statements), *Find_Basic_Blocks>*) then, to assemble the basic blocks into trees (<(Product Structure, Basic Blocks), *Build _Trees>*) and, finally, to describe each context of the forest in detail (<(Contexts), *Specify_Forest>*).

The generation of basic blocks assumes the existence of the product structure for the method under construction as well as of the relevant types of decision for decision making. Therefore, the meta-method suggests a plan where the constructional factors are defined first (<(Method Statements), *Build_Product_Structure>*), then the decision types are identified <(Method Statements), *Identify_Types_ of_Decision>* and finally, the basic blocks are generated (<(Product Structure), *Generate_ Basic_Blocks>*).

The gathering of basic blocks in trees asks for a definition of the approaches. Therefore, the context <(Product Structure, Basic Blocks), *Build_Trees>* is further defined in the meta-method as a plan with two components, to choose the approaches <(Product Structure), *Choose_Approaches>*, and to achieve the gathering of basic blocks to generate the method trees <(Product Structure, Basic Blocks), *Generate_Trees>*.

The formal specification of the method consists of repeating the component (<(Context), *Specify_Context>*) to specify contexts.

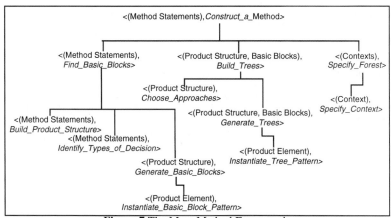

Figure 7 The Meta-Method Framework.

Frameworks often use patterns (Krasner, 1988) (this justified the composed-of relationship in Figure 1). As shown in Figure 7 our proposal is to support the generation of basic blocks by method construction patterns. Therefore, the application of the framework calls for the instantiation of the appropriate patterns. Generic patterns are classified into two : those which build basic blocks for each product element of the product structure (<(Product Element),

Instantiate_Basic_Block_Pattern>) and those which relate these blocks together (*<(*Product Element*), Instantiate_Tree_Pattern>*).

3   THE METHOD META-KNOWLEDGE LEVEL

Assuming that method chunks for components, patterns and frameworks exist, the question now is "how to deliver the relevant method chunks to the user?" We shall look at this question in two ways : first, by describing the semantic contents of the method base in a manner which eases the retrieval of chunks meeting the requirements of the user and, secondly, by providing query facilities.

Description of method knowledge is knowledge about method knowledge i.e. *method meta-knowledge*. We use the notion of *descriptor* (De Antonellis, 1991) as a means to describe method chunks. A descriptor plays for a method chunk the same role as a meta-class does for a class. The concept of descriptor is similar to the one of faceted classification schema (Prieto-Diaz, 1987) developed in the context of software reuse.

The knowledge that should be provided by the descriptor aims at facilitating the use of the method base. If we keep in mind that the knowledge base shall facilitate the construction of a method suitable for a specific project, then the descriptor must help in categorizing the situation in which a method chunk is relevant for a certain purpose. The method engineer, as a user of the method base, is faced to a certain *situation* which he/she looks upon with a certain *intention* in mind. He/she is placed in a certain *context* that he/she should be able to formulate as a query to the method base. Consequently, the descriptor shall also be organised in a contextual fashion. This means that a descriptor must categorize the situation in which the chunk can be used and describe the intention of its use.

Thus, we propose to extend our contextual approach to the representation of method meta-knowledge. A descriptor can be seen as a *meta-context* which links the situation in which a method chunk is relevant to the intention the chunk allows to fulfil. The situation part refers to the characteristics of the projects in the development of which the chunk can be used as part of the project method. The intention part refers to the engineering intention(s) that could be fulfilled when using the chunk.

A descriptor shall naturally be associated to every method chunk, irrespective of its granularity. However gathering of chunks into other chunks such as forests might be justified because these chunks have a unique context of use and, therefore, a unique descriptor. We consider it is the role of the method base administrator to reorganize the initial method chunks in the light of their description. This justifies a classification of forests (see 3.1) into *methods* (forests which represent methods) and *groups* (forests which gather trees having the same use). Similarly, for facilitating the use of the method base, the administrator can build hierarchies of descriptors associated with hierarchies of forests. This shall permit a hierarchical search in the method base by refining progressively the characterisation of the project situation and/or the method engineering intention.

In the next section we consider the method meta-knowledge in detail. In the subsequent section we shall illustrate its use by introducing the query language through examples.

3.1   Method meta-knowledge organisation

Figure 8 depicts the way the meta-knowledge is organized using the same ER like notations that have been used for the knowledge part in Figure 1. For the sake of readability, the representation of the knowledge part has been restricted to the elements required to understand the links with the meta-knowledge part.

As introduced before, a method chunk is placed and described in the context of its potential use in specific projects. A method chunk is said to be relevant *for* (relationship-type *for* in Figure 8) a certain *situation* (entity-type *situation*) *to* (relationship-type *to*) achieve a certain *intention* (entity-type *intention*). For example, Chunk c is applicable *for <u>high risk project</u>* (characterization of the situation) *to <u>a reengineering purpose</u>* (intention).

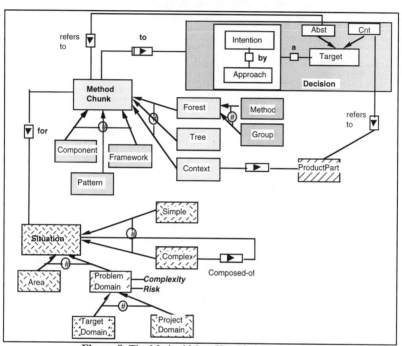

Figure 8 The Method Meta Knowledge Structure.

The NATURE contextual modelling approach refines the concept of *Decision* into *Intention* and *Approach* (Rolland, 1995). The intention is the goal to be achieved, the approach is the way to reach the goal. Further a Decision has a *Target* which is expressed in terms of *Product Parts*. As shown in Figure 8, all these aspects are relevant in a descriptor as they are discriminant criteria for the selection of method chunks. The intentional part of the descriptor can then express that a chunk is relevant *to* (relationship-type *to* in Figure 8) achieve *a* (relationship-type *a* in Figure 8) targeted intention *by* a given approach. Therefore the previous example can be refined in the following way : Chunk c is applicable *for <u>high risk project</u> to <u>reengineer</u>* (intention) *a <u>business process</u>* (target) *by <u>domain based approach</u>* (approach).

Targets in descriptors are either abstract targets -which refer to type level i.e. to one of the types of method chunks- or concrete targets -which refer to instances of method chunks. This is modelled in Figure 8 by sub-typing *Target* into two, *Concrete Target (Cnt)* and *Abstract Target (Abst)* A concrete target refers to a Product Part whereas an abstract target refers to a Method Chunk (relationship-types *refers to* in Figure 8). For example, the descriptor of the forest (a group) composed of the collection of constructional patterns such as *Describe, Identify, Define* etc. has <u>*generate*</u> as *intention* and an *abstract target* which is a <u>*tree.*</u> On the other hand, the descriptor of the OMT forest (a method) describes the *intention* of the forest as <u>*requirements engineering*</u> and the *concrete target* as an <u>*analysis schema.*</u> This classification is helpful to formulate recursive queries whose outputs are abstract targets i.e. method chunks that can, in turn, be subjects of embedded queries. This shall be exemplified in the following section.

The situation part of a descriptor aims at providing the means to evaluate the adequacy of the method chunk to the situation of project at hand while the intention part tries to ensure that the goal of the project matches the goal of the method chunk. As shown in Figure 8 we propose to characterise the situation in two ways : (a) by the *Area* (entity-type *Area*) of the project and, (b) by the *complexity* and *risk* (properties of the entity-type *Problem Domain)* as two situational factors evaluated for both the *Project Domain* (entity-type *Project Domain*) and the *Target Domain* (entity-type *Target Domain*).

Our characterisation of the Problem Domain is based on the results achieved by the EUROMETHOD project (Franckson, 1994). The term Target Domain refers to the system to be engineered or re-engineered and its evaluation comprises two parts, one for the information system and another one for the computer system. Each of the two parts is further refined into detailed factors such as *size* of target domain, *heterogeneity of actors, complexity of data, complexity of target technology* etc. There are four aspects of the Project to evaluate : *tasks, structure, actors* and *technology.* Complexity measure has three values, simple (S), moderate (M) and complex (C); similarly the risk values are low (L), moderate (M) and high (H).

It is clear that all these situational factors cannot be evaluated for every descriptor; some of them may not even be meaningful for some descriptor. Thus, in order to leave the required level of flexibility and freedom to the method base administrator the *Situation* is specialized into *Simple Situation* (entity-type *Simple Situation* in Figure 8) and *Complex Situation* (entity-type *Complex Situation* in Figure 8) - a situation composed of situations. This allows us to describe a Context for *geopolitical game Area* and *C complexity of Target Domain.size* and *C complexity of Target Domain.heterogeneity of actors* and *M risk of Project.actors.*

A method chunk descriptor includes instances of elements introduced in Figure 8 as parts of the situation and decision which form its context of use. As a brief summing up of this section, we can point out that the NATURE contextual approach provides an elegant frame to model the meta-knowledge supporting situational method engineering. The key notion of a context is used here to describe the type of project, the problem domain situation, as well as the engineering purpose for which a method chunk can be used. Besides the same frame is applicable to concrete components (method fragments) and abstract patterns and frameworks. In the next section we exemplify the query mechanism to access the method base.

3.2   Using meta-knowledge to retrieve method knowledge

Access to method knowledge is through the meta-knowledge i.e. the descriptors. Based on the structure of the descriptor presented in the previous section, we propose a query language which is exemplified in this section. Navigation in this language is through the structure of a descriptor and is based on key words corresponding to entity-type names and relationship-type names.

In order to query the method base, the user has access to dictionaries which contain the values of the entity-types which are parts of the descriptor structure. He can access, for instance, the *intentions* which have chunks corresponding to them in the method base. Similarly, access can be obtained to chunks according to the known *areas.* Dictionaries are organized like thesaurus, in a hierarchical manner in which, for instance, the intention *engineering* is refined into *requirements engineering, design* and *implementation.* Requirements engineering could itself be refined into *requirements representation, specification* and *agreement.* Dictionaries are automatically updated in an interactive way at the time the method base administrator adds, removes or changes descriptors.

Below are some examples of queries focusing on the decision part of the descriptor. Key words are bold letters and comments are put into brackets in the query itself

Select forest **with name** (property of the ET) = 'OMT'

Select tree **to** specify(intention)
    a schema (target) **with name** = 'OM'

Select method chunk
to requirements engineering•representation.(sub-intention)
    by reuse (approach)
and to requirements engineering•agreement (sub-intention)
    by cooperation (approach)

With is used to introduce a selection based on an Entity-Type (ET) property. **To** is the name of the Relationship-Type (RT) which links the ET Method Chunk to the ET Decision (Figure 8). It is used for expressing a selection based on decision values. **By** and **a** play a similar role. The notation • is the dotted convention of query languages. In the last example it is used to manipulate sub-intentions (representation is a sub-intention of requirements engineering).

Select framework
    to engineer (intention)
    a method (target)
        to requirements engineering (target intention)
        by domain reuse (target approach)

Select pattern
    to generate (intention)
    a tree (target)
        to construct (target intention)
        a schema (sub-target)

These two queries aim at selecting abstract method chunks; they have abstract targets (method and tree) which are subjects of further selection just as any other method chunk can be. This leads to queries with an embedded form where a **to-a-by** clause is embedded in another **to-a-by** selection clause.

The remaining examples focus on selections based on the situation part of a descriptor. The queries could complement some of the previous ones.

Select method.
    for real time (area)

Select framework
    for business system (area)
        with risk-of project domain•structure = H
        and with risk-of project domain•actors = H

Select method
    for information system (area)
    with complexity-of target domain•size = C
    and with complexity-of target domain•technology= C
    and with risk-of project domain•tasks = H

The key word **for** is the name of the relationship-type which links the ET method Chunk to the ET Situation. It introduces the selection part based on the project and domain situation. The notation • allows the user to characterise the complexity and risk of both the project and domain using the subdivisions proposed.

The query language is currently under development in the MENTOR environment. It is being implemented on top of the O2 (O2, 1993) query language.

4   CONCLUSION

The essence of the contextual method engineering approach developed in this paper lies in the emphasis on decision making in specific situations in a rational manner. At the centre of this approach is the notion of a context, which is applied both to method knowledge and method meta-knowledge.

The contextual approach advocates a move from method fragments to method modules. These modules are both cohesive and loosely coupled. Cohesiveness results in modules which can be used in specific situations in specific ways whereas loose coupling makes it possible to move away from a rigid, linear modular sequence to more dynamic module interaction.

Method knowledge at different levels of abstraction and granularity is all expressed in the same representation, that of a chunk modelled with the NATURE contextual formalism. This can been gainfully exploited to enact any chunk, whatever its abstraction or granularity, thanks to the enactment mechanism of the MENTOR environment which guides any process modelled in the terms of this formalism.

Future work shall concentrate on the discovery of new patterns and the implementation of the query language.

5   REFERENCES

Arango G (1989), *"Domain analysis : from art to engineering discipline"*, Proc. 5th Int. Workshop on Software Specification and Design, IEEE Computer Society Press, San Diego

Bubenko J., Rolland C., Loucopoulos P., DeAntonellis V. (1994), *"Facilitating "Fuzzy to Formal" Requirements Modelling"*, IEEE 1st Int. Conference on Requirements Engineering, ICRE'94, pp 154-158

De Antonellis V., Pernici B., Samarati P. (1991) *"F-ORM METHOD : A methodology for reusing specifications"*, in Object Oriented Approach in Information Systems, Van Assche F., Moulin B., Rolland C. (eds), North Holland

Franckson M. (1994), *"The Euromethod deliverable model and its contribution to the objectves of Euromethod"*, Proc. IFIP-TC8 Int. Conf. on Methods and Tools for the Information Systems Life Cycle, Verrijn-Stuart and Olle (eds), North-Holland, pp131-149

Gamma E., Helm R., Johnson R., Vlissides J. (1993), *"Design patterns : Abstraction and Reuse of Object-Oriented Design"*, Proc. of the ECOOP'93 Conf., Sringer Verlag

Harmsen F et al (1994), *"Situational method engineering for informational system project approaches"*, in Method and Associated Tools for the Information Systems Life Cycle, Verrijn-Stuart and Olle (eds.), North Holland, pp169-194

Hidding G.J. (1994), *"Methodology information : who uses it and why not?"* Proc. WITS-94, Vancouver, Canada

Jones T.C. (1984), *"Reusability in programming : a survey of the state of the art"*, IEEE Transactions on Software Engineering,SE Vol 10, No1

Johnson R. E., Foote B. (1988), *"Designing reusable classes"*, Journal of Object-Oriented Programming, Vol 1, No3

Johnson R.E., Russo F. (1991), *"Reusing object-oriented design"*, Technical report UIUCDCS 91-1696, May 1991, University of Illinois

Krasner G.E, Pope S.T (1988), *"A cookbook for using the Model-View Controller user interface in Smalltalk-80"*, Journal of Object-Oriented Programming, Vol 1, No3

Krogstie J., Lindland O.I., Sindre G. (1995 a),*"Defining quality aspects for conceptual models"*, in E.D. Falkenberg et al., editor, Information Systems Concepts, Proc. ISCO3, Marburg, Germany, North Holland

Krogstie J., Lindland O.I., Sindre G, (1995 b), *"Towards a Depeer Understanding of Quality in Requirements Engineering"* in Advanced Information Systems Engineering, CAISE'95, Iivari J. and Lyytinen K. (eds), Springer Verlag

Lyytinen K. (1987), *"Different perspectives on information systems : problems and solutions"*, ACM Computing Surveys, Vol 19, No1

O2 (1993) *"The O2 User Manual December"*,

Olle T. W., J. Hagelstein, I. MacDonald, C. Rolland, F. Van Assche, A. A. Verrijn-Stuart, (1988), *"Information Systems Methodologies : A Framework for Understanding"*, Addison Wesley

Plihon V. (1994), *"The OMT, The OOA, The SA/SD, The E/R, The O*, The OOD Methodology"* NATURE Deliverable DP2

Plihon V., Rolland C. (1995), *"Modelling Ways-of-Working"*, Proc 7th Int. Conf. on Advanced Information Systems Engineering, CAISE'95, Springer Verlag

Pohl K. (1993), *"The Three Dimensions of Requirement Engineering"*, 5th Int. Conf. on Advanced Information Systems Engineering, Paris, France, June 1993

Prakash N. (1994), *"A Process View of Methodologies"*, 6th Int. Conf. on Advanced Information Systems Engineering, CAISE'94, Springer Verlag

N. Prat (1995), *"Using learning techniques for process model improvement"*, Internal report, CRI (Centre de Recherche en Informatique), University of Paris-Sorbonne

Pree W. (1995), *"Design Patterns for Object-Oriented Software Development"*, Addison Wesley

Prieto-Diaz R., Freeman (1987), P., *"Classifying software for reusability"*, IEEE Software, Vol. 4, No. 1

Rolland C. (1994), *"A Contextual Approach to modeling the Requirements Engineering Process"*, SEKE'94, 6th International Conference on Software Engineering and Knowledge Engineering, Vilnius, Lithuania

Rolland C., Souveyet C., Moreno M. (Rolland, 1995), *"An Approach for Defining Ways-Of-Working"*, Information Systems, Vol 20, No4, pp337-359

Rolland C., Plihon V. (1996), *"Using generic chunks to generate process models fragments"* in Proc.of 2nd IEEE Int. Conf. on Requirements Engineering", ICRE'96, Colorado Spring

Tempora (1994), Tempora ESPRIT project : final report

Schmitt J.R. (1993), *"Product Modeling in Requirements Engineering Process Modeling"*, IFIP TC8 Int. Conf. on Information Systems Development Process, Prakash., Pernici and Rolland (eds) North Holland

Schmitt J.R. (1995), *"Méta-modélisation des démarches d'analyse"*, Phd thesis, University of Paris6 Jussieu

Schwer S., Rolland C. (1995), *"Theoretical formalization of the process meta-modelling approach"*, internal CRI report 95-08, University of Paris 1, France.

Si-Said S., Rolland C., Grosz G. (1996), *"MENTOR : A Computer Aided Requirements Engineering Environment"*, in Proc 8th Int. Conf. on Advanced Information Systems Engineering (CAISE'96), Springer Verlag .

Weinand A., Gamma E., Marty R. (1989), *"Design and implementation of ET++, a seamless oject-oriented applcation framework"*, Journal of Structured Programming, Vol 10, No2, pp63-87

Welke R, and Kumar K. (1991), *"Method engineering : a proposal for situation-specific methodology construction"*, in Systems Analysis and Design : A Research Agenda, Cotterman and Senn(eds), Wiley

Wilson D.A, Rosenstein L.S., Shafer D. (1991), *"Programming with MacApp"*, Addison-Wesley

Wirfs-Brock J., Johnson R. (1990), *"Surveying current research in Object-Oriented Design"*, Communications of ACM, Vol 33, No9

6   BIOGRAPHY

Colette Rolland is currently Professor of Computer Science in the Department of Mathematics and Informatics at the University of Paris-1 Panthéon/Sorbonne. Her research interests lie in the areas of information modelling, databases, temporal data modelling, object-oriented analysis and design, requirements engineering, design methodologies, development process modelling and CASE tools. She has extensive experience in participating to national and european research projects under the ESPRIT programme (projects TODOS, BUSINESS CLASS, F3, NATURE, TOOBIS, ELKD and CREWS) and conducting co-operative projects with industry. She is the French representative in IFIP TC8 on "Information Systems" and chairperson of the IFIP Working Group WG8.1.

Naveen Prakash is currently Professor of Computer Science and Dean of the Department of Information Technology in the Delhi Institute of Technology. His research interests are in object oriented analysis, methods, CASE and META-CASE tools and Method Engineering. He had an extensive professional experience in research and development as the R&D Director of CMC, one of the largest software houses in India. He is member of the IFIP Working Group WG8.1 and the co-ordinator of the group's activities in Asia.

14

Comparison of four Method Engineering languages

F. Harmsen[1], M. Saeki[2]

[1]University of Twente, Department of Computer Science
IS Design Methodology Group
P.O. Box 217, 7500 AE Enschede, Netherlands

[2]Tokyo Institute of Technology
Department of Computer Science
2-12-1 O-okayama, Meguro-ku, Tokyo, 152, Japan

Abstract

Currently, several languages to represent and manipulate parts of IS engineering methods, techniques and tools are being used. These so-called Method Engineering languages can be classified into four categories: product-oriented, object-oriented, process- and decision-oriented, and hybrid. In this paper representatives of each of these categories are being reviewed. Meta-models of the languages are given, and each description is illustrated by an example specification. Focus of comparison is expressive power. The Method Engineering languages are compared on the basis of a number of requirements, which are deduced from the notions used in the Method Engineering domain.

Keywords

Method specification languages, Comparisons

1 INTRODUCTION

Method Engineering is the discipline to construct new methods from parts of existing methods. In order to successfully apply Method Engineering principles (Kumar and Welke, 1992; van Slooten and Brinkkemper, 1993), a specification language is needed with which method fragments, i.e. components of IS development methods (Harmsen et al., 1994), can be described and manipulated. We define a *Method Engineering language* as a modelling technique with the purposes:

- to represent IS development and management methods and fragments thereof, and
- to enable the assembly of information systems development methods by offering constructs to manipulate method fragments.

If such a language is only able to represent method fragments, we call it a meta-modelling language. Brinkkemper claims that every conceptual modelling language is suitable to serve as a meta-modelling language (Brinkkemper, 1990), and therefore suitable to represent method fragments. Various meta-modelling applications of languages originally intended for other domains, such as LOTOS in software process modelling (Saeki et al., 1991), show the validity of this claim. However, the expressive power with respect to Method Engineering of the various conceptual modelling languages differ considerably, turning some modelling languages more suitable for method specification and manipulation than others. Moreover, Method Engineering projects have different goals and objectives, which, again, makes it hard to choose a language superior in all cases.

As Method Engineering is becoming more mature, different schools of thought have been established concerning representation and manipulation languages. One school adopts a data-oriented approach, stressing the representation of the product aspect of methods. Method Engineering languages of this type include (G)OPRR (Smolander, 1992; Kelly et al., 1996), PSM-LISA/D (ter Hofstede, 1993), NIAM Concept Structure Diagrams (Brinkkemper, 1990; Wijers, 1991), semantic data models (Sowa and Zachman, 1992), and ASDM (Heym and Österle, 1992). Others adopt an object-oriented approach, such as Telos (Mylopoulos et al, 1990), Metaview (Sorenson et al., 1988), and Object Z (Saeki and Wen-Yin, 1994). The third school consists of languages evolved from or direct towards software process modelling and capturing design rationale. Among these languages are Task Structure Diagrams (Wijers, 1991; Verhoef and ter Hofstede, 1995), HFSP (Katayama, 1989; Song and Osterweil, 1992), ALF (Benali et al., 1989), and MERLIN (Emmerich et al., 1991). A last category are the so-called hybrid languages, taking into account different aspects and offering often explicit operations for Method Engineering. MEL (Harmsen and Brinkkemper, 1995ab) is an example of this type of language.

In this work, we have taken from each category one representative. We compare Object-Z, MEL, GOPRR, and HFSP. We also review the data models (meta-models) of these four Method Engineering languages. For the comparison, we have listed a number of requirements, some of which are quite generic, applying to all conceptual modelling languages, whereas others only address Method Engineering.

Related research is performed in the area of comparison of methods and techniques and CASE tools. Hong et al. (1993) compare eight object-oriented methods by comparing their data models. A "super method" acts as a reference model for the methods compared. Iivari (1994) relies, in line with the "CRIS" approach (Olle et al., 1983, 1991), on a normative comparison of object oriented methods, as he draws up a number of requirements which are compared with the methods' properties. In contrast to this, Oei and Falkenberg (1994) define a set of basic transformations, called the Meta Model Hierarchy transformations, to transform method fragments, via a sequence of basic steps, into each other. Operations are associated with the quality attributes expressive power, genericity and liberality. Their main criticism on an approach using a reference technique is, that it would be easy to create yet another modelling technique, whose concepts are not or only partly covered by the framework. Song and Osterweil (1992) take a similar approach as Hong's, comparing different methods on the basis of their underlying models. However, Song and Osterweil concentrate on process models, which are represented in the process modelling language HFSP. Other related research focuses on normative comparison of conceptual data models (Venable, 1993), CASE tools (Wijers and van Dort, 1990) or meta-CASE tools (Marttiin et al., 1993).

We have adopted the traditional CRIS approach for comparing Method Engineering languages. We claim that in limited application domains, such as Method Engineering, normative comparisons are possible. Concepts and relationships are fairly stable, in contrast to general application domains which are continually subject to additions. In this paper we have investigated the Method Engineering domain, and translated the results of these investigations to requirements for Method Engineering languages.

This paper is structured as follows. Section 2 deals with the requirements that are to be imposed on Method Engineering languages. Section 3 reviews the four chosen languages, whereas in section 4 a comparison between these languages based on the requirements is made. The paper ends with conclusions and suggestions for further research.

2 REQUIREMENTS FOR METHOD ENGINEERING LANGUAGES

According to Oei and Falkenberg (1994), a conceptual modelling language should have the expressive power to model the application domain in an effective manner, and should be practical to apply with respect to convenience, efficiency, and learnability. The application domain is Method Engineering, in particular representation of methods. In general, a Method Engineering language should also enable the administration of method fragments in the method base, the selection of method fragments, and their assembly into a situational method, but these operational aspects will not be considered in this paper.

2.1 The Method Engineering domain

A Method Engineering Language should support representation and manipulation of all types of method fragments. Not only should, for instance, a complete method like OMT be represented, but also its elementary concepts, such as "Object", "Activity", and "State". Moreover, specification of both products and processes should be supported. We have developed a classification framework which clarifies the different types of method fragments. We classify method fragments along the three dimensions *perspective, abstraction,* and *granularity layer*.

The perspective dimension constitutes of the *product* perspective and the *process* perspective. Product fragments are deliverables, milestone documents, models, diagrams, or concepts. For instance, "Functional Specification" and "Data Flow Diagram" are product fragments. Process fragments represent the stages, activities and tasks to be carried out. Examples of process fragments are: "Create Data Flow Diagram", "Perform Requirements Analysis", or "Make Data Model".

Furthermore, we distinguish between *conceptual* method fragments and *technical* method fragments. Conceptual method fragments are objective descriptions of information systems development methods or part thereof. For instance, a set of guidelines in the Information Engineering book (Martin, 1990) to construct ERD's is a conceptual method fragment, as is the description of ERD's concepts and relationships. Technical method fragments are the operational parts of a method, i.e. the tool components. An Entity Relationship Diagram editor is an example of a technical method fragment, as is its associated repository or the hypertext ERD procedure in a CASE tool process manager. Some conceptual fragments are to be supported by tools, and must therefore be accompanied by corresponding technical fragments.

A method fragment can reside at one of five possible granularity layers:

- Method, which addresses the entire object system. For instance, the Information Engineering method resides at this granularity layer.
- Stage, which addresses an abstraction level of the object system. An example of a method fragment at the Stage layer is a Technical Design Report.
- Model, which addresses an aspect of an abstraction level. Examples of method fragments at this layer are the Data Model, and the User Interface Model.
- Diagram, addressing the representation of an aspect of an abstraction level. For instance, the Entity Relationship Diagram or the State Transition Diagram are at this granularity layer.
- Concept, which addresses the concepts and associations the method fragments on the Diagram layer, as well as the manipulations defined on them. Examples are: "Entity", "Entity is involved in Relationship", and "Identify entities".

2.2   Requirements

Based on the framework presented in   section 2.1, the expressive power and practicality requirements have been adapted for Method Engineering, resulting in a number of requirements for Method Engineering languages. The requirements can be viewed from three perspectives: *importance, genericity,* and *Method Engineering domain.* The perspective *importance* is introduced because some requirements have more impact on modelling systems development methods than others, or are a logical consequence of others. The *genericity* perspective focuses on the extent to which requirements are generic, or Method Engineering specific. The *Method Engineering domain* perspective encompasses the three dimensions introduced in section 2.1.

Prerequisite

To our opinion the most important requirement, and therefore a prerequisite to all other requirements, is *suitability*. This requirement implies that the Method Engineering language should be learnable, efficient, and convenient for the method engineer. The language should contain concepts and constructs corresponding with the method engineer's intuition and the Method Engineering domain. The products and processes are to be modelled in an efficient way.

Method Engineering Domain

A group of requirements of secondary priority, all of equal importance and addressing the Method Engineering domain, are:

- Support of representation of both method *processes* and method *products*. The functional and behavioural contents of each activity need to be represented. The components and structure of products need to be specified. Also, support for hierarchical decomposition of both process descriptions and product descriptions to enable specification of contents should be provided. For instance, OMT's Object Design activity, a process description, consists of activities like "Optimise access paths", "Adjust structures", and "Design attribute details". OMT's Object Model, a product description, consists of concepts like "Object" and "Class", their properties, and relationships between them. The Method Engineering language should provide notations and means to represent these activities and products.

- Support of representation of both *operational* (*development*) and *project management* aspects of methods. These aspects should be distinguishable, but relationships between them have to be identifiable. For instance, a "Plan Object modelling" activity is related to the Object modelling activity (which is planned by it), its sub-activities, and its products, although it addresses a different aspect of the method.

- Support of representation of the *conceptual* and the *technical* (i.e., tools) side of methods. As with the difference between development and project management, conceptual aspects and technical aspects are related, but should also be distinguishable. A conceptual description of Entity Relationship Diagrams, for instance, only contains the concepts "Entity", "Relationship", "Attribute", and so forth. Properties are "name" and "definition". An implementation of Entity Relationship Diagrams, for instance a diagram editor or part of a CASE tool repository, needs additional concepts and properties, such as specifications of the symbols with which concepts are represented (rectangle, diamond, circle), access paths to internal storage, etc.

- The ability to *formally express constraints and rules* concerning method fragments. The mere representation of process fragments and product fragments does not suffice. Relationships among method fragments are subject to constraints, and method fragments themselves behave according to rules. For instance, a rule is: each data flow in a DFD should be specified by an Entity Relationship Diagram. Such rules cannot be expressed by simple cardinality constraints, but are important for the consistent application of method fragments. In particular for effective tool support, rules should be formally expressed. It is necessary that a Method Engineering language provides support for such formalised constraints and rules.

- Support for representation of *actors* and *roles* in the systems development process. In order to assign responsibilities and duties to people (the key factor) involved in systems development, it is necessary to provide mechanisms for representing so-called actors and the roles they play. An actor is considered an actual person, such as Henk de Vries or Haruhiko Suzuki, which play roles like project manager, analyst, programmer, and so forth.

- Distinction between *instance level* and *meta-level*, and support of both of them. The instance level consists of the actual systems development processes, such as "Create Inventory control object model", and products, such as "Inventory control object model". The meta-level addresses the method to be used on the instance level. Method fragments, such as "Create object model", belong to this level. Actual development processes, including their products and tools, are therefore instances of method fragments. The distinction is important, as developers generally only deal with the instance level, which is the level where the actual job is done. The meta-level is prescriptive, and influenced by the instance level, because experience gained in the actual development process has to be captured by the method fragments.

- Support of *non-determinism*. Actual systems development generally takes not place according to strict sequences of processes. Usually, a lot of non-deterministic activities take place, for instance in joint application development or prototyping, for which no strict sequencing can be provided. Non-determinism is also used to handle exceptional or unforeseen cases, such as excessively running out of time.

- Support of *parallel* processes. Systems development is teamwork, which is reflected in the parallel nature of many method processes. A Method Engineering language should be able to support this parallelism, both on the meta-level, for instance the parallel execution of data modelling and process modelling activities, and on the instance level, e.g., the parallel execution of data modelling activities A and B.

- Support for recording *design rationale*. As was already noted before, the instance level constantly forces to make changes on the meta-level. Project experience should be accumulated in the method fragments, which are relatively dynamic notions. One of the main mechanisms to benefit from experiences made earlier, is to record design or decision rationale. This implies that not only the decisions are described, but also the reasons why decisions have been made, including their pro and con arguments, motivations, etc. Design rationale can be viewed both on the instance level, for instance the pro and con's of introducing an additional object class "Level" in an inventory control system specification, and on the meta-level, for instance the reasons why State Transition Diagrams have been chosen in a particular method.

Generic requirements

Besides the overall prerequisite of suitability, and requirements regarding the Method Engineering domain, some requirements for Method Engineering languages are applicable to any specification language. These generic requirements, which are of less priority than the other two groups, are:

- Support of *modularisation* of method fragments. Effective re-use of method fragments demands for a modularisation mechanism in the language. Method fragments are essentially black boxes, which are to be selected and assembled based on their external specification; internal details should be encapsulated as much as possible. Related to this is the need for effective characterisation of method fragments. A language should supply the means to valuate properties in such a way, that each method fragment is uniquely identifiable. For instance, an Entity Relationship Diagram can be characterised by a goal (such as: "Data modelling"), a maturity level, a description of the capabilities needed to apply the technique, a set of application domain descriptions, and so forth. A method engineer does not need to know which concepts and relationships play a role in ERD, but can select by investigating its properties. The properties also provide a fine-grained classification of method fragments to support modularisation, as opposed to the coarse-grained classification described in section 2.1.
- Support for defining *views*. A method comprises everything needed for performing systems development, be it for a general case or for a specific case, resulting in a huge amount of activity descriptions, product descriptions, tools, etc. However, each actor in the systems development process requires only a relatively small portion of the method, which is its view on the method. For instance, a project manager has a different view, including project management activities, products and tools, than a programmer, who needs other parts of the method. The definition of views reduces complexity for a single actor, and increases learnability.
- Unambiguity, implying that a Method Engineering language should be formally, mathematically defined to avoid multiple interpretations and to be able to enact the method.

Venable (1993) uses a similar classification for evaluation of conceptual data models. He distinguishes between *criteria for semantic concepts*, *criteria for syntactic constructs*, and *criteria for relationships to other areas*. The first group contains criteria such as *richness* (expressive power), *minimality* (suitability, in particular efficiency), and problem domain correspondence (all the requirements concerning the Method Engineering domain). The criteria for syntactic constructs relate to the graphical representation of concepts and the relationship between syntax and semantics. The third group roughly corresponds to the *generic* requirements described above.

3 REVIEW OF METHOD ENGINEERING LANGUAGES

In this section four representative Method Engineering languages are reviewed. The concepts and relationships of each language are described in a data model or *meta model* (Brinkkemper, 1990). Meta models are depicted in an Entity Relationship Diagram notation, consisting of entities and relationships. This notation is used for the sake of presentation, to provide a quick overview. To get a further impression of each language, a small example concerning Entity Relationship Diagramming has been conceived.

3.1 Object-Z

The formal specification language Object-Z (Duke et al., 1991; Saeki and Wen-Yin, 1994) is an object oriented extension of the Z language semantically based on ZF set theory. In the object oriented paradigm, the system to be specified is considered as a collection of individual objects having internal states. Object-Z defines the objects by using class concepts where the definitions of their states (state variables), initial states, and the operations related to them are encapsulated. The class schema for the specification of a class may contain schema's for defining operations permitted on the objects. A class can inherit states and operations from other classes.

Figure 1 depicts the meta-model of Object-Z. In this figure, method fragments are modelled from the product and the process perspective. From the product perspective, the structures or types of the produced products and constraints on the product components are specified. To specify the processes, permitted manipulations on the method products are defined as operations. Behavioural constraints, such as execution ordering, are specified as pre- and post-conditions of the operations.

Method fragments are defined with the class schema of Object-Z. For defining product structures, a *method fragment* has *attributes* as state variables and *constraints* as logical formulas. Similarly, *operation*, defined by an operation schema of Object-Z for specifying manipulations on the products, has *variables* as input and output parameters and *predicates* as logical formulas which define the effect of the operations. Pre-conditions and post-conditions of the operation belong to predicate. Note that a method fragment has two relationships *inheritance* and *reference* with other method fragments. In this respect, Object-Z is remarkably different from other, non-object-oriented, Method Engineering languages.

The example in figure 2 depicts an Object-Z specification of a simple variant of Entity Relationship Diagramming. The class schema ERD_in_ConceptualLevel starts with the declaration of the conceptual structure of Entity Relationship Diagram. It contains a number of state variables, whose values express an instance of Entity Relationship Diagram class. They address the definition of the concepts of ERD, i.e. Entity, Relationship and Attribute. A
state variable is defined by its name and its type, for instance a powerset of the abstract basic type entity. The associations between them can be defined by maps, in the example of the association between entities and attributes a finite map from attribute to entity (EntityAttribute). The state variable declarations, i.e. attribute declarations are separated with a horizontal line from the state invariants, which denote constraints with respect to the state variables.

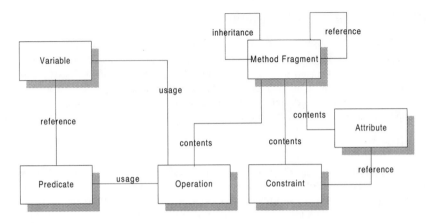

Figure 1 Meta-model of Object-Z.

For each permitted operation on the ERD_in_ConceptualLevel, such as IdentifyEntities, an operation schema is defined. Such a schema consists of variable declarations called signatures and predicates. The latter denote pre- and post-conditions for the operation. The Δ symbol indicates from which variables the values are changed by the operation. The ? symbol depicts input variables, and the variables with the prime represent the state after the operation.

The operations IdentifyEntities and IdentifyRelationships are for constructing conceptual ERDs and updating the state variables. For example, IdentifyEntities needs an input as a newly identified entity and adds it to the state variable Entity after its execution. This operation corresponds to the activity of identifying entities. The identified entities are stored in the state variable Entity. The operation IdentifyRelationships has a newly identified relationship and two entities participating in it as input parameters. The pre-condition, the first.formula below the horizontal line of the operation schema, specifies that the two entities should be already identified before its execution. Therefore, this formula specifies implicitly the execution order of IdentifyEntities and IdetifyRelationships, IdentifyEntities should be executed before IdentifyRelationships. EntityRelationship_1 and EntityRelationship_2 stand for the association between identified entities and relationships.

The class schema ERD_in_ConceptualLevel does not include sufficient information to specify Entity Relationship Diagrams. For example, the schema did not have the information that an entity can be represented with a rectangle. The class schema ERD_in_TechnicalLevel , depicted in figure 3, specifies this *notational* information of ERD. It inherits state variables and operations from ERD_in_ConceptualLevel. The inheritance mechanism allows us to specify various level descriptions of method fragments separately. We define new state variables which include the information of graphical components standing for the ERD concepts. For example, entities in this level are defined by a map from conceptual entities to rectangles. Each Entity is represented with a rectangle. A graphical component such as a rectangle consists of x co-ordinate, y co-ordinate and a label, i.e. location information and its identifier. The operations, e.g. CreateEntity and MoveEntity are editorial manipulations of these graphical components. For example, MoveEntity moves the entity e? to x-axis-direction dx and y-axis direction dy.

```
┌─ ERD_in_ConceptualLevel ──────────────────────────────────────────
│
│  ┌──────────────────────────────────────────────────────────────
│  │ Entity : ℙ entity
│  │ Relationship : ℙ relationship
│  │ Attribute : ℙ attribute
│  │ EntityRelationship_1 : relationship ⇸ entity
│  │ EntityRelationship_2 : relationship ⇸ entity
│  │ EntityAttribute : attribute ⇸ entity
│  │ RelationshipAttribute : attributes ⇸ relationship
│  │ Cardinality : Relationship ⇸ (ℕ × ℕ)
│  ├──────────────────────────────────────────────────────────────
│  │ dom EntityAttribute ⊆ Attribute ∧ ran EntityAttribute ⊆ Entity
│  │ dom RelationshipAttribute ⊆ Attribute ∧ ran RelationshipAttribute ⊆ Relationship
│  │ dom Cardinality ⊆ Relationship
│  │ status = "completion" ⇒
│  │     ∀ e : Entity ∃ r : Relationship • EntityRelationship_1(r, e) ∧ EntityRelationship_2(r, e)
│  └──────────────────────────────────────────────────────────────
│
│  ┌─ IdentifyEntities ───────────────────────────────────────────
│  │ Δ(Entities)
│  │ new_entity? : entity
│  ├──────────────────────────────────────────────────────────────
│  │ Entity' = Entity ∪ {new_entity?}
│  └──────────────────────────────────────────────────────────────
│
│  ┌─ IdentifyRelationships ──────────────────────────────────────
│  │ Δ(Relationship, EntityRelationship_1, EntityRelationship_2)
│  │ new_relationship? : relationship
│  │ domain_entity?, range_entity? : entity
│  ├──────────────────────────────────────────────────────────────
│  │ domain_entity? ∈ entities ∧ range_entity? ∈ entities
│  │ Relationship' = Relationship ∪ {new_relationship?}
│  │ EntityRelationship_1' = EntityRelationship_1 ∪ {new_relationship? ⇸ domain_entity?}
│  │ EntityRelationship_2' = EntityRelationship_2 ∪ {new_relationship? ⇸ range_entity?}
│  └──────────────────────────────────────────────────────────────
│
│  . . .
└────────────────────────────────────────────────────────────────────
```

Figure 2 Description of conceptual ERD.

```
┌─ ERD_in_TechnicalLevel ──────────────────────────────────────────────
│ ┌─ ERD_in_ConceptualLevel ──────────────────────────────────────────
│ │
│ │  entity_symbols : Entity ⇸ Rectangle
│ │  attribute_symbols : Attribute ⇸ Circle
│ │  relatioship_symbols : Relationship ⇸ Diamond
│ │  . . .
│ │ ───────────────────────────────────────────────────────────────────
│ │  dom EntityGraphicalObject = Entity
│ │  ∀ e : Entity ∀ a : Attribute • EntityAttribute(a) = e ⇒
│ │      connected(entity_symbols(e), attribute_symbols(a))
│ │  ∀ r : Relationship ∀ a : Attribute • RelationshipAttribute(a) = r ⇒
│ │      connected(relationship_symbols(e), attribute_symbols(a))
│ │  ∀ e1, e2 : Entity ∀ rel : Relationship •
│ │      EntityRelationship_1(rel) = e1 ∧ EntityRelationship_2(rel) = e2 ⇒
│ │          connected(relationship_symbols(rel), entity_symbols(e1)) ∧
│ │          connected(relationship_symbols(rel), entity_symbols(e2))
│ └───────────────────────────────────────────────────────────────────
│ ┌─ CreateEntity ────────────────────────────────────────────────────
│ │ Δ(entity_symbols)x?, y? : Coordinate
│ │ label? : String
│ │ ───────────────────────────────────────────────────────────────────
│ │ IdentifyEntities
│ │ entity_graphical_oject' = entity_symbols ∪ {new_object? ↦ < x?, y?, label? >}
│ └───────────────────────────────────────────────────────────────────
│ ┌─ MoveEntity ──────────────────────────────────────────────────────
│ │ Δ(entity_symbols)
│ │ e? : Entity
│ │ dx?, dy? : Coordinate
│ │ ───────────────────────────────────────────────────────────────────
│ │ ∀ x, y : Coordinate, ∀ label : String • entity_symbols(e?) =< x, y, label >⇒
│ │     entity_symbols' = entity_symbols ∪ {e? ↦< x + dx?, y + dy?, label >}
│ │ . . .
│ └───────────────────────────────────────────────────────────────────
│ . . .
└──────────────────────────────────────────────────────────────────────
```

Rectangle ::= Coordinate × Coordinate × String
. . .

Figure 3 Description of technical ERD.

3.2 MEL

MEL (Harmsen and Brinkkemper, 1995ab) is a language to describe and manipulate parts of IS development methods, and designed to support Method Engineering. The language offers representation mechanisms to describe methods on different levels of granularity. MEL facilitates both representation of method processes and method product models, as well as the tools that accompany a method. It is founded upon a definition in first order predicate logic. The product models, called product fragments, can be related to the process representations (process fragments) through relationships, represented by MEL keywords. Such relationships include: *prerequisite*, which relates the product fragments required by a process fragment, and *manipulation*, relating the product fragments manipulated by a process fragment in a certain *role*, such as update, production, or usage. Product fragments can be involved in an *association*, or can *precede* each other. A product fragment can be associated to one or more *rules*, specifying a static constraint, and can be, on a higher granularity level, represented by a graphical symbol. Product fragments can be described in terms of *ontology* concepts and associations which is especially useful when assembling product fragments from different methods.

For process fragments, *decision* and *iteration* constructs are provided. Moreover, it is possible to specify parallelism. Process and product fragments are characterised by a number of predefined *property types* and *values*, the latter being taken from a number of pre-defined methodology-related value *domains*. Process and product fragments can be specialised, and it is possible to specify *abstract*, polymorphic product fragments (cf. templates) , which can be parametrised in the specialisation. Such polymorphic method fragments are also used to define role-specific *views*. Such a view is a specialisation which only contains the relevant parts for a specific actor type. Tool aspects are handled by providing special constructs, such as **SYMBOL**, and property types, such as colour and coordinates.

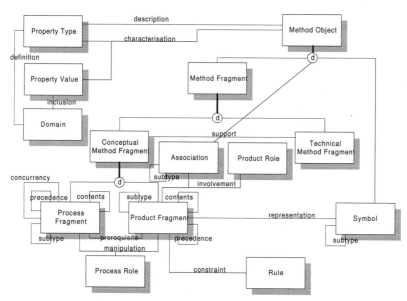

Figure 4 Meta model of MEL.

Figure 4 depicts a simplified meta model of the representational aspects of MEL. To improve readability, properties of the concepts, and cardinalities and role names of the relationship types are not shown. A *method object* can be a method fragment, an association, or a symbol. There are two relationship types between method object and property type: the ternary *characterisation* relationship, which is used to denote intrinsic properties of the method object along with their values, and the binary *description* relationship, used to indicate properties of method object instances.

```
PRODUCT Simple EntityRelationshipDiagram:
  IS_A Product;
  LAYER Diagram;
  CREATOR TYPE Information Analyst;
  NAME TEXT;
  CREATION DATE DATE;
  DEFINITION TEXT;
  MANIPULATED BY {(Create ERD, Production), (Modify ERD, Update), (Create DFD, Usage)};
  (
  - Entity;
  - Attribute;
  - Relationship
    RULE r1: forall d in EntityRelationshipDiagram forall e in Entity exists r in Relationship [status(d) = 'completion' implies
    domain_of(e,r) or range_of(e,r)]
  # all entities are connected if ERD is completed #
  ).

PRODUCT Entity:
  LAYER Concept;
  SYMBOL Rectangle;
  MANIPULATED BY {(Identify provisional entities, Production), (Identify entities, Update), (Identify relationships, Usage)};
  ASSOCIATED WITH {(EntityRelationship_1, domain_of),(EntityRelationship_2, range_of), (EntityAttribute, has)}.

PRODUCT Attribute:
  LAYER Concept;
  SYMBOL Circle;
  ASSOCIATED WITH {(EntityAttribute, is_of),(RelationshipAttribute, is_of)}.

PRODUCT Relationship:
  LAYER Concept;
  SYMBOL Diamond;
  ASSOCIATED WITH {(EntityRelationship_1, has_domain), (EntityRelationship_2, has_range), (RelationshipAttribute, has)}.

ASSOCIATION EntityRelationship_1:
  ASSOCIATES(Entity, Relationship);
  CARDINALITY(1,n; 1,1) # the example requires only binary relationships #.

ASSOCIATION EntityRelationship_2:
  ASSOCIATES(Entity, Relationship);
  CARDINALITY(1,n; 1,1).

ASSOCIATION EntityAttribute:
  ASSOCIATES(Entity, Attribute);
  CARDINALITY(1,n; 0,n).

ASSOCIATION RelationshipAttribute:
  ASSOCIATES(Relationship, Attribute);
  CARDINALITY(1,n; 0,n).
```

Figure 5   Product representation in MEL.

Besides a representational part, which is the focus of this paper, MEL contains *operations* to administrate method fragments in the method base, to query them, and to assemble method fragments into a situational method. The examples below depict a product fragment and a process fragment. The simple ERD inherits all properties from a product fragment called "Product". Furthermore, it has the characterising properties layer and creator type. To enable further specification of its instances, it also has a number of properties which are not known until method application, such as name and creation date. It has some relationships with other method fragments, and it consists of three concepts, which are, together with their associations, specified further on.

The activities to produce the ERD are described in a process fragment specification. In process fragments, hyphens before activity names indicate sequential activities. By means of the **REQUIRED** and **DELIVERABLES** sections the input and output products, respectively, are indicated. Constructs not shown in the examples include parallelism, **DECISION**, to denote optionality and decisions, **REPEAT...UNTIL**, to denote iteration, and **AT LEAST ONE OF**, to denote non-determinism with respect to the required products.

```
PROCESS Create ERD:
  LAYER Diagram;
  REQUIRED Interview results
  (
   - Identify Entities;
   - Identify Relationships
  )
  DELIVERABLES Simple EntityRelationshipDiagram.
```

Figure 6 Process representation in MEL.

3.3 GOPRR

GOPRR (Kelly et al., 1996) focuses on the modelling of the conceptual structure of techniques and relationships between these, supporting:
- Decomposition and complex objects,
- Generalisation and specialisation of modelling concepts,
- Polymorphic modelling concepts,
- Representation independence, and
- Rules for checking the model integrity.

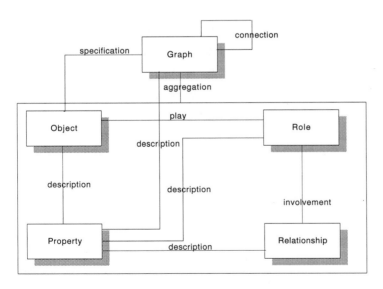

Figure 6 Meta model of GOPRR.

GOPRR-p (Koskinen, 1996) is used to model *process* structure of methods. It is an extension of GOPRR that conceptualises also the behavioural aspects of processes, in particular for automating the process model enaction. GOPRR-p is not taken into consideration in this comparison.

GOPRR distinguishes between objects, properties, relationships, roles, and graphs An *object* is used to model high granularity method products or concepts. A *relationship* is a connection between a set of objects. A *role* specifies how an object is connected to a relationship. A set of elements is collected using a *graph*, which enables the coupling of diagrams to diagrams, as well as concepts to diagrams. The relationships between property and the other concepts all relate to the instance level, and are therefore similarly named as in the **MEL** meta-model.

In the example below, boxes represent objects. Circles represent roles, diamonds represent relationships, and ellipses represent properties describing instances of objects. Properties characterising an object (method fragment) are placed within a dotted rectangle. For instance, the object Entity has three roles (domain_of, range_of, and has), which are associated with relationships. The entire model, a graph, has three descriptive properties: Name, Creation Data and Definition, which are used to characterise an instance of this graph. It has two characterising properties: Layer, and Creator Type. These properties characterise the graph itself. Something which is not shown in the example is, that properties can be shared by several objects and relationships.

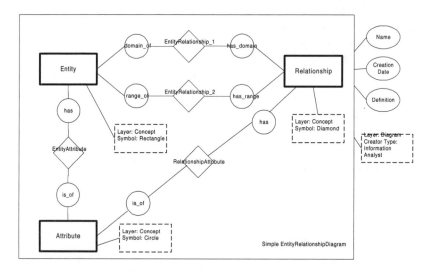

Figure 7   Product representation in GOPRR.

3.4   HFSP

HFSP (Katayama, 1989; Song and Osterweil, 1992) provides a language for describing software process programs in a process-centred style. It is based on attribute grammars. The descriptions, i.e. HFSP programs, consist of two parts - declarations of data types and the definition of derivation rules that specify the activities and the computation of products in the processes. Data types are defined in a similar way as in well-known program languages, such as record type, set type, enumeration type and so on.

The meta model of HFSP is shown in Figure 8. A *type* is a definition of a product type and specifies the type of *attribute* values associated with *activity*. An activity corresponds to a non-terminal symbol or a terminal symbol in grammatical *derivation rules*. Typical derivation rules have the following form:

$A \Rightarrow B_1 B_2 ... B_n$
when *conditions*
where *computation rules*

The activity A is decomposed to sub activities B_1, B_2, ... and B_n. A is a non-terminal symbol and each B_i ($1 \le i \le n$) corresponds to non-terminal or terminal symbols. A and each B_i can have inputs and outputs as their attributes. When A has several inputs and outputs, we write $A(in_1, in_2, ..., in_m \mid out_1, out_2, ..., out_k)$. Intuitively speaking, $in_1,..., in_m$ are inherited atributes, while $out_1, ..., out_k$ are synthesised attributes, because they are computed from the values associated with $B_1, ..., B_n$ and $in_1, ... , in_m$.

We use the term *decomposition rule* to denote the right hand side of derivation rules that have on the left hand side the activities in which an activity can be decomposed. Thus, a decomposition rule consists of a sequence of *activities*, and the *usage* relationship expresses which activities occur in the decomposition rule. *Computation rule* and *condition* are associated with a derivation rule. The former is for computing an output attribute value associated with the activity when it is decomposed. The latter specifies the condition which should hold when the activity is decomposed, i.e. executed.

In the example depicted in figure 9, which is part of an ER diagram description in HFSP, we define the structure of ER diagram by using set type and record type constructions. For example, EntityRelationship_1 (association between Entity and Relationship) is defined as a pair (record type) of entities and relationships. Conceptual ER diagrams consist of a set of entities, a set of relationships, a set of attributes and their associations (named EntityRelationship_1, EntityRelationship_2, EntityAttribute and RelationshipAttribute). To attach graphical information to entity, relationship and attribute components on diagram notation, we introduce the other types entity_symbols, relationship_symbols and attribute_symbols using record type construction. They have graphical components such as a rectangle, a diamond and a circle.

The activities for constructing ER diagrams are specified by derivation rules associated with conditions and computation rules. As mentioned before, conditions specify the constraints for application of the derivation rule. The input and output values are computed following the computation rules. In the example of the second rule of IdentifyEntity, only if the value of Entity.e is not included in entities.in, the rule is applied and then the value of entities.out is computed as the union of entities.in and {Entity.e}. Note that we use the variables for denoting the attribute values, i.e. the variables keep the referential transparency. Because of this property, we often write many copy rules to propagate the attribute values that are globally used. A variable name may be prefixed with its type. For example, entities.in stands for the variable "in" whose type is entities.

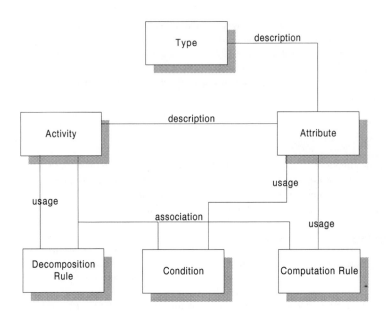

Figure 8   Meta model of HFSP.

As the execution of activities proceeds, the derivation tree becomes larger. The derivation tree records the execution history. The execution order of activities is the derivation order of the rules and the derivation order is specified by the conditions and the computation rules. When the conditions are satisfied and where the values necessary for the computation are already determined, we can execute the derivation, i.e. the corresponding activity. Thus it means that HFSP specifies the execution order of activities implicitly. Furthermore HFSP can specify concurrency and non-determinism on activity execution. Suppose there is more than one node the derivation rules can be applied   in the derivation tree. They can be derived concurrently, i.e. parallel parsing, or one or some of them can be selected and derived in a non-deterministic way.

As shown in the example, method-descriptions cannot be separated among different levels. Therefore, notational information of ERD is scattered in its conceptual description.

Note that it is difficult in HFSP to specify constraints on products because its data type definition part has no syntactic devices to specify them. If a constraint has to be specified on the products, it has to be associated with derivation rules. This is also one of the reasons why the method descriptions in HFSP are not so comprehensive.

type
  entities : **set of** Entity
  relationships : **set of** Relationship
  attributes : **set of** Attribute
  EntityRelationship_1, EntityRelationship_2 : (Entity, Relationship)
  EntityAttribute : (Entity, Attribute)
  RelationshipAttribute : (Relationship, Attribute)
  entity_symbols : **set of** (Entity, Rectangle)
  relationship_symbols : **set of** (Relationship, Diamond)
  attribute_symbols : **set of** (Attribute, Circle)
  Rectangle, Diamond, Circle : (Coordinate, Coordinate, Label)
  ERDiagram : (entity_symbols, relationship_symbols, attribute_symbols,
        EntityRelationship_1, EntityRelationship_2,
        EntityAttribute, RelationshipAttribute)

activity
  MakeERDiagram(| ERDiagram.out) $\Rightarrow$
    DrawEntity(| entity_symbols)
    DrawRelationship(entity_symbols.out | relationship_symbols.out,
          EntityRelationship_1.out, EntityRelationship_2.out)
    DrawAttribute(entity_symbols.out, relationship_symbols.out |
        attribute_symbols.out, EntityAttribute.out,
        Relationship_attribute.out)
    where
    ERDiagram.out = (entity_symbols.out, relationship_symbols.out,
         attribute_symbols.out, EntityRelationship_1.out,
         EntityRelationship_2.out, EntityAttribute.out,
         RelationshipAttribute.out)

  DrawEntity(| entity_symbols.out) $\Rightarrow$
    IdentifyEntity(| entities.out)
    CreateEntity(entities.out | entity_symbols.in)
    MoveEntity(entity_symbols.in | entity_symbols.out)

  IdentifyEntity(| entities.out) $\Rightarrow \varepsilon$
    where entities.out = { }

  IdentifyEntity(| entities.out) $\Rightarrow$ IdentifyEntity(| entities.in)
    when Entity.e $\notin$ entities.in
    where entities.out = entities.in $\cup$ {Entity.e}

  CreateEntity(entities.in | entity_symbol.out) $\Rightarrow \varepsilon$
    when entities.in = { }
    where entity_symbols.out = { }

  CreateEntity(entities.in | entity_symbols.out) $\Rightarrow$ CreateEntity(entities.out | entity_symbols.in)
    when entities $\neq$ { } $\wedge$ entity.e $\in$ entities.in
    where entities.out = entities.in - {Entity.e}
      entity_symbols.out = entity_symbols.in $\cup$ {(Entity.e, (x,y,label)}

  MoveEntity(entity_symbols.in | entity_symbols.out) $\Rightarrow \varepsilon$
    where entity_symbols.out = entity_symbols.in

  MoveEntity(entity_symbols.in | entity_symbols.out) $\Rightarrow$ MoveEntity(entity_symbols.in | entity_symbols.mid)
    when (Entity.e, (x,y,label)) $\in$ entity_symbols.mid
    where entity_symbols.out = entity_symbols.mid - {(Entity.e, (x,y,label))}
             $\cup$ {(Entity.e, (x+dx,y+dy,label))}

Figure 9 Method fragment representation in HFSP.

4   COMPARING THE METHOD ENGINEERING LANGUAGES

In table 1 the four languages are characterised on the basis of the following aspects:
- *Basis*, which is the underlying -mathematical- formalism or modelling language.
- *Scope*, which denotes the range of applications for which the language is being used.
- *Paradigm*, addressing the philosophy or "way of thinking" a Method Engineering language adopts.
- *Explicitness*, which indicates whether method fragments are completely described, or that part of the method fragment specification should be derived. For instance, the activity sequence can be derived from pre- and post-conditions associated with process fragments.
- *Focus*, indicating which part or aspect of a method specification is particularly emphasised by the language.
- *Size*, which gives an indication of the average size of a method specification in a language.

Table 1   Characterisation of Method Engineering languages

	Object-Z	*MEL*	*GOPRR*	*HFSP*
basis	ZF set theory	predicate logic	extended ER model	attribute grammars
scope	general-purpose	Method Engineering	meta-modelling	process modelling
paradigm	object-oriented	data/process-oriented	data-oriented	functional
explicitness	process order implicit	explicit	explicit	implicit
focus	method products	method products	method products	method processes
size	moderate	large	moderate	large

Table 2 represents an comparison of the four languages by assessing the extent to which each language meets the requirements stated in section two.

Object-Z does support process representation, but, due to its object-oriented roots, only in combination with a product description. HFSP only supports record-like product descriptions, and is therefore less suitable for representing products. All languages can support both the development and the project management perspective, but none of them offers special constructs to distinguish or relate the two. Only MEL offers support for representation of technical method fragments by providing the **SYMBOL** object class and several property types for technical method fragments. However, all other language are capable of representing them, as has been shown in some examples. Only GOPRR is not able to express formal rules; HFSP offers conditions, MEL rules, and Object-Z formulas. Modularisation is a weak point of HFSP; all other languages have constructs to support this feature: Object-Z by class schema's and their instances, MEL by method objects, and GOPRR by graphs. The investigated Method

Table 2 Comparison of Method Engineering languages

	Object-Z	MEL	GOPRR	HFSP
suitability	no methodology-specific concepts, relatively hard to learn	many methodology-specific concepts, relatively hard to learn	concepts for modelling techniques, easy to learn	non-determinism, simulation, hard to learn
processes & products	both, but processes less well supported	both	products	both, but products less well supported
development & proj. mgmt.	mainly development	mainly development	development	mainly development
conceptual & technical	both	both, special constructs and property types	both	both
formal rules	yes	yes	no	yes
actors	no, but can be user-defined	as pre-defined property types	no	no
type/instance	yes	no	no	no
non-determinism	yes	no	no	yes
parallellism	yes	yes	no	yes
design rationale	no, but can be user-defined	no	no	no
modularisation	yes (objects, classes)	yes	yes (composite concepts)	no
views	no	yes	no	no
unambiguity	unambiguous	unambiguous	unambiguous	unambiguous

Engineering languages do not provide explicit support for actors or roles. MEL features pre-defined property types such as "creator" or "responsible" which serve as actor and role representations. In Object-Z, actors and roles can be represented by object classes. Only in Object-Z, the difference between types and instances is handled well. GOPRR and HFSP can represent both types and instances, but not their relationships. MEL is not able at all to represent method fragment instances. Non-determinism of operation sequence is supported in Object-Z and HFSP. GOPRR does not operations at all, in MEL the sequence of operations is explicitly defined. Parallelism is supported by all three languages that provide representation for process fragments. None of the investigated languages provides support for capturing design rationale, although in Object-Z object class schemata to serve that purpose can be defined. MEL supports the explicit definition of views by specialisation of generic method fragments, the other languages do not. All of the languages are unambiguously and formally defined by their authors, leaving no room for misinterpretations. Object-Z provides no methodology-specific concepts, which causes the language somewhat harder to learn for methodologists. Due to the compact representation, the size of Object-Z specifications does not suffer from this fact. MEL provides a lot of methodology-specific concepts and properties. This huge number makes the language also harder to learn. GOPRR only addresses product representation (GOPRR-p was not yet taken into consideration), but does this in an easy and elegant fashion. GOPRR is in particular suited for modelling modelling techniques, and not complete methods, although the graph concept enables to do so. HFSP is particularly suitable for modelling non-deterministic processes. Due to the precise description of processes, HFSP is executable and can be used for simulation purposes. This language is relatively difficult to learn.

5   CONCLUSION

In this paper we proposed a number of requirements for Method Engineering languages. From each of the four identified categories of Method Engineering languages we have taken one example, which have been described with meta-models and illustrated with example specifications. We have compared the four languages on the basis of the requirements.

A general conclusion that can be drawn is that there is no ultimate Method Engineering language. Choice of the language depends on the desired purpose and goals one wants to reach. Also in this respect, Method Engineering languages and their usage are very similar to IS modelling techniques. Object-Z provides compact, elegant specifications underpinned by the object-oriented paradigm. If only the process aspects of a method need to be represented, Object-Z is less suitable. MEL tries to combine the product and process aspects and uses methodology-specific terms, particularly in its pre-defined properties. Because MEL was designed by looking at advantages of other Method Engineering languages, it is probably the best all-round language around. However, the huge number of concepts and properties make the language hard to learn, which counteracts the advantage of being methodology-specific for a part. GOPRR is not so hard to learn, but addresses only the product aspect. This language is best suited for modelling and representing modelling techniques and their interrelationships. HFSP is particularly suited for modelling processes, the product representation support by record types is quite rudimentary. HFSP is at its best if processes need to be simulated, for instance to calculate various alternative project plans.

The conclusion that there is no ultimate Method Engineering language could lead to a situation in which Method Engineering languages are composed of fragments originating from several Method Engineering languages, to obtain a purpose-fit language. We call this *Method Engineering of Method Engineering languages.*

Further research focuses on refining the various categories and comparing more languages. Purposes of Method Engineering will be related to the various languages around. The comparison techniques will be sophisticated and formalised. Currently a reference framework and associated comparison metrics for Method Engineering languages is under development. This framework is developed towards a Method Engineering ontology, i.e. a formal data model containing basic concepts of IS engineering methods, while taking into account earlier results (described in (Olle et al., 1991) and (Heym and Österle, 1992)) regarding such data models.

6 REFERENCES

Benali, K., Boudjlida, N., Charoy, F., Derniame, J.-C., Godart, C., Griffiths, Ph., Gruhn, V., Jamart, Ph., Oldfield, D. and Oquendo, F. (1989) Presentation of the ALF project. *Proceedings of the International Conference on System Development Environments and Factories*, Berlin.

Brinkkemper, S. (1991) Formalisation of Information Systems Modelling, Dissertation University of Nijmegen, Thesis Publishers, Amsterdam.

Duke, R., King, P., Rose, R. and Smith, G. (1991) The Object-Z Specification Language, Technical Report 91-1, Software Verification Centre, University of Queensland.

Emmerich, W., Junkermann, G. and Schäfer, W. (1991) MERLIN: knowledge based process modelling. *First European Workshop on Software Process Modelling*, Milan.

Harmsen, F., Brinkkemper S. and Oei H. (1994) Situational Method Engineering for Information System Projects. *Proceedings of the IFIP WG8.1 Working Conference CRIS'94* (Eds. T.W. Olle and A.A. Verrijn-Stuart), North-Holland Publishers, Amsterdam, pp. 169-194.

Harmsen, F., and Brinkkemper, S. (1995a) Description and Manipulation of Method Fragments for Situational Method Assembly. *Proceedings of the Workshop on Management of Software Projects*, Pergamon Press, London.

Harmsen, F. and Brinkkemper S. (1995b) Design and Implementation of a Method Base Management System for a Situational CASE Environment. *Proceedings of the 2nd Asian-Pacific Software Engineering Conference (APSEC'95)*, IEEE Computer Society Press, Los Alamitos, CA, pp. 430-438.

Heym, M. and Österle, H. (1992) A reference model of information systems development. *The Impact of Computer Supported Technologies on Information Systems Development* (Eds. K.E. Kendall, K. Lyytinen and J.I. DeGross), Amsterdam, North-Holland, pp. 215-240.

Hofstede, A.H.M. ter (1993), Information modelling in data intensive domains, dissertation University of Nijmegen, the Netherlands.

Hong, S., van den Goor, G., and Brinkkemper, S. (1993), A Comparison of Object-Oriented Analysis and Design Methodologies. *Proceedings of the 26th Hawaiian Conference on System Sciences (HICSS-26)*, IEEE Computer Science Press.

Iivari, J. (1994) Object-oriented information systems analysis: A comparison of six object-oriented analysis methods. *Proceedings of the IFIP WG8.1 Working Conference CRIS'94* (Eds. T.W. Olle and A.A. Verrijn-Stuart), North-Holland Publishers, Amsterdam, pp. 85-110.

Katayama, T. (1989) A hierarchical and functional software process description and its enaction. *Proceedings of the 11th Int. Conf. on Software Engineering*. pp.-343-352.

Kelly S., Lyytinen, K. and Rossi, M. (1996) MetaEdit+ A Fully Configurable Multi-User and multi-Tool CASE and CAME Environment. *Proceedings of the CAiSE'96 conference*, 20-24 May, Heraklion, Crete, Greece.

Koskinen, M. (1996) Designing Multiple Process Modelling Languages for Flexible, Enactable Process Models in a MetaCASE Environment, *Proceedings of the 7th European Workshop on Next Generation CASE Tools (NGCT'96)*, Heraklion, Crete, Greece.

Kumar, K. and Welke, R.J. (1992) Methodology Engineering: A proposal for Situation-specific Methodology Engineering. *Challenges and Strategies for Research in Systems Development* (Eds. W.W. Cotterman and J.A Senn), John Wiley and Sons Ltd., pp. 257-269.

Martin, J. (1990) Information Engineering, Book II - Planning and Analysis, Prentice-Hall, Englewood Cliffs.

Marttiin, P., Rossi, M., Tahvanainen, V.-P. and Lyytinen, K. (1993) A Comparative Review of CASE Shells: a preliminary framework and research outcomes. *Information and Management*, **25**, pp. 11-31.

Mylopoulos, J., Borgida, A., Jarke, M., Koubarakis, M. (1990) Telos: Representing Knowledge About Information Systems. *ACM Transactions on Information Systems*, **8**, 4, pp. 325-362.

Oei, J.L.H. and E.D. Falkenberg (1994) Harmonisation of Information System Modelling and Specification Techniques. *Proceedings of the IFIP WG8.1 Working Conference CRIS'94* (Eds. T.W. Olle and A.A. Verrijn-Stuart), North-Holland Publishers, Amsterdam, pp. 151-168.

Olle, T.W., Sol, H.G. and Tully, C.J. (Eds.) (1983) *Information Systems Design Methodologies: A Feature Analysis*. Elsevier Science Publishers, North-Holland, Amsterdam.

Olle, T.W., Hagelstein, J., MacDonald, I.G., Rolland, C., Sol, H.G., Van Assche, F.J.M. and Verrijn-Stuart, A.A (1991) *Information Systems Methodologies: A framework for understanding*. Addison-Wesley Publishing Company, Wokingham, England.

Saeki, M., Kaneko, T., and Sakamoto, M. (1991) A Method for Software Process Modeling and Description using LOTOS. *Proceedings of the 1st International Conference on the Software Process* (Ed. M. Dowson), IEEE Computer Society Press, Los Alamitos, CA, pp. 90-104.

Saeki, M., and Wen-yin, K. (1994) Specifying Software Specification and Design Methods. *Advanced Information Systems Engineering* (Eds. G. Wijers, S. Brinkkemper and T. Wasserman), LNCS#811, Springer-Verlag, pp. 353-366.

Smolander, K. (1992) OPRR - A Model for Methodology Modeling. *Next Generation of CASE Tools* (Eds. K. Lyytinen and V.-P. Tahvanainen), Studies in Computer and Communication Systems, IOS press, pp. 224-239.

Slooten, K. van, and Brinkkemper S. (1993) A Method Engineering Approach to Information Systems Development. *Proceedings of the IFIP WG8.1 Conference on Information Systems Development Process* (Eds. N. Prakash, C. Rolland and P. Pernici), Como, pp. 167-186.

Song, X., and Osterweil, L.J. (1992), Towards objective, systematic design-method comparison. *IEEE Software*, **34**, 5, May, pp. 43-53.

Sorenson, P.G., Tremblay, J-P. and McAllister, A.J. (1988) The Metaview system for many specification environments. *IEEE Software*, **30**, 3, March, pp. 30-38.

Sowa, J.F., and Zachman, J.A. (1992) Extending and formalizing the framework for information systems architecture. *IBM Systems Journal*, **31**, 3, pp. 590-616.

Venable, J. (1993) CoCoA: A Conceptual Data Modelling Approach for Complex Problem Domains. Ph.D. dissertation, State University of New York, Binghampton.

Verhoef, T.F. and Ter Hofstede, A.H.M. (1995) Feasibility of Flexible Information Modelling Support. *Advanced Information Systems Engineering* (Eds. J. Iivari, K. Lyytinen and M. Rossi), LNCS #932, Springer-Verlag, pp. 168-185.

Wijers, G. and Dort, H. van (1990) Experiences with the use of CASE tools in the Netherlands. *Advanced Information Systems Engineering* (Eds. B. Steinholz, A. Sølvberg and L. Bergman), LNCS#436, Springer-Verlag, pp. 5-20.

Wijers, G. (1991) Modelling Support in Information Systems Development. Ph.D. dissertation, Thesis publishers, Amsterdam.

7 BIOGRAPHY

Frank Harmsen is a researcher in the Information Systems Design Methodology Research Group at the Computer Science Department of the University of Twente in the Netherlands. He holds a B.Sc and M.Sc in Mathematics and Computer Science from the University of Nijmegen. His research interests are information system methodology, meta-modelling, Method Engineering, and CASE tools, about which he has published several papers. Current research activities focus on defining formalisms and tools for representation and assembly of method fragments for Situational Method Engineering. He was co-editor of the 1993 edition of the Workshop on Next Generation of CASE Tools (NGCT), and served on the organisation committee of CAiSE'94 (Conference on Advanced Information Systems Engineering). He is a member of the Netherlands Society for Informatics.

Motoshi Saeki is an associate professor of Tokyo Institute of Technology, Tokyo, Japan. He received a Ph.D degree from Dept. of Computer Science, Tokyo Institute of Technology in 1983. He has worked for Dept. of Computer Science as a research associate and since 1988 as an associate professor. His current interests include specification & design methods, formal methods (in particular, application of formal methods), human factor in software development and CSCW in software development.

15

Method Engineering: Who's the Customer?

L. Mathiassen, A. Munk-Madsen, P. A. Nielsen and J. Stage
Department of Computer Science, Aalborg University
Fredrik Bajers Vej 7, DK-9220 Aalborg Ø, Denmark
{larsm, pan, jans}@iesd.auc.dk

Metodica, Nyvej 19, DK-1851 Fredriksberg C, Denmark
metodica@post4.tele.dk

Abstract

This paper reports from a large Danish effort to engineer an object-oriented method for analysis and design of computer systems. Over a period of six years a method was developed based on new ideas on how to learn object-orientation supplemented with well-known ideas of how to work object-oriented in systems development.

The experience from this method engineering effort is interpreted as an iterative process involving elements of theory, method and case records. These elements played different roles when engineering the method. But, what is more important, they became key elements in structuring and presenting the method to practitioners and students of the field.

This particular method engineering effort has thus been governed by a paradigm for learning methods rather than a paradigm for working with methods. We discuss this paradigm by exploring three issues involved in method engineering: (1) the relation between learning the method and working with the method; (2) the role of principles, patterns, and guidelines in explaining the method; and, finally, (3) the relation between concepts for reflection and modelling and concrete representations used to create texts and diagrams.

We suggest that the primary customers of method engineering are those studying methods eager to learn a class of new systems development practices. Those actually working with the method should be thought of in a secondary role when structuring and presenting a new method – even though they are the ultimate judges of the method's practical strengths and weaknesses.

Keywords

Method engineering, systems development, object-orientation, learning, working.

1   INTRODUCTION

One may take different approaches to method research and engineering: a comparative approach with particular focus on the features of methods (e.g. Olle *et al.* 1982, 1983 and 1986, Nielsen 1990a and 1990b), a tool-oriented approach with a particular focus on notation and CASE (e.g. Steinholtz *et al.* 1990, Andersen *et al.* 1991), or a mixed approach (e.g. Tolvanen and Lyytinen 1993, Verrijn-Stuart and Olle 1994). We have taken an experience-based approach as outlined in the following.

It has been the authors' privilege to work with systems development and systems development methods for a number of years, teaching methods to computer science and engineering students at the university and to practitioners in companies in the computing industry, experimenting with methods in companies and laboratories, and researching into the qualities of methods both in processes of learning them and working with them. This is reflected in our previous work (Mathiassen 1981, Stage 1989, Nielsen 1990a and 1990b, Kensing and Munk-Madsen 1993).

We have taught both structured and object-oriented methods to computer science and engineering students for several years, and during the last six years we have taught object-oriented methods to a large number of practitioners. In these efforts we have often experienced a gap between the way a specific method is structured and presented and the requirements and needs we experience when trying to convey the underlying new systems development practices to practitioners and students in the field. It is this dissatisfaction with the pedagogical weaknesses of many systems development methods that initiated the research reported in this paper.

For more than six years we have been involved with our students, companies in the computing industry and practitioners of systems development in engineering a new Danish method for object-oriented analysis and design, called OOA&D. The method is documented in two books (Mathiassen *et al.* 1993 and 1995). Evolving versions of the method have been taught to students and practitioners in different pedagogical contexts (university courses, open courses for practitioners, and in-house courses for specific companies). From this stems the experience that has driven the method engineering process: our method is based on new ideas on how to explain and learn object-orientation supplemented with well-known ideas of how to work object-oriented in systems development (Jackson 1983, Coad and Yourdon 1991, Booch 1991, Rumbaugh *et al.* 1991, Jacobson *et al.* 1992).

During the development of OOA&D two fundamental questions to method engineering have been addressed:

- What are the key elements of the method?

- What are the basic principles for structuring and presenting the method?

These questions are intrinsically related and answering them in our own method engineering effort required several iterations. Once the questions were answered the rest of the method fell in place more easily. In the engineering of OOA&D we made a fundamental decision, which helped us design the engineering process and answer the two questions:

- The underpinning paradigm of the method engineering process is that of learning and teaching object-oriented ideas to practitioners and students.

- The primary customers of the method engineering process are the practitioners and students that want to learn object-orientation.

This learning paradigm negates the conventional implicit assumption, that systems development methods should be structured and presented to reflect the way in which practitioners work when using the method.

The learning paradigm has had considerable implications for the engineering of our method and for the structure and documentation of the method. We suggest that this paradigm can help other method engineers overcome some of the difficulties involved in successfully engineering new methods. These difficulties include: hardship of teaching and learning the essentials of a method, difficulty in distinguishing the important differences between alternative methods, reluctance amongst practitioners and students to adhere to the method, and last but not least a slow adaptation of the method.

The structure of our discussion is as follows. The process through which we engineered OOA&D is described in Section 2. Our experience is interpreted as an iterative process involving elements of theory, method and case records as in (Checkland 1981). In Section 3, three major issues in designing OOA&D are then presented and discussed: learning and working with methods; the role of principles, patterns, and guidelines; and, finally, the relation between concepts for reflection and modelling and concrete representations used to create texts and diagrams. A summary of the learning paradigm and its implications for method engineering is given in Section 4.

2   THE ENGINEERING PROCESS

2.1   A Specific Case

Background: We have taught systems development methods to computer science and engineering students for a couple of decades. First, we taught a selection of state-of-the-art methods; then we used Jackson System Development (Jackson 1983) for a few years; later Modern Structured Analysis (Yourdon 1989) was used based on different course books; we have taught OOA and OOD (Coad and Yourdon 1991a, 1991b); and for the last three years, we have used different versions of our own method, OOA&D.

These methods are taught in a software engineering course introducing the students to software engineering in general and analysis and design of computer systems in particular. It is a one-term course with 20 sessions of lectures and related exercises of which the method part would cover more than half the sessions. The course runs in parallel to a programming course and a one-term project (half of the students' time) in which the students in groups of 6–7 would use the analysis and design method together with programming concepts and techniques to develop a computer system. Within the same term students are taught a method and required to use it for practical purposes. During the method engineering process this educational environment gave constant feed-back from the student projects.

In a different environment we have taught the same systems development methods to practitioners. Some of these activities have been general courses with participants from different companies and others have been in-house courses tailored to the needs of specific projects and companies. In particular, starting in 1991, we have taught OOA and OOD based on Coad and Yourdon's method (1991a, 1991b). Typically the analysis part and the design part were taught in two separate 3-day courses with a series of lectures in combination with a mini-project in which the participants used the method on a small, but realistic case.

Experiences

We have different experiences teaching the various methods. Jackson System Development (Jackson 1983) was fairly easy to explain because of its emphasis on clear concepts, the elaborate examples, and the combination of well-defined activities and fundamental principles (e.g. model before function). The implementation part of the method was too elaborate with many technical details, the notion of entity was too simple, and some of the graphical representations of concepts were difficult for the students and practitioners to use.

Modern Structured Analysis (Yourdon 1989) is based on easy-to-understand concepts and intuitively appealing representations. The concepts and representations are, together with a few heuristics, the key elements of the method. There are no, or very few, fundamental principles. We found it easy to organize good lectures based on examples, but it was difficult for students and practitioners to combine the various models into coherent practical cases.

OOA and OOD (Coad and Yourdon 1991) attempt to overcome this difficulty by introducing object-orientation. The concepts are easy to understand, but the representations are less intuitive. Moreover, it was difficult for the students and practitioners to see how this method could cover all traditional aspects of systems analysis. The approach is heavily oriented towards data models, it is not obvious how services (or methods) are used during analysis, and many practitioners were missing the traditional function-oriented approach to requirements specification.

Approach

On the basis of these experiences we decided to develop a new method for object-oriented analysis and design in which we would combine the strengths and if possible avoid the weaknesses of these methods.

Our approach to this method engineering effort consisted of a number of elements. First, the process was designed to develop a series of versions of the method, to document each version as a series of transparencies together with a still more elaborate text, to use each version in different pedagogical environments, and to systematically collect feed-back from each of these teaching experiences. This process helped us develop an answer to one of the fundamental method engineering questions (What are the basic principles for structuring and presenting the method?)

Second, to answer the other fundamental method engineering question (What are the key elements of the method?) our approach included detailed studies of published methods on object-oriented analysis and design. Selected methods were studied in detail, their elements were critically analysed, similarities and differences between methods were identified, and based on this analysis, we chose principles, concepts and representations that we found potentially useful in our method.

Third, we wanted to make sure, that the resulting method emerged as a coherent whole, not as a mere collection of selected elements from other methods. To that end we designed our own conceptual framework explicating a specific perspective (or theory, cf. Section 2.2) on the processes and key products involved in object-oriented analysis and design: a model of a computer system, a model of the context of a computer system, the fundamental concepts of objects and classes, the key activities involved in analysis and design, and, finally, an outline of the resulting documentation.

Finally, we stressed the development of realistic examples (or case records, cf. Section 2.2) of both the processes of analysis and design (i.e. chronological accounts and experiences) and of the resulting products (i.e. models, specifications, and documentation). These examples were typically developed through small experiments in which some authors were active while others observed and took notes.

The primary test-bed for the method engineering process was the different educational activities with students and practitioners, involving lectures, small exercises and large-scale student projects. Each time a version was tested, new insights were generated, and these insights were then accumulated as the key input to the development of the next version of the method.

Documenting each version of the method on transparencies allowed for relatively frequent changes and modifications. The complementary text describing elements of the method in greater detail were modified more seldom. In the end, the method was documented as two complete text books.

The method is presently being used as the standard text on object-oriented analysis and design in a number of Scandinavian universities and colleges. At the same time, the first large-scale industrial experiments have taken place.

2.2   A General Model

Stressing in method engineering, as we do, the context of learning the method at the expense of the context of working with the method, we run the risk of ending up with a wrongly balanced picture of the relation between methods and practices. To frame our discussion with a balanced view we use a general model by Anderton and Checkland (see Checkland 1981, p. 7–8). They argue convincingly that any development of a subject (in our case an object-oriented method including case records and underlying theories) has to be circular and has to contain the elements depicted in Figure 1.

In developing our method, the related area of reality (containing concerns, issues, problems, and aspirations) is object-oriented analysis and design practices. Together with other sources (e.g. experience with other types of analysis and design methods, general theories about design) these practices give rise to ideas about object-oriented analysis and design from which may be formulated substantive theories (about object-oriented models and systems) and methodological theories (about development of object-oriented models and systems). Such theories present problems (e.g. on how to understand the behaviour of objects) which may be analysed using models and related techniques.

The theories yield methodologies (in the context of this paper: systems development methods) which use the developed models and techniques. The methodologies are then used in action in the related area of reality. These applications of the methodology are documented in case records that support criticism of the theories.

This general model of development of a subject, or in this context, method engineering, emphasises a number of important points:

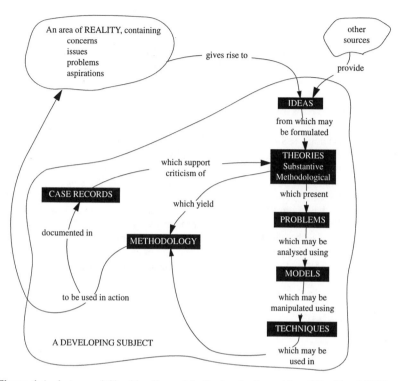

An area of REALITY, containing
concerns
issues
problems
aspirations

other
sources

gives rise to

provide

IDEAS

from which may
be formulated

THEORIES
Substantive
Methodological

which support
criticism of

CASE RECORDS

which present

which yield

PROBLEMS

documented in

METHODOLOGY

which may be
analysed using

MODELS

to be used in action

which may be
manipulated using

TECHNIQUES

A DEVELOPING SUBJECT

which may be
used in

Figure 1 Anderton and Checkland's model of a developing subject (Checkland 1981, p. 8).

1. The ultimate source of inspiration and the ultimate test-bed for a systems development method is the related area of reality, i.e. the practices related to the method (including individual learning, organisational adaptation, and practical use in projects).

2. Systems development methods are based on (implicit or explicit) theories about the products and processes involved in working within the related area of reality (in our case object-oriented systems development).

3. Case records (documented practices of working with the method) play an important role in evaluating the underlying theories and the related models and techniques.

These three characteristics of the iterative process are all expressions of fundamental relations between methods and practices. In the development of our method they all played important roles, cf. Section 2.1. The last two points correspond quite directly to the approach taken in developing our method. In the following, we will elaborate on the first point by concentrating on the importance of learning a method (which is also an integral part of the concerns in the related area of reality) as opposed to mainly focusing on working with the method.

3   DESIGN ISSUES

Three major issues, all related to the learning paradigm, have played a significant role in the design of the method. This section will discuss these and thus explicate the difference and the relationship between taking a learning and a working paradigm.

3.1   Learning and Working

Soft Systems Methodology (SSM) is a method[*] employing systems concepts and ideas to change organisations. It is a very general method that has nothing in particular to do with the development of computer-based information systems. SSM was engineered or rather it evolved from the action research by Peter Checkland and his colleagues at the Systems Department at Lancaster University from 1969 to the present. The evolution can be described as in Figure 2.

This cyclic process based on working with the method in projects where students and researchers engage in real problems in organisations has been very successful. SSM has by now been used in hundreds of such projects, but it has also taken 25 years to bring SSM to its present form. Engineering[†] a method in this way makes the eliciting of experience from the practice of working with the method the core activity. The engineering approach is thus characterised by:

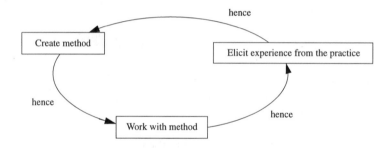

Figure 2 The evolution of a method through action research (Checkland 1981, p. 254)

- Experience is elicited from *working* with the method.
- There is a slow turn-around in the cyclic process as it is the real-world setting that forms the problems and therefore also the time-span.
- The usefulness of the method is judged on its strength as a working device in processes of development and change.
- It is difficult to evaluate 'working with a method' in real-world settings.

---

[*]Checkland actually makes a point of calling SSM a methodology (Checkland 1981, p. 162); but to avoid unnecessary confusion in this paper we call it a 'method' though he undoubtedly is right in his phrasing of the construct as something which is in between a philosophy and a technique.
[†]Engineering here to be understood in its broadest sense.

This model of method engineering is expanded in Figure 3 to embrace the method learning cycle. Figure 3 highlights the cyclic process where the learning of a method forms the practice from which experience is elicited such that the method can be re-created to become a better device for learning the method.

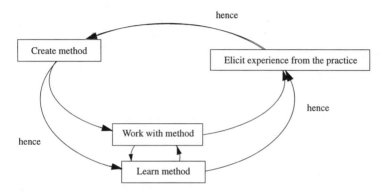

Figure 3 The learning cycle and its relationship with the working cycle

This expanded engineering approach is characterised by:

- Experience is elicited from *learning* the method.
- There is a fast turn-around in the cyclic process as it is the class-room setting that forms the problems and the time-span.
- The usefulness of the method is judged on its strengths as a learning device in processes of teaching and acquiring knowledge on the relationship between the method and practice.
- It is easier to evaluate 'learning a method' in a class-room setting.

To elaborate on this distinction between learning and working we take a 'method' to be an abstract account of possible ways in which activities in systems development may be performed. Viewed from the perspective of learning, a method is a framework for learning a class of systems development practices. Viewed from the perspective of working, a method is a set of guidelines and underlying theories for working within a class of systems development practices. Use of a method will in this sense encompass both the learning perspective and the working perspective. To acquire eloquence in a method one needs to be involved in both. Working with a method enables the learning of the method; and learning a method enables the work with the method. In both cases, as part of the practical use of a method, it is adapted to the specifics of the use situation and supplemented with other approaches.

In our engineering of OOA&D we have chosen a basic structure and presentation primarily suited for learning. This is in part due to the fact we have to define the structure in which the method is presented while working with the method may well follow various structures depending on the specifics of the situation. A book has a fixed structure, a series of lectures and exercises has a fixed structure and even a single lecture has a fixed structure. A pertinent question for us as method engineers was therefore: In which sequence should the story of object-orientation be told? We chose a sequence which we followed in both the transparencies documenting the courses and in the text-book. For example, from our learning perspective one has to learn about objects and classes and how to take decisions on which classes to include in a model and which to exclude before anything else. Then one can learn about object and class structures and how to model such structures. Then one can learn about object dynamics and how to model that in classes. We could, of course, have chosen another sequence based on other pedagogical ideas.

In taking these fundamental decisions on sequence the method engineer has to apply pedagogical arguments rather than arguments of the type "this is how it works in practice". A presentation of a method is like a story with good explanations of the complexities of its subject (like object-orientation in analysis and design) and with explanations that are understandable by novices with respect to the subject (e.g. students and practitioners not mastering object-orientation). Different pedagogies may be chosen, but it is still a pedagogical decision.

In the presentation of OOA&D we have made a particular point of giving such a sequence that is good for learning our method; but we have also explained in more general terms and using examples how that sequence differs from actually working with OOA&D in practice.

A method engineer should not forget the working perspective and neglect the experience elicited from the practice of working with the method. Any presentation and good explanation of a method will also have to encompass guidance on how to relate learning and working. The crux of the matter is that the basic structure of a method should primarily be suitable for learning and secondarily for working.

3.2 Principles, Patterns and Guidelines

A method contains descriptions of processes and products involved in the related class of systems development practices. These descriptions can be given in reasonably abstract forms. Guidelines are rather concrete expressions of ways of doing things. They typically include ways of representing concepts combined with techniques or procedures for how to apply these representations to develop models. Principles and patterns are more abstract descriptions. Principles are understood as abstract accounts of approaches to specific processes. Patterns are abstract descriptions of partial solutions to modelling the products.

In the engineering of OOA&D and most prominently in the presentation of OOA&D, guidelines are, of course, used to illustrate and explain. But principles and patterns are at the very centre. Each of the core chapters in the text-books and each of the core lectures in the courses explains an activity in the method. Figure 4 shows part of the front-page of Chapter 5 in the text-book on analysis. This chapter explains the activity 'Dynamics' and it puts strong emphasis on the purpose of the activity, the concepts to be explained in the chapter as well as being used during performing the activity, the principles giving abstract accounts of processes, and the product of the activity.

Similarly, patterns are frequently used to explain solutions to modelling problems or product development. The activities on architectural design are mainly explained in terms of different patterns (e.g. layered architecture and client-server architecture). Another chapter gives a pattern (template) for the analysis and design documentation and these are complemented with specific examples of full analysis and design documents. Basically, there are two ways of using patterns in a description of a method: as exemplars and masterpieces to be plagiarised, and as gen-

Dynamics

Purpose	• To describe the dynamics of the object system i terms of behaviour of objects.
Concepts	• Event lifecycle: A concrete sequence of events which an object during a particular time-span is involved in. • Behavioural pattern: An abstract pattern of events that stipulates the possible and desirable event lifecycles for all objects in a class. • Attribute: The name of a data property for a class or an event.
Principles	• Describe the behaviour of objects by a behavioural pattern for their class. • Consider particularly events which are common for several objects. • Deduce the attributes for a class from its behaioural pattern.
Results	• Behavioural pattern and attributes for each class.

Figure 4 Sample of a front-page from Chapter 5 in (Mathiassen *et al.* 1993)

erally applicable solutions that have been shown to solve partial problems. Principles and patterns supplement each other nicely as the principles provide abstract accounts to guide and understand processes and the patterns provide abstract accounts of (partial) products without any of the two over-emphasising particular ways of performance.

Principles and patterns are important means for learning a systems development method. Guidelines are useful, of course, as they provide possible concrete ways to apply principles and patterns. What matters, though, is often what is done, not precisely how it is done. Explanation in terms of principles and patterns focuses on the important and the essential rather than on the many and sometimes obscure details. Moreover, such explanations encourage the method engineer to explicate the ideas, theories, and problems underlying the method, cf. Figure 1. This insight will help practitioners and students trying to learn the method to understand and appreciate, not only what should be done, but also why it should be done. For practitioners working with the method this level of appreciation is useful to understand how the method can be combined with other methods and tailored to different situations, maintaining the essentials and reshaping the specifics.

3.3   Concepts and Representations

A systems development method supports the modelling of computer-based systems through concepts and means of representation. From a working perspective it is important to provide a full notation and all that comes with a notation, e.g. symbols, semantics, rules for applying the symbols, ways of manipulating texts or diagrams written with the notation. This embodies both concepts and means of representation, but with a leaning towards the means of representation.

From a learning perspective concepts are more important elements of a method than the related means of representation. Means of representation are not neglected, but they play a different role in learning the modelling techniques compared to the concepts. In particular, specific means of representation are needed to explain and illustrate a method. This is done for various reasons: examples of products are given in a representation, ways of modelling and modifying models are given in a representation, etc. In presenting a method it is useful to adhere to a few, preferably coherent representations.

In the engineering of OOA&D we put more emphasis on which concepts we chose to be part of the method than on the representation of the concepts in models. Our means of representation were taken from (Coad and Yourdon 1991a, Jackson 1983, Harel 1987, Jacobson *et al.* 1992). What we didn't find there we invented our own representations of. Having decided which concepts it should be possible to use in creating a model it was fairly easy to go through the available notations used by others and find suitable representations.

After having written the two text-books we were asked by a company within telecommunications and associated with major foreign companies all using Rumbaugh *et al.*'s method (1991) to give a course on object-oriented analysis. They wanted to stick to Rumbaugh *et al.*'s means of representation but wanted our method in the learning of object-oriented practices. Because the key elements of OOA&D are independent of the chosen means of representation it was fairly easy to change the means of representation in a whole 3-day course to those used by Rumbaugh *et al.* It took 7 hours to change the transparencies and none of the concepts in OOA&D had to be changed in the process.

All in all, concepts are more important elements of a method than the related means of representation.

4   SUMMARY

This paper has reported experiences from a method engineering effort that was governed by a paradigm for learning methods rather than a paradigm for working with methods. We have discussed this paradigm by exploring three issues involved in method engineering: (1) the relation between learning the method and working with the method; (2) the role of principles, patterns, and guidelines in explaining the method; and, finally, (3) the relation between concepts for reflection and modelling and concrete representations used to create texts and diagrams. The main points to consider for other method engineers are:

- When experience is elicited from learning the method there is a fast turn-around in the cyclic process of development and it becomes easier to evaluate new versions of the method.

- Principles and patterns are important means for learning a systems development method. Guidelines are useful, of course, as they provide possible concrete ways to apply principles and patterns. But what matters is often what is done and why it is done, not precisely how it is done.

- From a learning perspective concepts are more important elements of a method than the related means of representation. In addition, when the key elements of a method are independent of the chosen means of representation it was fairly easy to change the means of representation when adapting the method to new situations.

In summary, we suggest that the primary customers of method engineering are those studying methods eager to learn a class of new systems development practices. Those actually working with the method should only play a secondary role in structuring and presenting a new method – even though they, of course, are the ultimate judges of the method's practical strengths and weaknesses.

5 REFERENCES

Andersen, R., J. A. Bubenko Jr. and A. Sølvberg (1991). *Advanced Information Systems Engineering. Proceedings from CAiSE '91*. Springer-Verlag, Berlin.

Booch, G. (1991). *Object-Oriented Design with Applications*. Benjamin/Cummings, Redwood City, California.

Checkland, P. B. (1981). *Systems Thinking, Systems Practice*. Wiley, Chichester.

Coad, P. and E. Yourdon (1991a). *Object Oriented Analysis*. Prentice-Hall, New York. 2nd edition.

Coad, P. and E. Yourdon (1991b). *Object Oriented Design*. Prentice-Hall, New York.

Fichman, R. G. and C. F. Kemerer (1993). Adoption of Software Engineering Process Innovations: The Case of Object Orientation. *Sloan Management Review*, **34**, 2, 7-22.

Harel, D. (1987). Statecharts: a visual formalism for complex systems. *Science of Computer Programming*, **8**, 231–274.

Jackson, M. (1983). *System Development*. Prentice-Hall, Englewood Cliffs, New Jersey.

Jacobson, I., M. Christerson, P. Jonsson and G. Övergaard (1992). *Object-Oriented Software Engineering*. Addison-Wesley, Wokingham.

Kensing, F. and A. Munk-Madsen (1993). Participatory Design: Structure in the Toolbox. *Comm. ACM*, **36**, 6, 78–85.

Mathiassen, L. (1981). *Systems Development and Systems Development Method*. In Danish. Dr.scient. Thesis, Oslo University.

Mathiassen, L., A. Munk-Madsen, P. A. Nielsen and J. Stage (1991). Soft Systems in Software Design, in *Systems Thinking in Europe* (eds. M. C. Jackson *et al.*), 311–317, Plenum Press, New York.

Mathiassen, L., A. Munk-Madsen, P. A. Nielsen and J. Stage (1993). *Object-Oriented Analysis*. In Danish. Marko, Aalborg.

Mathiassen, L., A. Munk-Madsen, P. A. Nielsen and J. Stage (1995). *Object-Oriented Design*. In Danish. Marko, Aalborg.

Nielsen, P. A. (1990a). Approaches for Appreciating information systems methodologies: A soft systems survey. *Scandinavian Journal of Information Systems*, **2**.

Nielsen, P. A. (1990b).*Using and Learning IS Development Methodologies*. Ph.D. Thesis, Lancaster University.

Olle, T. W., H. G. Sol and A. A. Verrijn-Stuart, editors (1982). *Information Systems Design Methodologies: A Comparative Review*. North-Holland, Amsterdam.

Olle, T. W., H. G. Sol and C. J. Tully, editors (1983). *Information Systems Design Methodologies: A A Feature Analysis*. North-Holland, Amsterdam.

Olle, T. W., H. G. Sol and A. A. Verrijn-Stuart, editors (1986). *Information Systems Design Methodologies: Improving the Practice*. North-Holland, Amsterdam.

Rumbaugh, J., M. Blaha, W. Premerlani, S. Eddy and W. Lorensen (1991). *Object-Oriented Modelling and Design*. Prentice-Hall, Englewood Cliffs, New Jersey.

Stage, J. (1989). *Between Tradition and Transcendence: Analysis and design in systems development*. In Danish. Dr.scient. Thesis, Oslo University.

Steinholtz, A. Sølvberg and L. Bergman (1990). *Advanced Information Systems Engineering. Proceedings from CAiSE '90*. Springer-Verlag, Berlin.

Tolvanen, J.-P. and K. Lyytinen (1993). Flexible Method Adaptation in CASE: The metamodeling approach. *Scandinavian Journal of Information Systems*, **5**, 51–78.

Verrijn-Stuart, A. A. and T. W. Olle, editors (1994). *Methods and Associated Tools for the Information Systems Life Cycle*. North-Holland, Amsterdam.

Yourdon, E. (1989). *Modern Structured Analysis*. Prentice-Hall, New York.

6   BIOGRAPHY

Lars Mathiassen is currently professor in Information Systems at the Department of Computer Science, Institute for Electronic Systems, at Aalborg University. For the last twenty years he has done research in the intersection between software engineering and iInformation systems. His reaearch interests include obejt-oriented software engineering, risk-based project management, IT management and strategy, and the philosophy of computing. Lars Mathiassen has published several scientific papers on these subjects and he has co-authored a number of books on software engineering and information systems, including two books in Danish on object-oriented analysis and design.

Andreas Munk-Madsen is partner in Metodica, a Copenhagen-based company specialised in software methods. He has a broad experience in research, education, and consultancy. He has a PhD in computer science. He is co-author of several books on system development methods and is currently completing a book on strategic project management. His current interests include requirement management, project management, methods implementation, and object-oriented analysis and design.

Peter Axel Nielsen is currently associate professor in Information Systems at the Department of Computer Science, Institute for Electronic Systems, at Aalborg University. Over the past years he has been engaged in understanding the use of information systems development methodologies. His research interests include analysis and design techniques, object-orientation, domain modelling, the modelling process with a particular focus on recurrent and reusable patterns as well as IT management. He is currently the editor of Scandinavian Journal of Information Systems. Peter Axel Nielsen is co-author of two books in Danish on object-oriented analysis and design.

Jan Stage is currently associate professor in Information Systems at the Department of Computer Science, Institute for Electronic Systems, at Aalborg University. His research interests include theoretical and methodological aspects of information systems development, especially development of new object-oriented methods and techniques for analysis and design. He is teaching graduate and undergraduate students in computer science and information systems and giving industry courses on analysis, design, and programming for software professionals. Jan Stage is co-author of two books in Danish on object-oriented analysis and design.

16

Simulation-Based Method Engineering in Federated Organizations

P. Peters, M. Mandelbaum, M. Jarke
Informatik V, RWTH Aachen,
Ahornstr. 55, 52056 Aachen, Germany
email: {peters,mandel,jarke}@informatik.rwth-aachen.de
Phone/Fax: +49 241 8021512/ +49 241 8888321

Abstract

The decentralization of organizations influences method engineering in two ways: Firstly, the distributed IS development process has to be supported by flexible, modular methods. Secondly, the interaction among methods and their users in the organizational network must be facilitated in order to ensure and improve process quality and efficiency. Our research starts from the observation that recent research in method engineering focusses on flexible, process-oriented integration of methods than on the organizational coupling of information flows between established methods that ensure high quality information exchange and continuous process improvement along feedback cycles. In order to show how organizational feedback cycles influence the efficiency and quality, we identified three kinds of information flows which can be categorized as task information, corporate memory and strategy information. Taking advantage of this categorization, we present a formal approach to method engineering in-the-large. This approach combines conceptual modeling of information flow models between federated methods and quantitative analysis of their short-term and long-term impacts on organizational performance by simulation. Technically, this is achieved by a two-fold application of meta modeling: firstly, to make short-term and long-term simulation techniques interoperate; and secondly, to link conceptual method models to the simulation models. These two links have been implemented in the MultiSim environment on top of the ConceptBase meta data manager. A case study that takes place in a setting of federated manufacturing methods shows how a change of methods influences the behavior of the overall company and how information flows along and across processes must be engineered to achieve a positive net outcome.

Keywords

Information Quality, Conceptual Modeling, Simulation, System Analysis

This work was supported by the German Ministry of Research under contract 02PV71025, the DFG Graduate College 'Computer Science and Technology' at RWTH Aachen, and by the European Community under Information Systems Interoperability Project No ECAUS003 and Basic Research Working Group No.8319 (ModelAge)

1 COOPERATION AMONG FEDERATED METHODS

No matter where you look in information systems (IS) application areas (e.g. Computer Integrated Manufacturing, financial markets, or scientific community) the evolution of systems is taking the step from closely integrated, monolithic systems to modular, distributed systems. One reason for this development is a change in focus: although business efficiency is still a major driver for IS development, flexibility and changeability have been named as important attributes of both business processes and IS [Heinzl and Srikanth, 1995; Scott-Morton, 1994]. The second reason is a change of IS usage: The information system is no longer seen as an extension of a calculator that stores and manipulates data but as an extension of the telephone, by which autonomous agents communicate along and across business processes [Jarke and Ellis, 1993].

IS development has to deal with the problems that result from this change [Brodie and Ceri, 1992; Klein and Lyytinen, 1992; Lyytinen, 1987] in two ways:

1. It has to provide methods for capturing and analysis of requirements in federated environments and methods for designing appropriate IS solutions. Methods, and the supporting tools, must focus specifically on the interaction of information system and organization.
2. The IS development process itself should be organized and supported according to the changing demands. While flexibility and changeability have been tackled by recent research on process-centered engineering environments [Marttiin, 1994; Pohl, 1994] or situational method modeling [Harmsen *et al.*, 1994], the distribution of IS design is reduced to **formal interfaces along processes** that define the exchange of documents between methods.

But system quality is not only determined at the **process level** where the execution of processes is supported by more or less adapted methods and might be connected by formal documents. At the **organizational level**, the implementation of information feedback loops that provide accumulated experiences across team borders ensure organizational learning and thus continuous process improvement. Furthermore, at the **communication level**, the way of presenting information influences the degree of uncertainty and equivocality among cooperating agents involved in the process [Daft and Lengel, 1986].

Our research starts from the assumption that **information flows** provide the glue that combines methods on all three levels in order to perform business processes [Peters, 1996] as well as organizational feedback loops. This paper presents an approach for the conceptual description and impact analysis of three types of information flows. It can be used by the method engineer to capture and analyze information flows in federated organizations as a basis to analyze and engineer the cooperation among federated methods. It therefore does not focus on analyzing the method structure itself but on suitable ways to combine methods with respect to the three levels.

In the next section we describe the conceptual modeling approach that focuses on the communication among methods by information flows. A categorization of information flows is the foundation for a discussion of the impact of information flows on organizational performance. Starting from this discussion, Section 3 presents a multi-simulation approach to evaluate information flow design alternatives in their short-term and long-term effects. A case

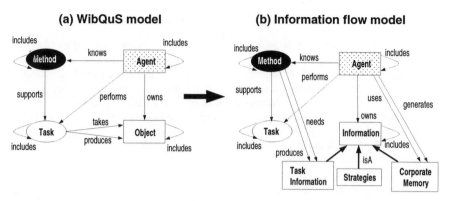

Figure 1 A language model for method interaction

study in a manufacturing company serves as an initial empirical validation of the approach and shows how local changes of methods influence the performance behavior of the overall method network. The results of the case study are finally related to the IS development process with respect to the trade-off between flexibility and the quality of process results.

2 THE MODELING APPROACH: CAPTURING INFORMATION FLOWS

To better understand the main idea of this paper, it may be instructive to compare our meta-modeling approach to its predecessor, a meta model developed in the project WibQuS ([Jarke *et al.*, 1993], cf. Figure 1a). This model was defined originally to describe processes within and among industrial quality management methods and their interactions as a starting point for distributed development of federated IS.

In the tradition of the CRIS methodology [Olle *et al.*, 1991] the business process description consists of **tasks** and **objects** consumed and produced by those **tasks**. Additionally, it refers to the **agent** as the responsible performer of a specific **task** to whom a supporting IS should be adapted. Finally, the concept of **method** was introduced, because the method provides the way-of-working for a specific task and supports its execution. Methods and tasks form an AND/OR decomposition structure in that a task can be supported by one or several methods while a method consists of a partial order of tasks.

The resulting models of quality management methods were the starting point for the **detection and definition of interfaces among those methods**. After an integration process, the integrated method models were stored in a repository and served as the structural and conceptual framework for a federated IS design controlled by a information trading mechanism. On top of this repository/trader combination several tools were developed which make use of the model in information management and access or communication processes [Peters *et al.*, 1995].

A case study of the distributed modeling process in the WibQuS project [Peters and Jeusfeld, 1994] identifies two major shortcomings of the modeling language:

1. While the contents of interfaces between methods were identified quite well, the communication channels that connect methods could not be specified explicitly within the language. We changed the model by adding three attributes to every object that describe the content of an information, its representation within the organization and the presentation types supported by the representation. This change allowed to model information flows not only by data but also by explicitly describing the communication channel used. Differing media and information understanding between communicating groups can now be detected quite early in the IS development process.

2. Different qualities of information flows could not be distinguished within the model. The modeling teams had the feeling that there were categories of information that had to be handled differently with respect to representation, presentation and communication channel. For instance, very formal and commonly used definitions like product structures were specified well by ER-diagrams and, after being transferred into database tables, exchanged directly between the involved databases. Other, quite specific knowledge on system failures or product malfunctions needed richer representation and direct involvement of the agents performing the tasks.

The second problem led to the reorganization of the language model based on results from the literature on information management and organizational IS in industrial environments [Peters, 1996]. The revisited meta-model distinguishes three major groups of information flows within organizations, which are to be implemented and supported differently:

1. **Task Information**:
   This kind of information is the one usually handled by "classical" method engineering. It drives and controls the operational business processes in organizations [Hammer, 1992; Olle *et al.*, 1991; Harmsen *et al.*, 1994] . Like e.g., the structure of a product in manufacturing industries, this information is commonly understood within an organization. Its transfer between departments or tasks is based on standardized formats. The contents of this kind of information is currently subject of international standardization approaches (STEP [Shaw, 1991], ISO 9000 [ISO, 1987], or CMM [Paulk *et al.*, 1993]). Its production described by reference models for business processes [Österle, 1995; Scheer, 1993].

2. **Corporate Memory**:
   Important organizational knowledge about products and processes results from accumulated execution and analysis of business processes [Senge, 1990; Vennix *et al.*, 1994; Harmsen *et al.*, 1994]. Other than with task information, the transfer of or communication about corporate memory cannot be formalized easily. It can consist of very informal documents like experience collections or stories and of formal ones like design rules or process models. It needs rich communication support in order to reduce equivocality, uncertainty and ambiguity between the communicating partners [Daft and Lengel, 1986].

3. **Strategies**:
   The goal of a strategy[2] is the definition of a common context according to which tasks are

---

[2]   The words philosophy or paradigm can be used equivalently. In a modeling context the idea of meta-modeling captures best what can be formalized of a strategy.

organized and information is interpreted [Hammer, 1992]. It consists of a set of visions, policies and goals under which an organization or department operates. Examples are TQM or OO-Design and Analysis

The identification of these categories led to a change of the modeling language as depicted in Figure 1b: The categories are explicitly embedded into the language and related to the producers or users of the information represented. This distinction supports explicit analysis and management of information flows according to the attributes and the ways-of-usage of the information categories. In this paper we focus on the analysis of information flows within a distributed environment.[3]

In the following, we present an integrated approach for analyzing the impact of corporate memory and task information under the given strategy of TQM [Feigenbaum, 1991] which advocates feedback loops as a major element of process quality and improvement. The effects analyzed are the effectiveness and quality of method performance related to the information flows existing among the methods.

3 ANALYSIS APPROACH: SIMULATION OF INFORMATION IMPACT

3.1 The Problem of Analyzing Information Flows

If you want to analyze the impact of information exchange on performance in federated organizations, the differing contents and ways of processing of task information and corporate memory have to be analyzed using different criteria. The impact of task information is determined by short term effects like transaction costs, timeliness, and completeness. The exchange of corporate memory influences performance by long term effects on process quality, effectiveness, or personnel qualification.

Task information criteria are defined in recent approaches by discrete, quantitative measures, because they describe short-term, local effects which relate directly to the business process (and therefore monetary or time-related business criteria). The analysis of such criteria is usually performed by Petri-Net or Queuing System simulation [Deiters *et al.*, 1995; Oberweis *et al.*, 1994].

The analysis of corporate memory is much harder, because its effects are related to long-term feedback loops within an organization: information has to be accumulated, condensed and then transferred to the organizational units where its effects are supposed to happen. The impact of those processes is not related to the business workflows and cannot be measured by hard business variables in time and money, but by **the way they influence** the variables that produce those time-and-money effects, like task performance, error rate, or document production rate.

Typically, these effects cannot be described by the exchange of discrete units of information. They are represented as a constant flow of influence, whose rate is determined by the availability of corporate memory and its common understanding by the communicating partners. A classical method for the analysis of such systems is System Dynamics (SD) [Forrester, 1961]. The philosophy of SD is that people can describe structure and local behavior

---

[3]   Implementation strategies and examples can be found in [Peters, 1996]

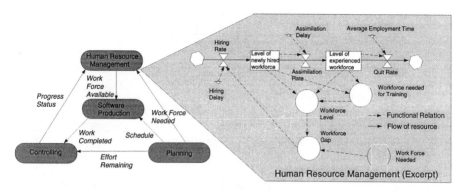

Figure 2 Software development subsystems (adopted from [Abdel-Hamid and Madnick, 1991])

of a system very well, but fail to predict global behavior, especially if feedback loops of different length and complexity are part of the system. This is exactly the situation under which we analyze the impact of information flows. SD describes a system by a flow of resources between levels. The quantity of the flow is determined by flow rates, which in turn are defined by information about levels from different areas of the system aggregated by functions in the so-called auxiliaries (cf. Figure 2, right side).

In his work on software project dynamics, Abdel-Hamid [Abdel-Hamid and Madnick, 1991] showed that SD simulation is well-suited for the analysis of multiple cause-effect feedback loops that describe the productivity behavior of a software development team performing a specific project. Abdel-Hamid developed and validated a set of models for the major factors related to software development productivity and established the feedback loops within and among them (see Figure 2 for a overview of the model structure). As an example, consider the simulation of an effect called Brooks Law: If schedule pressure is detected in the *Controlling* submodel the *Planning* module is defining the *workforce needed* to meet the schedule. This workforce needed determines the current workforce gap and influences the hiring rate. Addition of new workforce to *newly hired workforce* leads to additional *workforce needed for training*. This reduces the overall workforce available, since newly hired workforce is considered being of significantly lower availability. The result is a lower productivity and even more schedule pressure.

Abdel-Hamid's ideas were the starting point for our own simulation model. However, while his approach deals with *one* team performing *one* project, our goal is to analyze cooperating methods. Therefore, we had to widen the scope with respect to contents, focus and scale:

1. Communication and cooperation was not an issue in the single team situation described by Abdel-Hamid. We had to develop an additional model that describes the manpower needed for information management, document creation, or communication and the effects that result from the existence and quality of information flows. With this model we relate the effort spent on information exchange to the effects that information flows can have on the overall productivity in the development process.

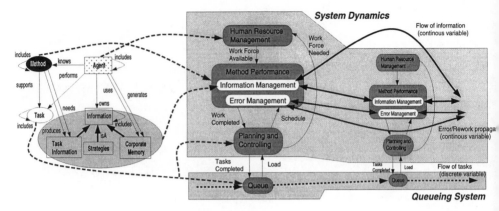

Figure 3 Mapping of the conceptual to the simulation model

2. We had to adapt to a multi-team-multi-project situation to describe the cooperation aspects that define the context of the information flow analysis. This led to a system structure, where

   a. one SD model that describes the productivity of every unit in the organizational network and

   b. coupling mechanisms among the method SD models were defined. A Queueing System was coupled to the SD model in order to simulate the flow of discrete tasks that define the schedule and the amount of task information. SD variables were defined to couple the models with respect to efforts on and effects of information flows, the propagation of errors, and rework effort needed

These requirements led to an overall model structure where one SD performance model in the sense of Abdel-Hamid exists for every method and those models are coupled by the flow of tasks, information and errors through the modeled system. In the next subsections, we discuss this structure and its representation in a conceptual meta modeling environment.

3.2 The Method Simulation Model

In order to relate the conceptual structure of the information flow model in Section 2 to the simulation model one has to define a mapping between the described concepts and a formal coupling between their representations (Section 3.2). The mapping of the information flow model onto the simulation model that fulfills the requirements of Section 3.1 is realized as shown in Figure 3.

1. Every **agent** is represented by a **Human Resource Management** model. This is based on the idea that the role of the agent in method execution can be filled by the workforce of this department. Cross-method teams cannot be modelled using this approach.

2. The **tasks** performed by the methods are represented by the **Planning and Controlling/Queue** models. The task in the conceptual model describes what has to be done (the workload) and the method describes how things are to be done (the performance of work).

System	Purpose of Analysis	Resource	Input	Output
Human Resouce Management	- integration of new hires - structure of workforce -training effort	- workforce	- workforce needed - training info avail.	- workforce avail. - manpower avail.
Planning and Controlling	- definition and control of schedule	- tasks	- workload	- schedule - workforce needed
Queue	- description of task flow	- tasks	- new tasks - state of schedule	- workload - performed tasks
Method Performance	- allocation of manpower - task productivity - effects of schedule pressure	- tasks	- workforce - schedule - corporate memory	- performed tasks
Error Management	- error and rework rate with respect to workforce, schedule pressure, available information	- errors	- tasks performed - corporate memory - schedule pressure	- errors not found - rework effort needed
Information Management	- manpower needed for task information production, - manpower needed for information management, - effects of reuse of information	-Corporate Memory - Task Information	- tasks performed - manpower available	- Information avail., - manpower needed

Table 1 The role of the models in the simulation approach

3. The **method** is mapped on the **Method Performance** model. This model describes how manpower made available by the human resource management is spent on various parts of a task. It consists of submodels concerning task productivity, manpower allocation and the models under point 4. and 5.
4. The **Error Management** is a submodel of **Method Performance**. It provides the means to analyze the rate by which errors are generated, detected and reworked within a method and the resulting effort in needed manpower. The propagation of errors is described by a variable that couples the Error Management models for every method along the business process.
5. The **Information Management** model describes the amount of work necessary to access, provide and manage the information flows defined in the conceptual model. It also provides the corporate memory as a resource that influences the productivity of other tasks in the model, e.g. training effort, task productivity, error generation, etc. The information flows identified and the effort and impact connected to them are described by input and output variables in every Information Management model along the business process.

The complete structure of the SD model is explained in detail in [Peters, 1996]. Table 1 shows the roles and relations of the models.

A SD/Queueing model for a method consists of about 100 variables. The model is typically underspecified, which means that even 'driving the wrong screws' could lead to acceptable overall results with respect to the variables of interest. Careful calibration and validation is necessary, before the models can be used as a testbed for analyzing organizational information flows. Fortunately, a lot of validation work for the Human Resource Management, Method Performance, and partially the Planning and Controlling submodel has been performed

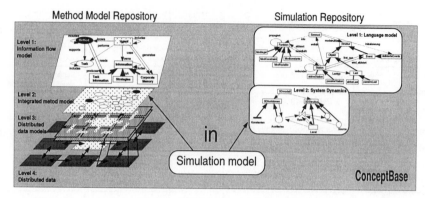

Figure 4 Repository-based integration of conceptual and simulation models

by Abdel-Hamid. Therefore, we could concentrate on validating the specific models and connections added by our approach. Before we describe a first model validation and experimentation case study, we give an overview of the modeling and execution environment which we developed to define the simulation models and to connect them to the conceptual models.

3.3 The MultiSim Environment

Our model demands a heterogeneous simulation that allows the coupling of discrete (Queueing Systems) and continuous (SD) simulation techniques. The implementation idea is based on the observation that every quasi-continuous simulation technique can be mapped on a discrete-event technique if the time increment is sufficiently small. System modeling concepts which lead to the coupling of different simulation techniques in one executable model have been realized and tested recently by Fishwick in his work on multi-simulation [Fishwick, 1995]. We enlarged his approach by developing a graphical system modeling environment which interprets the developed models at runtime [Mandelbaum, 1995]. In order to enable high usability and high model quality, the model editor is customized automatically not only to the graphical symbols and modeling elements but also to the modeling constraints defined for a specific simulation technique.

The kernel of this environment is an IRDS repository for simulation techniques which is, like the method model repository, realized in the ConceptBase meta data manager [Jarke *et al.*, 1995]. We developed a definition language for simulation techniques by which simulation languages like SD, Queueing Systems, or Petri-Nets can be modelled and connected. The simulation model is defined on the third level of this repository.

While the simulation techniques specify the representation of the simulation model, the method models between methods specify their contents. As mentioned before, the method models form the second level of a repository for IS based on the information flow model. By coupling the simulation and method model repositories we are in the position to relate the simulation model directly to the conceptual model of information flows and the simulation

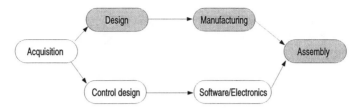

Figure 5 Basic business process in the company of the case study

techniques by using the multiple instantiation principle (cf. Figure 4). This allows for the direct relation of information flow changes to simulation experiments and, vice versa, from simulation results to information flow structure.

In the following, we describe a first validation of the simulation model in an industrial environment. After describing the validation process we give an example on how the models and the simulation environment MultiSim were used for analyzing how information exchange and overall performance are influenced by method changes.

4 ANALYZING THE PERFORMANCE IMPACT OF METHOD CHANGES

The case study was performed in a medium-sized manufacturing company, which provides system solutions for packaging machines. Since those machines consist of mechanical parts and of control software, there are two main business processes (cf. Figure 5). One consists of the mechanical design and the manufacturing of components which then are assembled and tested together with the developed control software that is developed in a parallel process. In the case study we concentrated on the manufacturing process highlighted in gray.

The company was applying for ISO 9000 certification, and therefore needed to analyze and reorganize their business processes. We were asked to support information management organization. During the interviews we did to define the information flows and information structure we were able to do a first validation of the simulation models. Afterwards we used the model as a kind of process management flight simulation, by which the process manager could experiment with possible impacts of changing methods or information flows on the overall system performance.

The philosophy of our method modeling approach is that structure and local behavior of processes can be defined with high quality by the involved agents. The emanating global dynamics have to be simulated and compared with the company's reality. We therefore initiated a three step validation process.

In the first step we validated the model structure by asking the engineers and workers about the relevance and correctness of the variables, their relations, and the resources. Afterwards a questionnaire about the value of the variables was filled in by other engineers who were not involved in the interviews. Multiple statements per were collected about

1. the self estimation of workload and overwork rates, the allocation of time to their jobs, their personal error management
2. assimilation time of new hirees and effort for training

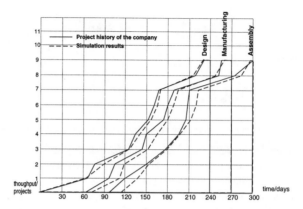

Figure 6 Simulation of company performance (base case)

3. task spectrum, time per task, meeting of schedules
4. information access along business processes
5. IS structure and usage

In a second step, the dynamics of the resulting submodels were validated using black-box and plausibility tests with example processes. Finally, the whole model for one business process (design — manufacturing — assembly) was tested using real production data of the previous year as a base case. At that time, the information flow situation in the company was mainly a flow of task information along the business process.

The simulation model was initialized with *planned* production schedules and the information from the interviews. The simulated throughput at the **Queue** submodel (see Table 1) of the departments was then compared to the *real* throughput of the company. Figure 6 shows this comparison of project throughput. The simulation result resembles the original throughput with respect to the structure and scale of the curves.[4]

For a *general* validation of the model structures and dynamics the case study was only a first step. Nevertheless, the models are good enough to analyze effects of information management and method changes **within this specific company**: Related to the ISO 9000 certification, the company wanted to solve problems with meeting their schedules in the design department. The introduction of a CAD method was considered as a possible solution (cf. Figure 7a). Together with the system, a faster distribution of drawings and support for the collection of drawings that were changed throughout the process was planned. Those drawings were often changed during manufacturing and assembly due to design errors. The collection of corporate memory information about changes should lead to the reduction of design errors by reuse of previously corrected designs.

---

[4]   An exception are some 'holes' (e.g., *design* around day 76, *manufacturing* around day 150, or *assembly* around day 210). At these points one task passed another one in the company which could not be modeled in the queueing system. Therefore, the simulation is late at first and then catches up after the next task.

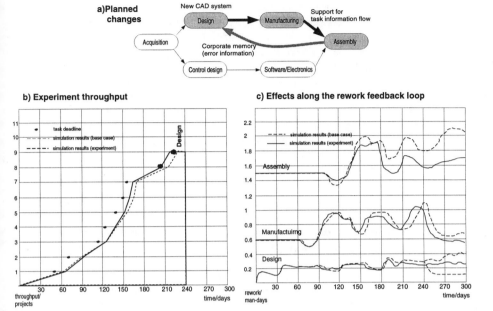

Figure 7 Prognosis on IS changes

We interviewed the engineers on the anticipated local effects that these changes might produce with respect to information management and error production. With conservative interviewees answers we performed a set of experiments. Two sample results are depicted in Figure 7b and c.

Figure 7b shows the simulated changes in throughput. The results indicate that the implemented changes show no positive effects on design throughput in the first half year. Afterwards the throughput is significantly better than in the base case and finally, the deadlines defined for the tasks are met. A first analysis shows that these results stem from an overlay of two effects: Better support of task information flow rapidly leads to better performance. The additional effort needed to manage the collected design drawings might consume those positive effects at first. But after some time of collecting corporate memory the reuse of drawings and design error knowledge leads to an **acceleration of the design process**.

A closer look at the simulation results indicates that this description of the dynamics is still too simple. There are various other global effects that influence the design throughput. Additionally, there are positive effects resulting from outside the design department. Our simulation approach allows for a deeper and more global analysis of the changes, as the example in Figure 7c shows.

The figure depicts the manpower needed for rework in all three departments. The first effect of the change is one across departments in the direction of the production process. The reduction of errors in the design phase leads a reduction of manpower spent on rework in the late steps of the production process. Even if the manpower needed for managing the corporate memory on errors would add to the overall manpower needed in design, the strong positive effect on other steps of the process justifies the change.

The second observation is a feedback effect that influences the productivity of the design department. If you take a closer look at the graph for rework in design, you see that a lot of tasks are sent back to design. Otherwise the base case line would go down to the initial value after day 240, the end of the planned design jobs (as indicated by the forking of the base case graph). Even if the corporate memory could not show its full effect after nine projects, it is clear that rework in the design department is reduced significantly. Avoiding past errors led to less rework in the assembly and therefore in the design department, too. This in turn leads to higher productivity and less errors per task. Therefore, there is a positive effect on the design process because of the **higher quality of the overall process**.

There are two major results drawn from this case study:

1. The impact of changing methods on productivity should not be analyzed with respect to the isolated task the method supports, but should be seen in the global context of the network of methods in order to define the long term net effect of method introduction. In our case the introduction of a method and new information flows led to a positive effect, but it might also be that, although the method fits perfectly into the process, important feedback loops are no longer support, either because information is no longer available or because it is not exchanged properly anymore. Furthermore, it always takes time to accumulate new experiences with a method and to spread them in the organization. This time gap often leads to non acceptance of a new method if it becomes to large.
2. The simulation method itself allows the method engineer to gain better knowledge about the dynamics of his environment and effects of changes. The tool was considered as fun to play with by the engineers and motivated them to test hypotheses our fill knowledge gaps.

5 CONCLUSION

In this paper, we presented a formal approach to method engineering in-the-large, integrating conceptual modeling and simulation technology. The approach focuses on the modeling of information flows among methods. The identification of three information categories led to an analysis method based on conceptual models of information flows. It relates information exchange requirements defined in the information flow models to design decisions by simulating the impact of those decisions on organizational performance. The conceptual and simulation models are formally linked by a common repository concept. We demonstrated the possibilities of the simulation approach by performing some experiments in a manufacturing company.

Currently we are trying to generalize the applicability of the models by additional case studies. We are aiming at an experimenting environment in the style of a 'management flight simulator' for flexible information management in federated organizations, which can be used in IS requirements definition, IS management education and the like. The link between the analysis tool and system design will be supported by a tool that guides the developer according to a methodology organized with respect to the three information flow categories.

Even now, our findings seem to put in question some established wisdoms in Method Engineering and Business Process Reengineering: It is definitely necessary to have a flexible, configurable IS development process because of varying product requirements or steadily changing IS development methods. But you have to be careful not to reduce the process to a set of configurable methods with well-defined interfaces for two reasons. First, consider a really new method, i.e. not only a varying notation or tool with the same semantics. Such a method should not be embedded into the process by adapting the interfaces. The information flows and methods along the whole process have to be analyzed with respect to the impact of the new method. The case study is an example. Second, on-going radical change of methods does not allow to establish a corporate memory about the way-of-working and the experiences resulting from that. Higher quality of a specific method might be reduced or totally consumed by the lack of knowledge about how the method works in the specific context of an organization. In short, the introduction of a new method has to be analyzed globally and not only according to its direct interfaces in the business process.

6 ACKNOWLEDGMENT

The authors would like to thank the people at the OSTMA company for answering all our questions and being patient even if they had other important work to do. Furthermore, we would like to thank the referees for their valuable remarks and suggestions. We hope that we fixed the problems named.

7 REFERENCES

[Abdel-Hamid and Madnick, 1991]
T. Abdel-Hamid and S. Madnick. *Software Project Dynamics*. Prentice Hall, Englewood Cliffs, NJ, 1991.

[Brodie and Ceri, 1992]
M. Brodie and S. Ceri. On Intelligent and Cooperative Information Systems: A workshop summary. *Int. Jour. on Intelligent and Cooperative Information Systems 1*, 2 (1992), pp. 249–290.

[Daft and Lengel, 1986]
R. Daft and R. Lengel. Organizational Information Requirements, Media Richness and Structural Design. *Management Science 32*, 5 (1986), pp. 554 – 571.

[Deiters *et al.*, 1995]
W. Deiters, V. Gruhn and R. Striemer. The FUNSOFT Approach to Business Process Management. *Wirtschaftsinformatik 37*, 5 (1995), pp. 459 – 466.

[Feigenbaum, 1991]
A. Feigenbaum. *Total Quality Control*. McGraw-Hill Inc., 1991.

[Fishwick, 1995]
P. Fishwick. *Simulation Model Design and Execution*. Prentice Hall, Englewood Cliffs, N.J., 1995.

[Forrester, 1961]
J. Forrester. *Industrial Dynamics*. MIT Press, Cambridge, Mass., 1961.

[Hammer, 1992]
  D. K. Hammer. Lean Information Management: The Integrating Power of Information. In H. J. Pels and J. C. Wortmann (Eds.), *IFIP Transactions: Integration in Production Management Systems*, pp. 147–163. Elsevier Science Publishers B.V., 1992.

[Harmsen *et al.*, 1994]
  F. Harmsen, S. Brinkkemper and H. Oei. Situational Method Engineering for Information System Project Approaches. In *Methods and Associated Tools for the Information Systems Life Cycle*, pp. 169 – 194. Elsevier Science B.V., 1994.

[Heinzl and Srikanth, 1995]
  A. Heinzl and R. Srikanth. Entwicklung der betrieblichen Informationsverarbeitung. *Wirtschaftsinformatik* 37, 1 (1995), pp. 10 – 17.

[ISO, 1987]
  ISO. ISO9000, Quality Systems - Model for Quality Assurance in design/development, production, installation, and servicing. Technical report, International Organization for Standardization, Geneva, Switzerland, 1987.

[Jarke and Ellis, 1993]
  M. Jarke and C. Ellis. Distributed Cooperation in Integrated Information Systems. *Int. Jour. of Intelligent and Cooperative Information Systems* 2, 1 (1993), pp. 85 – 103.

[Jarke *et al.*, 1993]
  M. Jarke, M. Jeusfeld and P. Szczurko. Three Aspects of Intelligent Cooperation in the Quality Life Cycle. *Int. Jour. of Intelligent and Cooperative Information Systems* 2, 4 (1993), pp. 355–374.

[Jarke *et al.*, 1995]
  M. Jarke, R. Gallersdörfer, M. Jeusfeld, M. Staudt and S. Eherer. ConceptBase – A Deductive Object Base for Meta Data Management. *Journal of Intelligent Information Systems 4*, 2 (1995).

[Klein and Lyytinen, 1992]
  H. Klein and K. Lyytinen. Towards a New Understanding of Data Modeling . In C. Floyd, H. Zullighoven, R. Budde and R. Keil-Slawik (Eds.), *Software Development and Reality Construction*, pp. 203 – 219. Springer-Verlag, 1992.

[Lyytinen, 1987]
  K. Lyytinen. A Taxonomic Perspective on Information Systems Development: Theoretical Constructs and Recommendations . In R. Boland and R. Hirschheim (Eds.), *Critical Issues in Information Systems Research*, pp. 3 – 42. John Wiley and Sons, 1987.

[Mandelbaum, 1995]
  M. Mandelbaum. Modellierung und Durchfürung von Informationsflussimulationen auf der Basis eines Simulationsrepositories. Master's thesis, Lehrstuhl für Informatik V, RWTH Aachen, 1995.

[Marttiin, 1994]
  P. Marttiin. Towards Flexible Process Support with a CASE shell. In G. Wijers, S. Brinkkemper and T. Wassermann (Eds.), *Proc. of the 6th Int. Conf. on Advanced Information Systems Engineering (CAiSE'94)*. Springer-Verlag, Heidelberg, Germany, 1994.

[Oberweis *et al.*, 1994]
  A. Oberweis, G. Scherrer and W. Stucky. INCOME/STAR: Methodology and Tools for the Development of Distributed Information Systems. *Information Systems 19*, 8 (1994), pp. 643 – 660.

[Olle *et al.*, 1991]
  T. Olle, J. Hagelstein, I. MacDonald, C. Rolland, H. Sol, F. van Assche and A. Verrijn-Stuart. *Information Systems Methodologies - A Framework for Understanding*. North-Holland, Amsterdam, 1991.

[Österle, 1995]
  H. Österle. *Prozess- und Systementwicklung (Band 1: Entwurfstechniken*. Springer-Verlag, Berlin, Heidelberg,...., 1995.

[Paulk *et al.*, 1993]
> M. Paulk, B. Curtis, M. Chrissis and C. Weber. Capability Maturity Model for Software, Version 1.1. Technical Report SEI-93-TR-24, Software Engineering Institute, Carnegie Mellon University, Pittsburgh, PA, February 1993.

[Peters and Jeusfeld, 1994]
> P. Peters and M. Jeusfeld. Structuring Information Flow in Quality Management. In *Int. Conf. on Data and Knowledge Systems for Manufacturing and Engineering*, pp. 258 – 263, Hong Kong, 1994.

[Peters *et al.*, 1995]
> P. Peters, P. Szczurko, M. Jarke and M. Jeusfeld. A Federated Information System for Quality Management Processes. In *IFIP WG8.1 Working Conference on Information Systems for Decentralized Organizations*, pp. 100 – 117, Trondheim, Norway, 1995.

[Peters, 1996]
> P. Peters. *Planning and Analysis of Information Flow in Quality Management*. PhD thesis, RWTH Aachen, 1996.

[Pohl, 1994]
> K. Pohl. *A Process Centered Requirements Engineering Environment*. PhD thesis, RWTH Aachen, 1994.

[Scheer, 1993]
> A.-W. Scheer. *Wirtschaftsinformatik (Reference Models for Industrial Business Processes (in German)*. Springer Verlag, Berlin, Heidelberg,..., 1993.

[Scott-Morton, 1994]
> M. Scott-Morton. The 1990s research program: Implications for Management and the Emerging Organization. *Decision Support Systems 12*, 2 (1994), pp. 251–256.

[Senge, 1990]
> P. Senge. *The Fifth Discipline: The Art and Practice of the Learning Organization*. Currency, New York, 1990.

[Shaw, 1991]
> N. Shaw. STEP Part 1 – overview and fundamental principles, ISO TC184/SC4/Editing Document No. N-11. Technical report, 1991.

[Vennix *et al.*, 1994]
> J. Vennix, D. Andersen, G. Richardson and J. Rohrbaugh. Model Building for Group decision Support: Issues and Alternatives fir Knowledge Elicitation. In J. Morecroft and J. Sterman (Eds.), *Modeling for Learning Organizations*. Productivity Press, 1994.

8 BIOGRAPHY

Peter Peters studied computer science and medical informatics at the University of Dortmund, Germany. He is currently a doctoral student at the 'Graduate College for Computer Science and Engineering' and a member of the Information Systems group at the Technical University of Aachen. In his research he investigates the modeling, enactment, and analysis of information flow and communication in distributed organizations and has just finished his doctoral thesis on 'Planning and Analysis of Information Flows in Quality Management'. During this work he has been participating in the interdisciplinary project WibQuS and FoQuS funded by the German Ministry of Research.

Matthias Jarke is professor of Information Systems and chairman of the computer science department at the Technical University of Aachen, Germany. After obtaining a doctorate from the University of Hamburg, Germany, in 1980, he held faculty positions at New York

University and the University of Passau prior to joining Aachen. His research interests lie in the development and usage of meta information systems for design applications. He has been coordinator of two European ESPRIT projects in this field, DAIDA (knowledge-based information system environments) and NATURE (requirements engineering environments), and was principal investigator in collaborative projects concerning IS applications in mechanical engineering (WibQuS) and medicine. He is editor-in-chief of the journal 'Information Systems'

Markus Mandelbaum has been a student of the Technical University of Aachen. During his diploma thesis he has co-designed and implemented the MultiSim system. After his graduation he has founded a company that provides computer solutions for manufacturing process and data management in small and medium sized enterprises.

17

Information systems development methodologies: a broader perspective

D E Avison
Department of Management, University of Southampton
Southampton SO17 1BJ, UK, tel: 44 1703 592563, fax: 44 1703 593844
e-mail: dea@socsci.soton.ac.uk

Abstract

This paper first provides a historical perspective on approaches to developing information systems and argues that there are major weaknesses associated with the conventional waterfall model and the methodologies which followed. The paper suggests that a contingency approach to information systems development has much to offer and looks at Multiview, which is described as an exploration in information systems development. Some strengths and weaknesses of this contingency approach are highlighted and a new version of Multiview offered. This description enables a further discussion of information systems development and suggests that human and organisational aspect are at least as important as the technical ones which tend to be emphasised. Information systems development is seen as first a social process, though it will contain technical aspects. This social process is examined in more detail illustrating the arguments, for example, with different views of the systems analyst and the problem situation in this process. Such a broad approach also suggests that the area of which information systems development is a part, is multi-disciplinary where technology and computing are by no means dominant.

Keywords

Action research, contingency, Multiview, social process, soft systems, information systems development

1 AN HISTORICAL PERSPECTIVE

1.1 Pre-methodology era

Early computer applications were implemented without an explicit information systems development methodology. The emphasis of computer applications development was on programming, with systems developers technically trained but rarely good communicators, nor were they systems analysts. The needs of the users were rarely well established with the consequence that the design was frequently inappropriate to the application. The dominant 'methodology' was rule-of-thumb and experience. This led to poor control and management of the project. Most emphasis was placed on maintaining present systems to get them right rather than developing new ones. Management were not getting value for money, and there was a growing appreciation of the potential role of the systems analyst and the need for a methodology to develop information systems.

1.2 The waterfall model

The life cycle or waterfall model (for example, Daniels & Yeates, 1971) of feasibility study, systems investigation, analysis, design, and implementation, followed by review and maintenance, became that methodology. It was widely used in the 1970s and is the basis for many methodologies that followed. It is well tried and tested. The feasibility study attempts to assess the costs and benefits of alternative proposals enabling management to make informed choices. The use of documentation standards helps to ensure that proposals are complete and that they are communicated to users and computing staff. The approach also ensures that users are trained to use the system. There are controls and these, along with the division of the project into phases of manageable tasks, help to avoid missed cutover dates. Unexpectedly high costs and lower benefits are also less likely.

However, there are serious limitations to the approach along with limitations in the way it is used. Some potential traps are (Avison & Fitzgerald, 1995):

- Failure to meet the needs of management (due to the concentration on single applications, particularly at the operational level of the organisation)
- Unambitious systems design (due to the emphasis on the existing system as a basis for the new computer system)
- Instability (due to the modelling of processes which are unstable because businesses and their environments change frequently)
- Inflexibility (due to the output-driven orientation of the design processes which makes changes in design costly)
- User dissatisfaction (due to problems with the computer-orientated documentation and the inability for users to 'see' the system before it is operational)
- Problems with documentation (due to its computer rather than user orientation and the fact that it is rarely kept up-to-date)
- Application backlog (due to the maintenance workload as attempts are made to change the system in order to reflect user needs).

As an answer to these criticisms, there have been a number of movements. The first is to reject methodologies by either playing lip-service to their use or fail to do even that. The second is to improve the traditional waterfall model by the inclusion of techniques and tools along with improved training so as to reduce the potential impact of these problems. A third movement is the proposal of new methodology themes and methodologies which are very different to the traditional waterfall model. A fourth movement is to suggest a more flexible contingency approach to information systems development reflecting the different problem situations that occur. We will look at each of these in turn.

1.3 Rejecting the methodology approach

One reaction to the unsatisfactory use of methodologies is the overt decision not to use any methodology when developing information systems (or the covert decision to pay only lip-service to them). A chosen methodology may not have been appropriate for the organisation and there has been a backlash against formalised methodologies. Their use has not always led to productivity gains. Methodologies have also been criticised for being over complex, for requiring significant people skills and expensive tools, and being inflexible and difficult to adopt.

More fundamentally, it has frequently been found that the existence of a methodology standard in an organisation leads to its unthinking implementation and to a focus on following its procedures to the exclusion of the real needs of the project being developed. In other words, the methodology obscures the important issues. De Grace and Stahl (1993) have termed this 'goal displacement' and talk about the severe problem of 'slavish adherence to the methodology'.

Wastell (1996) talks about the 'fetish of technique' which inhibits creative thinking. He takes this further and suggests that the application of a methodology in this way is the functioning of methodology 'as a highly sophisticated social device for containing the acute and potentially overwhelming pressures of systems development'. He is suggesting that systems development is such a difficult and stressful process, that developers often take refuge in the intense application of the methodology in all its detail as a way of dealing with these difficulties. Developers can be seen to be working hard and diligently, but this is in reality goal displacement activity because they are avoiding the real problems of effectively developing the required system. Users, analysts and managers thus find that the great hopes of some in the 1980s that methodologies would solve most of the problems of information systems development have not come to pass and this has led some to reject methodologies completely and others to use them as a social defence only.

1.4 Improvements to the waterfall model

Since the 1970s, there have been a number of developments in techniques and tools and many of these have been incorporated in the methodologies exemplifying the modern version of the waterfall model. Techniques incorporated include entity-relationship modelling, normalisation, data flow diagramming and entity life cycles. Tools include project management software, data dictionary software, drawing tools and computer-assisted software engineering (CASE) tools. The incorporation of these developments address some of the criticisms discussed in section 1.2, but give grounds to the potential criticisms of Wastell (1996). The data modelling techniques suggest that the waterfall models now are more balanced between process and data modelling rather than having a purely process modelling emphasis. The documentation has improved, thanks to the use of drawing and CASE tools, and it is more likely to be kept up to date and be more understandable by non-computer people. Further, CASE tools can be used to develop prototypes which enable users to assess the proposed information system in a far more tangible way and can speed up delivery of the operational system. The blended methodologies SSADM (Eva, 1994) and Merise (Quang & Chartier-Kastler, 1991) could be said to be updated versions of the waterfall model, and this updated waterfall model is the basis of many modern student texts and courses in information systems. Although these improvements have brought the basic model up to date, many users have argued that the inflexibility of the life cycle remains and inhibits most effective use of computer information systems.

1.5 New methodology themes and methodologies

Over the last ten or fifteen years, there have been many methodologies, some of which are as structured as the waterfall model, but reflect different movements in information systems development. They include incorporating ideas from systems thinking, typified by soft systems methodology (SSM) (Checkland, 1981 and Checkland & Scholes, 1990) which addresses the needs of management and the organisation as a whole; considering strategic issues, such as critical success factors (Bullen & Rockart, 1984), again, addressing the needs of management; business process re-engineering (Hammer & Champy, 1993), looking more fundamentally at the way the organisation does things (traditional information systems development is often accused of merely computerising present ways of doing things rather than improving things more fundamentally); object-orientation (Booch, 1991 and Coad & Yourdon, 1991) which unifies many aspects of the information systems development process and thus avoids the difficult combination of process and data approaches in one methodology; participation, such as ETHICS (Mumford, 1995) and joint requirements planning (JRP) and joint applications design (JAD) (Martin, 1991), where major consideration is given to the role of users and other stakeholders in the information systems development process, indeed, where the users rather than the technologists drive the process and therefore address the problem of user dissatisfaction that was inherent in traditional systems analysis; and the related emancipatory approaches where systems are developed which permit emancipation through rational discourse, typified by the UTOPIA project (Bodker *et al.*, 1987). All these approaches address some of the weaknesses of the traditional waterfall model and have been adopted by organisations. However, many users find some of them either unnecessarily complicated, expensive (in skills required and tools used) and difficult to adopt or, if this is not the case, narrow in their applicability and scope.

1.6 Contingency approaches to information systems development

Many users of methodologies have found the waterfall model and the alternative methodologies unsatisfactory. Most methodologies are designed for situations which follow a stated or unstated 'ideal type'. The methodology provides a step-by-step prescription for addressing this ideal type. However, situations are all different and there is no such thing as an 'ideal type' in reality. Situations differ depending on, for example, their complexity and structuredness, type and rate of change in the organisation, the numbers of users affected, their skills, and those of the analysts. Further, most methodology users expect to follow a step-by-step, top-down approach to information systems development where they carry out a series of iterations through to project implementation. In reality, in any one project, this is rarely the case, as some phases might be omitted, others carried out in a different sequence, and yet others developed further than espoused by the methodology authors. Similarly, particular techniques and tools may be used differently or not used at all in different circumstances.

A contingency approach is therefore suggested as a more realistic and useful methodology. Multiview (Avison & Wood-Harper, 1990) is an example of such an approach and this paper looks at this in more detail in the next section. It is a contingency framework in that it will be adapted according to the particular situation in the organisation. The authors are concerned to show that information systems development theories should be contingent rather than prescriptive, because the skills of different analysts and the situations in which they are constrained to work always has to be taken into account in any project. Each application of Multiview forms a new and original methodology. There are potential problems of the contingent approach and in examining Multiview, these potential criticisms ought to be considered. First, some of the benefits of standardisation might be lost. Second, there is a wide range of different skills that are required to handle many approaches. Third, the selection of approach requires experience and skills to make the best judgements. Fourth, they implicitly or explicitly follow a waterfall model and therefore they suffer the same criticisms of that approach. Finally, authors have suggested that any combination of approaches is untenable because each has different philosophies and therefore cannot be blended.

2 MULTIVIEW: A CONTINGENT FRAMEWORK

2.1 Background to Multiview

Multiview (Avison & Wood-Harper, 1990) was proposed as a framework for information systems development. Information systems development is perceived as a hybrid process involving computer specialists, who will build the system, and users, for whom the system is being built, with the help of a methodology. The methodology looks at both the human and technical aspects of information systems development. In this aspect and others, it has been greatly influenced by Soft Systems Methodology (Checkland, 1981) and ETHICS (Mumford, 1995) but has fused these ideas with those found in 'hard' methodologies, such as Yourdon Systems Modeling (Yourdon, 1993) and Information Engineering (Martin, 1989).

The approach adopted has been used on a number of projects, and the methodology itself has been refined using 'action research' methods (Checkland, 1981; Lewin, 1946; Susman & Evered, 1978; and Warmington, 1980), that is the application and testing of ideas developed in an academic environment into the 'real world'. It is a contingency approach in that it will be adapted according to the particular situation in the organisation. The authors are concerned to show that information systems development theories should be contingent rather than prescriptive, because the skills of different analysts and the situations in which they are constrained to work always has to be taken into account in any project. Avison and Wood-Harper (1986) describe Multiview as an *exploration* in information systems development. It therefore sets out to be flexible: a particular technique or aspect of the methodology will work in certain situations but is not advised for others.

The methodology includes many of the techniques used in other methodologies. The authors of Multiview claim, however, that it is not simply a hotchpotch of available techniques and tools, but an approach which has been tested and works in practice. It is also 'multi-view' in the sense that it takes account of the fact that as an information systems project develops, it takes on different perspectives or views: organisational, technical, human-orientated, social, economic and so on.

2.2 The original Multiview framework

The five stages of Multiview are as follows:

- Analysis of human activity
- Analysis of information
- Analysis and design of socio-technical aspects
- Design of the human-computer interface
- Design of technical aspects.

They incorporate five different views which are appropriate to the progressive development of an analysis and design project, covering all aspects required to answer the vital questions of users. These five views are necessary to form a system which is complete in both technical and human terms. The five stages move from the general to the specific, from the conceptual to hard fact and from issue to task. Outputs of each stage either become inputs to following stages or are major outputs of the methodology.

The authors argue that to be complete in human as well as in technical terms, the methodology must provide help in answering the following questions:

1. How is the computer system supposed to further the aims of the organisation installing it?
2. How can it be fitted into the working lives of the people in the organisation that are going to use it?
3. How can the individuals concerned best relate to the machine in terms of operating it and using the output from it?
4. What information system processing function is the system to perform?
5. What is the technical specification of a system that will come close enough to doing the things that have been written down in the answers to the other four questions?

Multiview attempts to address all these questions and to involve all the role players or stakeholders in answering these questions. The emphasis in information systems, it is argued, must move away from 'technical systems which have behavioural and social problems' to 'social systems which rely to an increasing extent on information technology'.

The distinction between issue and task is important because it is too easy to concentrate on tasks when computerising, and to overlook important issues which need to be resolved. Too often, issues are ignored in the rush to 'computerise'. Issue-related aspects, in particular those occurring at stage 1 of Multiview, are concerned with debate on the definition of system requirements in the broadest sense, that is 'what real world problems is the system to solve?'. On the other hand, task-related aspects, in particular stages 2-5, work towards forming the system that has been defined with appropriate emphasis on complete technical and human views. The system, once created, is not just a computer system, it is also composed of people performing jobs.

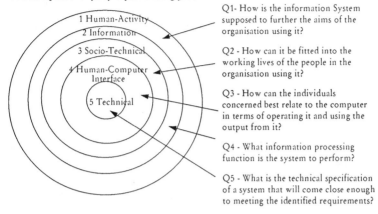

Q1- How is the information System supposed to further the aims of the organisation using it?

Q2 - How can it be fitted into the working lives of the people in the organisation using it?

Q3 - How can the individuals concerned best relate to the computer in terms of operating it and using the output from it?

Q4 - What information processing function is the system to perform?

Q5 - What is the technical specification of a system that will come close enough to meeting the identified requirements?

Figure 1 The Multiview framework (version 1)

One representation of the methodology is shown in figure 1. Working from the middle outwards we see a widening of focus and an increase in understanding the problem situation and its related technical and human characteristics and needs. Working from the outside in, we see an increasing concentration of focus, an increase in structure and the progressive development of an information system. This diagram also shows how the five questions outlined above have been incorporated into the five stages of Multiview.

The first stage looks at the organisation - its main purpose, problem themes, and the creation of a statement about what the information system will be and what it will do. It is based on SSM (mode 1), described in Checkland, 1981, using the techniques of rich picture building, CATWOE definition and the creation of root definitions, and conceptual models. Possible changes are debated and agendas drawn up for change. The second stage is to analyse the entities and functions of the problem situation described in stage one. This is carried out independently of how the system will be developed. The functional modelling and entity-relationship modelling found in most methodologies are suggested as modelling techniques.

The philosophy behind the third stage is that people have a basic right to control their own destinies and that if they are allowed to participate in the analysis and design of the systems that they will be using, then implementation, acceptance and operation of the system will be enhanced. Human considerations, such as job satisfaction, task definition, morale and so on are seen as just as important as technical considerations. This stage emphasises the choice between alternative systems, according to important social and technical considerations. The fourth stage is concerned with the technical requirements of the user interface. Choices between batch or on-line and menu, command or soft form interfaces are made. The design of specific conversations will depend on the background and experience of the people who are going to use the system, as well as their information needs.

Finally, the design of the technical subsystem concerns the specific technical requirements of the system to be designed, and therefore to such aspects as computers, databases, application software, control and maintenance. Although the methodology is concerned with the computer only in the latter stages, it is assumed that a computer system will form at least part of the information system. However, the authors do not argue that the final system will necessarily run on a large mainframe computer. This is just one solution, and many cases of Multiview in action show applications being implemented on a microcomputer.

2.3 The strengths and weaknesses of Multiview

Conventional information systems development methodologies have a number of weaknesses including:

- Narrow scope
- Rigidity in use
- Adherence to the waterfall model.

The authors argue that the first two aims are achieved in Multiview. The five parts of the approach encompass the aims of the organisation and how the information system can be fitted into the working lives of the people in the organisation that are going to use it, as well as addressing the user-computer interface, the functional requirements and the technical design. This is a much broader framework than that provided by more conventional methodologies.

A main tenet of Multiview is that it is a contingency approach, the techniques and tools suggested are to be used where appropriate and the phases and sub-phases may also be omitted or reduced in scope or executed in a different sequence than that shown in figure 1. Multiview is, however, not unstructured. An unstructured approach is offered by Benyon & Skidmore (1987) who suggest that information systems development should be a process of choosing techniques and tools as thought appropriate by the analysts at the time from a 'tool-kit'. Multiview provides a flexible framework and suggests (but does not put it stronger) a choice of techniques and tools at each phase in the development of a system. It allows the benefits of the experience and expertise embodied in good methodologies to be focused on the particular needs of the situation.

Although we have stated that phases might be omitted or reduced in scope or executed in a different sequence, the description of Multiview is in terms of 'layers in an onion' (as in figure 1) or as a series of five broad steps. However, this is described as an 'ideal type' which will guide the analyst who will redesign it for any practical situation. Nevertheless, the description gives the impression of a waterfall model, despite denials from the methodology authors using Multiview in practice. This led to difficulties where, for example, users required further explanation on how to go from stage 1 (essentially a description of the problem situation using SSM rich pictures, root definitions and conceptual models) to stage 2 (a combination of data modelling used in IE and process modelling used in STRADIS). A further refining of Multiview has led to another definition, and this is described in the next section. It is more explicitly an antithesis of the waterfall model.

2.4 The development of Multiview

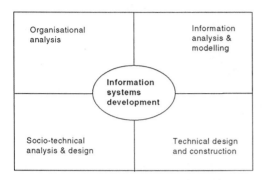

Figure 2 The Multiview framework (version 2)

In Multiview2 (Avison *et al.*, 1996), the five stages have been reduced to a four-box structure of organisational analysis, information analysis and modelling, socio-technical analysis and design, and technical design and construction. The proposed new framework for Multiview is given in figure 2 and it shows the four parts of the methodology mediated through the actual process of information systems development. The four parts of human activity systems analysis or organisational analysis (which examines organisational behaviours), socio-technical systems analysis and design (which examines work systems), and technical design and construction (which examines technical artefacts) are integrated through the information analysis and modelling stage which acts as a bridge between the other three, communicating and enacting the outcomes in terms of each other. In this way Multiview offers a systematic guide to any information systems development intervention, together with a reflexive, learning methodological process. Emphasis placed in each of the four parts of Multiview will change as the information system is being developed and contingent on the particular situation.

There are also differences in detail between the two versions of Multiview which reflect published research over the intervening years and more importantly experience in using Multiview during this period. Thus, for example, stakeholder analysis strengthens the conceptual analysis of SSM and ethical analysis in organisational analysis; there is a migration from structured methods to object-oriented analysis in information analysis and modelling; ethnographic approaches supplement ETHICS in socio-technical systems analysis and design; and prototyping, CASE, evolutionary and rapid development approaches are more strongly suggested in technical design and construction.

However, although the authors recommend a contingent approach to ISD, Multiview2 should not be used to justify random or uncontrolled development. The terms 'methodology' and 'method' tend to be used interchangeably, although they can be distinguished insofar as a method is a concrete procedure for getting something done while a methodology is a higher-level construct which provides a rationale for choosing between different methods (Oliga 1988). In this sense, an IS methodology, such as Multiview2, provides a basis for constructing a situation-specific method (figure 3), which arises from a genuine engagement of the analyst with the problem situation (Wastell 1996).

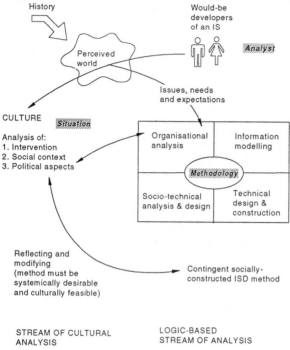

Figure 3 Constructing the information systems development methodology (adapted from Checkland & Scholes, 1990, Wood-Harper & Avison, 1992)

3 OBSERVATIONS AND CONCLUSIONS

3.1 Contingency

Strictly speaking, a distinction should be made in the criticisms of methodologies made earlier between poor application and use of a methodology on the one hand and an inadequate methodology itself. A defence made by a number of methodology vendors implies that the methodology is not being correctly implemented by some organisations. Whilst this may be true in some cases, it is not an argument that seems to hold much sway with methodology users. They argue that the two issues are much the same and for whatever reason they have experienced disappointments in the use of methodologies whether they represent improvements in the waterfall model (section 1.4) or new methodologies (section 1.5).

However, to respond to this by developing information systems without any methodology (section 1.3) is not the answer, as it will lead to the problems of poor control of the project, and management not getting value for money which were discussed in section 1.1 and, to some extent 1.2. Some authors (e.g. Benyon & Skidmore, 1987) advocate a 'tool-kit' approach, but it is argued elsewhere (Avison, Fitzgerald & Wood-Harper, 1988) that a tool-kit without any supporting advice and structures is indeed 'not enough' as it will lead to information systems that are likely to be idiosyncratic and difficult to maintain and therefore be of variable value.

One potential solution, outlined in section 1.6 and exemplified by Multiview which is described in section 2, is a more flexible approach, but within a framework, adaptable according to the characteristics of the project or domain. These contingent factors include the type of project, whether it is an operations-level system or a management information system, the size of the project, the importance of the project, the projected life of the project, the characteristics of the problem domain, the available skills and so on. As Mitroff & Linstone (1993) concluded, whilst any *inquiring system* can be used to generate evidence for any problem, it does not follow that each such system is equally valid or appropriate as a way of representing all kinds of problems.

A contingency approach to ISD is not new, indeed, was suggested in Davis (1982). Contingency is often seen as applying to techniques and tools only, however, it also applies to the general approach to information systems development, and that implies rejection of the waterfall model (except as a *special case* of applying a contingency approach). Multiview2 is more explicitly an antithesis of the waterfall model.

A contingent approach needs to be flexible enough to be appropriate for most situations. This implies that a broader, as well as more numerous, set of tools and techniques is available to the user of the contingency approach. But, it also implies that the approach carries within it the many 'philosophies' of the various approaches to information systems development suggested in section 1.4. Thus, such an overall approach might be a blend of human, technical, organisational, and other approaches to information systems development as found in the many methodologies proposed. Again, Multiview attempts to provide that broad-based framework. The method engineering movement also suggests a contingent and blended view of information systems development, but frequently a mainly (or even uniquely) technical view of the process. The authors of Multiview see information systems development as a social process containing technical aspects.

3.2 Information systems development as a social process

Defining an information system can be regarded as a social process with three aspects. These are the role of the systems analyst and the paradigm of assumptions constructed in practice; the political nature of the change process; and how methodologies are interpreted. These aspects are described in Wood-Harper & Avison (1992).

The theory about the role of the systems analyst and the paradigm of assumptions constructed in practice (Burrell & Morgan, 1979) can perhaps be explained best by giving examples of systems analysts in different situations. Four different stereotypical views of the systems analyst may be given as functionalist, interpretive, objective and subjective. The last three, to a greater or lesser degree, suggest that ISD is more of a social than a technical process. Roles, ideals and metaphors for each might be as follows:

- In the functionalist perspective, the information system consists of interactions which function independently of outside manipulation. The analyst assumes that the situation can be readily understood, indeed there is an assumption of rational behaviour by the actors which makes understanding easier. The systems are well controlled, can be well understood and can be formally defined. The systems analyst might be seen as technical expert, the ideals are objectivity, rigour and formality and a metaphor of the analyst might be a medical doctor. This is very much a technical and process view and one where ISD is seen as a technical rather than as a social process.

- In the interpretive perspective, it is assumed that the analyst is subjective and interprets the problem situation. The analyst hopes to understand the intentions of the actors in the situation. Participation and involvement will be the best way to obtain detailed information about the problem situation, and later to be able to predict and control it. The systems analyst might be seen as facilitator, the ideal might emphasise the importance of meaning and a metaphor of the analyst might be a liberal teacher.

- In the radical structuralist view, the situation will appear to have a formal existence but require radical change due to, for example, contradictory and conflicting elements. The systems analyst is assumed to be an agent for change and social progress, emancipating people from their socio-economic structures. The systems analyst might be seen as an agent for social progress, the ideals lean towards change of the socio-economic class structures and a metaphor of the analyst might be a warrior.

- Finally, in the radical humanist view, the situation is seen as external and complex. There is an emphasis on participation to enable a rapport between the actors and leads to emancipation at all levels, including the socio-economic and psychological. The systems analyst might be seen as change analyst, the ideals lean towards change of the socio-economic structures and psychological barriers and a metaphor of the analyst might be an emancipator.

Kling & Scacchi (1982) identified four perspectives within which problem solvers may view the content of the problem situation in which information technology is embedded. The importance of these perspectives for the information systems definition is that different strategies should be adopted based on the perspective embraced. The first is the formal rational perspective, which emphasises the formal organisational structure and procedures. With this perspective, we see the extreme of reductionist thought. Again, this is a traditional technical perspective. The second perspective, the structural perspective, includes considerations of the situation's formal subunits and recognises that communication must occur between them. The third perspective is the interactionist viewpoint which recognises that the pieces of the information resource are not independent nor formally defined. The social groups of interest cross intra-organisational and inter-organisational boundaries and are possibly in a constant state of flux. The process of change is founded on negotiation. The fourth perspective, organisational politics, assumes that interactions in the organisation are based on the political machinations and resulting manifestations of power. Again, as we progress through the four perspectives, we see less emphasis on the technical and structural and more emphasis on the social and potentially emancipatory.

Defining an information system can be thought of as metaphorical activity with, for example, the Multiview methodology as a non-prescriptive description of a real-world process. The essence of a metaphor is in the understanding and experiencing of one kind of thing in terms of another and, in this context, the methodology is a useful, epistemological device for the process of defining an information system (Lakoff & Johnson, 1980). This means that there is support from fieldwork that the Multiview methodology is a metaphor which is interpreted and developed in the situation. Consequently, the Multiview methodology can be thought of as being an 'open theory' where people close the theory in action.

3.3 The inter-disciplinary nature of information systems

Avison & Nandhakumar (1995) argue that information systems is a pluralist field and evidence this view through information systems development. There is a wide variety of approaches to information systems development and a large number of methodologies based on each of the general approaches. Longworth (1985) identifies over 300 information systems development methodologies. Wood-Harper & Fitzgerald (1982) discuss two basic differences of approaches as lying either within a systems paradigm or scientific paradigm, illustrated by soft systems method (Checkland, 1981) and structured analysis and design (DeMarco, 1979 and Gane & Sarson, 1979) respectively.

Avison & Fitzgerald (1995) widen the basis for comparison and suggest that information systems development methodologies can be compared on the basis of philosophy, model, techniques, tools, scope, outputs, practice and product, and they classify approaches within a number of broad themes including:

- Systems
- Strategic
- Participative
- Prototyping
- Structured
- Data
- Object-oriented.

None of these approaches can be described as different flavours to well accepted approach. They represent radically different approaches to information systems development and ways to perceive the information systems development process. They require different expertise: some emphasise people and stress the need for inter-personal skills; others require engineering skills and stress skills in the use of techniques; and yet others stress organisational issues. They represent different 'philosophies'.

If we consider the themes identified above as approaches to information systems development, disciplines relevant would seem to include, for example, computer science (prototyping tools and software engineering), mathematics (formal methods), sociology (participation) and business and management (planning). We may add applied psychology, economics, linguistics, politics, semiology, ethics, ergonomics, culture studies and probably others to the list of foundation disciplines. Information systems development has a multi-disciplinary nature, and technology and computing are by no means dominant. Unfortunately, it is clear that the majority of research into information systems development concentrates on the technical aspects, and this includes the languages and formalisms of the method engineering movement.

Mitroff & Linstone's 'Fifth Way of Knowing', which they call Unbounded Systems Thinking, subsumes all the other inquiring systems within it since every information system or inquiry presupposes all the others. In this way, each information system is mutually dependent upon the other and hence there is no sense in which they can be seen as having a distinct and separate existence, one from another. Unbounded systems thinking argues that complex problem solving requires the application of as many disciplines, professions, and branches of knowledge as possible, with each one employing different paradigms of thought.

ACKNOWLEDGEMENTS

I am grateful to my friends and colleagues who have contributed greatly to discussions which have led to this paper, in particular, Guy Fitzgerald, Richard Vidgen, Bob Wood and Trevor Wood-Harper.

REFERENCES

Avison, D. E. & Fitzgerald, G. (1995) *Information Systems Development: Methodologies, Techniques and Tools.* 2nd edition, McGraw-Hill, Maidenhead.

Avison, D. E., Fitzgerald, G. & Wood-Harper, A. T. (1988) Information systems development: a tool-kit is not enough. *Computer Journal, 31, 4.*

Avison, D. E. & Nandhakumar, J. (1995) The discipline of information systems: let many flowers bloom!, in *Information Systems Concepts: Towards a Consolidation of views* (eds. E. D. Falkenberg, W. Hesse, & O. Olivé) Chapman and Hall.

Avison, D. E. & Wood-Harper, A. T. (1986) Multiview - an exploration in information systems development. *Australian Computer Journal,* 18, 4.

Avison, D. E. & Wood-Harper, A. T. (1990) *Multiview: An Exploration in Information Systems Development.* McGraw-Hill, Maidenhead.

Avison, D. E., Wood-Harper, A. T., Vidgen, R. & Wood, R. (1996) *Multiview: A Further Exploration in Information Systems Development,* McGraw-Hill, Maidenhead.

Benyon, D. & Skidmore, S. (1987) Towards a tool-kit for the systems analyst. *Computer Journal.* 30, 1.

Bodker, S., Ehn., Kammersgaard, J., Kyng. M. & Sundblad, Y. (1987) A UTOPIAN experience: on design of powerful computer-based tools for skilled graphic workers, in: Bjerknes, G., Ehn. & Kyng. M. (eds.), *Computers and Democracy: A Scandinavian Challenge,* Avebury, Aldershot.

Booch, G. (1991) *Object Oriented Design with Applications.* Benjamin/Cummings, Redwood City, California.

Bullen, C. V. & Rockart, J. F. (1984) *A Primer on Critical Success Factors.* CISR Working Paper 69, Sloan Management School, MIT, Boston, Mass.

Burrell, G. & Morgan, G. (1979) Sociological Paradigms and Organisational Analysis. Heinemann, London.

Checkland P. B. (1981) *Systems Thinking, Systems Practice.* Wiley, Chichester.

Checkland, P. & Scholes. J. (1990) *Soft Systems Methodology in Action.* Wiley, Chichester.

Coad, P. & Yourdon, E. (1991) *Object Oriented Analysis.* 2nd ed., Prentice Hall, Englewood Cliffs, New Jersey.

Daniels, A. & Yeates, D. A. (1971) *Basic Training in Systems Analysis.* 2nd ed., Pitman, London.

Davis, G. B. (1982) Strategies for information requirements determination, *IBM Systems Journal*, 21, 2.

De Grace, P. & Stahl, L. (1993) *The Olduvai Imperative: CASE and the State of Software Engineering Practice.* Prentice Hall, Englewood Cliffs, New Jersey.

Hammer, M. & Champy, J. (1993) *Reengineering the Corporation: A Manifesto for Business Revolution.* Harper Business, New York.

Eva, M. (1994) *SSADM Version 4: A User's Guide.* 2nd ed., McGraw-Hill, Maidenhead.

Kling, R. K. & Scacchi, W. (1982) The web of computing: computing technology as social organization, *Advances in Computers*, 21.

Lakoff, G. & Johnson, M. (1980) *Metaphors We Live By*, The University of Chicago Press, Chicago.

Martin, J. (1991) *Rapid Application Development.* Prentice Hall, Englewood Cliffs, New Jersey.

Mitroff, I., & Linstone, H. (1993). *The Unbounded Mind, breaking the chains of traditional business thinking.* Oxford University Press, New York.

Mumford, E. (1995) *Effective Requirements Analysis and Systems Design: The ETHICS Method.* Macmillan, Basingstoke.

Quang, P. T. & Chartier-Kastler, C. (1991) *Merise in Practice.* Macmillan, Basingstoke (translated by D. E. and M. A. Avison from the French *Merise Appliquée.* Eyrolles, Paris, 1989).

Wastell, D. (1996) The Fetish of Technique: methodology as a social defence. *Information Systems Journal*, 6, 1.

Wood-Harper, A. T. & Avison, D. E. (1992) Reflections from the experience of using Multiview: through the lens of soft systems methodology, *Systemist*, 14, 3.

18

A Classification of Methodological Frameworks for Computerized Information Systems Support in Organizations

John Krogstie
Andersen Consulting phone: +4722928200, fax: +4722928900,
email: John.Krogstie@ac.com

Arne Sølvberg
Faculty of Electrical Engineering and Computer Science
The Norwegian Institute of Technology
University of Trondheim, Norway

Abstract

Although many conceptual frameworks for development and maintenance of information systems in organizations have been proposed, we experience a lack of integrated support of the evolutionary nature, the interconnectedness, and the social processes for developing such systems. This paper present a classification of methodological frameworks for evaluating important aspects of methodologies having this in mind. Contrary to most classification frameworks presented in literature which look solely upon different ways of supporting development of new information systems, we have in our framework a broader view, including larger parts of what we term computerized information systems (CIS) support in organizations.

In the end of the paper, we present the result of classifying a set of approaches to CIS-support in organizations described in academia and practice. No methodology is found to be sufficient in all respects, although newer approaches take more aspects into account.

Keywords

Methodology, classification

1 INTRODUCTION

Several frameworks for the classification of methodological frameworks have been developed through the years e.g. (Blum, 1994; Davis, 1988; Lyytinen, 1987). A weakness of these is in our view their limited scope, basically looking upon the development of a single application system in a comparatively stable environment. Organizations are continuously under the pressure of change from both internal and external forces. Most organizations of some size are supported by and depend upon a portfolio of application systems who likewise has to be changed, often in a comparatively stable environment. Organizations are continuously under the pressure of change from both internal and external forces. Most organizations of some size are supported by and depend upon a portfolio of application systems who likewise has to be changed, often rapidly, for the organization to be able to keep up and extend their activities. The portfolio usually consist of a set of individual, but often highly integrated application systems whose long term evolution should be looked upon as a whole. Change is the norm, not the exception for both portfolios and their individual information systems (Alagappan and Kozaczynski, 1991; Williams et al., 1988). A first step towards facing this is to accept change as a way of life, rather than as an untowarded and annoying exception.

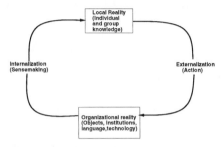

Figure 1: Social construction in an organization.

According to (Gjersvik, 1993) organizations are realities socially constructed through the joint actions of all the social actors in the organization. This process is illustrated in Figure 1. An organization consists of individuals who see the world in a way specific to them. The *local reality* is the way the individual perceives the world that he or she acts in. When the social actors of an organization act, they *externalize* their local reality. The most important ways social actors externalize their local reality, are to speak and to construct languages, artifacts, and institution. What they do is to construct *organizational reality*: To make something that other actors have to relate to in their work. This organizational reality may consist of different things, such as institutions, language, knowledge, artifacts and technology. Finally, *internalization* is the process of making sense out the organizational reality and making this part of the individual local reality.

We claim that the evolutionary aspects of computerized information systems (CIS) support are insufficiently covered by traditional approaches and tools. In addition, the process of social construction of the organizational reality is neglected in most development methodologies.

On this background, we will in this paper present a classification of methodological frameworks that takes also these aspects into account. We will in the end of the paper present the main results from an evaluation of a host of methodologies using the framework.

2   CLASSIFICATION OF METHODOLOGIES FOR COMPUTERIZED INFORMATION SYSTEMS SUPPORT

When deciding on relevant dimensions for a classification frameworks, we have tried to ask the questions *why, when, what, how, who, where* and *for how long* in the context of CIS support and

- *Why* do we attack the problem as we do? This is covered by the "Weltanschauung", i.e. underlying philosophical view of the methodology.
- *When* is the methodology applied? We have termed this aspect coverage in process indicating the main tasks that are covered by the methodology.
- *What* part of the portfolio is supported by the methodology? We have termed this aspect coverage in product.
- *How* do it help achieving the goals of CIS support? Based on the discussion in the introduction, we have concentrated on reuse and representation of product and process in the methodology with emphasis on conceptual modeling.
- *Who* is involved and where do changes take place? This is discussed under the area of stakeholder participation.
- *For how long* has the methodology been used. We term this aspect maturity: Is the methodology mature, being used for a long time in many organizations, with tool-support and support for evolution of the methodology.

Below, we will define and discuss each area in more detail.

2.1 "Weltanschauung":

FRISCO (FRISCO, 1995) differentiate between three different views:

- Objectivistic: "Reality" exists independently of any observer and merely needs to be mapped to an adequate description. For the objectivist, the relationship between reality and models thereof is trivial or obvious.
- Constructivistic: "Reality" exists independently of any observer, but what each person possess is a restricted mental model only. For the constructivist, the relationship between "reality" and models of this reality are subject to negotiations among the community of observers and may be adapted from time to time.
- Mentalistic: To talk about "reality" as such does not make sense because we can only form mental constructions of our perceptions. For the mentalist, what people usually call "reality" as well as its relationship to any model of it is totally dependent on the observer.

The methodologies that is found in literature can be characterized as being objectivistic or constructivistic. The "Weltanschauung" of a methodology is often not explicitly stated, but often appears only indirectly. Since different underlying philosophies may lead to radically different approaches, it is important to establish this. The distinction into objectivistic and constructivistic is parallel to the distinction between objectivistic and subjectivistic in the overview of Hirschheim and Klein (Hirschheim and Klein, 1989). Hirschheim and Klein also distinguish along the order-conflict dimension. In this dimension, the order or integration view emphasizes a social world characterized by order, stability, integration, consensus, and functional coordination. The conflict or coercion view stresses change, conflict, disintegration, and coercion. These two dimensions were originally identified by Burrel and Morgan (Burrel and Morgan, 1979) in the context of organizational and social research.

Based on the discussion in the introduction, it should come as no surprise that we find it beneficial to adapt a constructivistic world-view. Both the order and the conflict view combined with constructivism acknowledges a situation of continuous change.

2.2   Coverage in process

Do the methodology address:
- Planning of CIS-support
- Development of application systems
- Use and operation of application systems
- Maintenance of application systems

One or more of the above areas can be covered, more or less completely and in varying degrees of detail. More detailed specifications of dimensions of development methodologies are given by Blum (Blum, 1994), Davis (Davis, 1988) and Lyytinen (Lyytinen, 1987). Whereas Davis classifies a methodology according to the way it is able to address varying user-needs over time, Blum classifies development methodologies in two dimensions; if they are product or problem-oriented, and if they are conceptual or formal. We will only look upon the use of conceptual models and if these models are formal or not below. The product vs problem-oriented dimension as discussed by Blum is in our view a distinction on the *part* of development that is covered. Generally, every more detailed effort can be looked upon as a modeling task, where we differentiate based on the domain of modeling (Krogstie, 1995).
- The existing IS as it is perceived.
- The future IS as it is perceived.
- The future CIS as it is perceived.
- The (future) CIS in itself.

This correspond to what (Davis, 1995) term *understand problem, specify external behavior, design system,* and *implement system* respectively.

Lyytinen includes aspect covered by "Weltanschauung" and representation of product and process, in addition to linking technical, linguistic, and organizational aspects in a development methodology.

We claim that a comprehensive methodology should cover both planning, development, use, and maintenance in an integrated manner. The emphasis will be put on development and maintenance, but also the usage aspect is important, enabling the different end-users to make sense of the existing applications system in the organization, to both be able to use them more efficiently, and to be able to come up with constructive change-request and ideas for more revolutionary changes in the CIS support of the organization when the environment of the organization is changing. Planning aspects are important to be able to link the CIS-support of the organization up to strategic planning efforts in the organization, both to be able to implement the strategic plan, and to exploit information technology to the fullest in continuous development of the organization.

We claim that it is beneficial to not differentiate between development and maintenance in most cases, having a released based approach to CIS-support. This is partly based on figures appearing in our survey-investigation and in accompanying work presented in (Krogstie, 1995).

Maintenance has traditionally been looked upon as a more boring and less challenging task than development (Glass, 1992). Even if there are indications that this view might be changing e.g. (Layzell and Macauley, 1994) this still appears to be the prominent view among practitioners. According to our discussion in the introduction, it is both natural and desirable for CISs to change. As shown both in our own and other surveys, approximately half of the work which is normally termed maintenance is in fact further development of the information systems portfolio, and should be given credit as such. On the other side, almost half of the new systems being developed are replacement systems, not extending what the users can do with the portfolio of systems. Thus seen from the end-users point of view, a better assessment of information system support efficiency seems to be found by blurring the old temporal distinction between maintenance and development. This is difficult to achieve when having a large mental and organizational gap between development and maintenance, even though the actual tasks being done have many similarities.

Swanson in (Swanson and Beath, 1989) recognizes the similarities of the tasks of development and maintenance, but still argues for keeping the old distinction based on the following perceived differences:

- As also noted in (Glass, 1992), a large proportion of traditional maintenance work is to perform un-design of existing systems, finding out what the system does. We will argue that with modern development approaches where as much as possible of the work should take place on a specification and design level, the difference will be smaller. Supporting this is the results of a survey reported on in (Dekleva, 1992b) which gave no conclusive evidence that organizations using modern development methods used less time on maintenance activities. On the other hand, time spent on emergency error corrections as well as the number of system failures decrease significantly with the use of modern development methods. Systems developed with modern methodologies seemed to facilitate making greater changes in functionality as the systems aged, and the request from users seemed more reasonable, based on a more complete understanding of the system. We also note that because of the large amount of replacement work of often poorly documented application systems, code understanding problems are often just as important when developing "new" systems as when maintaining old systems today. Code and design understanding will also often be an issue when reusing the products from other projects, and during traditional development, when due to changing work load, developers have to work on other peoples code for instance during system-test.

- It is generally believed that "Maintenance of systems is characterized by problems of unpredictable urgency and significant consequent fire-fighting. In difference to new systems development, which is buffered from the day to day tasks of the users, the systems in production is much more visible" (Swanson and Beath, 1989). First of all, also development projects with tight schedules has its share of fire-fighting. Traditionally, it has been found that approximately 20% of the maintenance work is corrective maintenance (Lientz and Swanson, 1980), and our result of 26% seems to build up on the importance of this. On the other hand, if we look upon the percentage of work that is performed to do immediately necessary corrective maintenance on the application level, we found in our own investigation (Krogstie and Sølvberg, 1994) a percentage of 6%, the similar figure in Lientz/Swanson being 12%. The total amount on corrective maintenance on the individual systems in our investigations was 15%. (Jørgensen, 1994) indicate that the assessed corrective percentage of the work used on maintenance often might be exaggerated since these kind of problems are more visible for management. They found in their investigation of individual maintenance tasks that even if 38% of the changes were corrective, this took only up 9% of the time used for maintenance. Management assessed the percentage of corrective maintenance to be 19%. Those managers who based their answers on good data had a result of 9% corrective maintenance. Also in our investigation, we found a similar tendency, on the data of the maintenance task of the individual systems, those reporting to have good data, reported that only 8% of the work effort was corrective maintenance, 4% being emergency fixes. The same effect on over-assessing the amount of corrective maintenance has been reported earlier in (Arnold and Parker, 1982).

The problem of many small maintenance tasks done more or less continuously seems to be increased by how maintenance is often done, in an event-driven manner. In the Jørgensen investigation (Jørgensen and Maus, 1993), where 38% of the tasks were of an corrective nature, as much as 2/3 of the tasks where classified to have high importance by the maintainers themselves. The problem of changing priorities as described by Dekleva (Dekleva, 1992a) is closely related to this.

Even if the problem of emergency fixes seems to be smaller than earlier perceived, a methodology uniting development and maintenance must take into account that one has to be able to perform rapid changes to software artifacts.

2.3 Coverage in product

Is the method concerned with the development, use, and maintenance of
- One single application system.
- A family of application systems.
- The whole portfolio of application systems in an organization.

Also finer classifications can be perceived, i.e. methodologies that are specifically geared towards the use of specific technology, or to solve problems within specific domains, but we regard this as extensions of a general methodology rather than as independent methodologies. We will argue that it is beneficial for a complete methodology to be able to consider the whole portfolio in an integrated manner and not only the single application system. For the end-users, it is not important which application system that is changed. What is important is that their perceived needs are supported by the complete portfolio. This do obviously not mean that one always need to consider the whole portfolio when enhancing the CIS-support of the organization.

Application systems are not developed in a vacuum. They are related to old systems, by inheriting data and functionality, and they are integrated to other systems by data, control, presentation philosophy, and process (Thomas and Nejmeh, 1992). As reported in our investigation, the most important reason for replacements apart from systems being unmaintainable, was integration of application systems. Often when doing this kind of integration, it can be useful to collect the functionality of several existing application systems into a new application system, something which is not well supported when having strict borders for what is regarded as inside and outside of an application system.

As noted in (Swanson and Beath, 1989) the CISs of an organization tend to congregate and develop as families. By original design or not, they come to rely upon each other for their data. In Swanson/Beath 56% of the systems where connected to other systems through data integration. In our survey, we found that 73% of the main information systems in the organizations surveyed were dependent on data produced by other systems. In 40% of the responses to this question *all* the main system which the organization depended upon on a daily basis were dependant on data produced by other systems.

Over time, newer application systems originate in niches provided by older ones, and identifiable families of systems come to exist. Relationships among families are further established.

In the long run, an organization is served more by its CISs as a whole than it is by the application systems taken individually.

2.4   Reuse of product and process

Reusing experience is a key ingredient to progress in any discipline. Without reuse everything must be re-learned and recreated; progress in an economical fashion is unlikely. The need to utilize extensive reuse is based on the need for evolutionary and rapid changes in the CIS of an organization as discussed in the introduction.

An comprehensive overview of dimensions of reuse is given y (Prieto-Diaz, 1993):

- By substance: The essence of what is reused:
    - Idea reuse involves reusing formal notions, such as a general solution to a class of problems.
    - Artifacts reuse: Examples of artifacts are code, conceptual models, design, specifications, objects, text, architectures, and test data.
    - Procedures reuse: Formalizing and encapsulating software development procedure. Procedures reuse also means reusing skills and know-how, i.e. having a development and maintenance methodology can be looked upon as reuse in this sense.
- By scope: The form and extent of reuse:
    - Vertical reuse is reuse within the same application area.
    - Horizontal reuse is reuse across application areas.
- By mode: How reuse is conducted:
    - Planned reuse: The systematic and formal practice of reuse. Guidelines and procedures for reuse have been defined, and metrics are being collected to assess reuse performance.
    - Ad-hoc reuse: An informal practice, in which components are selected from general libraries.
- By technique: How reuse is implemented:
    - Compositional reuse is the use of existing artifacts as building blocks for new systems.
    - Generative reuse is reuse at the specification level by means of design and code-generators.
- By intention: Defines how elements will be reused:
    - As-is or black-box reuse is reuse without modifications.
    - Modified or white-box reuse involves modifications of what is reused.

It is usual to differentiate between methodologies being *for reuse* and those being *with reuse* (Karlsson (ed.), 1995; Wilkie, 1993). Another distinction is between reuse-in-the-large and reuse-in-the-small, where reuse in the large refers to the use of packaged solutions and frameworks. We will restrict the use of the term in the evaluations to include the planned reuse of artifacts, i.e. not including that using a methodology is an example of reusing procedures.

2.5   Representation of product and process

Knowledge about the process and the product of CIS development and maintenance can be represented using different kinds of languages. These languages can be informal, semi-formal, or formal, having a logical and/or a executional semantics. These terms are defined as follows:

Language : A set of *symbols*, the **graphemes** of the language being the smallest units in the writing system capable of causing a contrast in meaning, a set of **words** being a set of related *symbols* constituting the **vocabulary** of the language, rules to form **sentences** being a set of related words (**syntax**), and some inter-subjectively agreed definitions of what the different sentences mean (**semantics**).

A **formalism** is a formal *language*, i.e. a *language* with a precisely defined *vocabulary*, *syntax*, and *semantics*. If the semantics is based on mathematical logic, we use the term **logical formalism**. If it is possible to execute a set of sentences in the language on a computer, the language is said to have an operational semantics.

A **semi-formal language** is a *language* with a precisely defined *vocabulary* and *syntax*, but without a precisely defined *semantics*.

We will in this paper concentrate on conceptual modeling languages. As will be illustrated, conceptual modeling is believed to be an important technique for CIS support in organizations when combining development and maintenance having support for not only a single application systems, but the whole application system portfolio, being based around social construction theory and reuse. When discussing the benefits of using conceptual modeling below, we should have in mind that we are primarily talking about partly graphical languages which are semi-formal or formal, have a limited vocabulary, and which can be used in many areas on varying levels of formality and completeness.

- A conceptual model has the possibility of being a problem-oriented description of the requirements for CIS support, without being restrained too early by technical constraints. In this way we believe one can more easily support a process of social construction of information systems. A problem-oriented approach has been asked for by many researchers (Borgida et al., 1985; Bubenko jr., 1983; Hagelstein, 1988; van Assche et al., 1988) and conceptual modeling is looked upon as one way of achieving this.
- Due to the visual nature of many conceptual modeling languages they are believed to be more helpful in the sense-making process of what is modeled than the model which is implicit in the code of an application system. On the other hand, if we want to refine the conceptual models into a form that is suitable for automatic code-generation, the essential difficulty of complexity discussed by Brooks (Brooks Jr., 1986) will again appear.
- Since the separate conceptual modeling languages only include a limited set of phenomena, this enable a focusing of concerns, and it is possible to deduce properties that are difficult if not impossible to perceive directly, by concentrating on only some aspect at the time. This is obviously also problematic if this makes one blind for other concern, or makes it impossible to externalize certain explicit knowledge. Based on this we will claim that one need a set of interrelated semi-formal and formal modeling languages which can cover different perspectives for conceptual modeling to be more generally useful.
- Conceptual models developed in early parts of development can be used as an outset for further design and implementation, supporting generative reuse. Conceptual models are also believed to be easier to maintain than textual documents that do not have any other mission than to serve as documentation, since they can be constructed as part of the process of developing and maintaining the application system in the first place, thus supporting

change and an integration of development and maintenance techniques. It is also easier to get an overview of the CIS-support of an organization if the languages for conceptual modeling are known and sufficient tool support for handling them exist, thus potentially supporting the long range planning and evolution of the whole portfolio.

According to our survey (Krogstie, 1995), most of the organizations having started to use CASE-tools for development and maintenance, use these for conceptual modeling.

2.6   Stakeholder participation

In general, stakeholders in CIS-support can be divided into the following groups (Macauley, 1993):

- Those who are responsible for its design, development, introduction and maintenance, for example, the project manager, system developers, communications experts, technical authors, training and user support staff, and their managers.
- Those with financial interest, responsible for the application systems sale or purchase.
- Those who have an interest in its use, for example direct or indirect users and users managers.

We focus here specifically on end-user participation.

A **user** of a *CIS* is defined as a person who potentially increases his *knowledge* about some *phenomena* other than the *CIS* with the help of the *CIS*. An **end-user** increases his and hers *knowledge* in areas which are *relevant* to him by *interacting* with the *CIS*. **Indirect users** increase their *knowledge* by getting results from the *CIS* without *interacting* directly with the *CIS*.

This is somewhat different from how 'user' is often defined, terming the system development and maintenance personell as 'primary users' (Hirschheim, 1984) or technical users. Not including these persons as users in the following discussion do not mean that they are not important stakeholders.

The term 'participation' means to take part in something. There exists different forms of participation:

- **Direct participation:**
  Every stakeholder has an opportunity to participate.
- **Indirect participation:**
  Every stakeholder participate more or less through representatives that are supposed to look after their interests. The representatives can either be:
  - Selected: The representatives are picked out by somebody, e.g. management.
  - Elected: The representatives are chosen from among their co-workers.

Many arguments for having participation have been given in the literature see e.g. (Greenberg, 1975; Mumford, 1983) for classifications. Here, user participation is basically motivated through a cost-benefit-perspective on the long run. Since all stakeholders have their individual local reality, everyone have a potential useful view of how the current situation can be improved. Including more people in the process will ideally increase the possibility of keeping up with the ever more rapidly changing environment of the organization. Added to this is the general argument of including those who is believed to have relevant knowledge in the area, and which are influenced by the solution. As indicated in several surveys, general participation appears to be a general indicator for (development) project success as perceived by all the different stakeholders. In Bergersen (Bergersen, 1990), the three most important factors for overall perceived project success were found to be the goal-setting, management support, and user-participation. In van Swede (van Swede and van Vliet, 1994) the main contributions of success in the sense of satisfaction of all stakeholders were a cooperative environment, presence of a win-win starting point by considering the interest of all stakeholder-group, quality of project staff, and quality of project management.

According to Heller (Heller, 1991), participation is sharing power and influence. He has divided the degree of influence and power into six categories as illustrated in Figure 2.

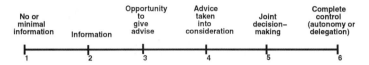

Figure 2: Scale of influence and power

We would claim that participation when applied should be in categories 4, 5, or 6 on this scale, and we will use this scale when classifying methodologies according to this aspect.

Due to the large number of potential stakeholders in a development effort, in most cases representative participation will be the only practical possibility. From the point of view of social construction, it is doubtful that a user representative can truly represent anyone else than himself. On the other hand, even if the internal reality of each individual will always differ to a certain degree, the explicit knowledge concerning a constrained area might be more or less equal, especially within groups of social actors (Gjersvik, 1993; Orlikowski and Gash, 1994). Another factor is the scope of participation, i.e. when do participation take place. Usually one would expect that user-participation would take place heavily in analysis and in acceptance testing, more lightly in design, and very little in implementation, but this will often depend on the chosen methodology. When it comes to suggesting improvements of the current information system of the organization, direct participation should be possible. Also in planning leading up to project establishment, a larger proportion of the stakeholders should be able to participate.

Another aspect related to this point, is where the changes of the portfolio takes place:

- In the user organization.
- In a data department, developing customized systems.
- Centrally, with one unit developing the core of the systems, which are then customized locally.
- Externally developed packages with large local adaptions.
- Externally developed packages with small local adaptions.
- By a different organization all-together (outsourcing)

Typically, one would expect a mix of these models within the support of a portfolio. We will not investigate this in detail here.

2.7 Maturity

Whereas some of the methodologies being presented in literature have been used for many years by many organizations, others are only described in theory, and never tried out in practice. When

discussing the maturity of a methodology, we can differentiate between the following factors:
- Is the methodology properly described? (vs. representation of process)
- Is the methodology supported by mature, high quality tools?
- Is the methodology (re)used and updated through practical application? Is it used by many organizations, supporting a large part of the portfolios in these organizations?
- Is the methodology undergoing a conscious evolution based on experience with the use of the methodology, being "annotated" with information about what parts of the methodology seems appropriate in a given situation?

Different parts of a methodology will typically be of varying maturity.

3   SUMMARY AND CONCLUSION

We have in (Krogstie, 1995) given an overview and classification of a host of existing methodologies and frameworks using the above classification. The following methodologies and frameworks were classified primarily based on the cited works.
- The conventional waterfall model (Royce, 1970).
- The structured life cycle (Yourdon, 1988).
- Iterative and throwaway prototyping (Carey, 1990).
- Incremental development (Davis et al., 1988).
- Transformational and operational development (Zave, 1982).
- Tempora (Loucopoulos et al., 1991).
- Method/1 (METHOD1:89, 1989).
- The spiral model (Boehm, 1988).
- The hierarchical spiral model (Iivari, 1990a).
- The fountain model (Henderson-Sellers and Edwards, 1990).
- OMT (Rumbaugh et al., 1991).
- REBOOT (Karlsson (ed.), 1995).
- CONFORM (Capretz and Munro, 1994).
- Maintenance as reuse-oriented development (Basili, 1990).
- Multiview (Avison and Wood-Harper, 1990).
- STEPS (Floyd et al., 1989).
- Systems devtenace (Krogstie, 1995).

Due to space limitation, we will here only summarize this work, noting that we have tried to include examples such that all aspects are covered in full by at least one approach. A short summary of our classifications is given in Table 3. It includes the first six aspects of the classification. The first column indicate the "Weltanschauung" as judged by what we have read on the methodologies. Process coverage indicates the areas that we judge the methodologies give comprehensive support in. Product coverage differentiate upon those methodologies which we regard as being useful for the support of more than one CIS at the time. Reuse is not discussed explicitly in many methodologies, which is indicated with - in the table. The 'conceptual modeling' column indicate the use and kind of languages used. 'OOA' refers to the use of languages for object oriented analysis, which are mostly semi-formal. Finally, the participation column indicates the strength of participation as indicated in the descriptions of the methodology.

Table 1 Classifications of methodologies

Methodology	Weltanschauung	Process coverage	Product coverage	Reuse	Conceptual modeling	Part. (range)
Waterfall	Objectivistic	Development +	one	-	Little	2-4
Structured	Objectivistic	Development	one	-	Semi-formal	2-4
Prototyping	Objectivistic	Development (early)	one	with	-	4-5
Operational	Objectivistic	Development	one	Generative	Formal	2-4
Tempora	Objectivistic	Development	one	Generative	Formal	2-4
Method/1	Objectivistic	Planning/ Development	one/ portfolio	In the large	Semi-formal	2-5
Spiral	Objectivistic	Development/ maintenance	one	with	-	3-5
Hierarchical spiral	Objectivistic	Development/ maintenance	one	-	Yes	3-4
Fountain	Objectivistic	Development (mainly)	one	for/with	OOA	-
OMT	Objectivistic	Development	one	for	OOA	2-4
REBOOT	Objectivistic	Development/ maintenance	one/ portfolio	for/with	OOA	2-3
CONFORM	Objectivistic	Maintenance	one	-	-	-
Basili	Objectivistic	Development/ maintenance	one/ portfolio	for/with	-	-
Multiview	Constructivistic	Development	one	-	Semi-formal	4-5
STEPS	Constructivistic	Development maintenance/use	one	-	-	4-5
Devtenance	Constructivistic	Development maintenance/use	One/ portfolio	Generative	Formal	4-5

According to our classifications we conclude the following:

- Weltansscahuung: As also noted in (Hirschheim and Klein, 1989), most earlier and current methodologies for application systems development and maintenance have an objectivistic outlook. Some exceptions illustrated are STEPS (Floyd et al., 1989), Multiview (Avison and Wood-Harper, 1990), and systems devtenance (Krogstie, 1995). Other examples are methodologies based on SSM (Checkland, 1981) and some PD-methodologies (Schuler and Namioka, 1993).
- Coverage in process: Most methodologies for CIS-support are focused on development, with maintenance being looked upon as a separate end-phase if considered at all. Several methodologies focused on maintenance also exist (e.g.CONFORM (Capretz and Munro, 1994), see also (Boldyref et al., 1994)), even if this part of CIS-support is not shown the same interest as development by researchers according to (Hale et al., 1990; Jørgensen, 1994). Some methodologies covers both development and maintenance in the same framework in an integrated manner (e.g. The Spiral Model (Boehm, 1988), the Hierarchical Spiral Model (Iivari, 1990a; Iivari, 1990b) and the framework presented by Basili (Basili, 1990) where also emergency error-correction is covered). STEPS (Floyd et al., 1989) and systems devtenance (Krogstie, 1995) also includes the usage aspect. Method/1 includes IT-planning in an integrated manner.
- Coverage in product: We have found few methodologies apart from system devtenance that cover traditional development or maintenance of the whole portfolio in a focused manner, even though maintenance can be said to often be performed in this way (Swanson and Beath, 1989). Several methodologies include organization-wide CIS-planning (e.g. METHOD/1 (METHOD1:95, 1995)).
- Reuse: Some methodologies explicitly addressing reuse exist (e.g. REBOOT (Karlsson (ed.), 1995)), even if few development and maintenance methodologies are geared towards conscious component reuse. Operational and transformational approaches as described in (Zave, 1982) are highly geared towards generative reuse. This is also the case with Tempora and systems devtenance.
- Use of conceptual models: Many methods use conceptual modeling to some extent, even if most use only semi-formal modeling languages. On the other hand, the use of operational conceptual models have received increasing interest as illustrated through Tempora and systems devtenance.
- Stakeholder participation: Increasingly looked upon as important both in objectivistic and especially constructivistic methodologies. This might be endangered by the current trend of more and more use of packages and outsourcing, although this might have economic advantages in the short run.
- Maturity: Most mature methodologies resembles traditional waterfall, but many of these are taking newer aspects into account e.g. Method/1 and extensions of this. Most methodological frameworks described in literature have a very low maturity. This especially applies to system devtenance, which is the framework which otherwise are meant to best cover the other six aspects.

4 CONCLUDING REMARKS

There seems to be an overall view that there are no right detailed methodology for all situation (Avison and Wood-Harper, 1990; Floyd et al., 1989; Glasson, 1989; Iivari, 1990a) something which are also recognized in more traditional methodologies like Method/1. The different development and maintenance efforts can vary according to several factors e.g.:

- The complexity of the application system (cf. (Brooks Jr., 1986)).
- The current rate of change(cf. the discussion on evolution in the introduction).
- The size, perceived importance, and risks of performing the changes (cf. (Boehm, 1988)).
- The number of stakeholders affected, skills needed and possessed.
- The number of different views of the situation (cf. social construction theory as described in the introduction).

Thus there is a need for flexibility, but in our opinion one still need a methodological framework of some sort to be able to deliver CIS-support in an organization. Taking into account the multitude of techniques, there is an obvious need for an integrative framework that can incorporate existing more detailed approaches and support their flexible situation-dependant use. The work presented in this paper is meant to give an indication of some of the main aspects that such a framework should cover.

Taking a philosophical standpoint neither reuse nor conceptual modeling nor having a defined methodology can be optimal, since all situations are unique, and thus in principle can best be attacked by using unique means. Reusing artifacts originally produced for some other purpose, in effect means to apply an externalization of the local reality of someone else than the current stakeholders, which thus can not be optimal. On the other hand, reuse is performed all the time. Using a commercial DBMS is for instance reuse, but it is not very wise to produce your own database management system when you perceive a need for this kind of functionality if you do not have very special needs. A balance between the different concerns brought up by our philosophical outlook is thus necessary.

5 REFERENCES

Alagappan, V. and Kozaczynski, W. (1991). The evolution of very large systems. In Lowry, M. R. and McCartney, R. D., editors, *Automating Software Design*, pages 1–24, California, USA. The MIT Press.

Arnold, R. S. and Parker, D. A. (1982). The dimensions of healthy maintenance. In *Proceedings of the 6th International Conference on Software Engineering (ICSE)*, pages 10–17. IEEE Computer Society Press.

Avison, D. E. and Wood-Harper, A. T. (1990). *Multiview: An Exploration in Information Systems Development*. Blackwell, Oxford, England.

Basili, V. R. (1990). Viewing maintenance as reuse-oriented software development. *IEEE Software*, 7(1):19–25.

Bergersen, L. (1990). *Prosjektadministrasjon i systemutvikling. Aktiviteter i planlegningsfasen som påvirker suksess (In Norwegian)*. PhD thesis, ORAL, NTH, Trondheim, Norway.

Blum, B. I. (1994). A taxonomy of software development methods. *Communications of the ACM*, 37(11):82–94.

Boehm, B. W. (1988). A spiral model of software development and enhancement. *IEEE Computer*, pages 61–72.

Boldyref, C., Burd, E. L., and Hather, R. M. (1994). An evaluation of the state of the art for application management. In (Müller and Georges, 1994), pages 161–169.

Borgida, A., Greenspan, S., and Mylopoulos, J. (1985). Knowledge representation as the basis for requirements specification. *IEEE Computer*, 18(4):82–91.

Brooks Jr., F. P. (1986). No silver bullet. Essence and accidents of software engineering. In Kugler, H. J., editor, *Information Processing '86*, pages 1069–1076. North-Holland.

Bubenko jr., J. A. (1983). On concepts and strategies for requirements and information analysis. In *Information Modelling*, pages 125–169. Chartwell-Bratt Ltd.

Burrel, G. and Morgan, G. (1979). *Sociological Paradigms and Organizational Analysis*. Heinemann.

Capretz, M. A. M. and Munro, M. (1994). Software configuration management issues in the maintenance of existing system. *Journal of Software Maintenance*, 6:1–14.

Carey, J. M. (1990). Prototyping: Alternative systems development methodology. *Information and Software Technology*, 32(2):119–126.

Checkland, P. B. (1981). *Systems Thinking, Systems Practice*. John Wiley & Sons.

Davis, A. M. (1988). A comparison of techniques for the specification of external system behavior. *Communications of the ACM*, 31(9):1098–1115.

Davis, A. M. (1995). Object-oriented requirements to object-oriented design: An easy transition? *Journal of Systems and Software*, 30(1/2):151–159.

Davis, A. M., Bersoff, E. H., and Comer, E. R. (1988). A strategy for comparing alternative software development life cycle models. *IEEE Transactions on Software Engineering*, 14(8):1453–1461.

Dekleva, S. M. (1992a). Delphi study of software maintenance problems. In *Proceedings of the Conference on Sofware Maintenance (CSM'92)*, pages 10–17.

Dekleva, S. M. (1992b). The influence of the information systems development approach on maintenance. *MIS Quarterly*, pages 355–372.

Floyd, C., Reisin, F.-M., and Schmidt, G. (1989). STEPS to software development with users. In Ghezzi, C. and McDermid, J. A., editors, *2nd European Software Engineering Conference (ESEC'89)*, pages 48–63, University of Warwick, Coventry, England.

FRISCO (March 1995). Personal communication with the FRISCO task group.

Gjersvik, R. (1993). *The Construction of Information Systems in Organization: An Action Research Project on Technology, Organizational Closure, Reflection, and Change*. PhD thesis, ORAL, NTH, Trondheim, Norway.

Glass, R. L. (1992). We have lost our way. *Journal of Systems and Software*, 18(2):111–112.

Glasson, B. C. (1989). Model of system evolution. *Information and Software Technology*, 31(7):351–356.

Greenberg, E. S. (1975). The consequences of worker participation: A clarification of the theorethical litterature. *Social Science Quarterly*, 56(2).

Hagelstein, J. (1988). A declarative approach to information systems requirements. *Knowledge Based Systems*, 1(4):211–220.

Hale, D. P., Haworth, D. A., and Sharpe, S. (1990). Empirical software maintenance studies during the 1980s. In *Proceedings of the Conference on Software Maintenance (CSM'90)*, pages 118–123. IEEE Computer Society Press.

Heller, F. (1991). Participation and competence: A necessary relationship. In Russel, R. and Rus, V., editors, *International Handbook of Participation in Organizations*, pages 265–281.

Henderson-Sellers, B. and Edwards, J. M. (1990). The object-oriented systems life cycle. *Communications of the ACM*, 33(9):142–159.

Hirschheim, R. A. (1984). A participative approach to implementing office automation. In *Proceedings from the Joint International Symposium on Information Systems*, pages 306–329, Sydney, Australia.

Hirschheim, R. A. and Klein, H. K. (1989). Four paradigms of information systems development. *Communications of the ACM*, 32(10):pages 1199–1216.

Iivari, J. (1990a). Hierarchical spiral model for information system and software development. Part 1: Theoretical background. *Information and Software Technology*, 32(6):386–399.

Iivari, J. (1990b). Hierarchical spiral model for information system and software development. Part 2: Design process. *Information and Software Technology*, 32(7):450–458.

Jørgensen, M. (1994). *Empirical studies of Software Maintenance*. PhD thesis, Department of Informatics, University of Oslo, Oslo, Norway.

Jørgensen, M. and Maus, A. (1993). A case study of software maintenance tasks. In *Proceedings of Norsk Informatikk Konferanse 1993 (NIK'93)*, pages 101–112, Halden, Norway.

Karlsson (ed.), E.-A. (1995). *Software Reuse: A Holistic Approach*. John Wiley & Sons.

Krogstie, J. (1995). *Conceptual Modeling for Computerized Information Systems Support in Organizations*. PhD thesis, IDT, NTH, Trondheim, Norway.

Krogstie, J. and Sølvberg, A. (1994). Software maintenance in Norway: A survey investigation. In (Müller and Georges, 1994), pages 304–313. Received "Best Paper Award".

Layzell, P. J. and Macauley, L. (1994). An investigations into software maintenance - perception and practices. *Software Maintenace: Research and Practice*, 6:105–119.

Lientz, B. P. and Swanson, E. B. (1980). *Software Maintenance Management*. Addison Wesley.

Loucopoulos, P., McBrien, P., Schumacker, F., Theodoulidis, B., Kopanas, V., and Wangler, B. (1991). Integrating database technology, rule-based systems and temporal reasoning for effective information systems: The TEMPORA paradigm. *Journal of Information Systems*, 1:129–152.

Lyytinen, K. (1987). A taxonomic perspective of information systems development: Theoretical constructs and recommendations. In Boland Jr, R. J. and Hirschheim, R. A., editors, *Critical Issues in Information Systems Research*, chapter 1, pages 3–41. John Wiley & Sons.

Macauley, L. (1993). Requirements capture as a cooperative activity. In *Proceedings of the First Symposium on Requirements Engineering (RE'93)*, pages 174–181.

METHOD1:89 (1989). *FOUNDATION - Method/1, Tools Reference Manual, Version 2.1*. Andersen Consulting.

METHOD1:95 (1995). *Method/1, System Development Management*. Andersen Consulting.

Müller, H. A. and Georges, M., editors (1994). *Proceedings of the International Conference on Software Maintenance (ICSM'94)*. IEEE COmputer Society Press.

Mumford, E. (1983). Participation - from Aristotle to today. In Bemelmans, T. M. A., editor, *Beyond Productivity: Information Systems Development for Organizational Effectiveness*, pages 95–104. North-Holland.

Orlikowski, J. W. and Gash, D. C. (1994). Technological frames: Making sense of information technology in organizations. *ACM Transactions on Information Systems*, 12(2):174–207.

Prieto-Diaz, R. (1993). Status report: Software reuseability. *IEEE Software*, pages 61–66.

Royce, W. W. (1970). Managing the development of large software systems: Concepts and techniques. In *Proceedings WESCON*.

Rumbaugh, J., Blaha, M., Premerlani, W., Eddy, F., and Lorensen, W. (1991). *Object-Oriented Modeling and Design*. Prentice-Hall, Englewood Cliffs, NJ.

Schuler, D. and Namioka, A. (1993). *Participatory design: Principles and Practices*. Lawrence Erlbaum.

Swanson, E. B. and Beath, C. M. (1989). *Maintaining Information Systems in Organizations*. Wiley Series in Information Systems. John Wiley & Sons.

Thomas, I. and Nejmeh, B. A. (1992). Definitions of tool integration for environments. *IEEE Software*, 9(2):29–35.

van Assche, F., Layzell, P., Loucopoulos, P., and Speltincx, G. (1988). Information systems development: A rule-based approach. *Knowledge Based Systems*, 1(4):227–234.

van Swede, V. and van Vliet, H. (1994). Consistent development: Results of a first empirical study of the relation between project scenario and success. In Wijers, G., Brinkkemper, S., and Wasserman, T., editors, *Proceedings of the 6th International Conference on Advanced Information Systems Engineering (CAiSE'94)*, pages 80–93, Utrecth, Netherlands. Springer Verlag.

Wilkie, G. (1993). *Object-Oriented Software Engineering - The Professional Developers's Guide*. Addison-Wesley.

Williams, G. B., Mui, C. K., Johnson, B. B., and Alagappan, V. (1988). Software design issues: A very large information systems perspective. Technical report, CStar, Arthur Andersen, Chicago.

Yourdon, E. (1988). *Managing the System Life Cycle*. Prentice-Hall.

Zave, P. (1982). An operational approach to requirements specification for embedded systems. *IEEE Transactions on Software Engineering*, 8(3):250–269.

6 BIOGRAPHY

- **John Krogstie** is a Senior Consultant with Andersen Consulting ANS in Norway. Krogstie received a MSc and a PhD in computer science from the University of Trondheim.
- **Arne Sølvberg** is a professor of computer Science at the University of Trondheim, NTNU. Sølvberg received a MSc in applied physics and a PhD in computer science from the University of Trondheim.

19

Method Engineering: Current research directions and implications for future research

Juha-Pekka Tolvanen, Matti Rossi and Hui Liu
Department of Computer Science and Information Systems
University of Jyväskylä
P.O. Box. 35, 40351 Jyväskylä, Finland
E-mail: {jpt, mor, huiliu}@ hyeena.jyu.fi

Abstract

In this study we investigate method engineering research by classifying studies into three contexts: technology, language and organization. Within each context we examine research bias, research outcomes and use of alternative research methods. This survey reveals the inherent bias of ME research towards tool and language development at the cost of empirical studies. We lack investigations of why organizations develop their own "variants" of system development methods, and how they manage their method engineering efforts. These observations lead us to suggest some directions for future research, which relate both to actual research questions and to the use of complementary research methods.

Keywords

Metamodeling, method engineering, system development methods, research methods

1. INTRODUCTION

From time to time every research domain should take a closer look at what kind of research efforts have been carried out, what have been the results so far, and where research is currently heading. This kind of survey reveals what kinds of research questions are emphasized, and more importantly, what questions are being ignored, and what research methods are used or should be used.

The starting point for this study is the obvious need to make a survey of past research in method engineering (ME). By ME we mean a discipline of designing, constructing and adopting methods and tools for information systems development (Kumar and Welke 1992, Brinkkemper 1995). The area of ME has grown from two observations: First there has been a need to describe different information system development (ISD) approaches by a common language in order to compare them (e.g. Olle et al. 1983). Second, there has been a need to develop support environments for methods (Kottemann and Konsynski 1984, Bubenko 1988). When the development of a CASE tool for a given method was observed to be too expensive, the idea of generic CASE environments, or CASE toolkits, emerged (Kottemann and Konsynski 1984, Kumar and Welke 1992).

The need of an investigation into ME research is motivated by some observations. First, there exists a relatively large body of research on ME for the basis of the survey. For example, significant research effort has recently been expended on developing new, or extending available languages for method modeling (e.g. Smolander 1991, Hofstede 1993, etc.). Another example is the emergence of several metaCASE tools (e.g. Sorenson et al. 1988, Smolander et al. 1991, Heym and Österle 1993 etc.). Second, research on ME has gathered growing interest during this decade, and this trend will most likely continue. Consequently, we face the need to solicit research questions that have remained unanswered, and to develop research methods that can improve the research being done. Finally, a survey to ME literature is important simply because such studies have not been made.

As the title of the paper indicates, the objective of the study is twofold. First, we will analyze what aspects and questions of ME have been studied, how they have been studied (i.e. which research methods have been applied), and what have been the most remarkable findings. The survey is conducted by analyzing ME literature within three different contexts: technology, language and organization context. Each context is also analyzed by the use of research methods. The results of the study clearly show a bias in current ME research, both related to the contexts (i.e. technology and language), and applied research (i.e. language construction and tool development) and basic research (i.e. theory building for ME). The second objective of our survey is to propose research topics that have remained unanswered. Similarly, we should examine the weaknesses in the use of various research methods and propose research approaches for future research on ME. We hope that the study will provide insights into current research directions in ME research as well as highlight areas in need of future research.

The paper is organized as follows. In the next section we shall discuss the foundations of ME and describe the framework used in analyzing ME research. Section 3 presents the survey, and Section 4 focuses on the use of research methods. Section 5 proposes future research directions and topics. Finally, Section 6 summarizes the study.

2. METHOD ENGINEERING: A DEFINITION AND A FRAMEWORK FOR THE STUDY

2.1 Foundation and definition

In its simplest form we can say that a *metamodel* is a conceptual model of a development method (Brinkkemper 1990). Consequently, metamodeling can be defined as a modeling process, which takes place one level of abstraction and logic higher than the standard modeling process (Gigch 1991). A metamodel captures information about the concepts, representation forms (or signs, cf. Leppänen 1994), and uses of a method. For example, in data-flow diagrams the concepts used to model systems are processes, data stores, external entities and various relationships between them. Moreover, the metamodel of data flow analysis defines how each object (concept) is represented (e.g. the symbol definition for an external entity is a square), and in what order the system model should be created (e.g. top-down structure). The relationships between modeling and metamodeling are illustrated in Figure 1 (cf. Brinkkemper 1990).

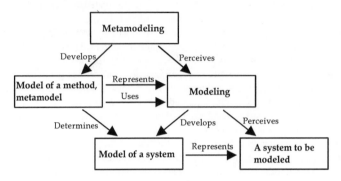

Figure 1. Metamodeling and modeling.

Configurable CASE tools, or CASE shells (Bubenko 1988), or metasystems (Sorenson et al. 1988) use a set of primitives, which allow them to describe a given method quickly and mechanisms to implement a tool to support the defined method. The first configurable CASE environments used complicated textual languages for method definition (e.g. see ISDOS 1985). It soon became evident that "Design of methodologies and applications systems are very comparable exercises in human endeavor. In both cases one has to decide what data is needed and what processes are to be supported. This recursivity (if that's the right word) means that one should be able to specify a design methodology in itself — an assertion that was made in earlier days about programming languages" (Olle et al. 1983 p.8). This recursivity led to the foundation of the area of method engineering (Kumar and Welke 1992).

Brinkkemper (1995) has defined *method engineering* as "a discipline to design, construct and adapt methods, techniques and tools for the development of information systems". If the method engineering process is supported by specific computer aided tools we call the engineering discipline *Computer Aided Method Engineering (CAME),* and the supporting tools *CAME tools.* A person responsible for developing and implementing method specifications is called a method engineer.

2.2 A taxonomy for ME research

Throughout this paper we shall apply a framework in surveying and analyzing ME research. The framework consist of two dimensions: the contexts of ME and research methods. The context dimension includes a technology context, a language context and an organization context (Lyytinen 1987), and they are used to classify the literature on ME. The technology context refers to various tools needed for processing, storing and retrieving descriptions of both ISD methods and system models. Thus, the technology provides a platform and supporting mechanisms for ME. The language context refers to the method modeling languages applied in ME. The languages are used for example in describing conceptual structures, representations and use situations of methods. Finally, the organization context connects method engineering with its purpose, goals, supporting organizational structures and mechanisms.

Although some other frameworks could also suit our survey, we believe that the three contexts selected are general and exhaustive enough to classify ME into distinct domains. For example the three contexts cover the domains of ME proposed by Kumar and Welke (1992), Heym and Österle (1993), Brinkkemper (1990), and Wijers (1991).

2.3 The use of research methods

The second dimension of the framework consists of research methods and allows us to examine the research in each context. The classification into research methods is important since ME is a relatively new research field in which complementary research efforts are needed to improve the quality of the research outcomes. In using this dimension of the framework we shall investigate the current use and the possible bias of research method use (Section 4), and later recommend topics for future research (Section 5).

The selected taxonomy of research methods includes the following types: survey, field study, laboratory experiment, case study, action research, applied, basic and normative. In principle other taxonomies could be applied but the selected one has been proven suitable for surveying similar research fields, such as CASE (Wynekoop & Conger 1991) and ISD methods (Wynekoop & Russo 1993). Each research method is briefly described below. A more thorough discussion of characteristics, strengths and weaknesses of different research methods can be found in Wynekoop and Conger 1991, Galliers 1991, Benbasat et al. 1987, Jenkins 1985, and WoodHarper 1985.

The first five research methods are empirical ones based on observation or interpretation. Survey is based on gathering field data using sampling and typically questionnaires and interviews. The data gathered focuses on a snapshot of practice, and independent variables are not manipulated. Field study focuses on evaluating changes in selected organizational systems. Here dependent variables are systematically measured, but not manipulated. Laboratory experiments allow researchers to create settings in which precise relationships between variables can be controlled and measured. By replicating experiments with multiple samples generalizations can be obtained that are valid outside the sample population. Case studies are evaluations of particular subjects, such as an organization, a group of people, or systems, at a point of time. They attempt to capture the "reality" in greater detail than any of the above research methods; typically no control of the phenomena is exercised. Action research can be understood as a case study with the exception that the researcher, using qualitative and "typical" representatives from the sample, participates in the area of study and simultaneously evaluates its results. Thus, in action research there is a possibility to obtain a deeper and first-hand understanding of the situation.

The last three research methods, i.e. applied, basic and normative, are based on researchers' ideas as well as on comparing them with other perspectives or ideas. Applied research can be characterized as goal-directed: a specific goal is known and the usefulness of the developed or designed outcome can be evaluated and compared to similar ones. Basic research deals with developing new theories based on the expertise and reasoning capabilities of the researcher.

Normative writing include attempts to concept development, presentation of ideas and applications, or ISD method descriptions. This paper clearly belongs to the normative category.

3. SURVEY INTO ME RESEARCH

In this section we shall apply the proposed framework to survey the literature of ME. Basically we tried to collect a representative set of papers for each category and, if possible, papers that also address the use of various research methods. For each context the following features are discussed: description of the context from the ME viewpoint, description of the research done, results of the research efforts, and questions that have been left unanswered.

3.1 Technology context

Lyytinen (1987) uses the term technology context to refer to "the view of how to efficiently process and store signs (data) in some material carrier". In ME this can be interpreted as a viewpoint of what kind of technical tool environments are used during method development, and how effectively ISD method representations can be transformed into CASE environment representations (Karrer and Scacchi 1993).

One major research stream in ME has traditionally focused on the development of tools for capturing method knowledge (cf. Heym and Österle 1993, Harmsen et al. 1994a, Verhoef et al. 1991), as well as on building generic CASE toolkits which can be customized for different methods (cf. Teichroew et al. 1980, Chen et al. 1989, Sorenson et al. 1988, Bergsten et al. 1989, Smolander et al. 1991, Rossi 1995, Grundy and Venable 1995).

The technology contexts can be further divided into two broad categories by how they model the object systems (Lyytinen 1987). These categories are data oriented and process oriented approaches. In ME a similar division can also be observed: there is a class of metalanguages and meta systems that model the data models of methods and support the storage of models made according to these definitions (Sorenson et al. 1988, Smolander 1991, etc.). In the process camp — with fewer representatives than data oriented — the research has focused on process representations and tools which support the enactment of these processes (Hofstede, et al. 1993, Wijers 1991, Hidding et al. 1993, etc.).

As in CASE research (cf. Wynekoop and Conger 1991) there is a bias towards building metaCASE and CAME environments rather than evaluating them. There are many articles that describe either principles and requirements for such environments (cf. Marttiin et al. 1995, Harmsen and Brinkkemper 1993, Goldkuhl and Cronholm 1993, Heym and Österle 1993), or represent how one particular metasystem has been implemented and how it works (cf. Teichroew et al. 1980, Sorenson et al. 1988, Bergsten et al. 1989, Chen et al. 1989, Smolander et al. 1991, Rossi 1995, Jarke et al. 1991). A number of articles describe individual aspects of metaenvironments for different purposes. See for example transformations (cf. Boloix et al. 1991a), metrics (cf. Boloix et al. 1991b), automatic diagram generation (cf. Protsko et al. 1989).

There is, however, a paucity of research that describes the use of these tools in practice. Only two empirical studies addressing the capabilities of adaptable environments were found: Cronholm and Goldkuhl (1992) studied method adaptations done with four different tools and five methods. Marttiin et al. (1993) made laboratory experiments by adapting the same method for three different CASE shells. These studies reveal that CAME tool developers have concentrated so far on techniques that allow tool customization and method adaptation rather than on developing techniques and principles for utilizing tool based knowledge about methods, for example in method selection, method composition, construction, and reuse. Hence, without proven ME principles on method construction and experience, the development of tool support for ME will be slowed down, and thus will remain in its infancy.

3.2 Language context

An IS language provides a means and an environment for linguistic communication which encompasses the use, nature, content, context and form of signs included in the IS (Lyytinen 1987). Seen in this light, the ME language context covers the language facilities for method construction, use and evaluation. The current research on ME languages has mainly focused on the following issues: (1) the metamodeling formalisms for data (i.e. product)-oriented models, process-oriented models of methods, or both; (2) mechanisms for integrating methods; (3) evaluation of the ISD methods; and (4) the effective representational paradigms of ME languages. Note that rather than being orthogonal to one another, these issues are internally related. Below we shall examine each category and summarize main topics of the research.

Metamodeling formalisms

The research in metamodeling formalisms has been so far one of the most intensively studied areas in ME. This is rational as it forms the basis for systematic ME. The general requirements for ME language can be found: Kottemann and Konsynski (1984), Marttiin et al. (1995), and Welke (1992) recognize the need of rich semantic constructs for modeling the conceptual structure and constraints of methods. Rolland et al. (1995) present a set of characteristics of process models which a meta-process model should cope with.

Starting from Teichroew et al. (1980), most of the *meta-data modeling* formalisms rely on an existing semantic model (Hull and King 1987). Two types of semantic models, ER-based models and NIAM-based models have been investigated in particular. Extensions to the ER model (Sorenson et al. 1988, Welke 1992, Smolander 1991) seek to improve the expressive power by directly enforcing certain integrity constraints (Welke 1992, Kelly and Tahvanainen 1994), or by representing complex objects (Welke 1992). The developed NIAM-based conceptual metamodeling formalisms (Bommel et al. 1991, Hofstede, et al. 1993, Hofstede and Weide 1993a) attain similar goals, but are founded on a more formal basis than the ER-based ones. The higher level degree of formality have made it easy to develop conceptual manipulation languages, like Lisa-D (Hofstede et al. 1993), to manage model (schema) evolution (Proper and Weide 1994), or to unify the object-role models (Bronts et al. 1995). For other metamodeling formalisms, Saeki and Wenyin (1994) have adapted an object-oriented modeling language called Object-Z. Ahituv (1987) introduces a formal metamodel, which views an information system as the data flow that moves from one state to another, and by which some existing methods can be modeled. The work of (Oei et al. 1992, Oei and Falkenberg 1994, Oei 1995) introduces a formal language for modeling methods and transforming them into a method hierarchy. The functionality of a method engineering language called MEL is sketched by Harmsen et al. (1994a) and Brinkkemper (1995). MEL is a specification and manipulation language for situational method construction.

Another aspect of ME, *meta-process modeling*, is less developed than the data aspect*. Nevertheless, the research can be classified into three categories of process modeling (Dowson 1987): activity-oriented, product-oriented, and decision-oriented. The formal model called "task structure" (Wijers 1991, Hofstede and Nieuwland 1993) has been developed to specify the relationships among the modeling tasks targeted to achieve certain objectives. The meta-process model of Tolvanen et al. (1993a) is able to specify activity models and agent models which specify, respectively, activities performed and the agents involved in utilizing a method. These two meta-process models are activity-oriented. The meta-process model proposed by Marttiin (1994) supports essentially both the specification of modeling products and the activities needed to make it evolve. It is, therefore, a product oriented model. The proposal of Rolland et al. (1995) focuses on the specification of successive transformations of the modeling product looked upon as consequences of decisions. Thus, this model falls in the last category. The strategies of integrating a meta-data model and a meta-process model are also addressed by Wijers and Dort (1990) and Tolvanen et al. (1993a).

Integration of methods

Integration of methods here refers to the capability of a ME language to associate multiple meta (data) models and to administrate, to cross-check, to reuse, to transform, or to compare them. To provide a comprehensive administrative functionality, the already mentioned modeling language MEL includes a set of operations for specifying, updating, selecting and assembling method fragments (Harmsen et al. 1994a). Kelly and Tahvanainen (1994a) introduce an approach based on the mechanisms of "property sharing" and type reuse to integrate methods that are used in parallel to model the same real-world domain. Motivated by the same goal, the proposal of Saeki and Wenyin (1994) associates interrelated semantic constructs (data types) to the same object (instances) domain. For reuse, two recent studies have suggested a framework for organizing "reusable" method fragments (Rossi and Tolvanen 1995, Brinkkemper 1995).

An approach for transforming specifications between different methods is reported in Boloix et al. (1991). Another approach for integrating methods, which is particularly well-suited for method comparison, is the aforementioned work of (Oei et al. 1992, Oei and Falkenberg 1994, Oei 1995). One of its distinct features is its rationale of harmonizing metamodels by transforming them into a common metamodel hierarchy (MMH) following certain criteria, thus providing a platform for comparing them.

Evaluation of methods

One driving force for ME is the need for a systematic and objective means[†] to compare or evaluate methods, with the aim of reducing the "YAMA (Yet Another Modeling Approach) Syndrome" (Oei et al. 1992) or "chopping down the methodology jungle." (Hofstede and Weide 1993b). Two types of research can be distinguished according to the aim of method

---

* Although numerous process models have been proposed for software engineering, some of which can be used in principle as meta-process models, we restrict our attention here to those process models explicitly developed for ME.

† We therefore focus on the formal systematic approaches for method evaluation, excluding the numerous studies using an *ad hoc* means for method comparison.

evaluation. One stream attempts to find prominent characteristics of methods by comparing a set of methods based on their meta-data model or meta-process model, or both (Hong et al. 1993, Song and Osterweil 1992, Song and Osterweil 1994, Oei 1995). These characteristics include similarities and differences among a set of methods (Hong et al. 1993, Song and Osterweil 1992), or even expressiveness, liability or generality (Oei 1995). Another type is aimed at analyzing the complexity-based features of methods based on a standardized method metrics standard, as proposed by Rossi and Brinkkemper (1995). An obvious benefit of this approach over the former is that it could easily be automated because of its formal and strict mathematical basis.

Representational paradigms of ME languages
Overall, metamodeling languages need a variety of representation forms. Research has shifted from the early textual style expressions as adopted in Teichroew et al. (1980) and Wijers (1991) to two-dimensional visual languages. The development of visual metamodeling languages has been heavily focused on diagrammatic paradigms, motivated by the fact that a large amount of methods are developed with diagrammatic representations. Hofstede and Weide (1993b) emphasize the importance of diagrammatic formalization in instantiating a method, and develop a general approach for such formalization. Sommerville et al. (1987), Smolander et al. (1991), Protsko et al. (1989), and Hofstede et al. (1992a) have proposed languages to represent graphical notations of a method, their connections, and/or graphical constraints. In addition, Kelly (1994) and Kinnunen et al. (1994) investigate the utilization of a matrix format as a visual representation form for metamodeling. A recent trend extends these developments to several representational paradigms, establishing a multiparadigmatic representational metamodeling environment. As an example, the MetaEdit+ metaCASE environment supports modeling of a method using a diagram, a matrix (Kelly 1994), or a table, and also a diagrammatic mode of querying method repository information (Liu 1995).

3.3 Organization context

The organization context is essential for ME because the development and use of ISD methods always involves organizational structures, processes and interactions between people. Within the organization context methods can be seen as organizational knowledge of ISD, which evolves and needs to be managed. Similarly, because ME is essentially the same kind of process as ISD it involves human interactions, such as decision making on method selection and assembly, training on methods, operative control on method use, collecting and sharing experience of method applicability.

Within the organization context several survey based studies (e.g. Wijers and Dort 1990, Aaen et al. 1992, Yourdon 1992, Russo et al. 1995) have revealed that ISD methods are developed or adapted locally. For example, a survey of over 100 organizations' use of ISD methods (Russo et al. 1995) shows that more than 2/3 of the companies have developed or adapted their methods in-house. Also, 89% of respondents believed that methods should be adapted on a project-by-project basis.

Although the surveys clearly reveal that local method engineering take place in practice they do not explain in more detail why and how local methods are produced and how the ME efforts are organized. If organizations make their own versions of methods, these issues must somehow be managed within the organizations, and this too could be studied empirically. The only research available on these issues consists of two field studies: Smolander et al. (1990) examined the adaptation of tools and methods in eight companies, and Cronholm and Goldkuhl (1993) studied five CASE tool adaptation projects. One of the main results of these studies showed the absence of general strategies in ME. In adaptation projects several factors, such as the size and skills of the organization as well as technology, can shape ME strategies. No systematic methods or use of metamodeling languages was encountered. Although these studies identify key organizational requirements (e.g. related to issues on management and user support, and on sufficient method knowledge) and problems (e.g. time and resources needed) related to ME they are still tool-focused. For example, most of the adaptation problems are related to the technical features and capabilities of the tools, rather than to organizational issues. Similarly, Bubenko (1988) inspected the situational factors that affect the choice of metaCASE technology: from the viewpoint of organizational context the factors claimed to favor metaCASE are experience of using a particular method, support for in-house methods, and better acceptance of the adapted tools.

Some studies have also reported experiences of ME (cf. WoodHarper 1985, Aalto 1993, van Slooten 1995, Tolvanen 1995, Vlasblom et al. 1995). They still tend to focus on describing developed methods and tools, rather than arguing for or against organizational support. Based on the experiences of ME efforts some studies have proposed frameworks (Slooten and Brinkkemper 1993, Tolvanen 1995), or metamodeling guidelines (Tagg 1990, Tolvanen and Lyytinen 1993b) for ME. These either follow a fairly narrow view of organizational support (e.g. the only unit is a ME/ISD project), or are limited to specific tasks of ME (e.g. tool adaptation). Finally and most importantly, the proposed frameworks have not been validated through the feasibility of metamodeling languages and tools.

To summarize, the research focus in the organizational context has been on tool-related aspects dealing with metaCASE selection, and on the identification of problems and requirements for tool customization. Accordingly, there is a paucity of research on tasks, organizational structures and mechanisms, and types of managerial coordination needed to carry out ME efforts. Researchers have so far focused mostly on proposing an organizational role for method engineers responsible for method management and redevelopment (e.g. Bubenko 1988, Kumar and Welke 1992).

4. USE OF RESEARCH METHODS

This section extends our survey by examining the use of research methods in ME research. In the following the use of research methods is discussed including references on published research. Table 1 summarizes the discussion. Some of the papers could not be classified into a single category: They focus on more than one context and apply multiple research methods. However, the aim of this survey is not to classify single papers but rather to find any overall bias in the use of research methods.

The majority of the *surveys* analyzed — although they have not focused specifically on ME rather on method use in general — falls into the organization context. However, these studies show only that organizations are developing methods in-house, rather than inspect how and why they are developed. In the technology context one survey was found (Karrer and Scacchi 1993)which examined the applications of meta-technology. Also, both of the *field studies* found (Smolander et al. 1990, Cronholm and Goldkuhl 1993) focus on tool and method adaptation, and thus investigated the capabilities of the customizable tools and organizational mechanism used during ME effort.

The role of the *case studies* is typically centered on describing the phenomena and their evolution in detail. In the language context Wijers (1991) conducted a case study using a knowledge acquisition approach to elicit method knowledge from three method engineers who had expertise for three different methods, and later using his modeling formalism to model each method. The finding shows the adequacy of the modeling formalism in coping with the three methods. We included also studies comparing ISD methods (cf. Song and Osterweil 1992, Song and Osterweil 1994) into case category, since they validate the framework through several method modeling cases. In the organization context, both case and action research studies have been carried out (cf. WoodHarper 1985, Slooten 1995, Tolvanen 1995). Many of the papers found describing ME projects, however, did not follow any case or action research method, and thus belong to the normative category.

Especially in the technology context, the dominant research approach has been *applied research*, to the degree that Nunamaker and Chen (1991) have developed a research approach, coined "software engineering research, which uses system building as a major research vehicle". Ever since the days of SEM (ISDOS 1985) tool research has focused on building environments (cf. reported environments: RAMATIC (Bergsten et al. 1989), MetaPlex (Chen et al. 1989), MetaEdit (Smolander et al. 1991), MetaView (Sorenson et al. 1988), and ConceptBase (Jarke et al. 1990)). Similarly in ME language development several papers seek to apply and extend existing theory or approaches from other closely related disciplines (databases, programming languages, software engineering, visual languages, and so on) to build and improve the capability of ME languages (Bronts et al. 1995, Liu 1995, Tolvanen et al. 1993a, Hong et al. 1993, Boloix et al. 1991a, Protsko et al. 1989, Saeki and Wenyin 1994).

Basic research has been densely concentrated in the language context (see table below). Although from the point of view of database modeling, some of the studies can be argued to be applied research (e.g. extensions to ER or NIAM), we believe that most of them (if not all) contribute to shape the theoretical basis of metamodeling. The numerous basic studies, on the other hand, reflect the fact that ME is still a young research area.

Normative writings can be found from each category. In the technology context some comparative research has emerged to categorize and compare features of available environments (e.g. see Marttiin et al. 1993) as well as to propose frameworks for designing environments (Goldkuhl and Cronholm 1993, Harmsen et al. 1994a). Several works in the language context make efforts either to generalize the requirements for ME languages, or to standardize the functionality of a ME language based on mathematics or conceptual framework (see table below). In the organization context some papers follow normative research since they propose a task of a method engineer (Kumar and Welke 1992), explains reasons for selecting customizable tools (Bubenko 1988), describe tool adaptation practices (Tagg 1990), or normative frameworks for ME (Slooten and Brinkkemper 1993).

Finally, and as important as the current use of research methods, there exist several research method and context combinations that have remained untouched (i.e. empty slots in the Table 1). First, there are fewer empirical studies than other research approaches; especially when compared to the use of applied research in tool development and basic research on language context. Second, the variety of research methods in the organization context is not being exploited to its full extent, since ME focused studies have used field studies and normative research.

	Technology context	Language context	Organization context
Survey	Karrer and Scacchi 1993	-	Wynekoop and Russo 1993, Yourdon 1992, Wijers and Dort 1990, Aaen et al. 1992, Kusters and Wijers 1993
Field	Smolander et al. 1990, Cronholm and Goldkuhl 1992		Smolander et al. 1990, Cronholm and Goldkuhl 1992
Laboratory	-	-	-
Case	-	Wijers 1991, Song and Osterweil 1992, Song and Osterweil 1994	Slooten 1995
Action	-	-	WoodHarper 1985, Tolvanen 1995
Applied	Brinkkemper 1990, Sorenson et al. 1988, Teichroew et al. 1980, Chen 1988, Chen et al. 1989, Chen et al. 1989, Bergsten et al. 1989, Smolander et al. 1991, Rossi et al. 1992, Rossi 1995, Rossi and Tolvanen 1995, Harmsen and Brinkkemper 1993, Harmsen et al. 1994b,Boloix et al. 1991b, Protsko et al. 1989, 1991	Bronts et al. 1995, Liu 1995, Tolvanen et al. 1993a, Hong et al. 1993, Boloix et al. 1991a, Protsko et al. 1989, Saeki and Wenyin 1994	N/A
Basic	Kottemann and Konsynski 1984	Ahituv 1987, Bommel et al. 1991, Harmsen et al. 1994a, Kelly 1994, Kelly and Tahvanainen 1994, Proper and Weide 1994, Rolland et al. 1995, Rossi and Brinkkemper 1995, Welke 1992, Sommerville et al. 1987, Sorenson et al. 1988, Teichroew et al. 1980, Hofstede, et al. 1993, Hofstede and Weide 1993a, Hofstede and Weide 1993b	-
Normative	Marttiin et al. 1995, Marttiin et al. 1993, Kelly and Smolander 1996, Bubenko 1988, Goldkuhl and Cronholm 1993, Harmsen and Brinkkemper 1993, Brinkkemper 1995, Jarke et al. 1990, Harmsen et al. 1994b, Kumar and Welke 1992, Tagg 1990, Tolvanen and Lyytinen 1993b, Verhoef et al. 1991	Kottemann and Konsynski 1984, Smolander 1991, Kelly 1995, Leppänen 1994, Kinnunen and Leppänen 1994, Welke 1992	Bubenko 1988, Kumar and Welke 1992, Slooten and Brinkkemper 1993, Tagg 1990, Vlasblom et al. 1995

Table 1. The use of research methods in method engineering research.

5. DIRECTIONS FOR FUTURE RESEARCH

The goal of any researcher is to generate "infallible" knowledge in his research field. In practice this means research collaboration, complementary research efforts, and use of a variety of research methods. For example, before building new metamodeling tools we need to have a good understanding of their current use and applicability. In the same vein, without research efforts towards developing new solutions and systems, there would be little opportunity for evaluative research (Nunamaker et al. 1991). In the following we shall contribute ideas for future ME research by proposing concrete research topics based on our survey: for each context and each research method some representative research questions will be raised (Table 2).

5.1 Technical context

Because earlier research has been mainly geared towards systems building, there is room for technical research that would verify the ideas put forth in the systems built. There is a huge amount of normative writing about the feasibility of different metamodeling approaches and environments, but no empirical (or even case based) research that could prove or refute these claims. Therefore, field research in particular should be encouraged, even though there are relatively few platforms that have so wide a user population that field research would be feasible. In addition to field studies based on several tools (such as Cronholm and Goldkuhl 1992) we also need case studies with detailed descriptions of tool use.

Because researchers have mainly built prototype systems, there have been few usability studies of the environments (e.g. Cronholm and Goldkuhl 1992). The usability of implemented CASE tools, as well as the usability of the method engineering tools, should be studied in practice.

5.2 Language context

For any modeling language, functionality and usability are always central issues, and ME languages are no exception. Future research on ME languages should thus concentrate on these aspects, either by extending existing research approaches or by creating new ones.

An obvious question concerning the functionality aspect is whether existing ME languages are sufficient to model *all* methods (according to the 100% principle of conceptual data modeling, see Griethuysen 1982). Although this question may never be answered with regard to the increasing emergence of "situational methods" we nevertheless need to answer it at some level. This necessitates the trial of ME languages using survey, field study, or case research. Another problem is weaknesses in existing ME languages to express constraints. Having evolved from general data modeling models or languages, existing ME languages are mainly capable of expressing specific semantic constraints imposed by the business data modeling domain. This constitutes a key deficiency in the functionality of ME languages, as the constraints in the method domain are quite different. Future work is needed on systematic study of ME-specific semantic constraints, and to develop a set of constraints for ME languages to cope with, ideally, an arbitrary set of constraints.

Reuse strategies form another research issue which needs further investigation. The central problem is how to model and organize reusable method fragments, and how to develop sufficient and effective means for retrieving promising reusable objects. Another important research question is ME languages' support for systematic and unbiased method comparison or characterization. Though the outcomes of the research in this problem area are encouraging, they address only a partial characterization of methods. A natural problem arises over whether it is feasible to standardize the *quality* of methods. Insofar as it is possible, such a standard could no doubt improve the ME process by allowing at least partial automation of the evaluation of a method supported by a ME language.

One (implicit) assumption for the shift from a textual ME language to a visual one lies in the belief of the improved user friendliness. No studies in the ME area have been found to support it, beyond a short comment in (Goldkuhl and Cronholm 1993). This necessitates empirical research, for example laboratory experiments, to evaluate not only this belief, but also investigate user preferences for different visual representational paradigms. The implementation of visual paradigms should also be improved to address the wide spectrum of the functionality of the ME languages support. This includes, for instance, the investigation of the role of visual languages for the querying and retrieval of reusable method fragments.

5.3 Organization context

As stated above there is a paucity of ME research in the organization context. Although several surveys of method use have been performed there is still a need for new ones. One reason for this is that existing studies (e.g. Wijers and Dort 1990, Aaen et al. 1992, Yourdon 1992, Russo et al. 1995) obtain different results: for example the popularity of method adaptation and thus in-house method development differs in the studies between 36% and 65%. Accordingly, it seems that there is no consensus on what method adaptation means (e.g. modification of phases on a general level or modification of the details of a method's concepts and notations). Similarly we do not know whether stakeholders are more satisfied with in-house methods than with methods taken as given.

The difficulty in survey studies is in the collection of detailed data. Field studies and case studies are more suitable for investigating in detail questions such as why in-house methods are developed, do in-house methods work and how ME efforts are organized. For the last question we can already find several alternatives for ME projects on the organizational level: ME can be done for a whole organization (cf. SDM by Turner et al.1988), for a single development project (cf. Vlasblom et al. 1995), or for a developed product (cf. Aalto 1993). Similarly the stakeholder's roles and tasks during ME efforts need to be studied: current research merely proposes a role of 'method engineer', although in-house method development also has other stakeholders. Field studies (Smolander et al. 1990, Cronholm and Goldkuhl 1992) have noted only a few of these stakeholders, and their roles have not been studied.

Finally, action research may be needed for examining what has caused success or failure in in-house method development, what decisions are made during ME, how frequently methods are changed, and how method evolution is controlled. These questions typically presuppose longitudinal research efforts as well as close interaction in method use and method development situations.

	Technology context	Language context	Organization context
Survey	How commonly are metaCASE tools used?	What metamodeling languages are used in practice?	How common are in-house methods? Are stakeholders satisfied with in-house methods?
Field	How do method engineers use CAME tools?	What are proper constructs for a metamodeling language?	Why are in-house methods developed? What strategies are applied in ME efforts? What stakeholders participate in ME efforts? What are the tasks and position of method engineers?
Laboratory	How well do current metaCASE tools support adaptation? How easy is the use of metaCASE tools?	What differences do metamodeling languages have? How can we compare metamodeling languages? Evaluation of the usability of visual ME languages	How do different method user groups develop and modify their methods?
Case	Study the use of CAME and metaCASE tools, particularly their usefulness and quality		What are the requirements for in-house methods? How is method evolution managed?
Action	Use a customizable CASE tool to develop a tool for a given method in a user organization	Assess a metamodeling language in a ME project	What causes success or failure in a ME effort? What kind of task and decisions are made during ME? What causes changes in methods and how are they controlled?
Applied			N/A
Basic		Development of a ME constraint language. What kind of inheritance structure is optimal for method fragments?	Development of a theory of how method knowledge is managed
Normative		A systematic classification of semantic constraints as observed in metamodeling. Study of the possibility and ways of standardizing the quality dimensions of methods. What constitutes a good ME language supporting "reuse"?	

Table 2. Sample research questions on future ME research.

6. SUMMARY

In this paper we conducted a survey of method engineering research approaches. Over 80 papers, found from journals and conference publications, were classified using Lyytinen's (1987) three contexts: technology, language and organization. A second dimension of classification was the chosen research paradigm(s) (i.e. survey, field study, laboratory experiment, case study, action research, applied, basic or normative) according to the framework of Wynekoop and Conger (1991).

Some interesting observations can be made from the amount of literature in each context and research approach. A pattern of distribution similar to that of Wynekoop and Conger can be found: most papers appeared in the applied, basic and normative categories. In the same vein the technical and language contexts predominate in the organizational context. Although a new field is often dominated by applied or constructive research, the now numerous available environments and languages call for evaluative research approaches. The lack of empirical studies can be partially explained by the relatively short time that method engineering tools have been used in ISD organizations.

For the field of method engineering to progress, we must widen the range of research methods we use. Many more empirical studies are needed to investigate the applicability of the tools and languages developed. Too often tools and languages are developed without empirical justification or evaluation outside the research group. The absence of studies in the organizational context must also be addressed, since organizational issues are essential for ME to achieve its purpose. Again, empirical studies are needed for obtaining a comprehensive view of ME practices. Alongside these empirical studies, new ideas and approaches are needed for organizational issues such as method management, method evolution, and use of method users' requirements to guide ME efforts.

Method engineering is an endeavor that takes place over time, extending over various method versions, ISD projects, and even tools. Research in ME should therefore also be directed towards longitudinal studies: research to date has mostly dealt with "snapshots" of ME. Finally, ME research is only a part of the research activities in IS, and it should therefore be tied in with research in other related disciplines in the field, such as IS development, computer-aided environments, software process improvement and requirements engineering.

ACKNOWLEGEMENTS

The authors would like to thank Steven Kelly for proofreading and valuable additions to the paper, and the anonymous referees for their constructive comments.

7. REFERENCES

Aaen, Ivan, Aila Siltanen, Carsten Sørensen and Veli-Pekka Tahvanainen (1992), "A Tale of Two Countries: CASE Experiences and Expectations," in *The Impact of Computer Supported Technologies on Information Systems Development*, K. E. Kendall, K. Lyytinen and J. I. DeGross (Ed.), North-Holland, Amsterdam, pp. 61-93.

Aalto, J.-M. (1993), "Experiences on Applying OMT to Large Scale Systems," in *Proceedings of the Seminar on Conceptual Modelling and Object-Oriented Programming*, A. Lehtola and J. Jokiniemi (Ed.), Finnish Artificial Intelligence Society, pp. 39-47 .

Ahituv, Niv (1987), "*A metamodel of information flow: a tool to support information systems theory,*" Communications of the ACM 30(**9**), pp.781-791.

Benbasat, I., D. Goldstein and M. Mead (1987), "*The Case Research Strategy in Studies of Information Systems,*" MIS Quartely (September), pp.369-386.

Bergsten, Per, Janis Bubenko jr., Roland Dahl, Mats Gustafsson and Lars-Åke Johansson (1989), "*RAMATIC - A CASE Shell for Implementation of Specific CASE Tools,*" Tempora T6.1 Report, first draft, SISU, Gothenburg.

Boloix, G., P. G. Sorenson and J. P. Tremblay (1991), "*On Transformations Using A Metasystem Approach To Software Development,*" TR 91-19, The University of Alberta, Edmonton, Alberta, Canada (November).

Boloix, G., P. G. Sorenson and J. P. Tremblay (1991), "*Software Metrics using a Metasystem Approach to Software Specification,*" Technical Report, The University of Alberta, Canada.

Bommel, P. van, A. H. M. ter Hofstede and Th.P. van der Weide (1991), "*Semantics and verification of object-role models,*" Information Systems 16(**5**) pp.471-495.

Brinkkemper, Sjaak (1990), "*Formalisation of Information Systems Modelling,*" Ph.D. Thesis, Univ. of Nijmegen, Thesis Publishers, Amsterdam.

Brinkkemper, Sjaak (1995), "*Method engineering: engineering of information systems development methods and tools,*" Information & Software Technology 37(**11**) pp.1-6.

Bronts, G.H.W.M., S.J. Brouwer, C.L.J. Martens and H.A. Proper (1995), "*A unifying object role modelling theory,*" Information Systems 20(**3**) pp.213-235.

Bubenko, J. A. (1988), "*Selecting a Strategy for Computer-Aided Software Engineering (CASE),*" 59, SYSLAB, University of Stockholm, Sweden.

Chen, Minder (1988), "The Integration of Organization and Information Systems Modeling: A Metasystem Approach to the Generation of Group Decision Support Systems and Compute-aided Software Engineering," PhD Thesis, University of Arizona, Tuscon, USA.

Chen, M., J. F. Nunamaker Jr. and E. S. Weber (1989), "*The Use of Integrated Organization and Information Systems Models in Building and Delivering Business Application Systems,*" IEEE Transactions on Knowledge and Data Engineering 1(**3**), pp.406-409.

Chen, Minder, Jr. Jay F. Nunamaker (1989), "METAPLEX: An integrated environment for organization and information systems development," pp. 141--151 in *Proceedings of the Tenth International Conference on Information Systems, December 4--6, 1989, Boston, Massachusetts*, J. I. DeGross, J. C. Henderson, and B. R. Konsynski (Ed.), ACM Press.

Chen, M., J. F. Nunamaker Jr. and G. Mason (1991), "*The Architecture And Design Of A Collaborative Environment For Systems Definition,*" Database (Winter/Spring) pp. 22-28.

Cronholm, S., G. Goldkuhl (1992), "*Meanings and motives of method customisation in CASE environments - observations and categorizations from an empirical study,*" Proceeding of the fifth workshop on the next generation of CASE tools, University of Twente, Twente.

Dowson, M. (1987), "Iteration in the software process," pp. 36-39 in *Proc of 9th Int. Conf. Software Engineering*, San Francisco.

Galliers, R. D. (1991), "Choosing Appropriate Information Systems Research Approaches: A Revised Taxonomy," pp. 327-348 in *Information Systems Research*, H.-E. Nissen, H. K. Klein and R. Hircheim (Ed.), North-Holland, Amsterdam.

Gigch, J. van (1991), *"Systems design and modeling and metamodeling,"* Plenum Press, New York.

Goldkuhl, Göran, Stefan Cronholm (1993), *"Customizable CASE Environments: A Framework for Design and Evaluation,"* Accepted to COPE IT '93. LiTH-IDA-R-93-42, Linköping University, Sweden.

Griethuysen, J.J. van (1982), *"Concepts and terminology for the conceptual schema and the information base,"* ISO/TC97/SC5-N695, ISO.

Grundy, J. C., J. R. Venable (1995), "Providing Integrated Support for Multiple Development Notations," pp. 255-268 in *Proceedings of the 7th International Conference on Advanced Information Systems Engineering, CAISE'95*, J. Iivari, K. Lyytinen and M. Rossi (Ed.), Springer-Verlag.

Harmsen, F., S. Brinkkemper (1993), "Computer Aided Method Engineering based on existing Meta-CASE technology," pp. 125-140 in *Proceedings of the Fourth Workshop on The Next Generation of CASE Tools*, Sjaak Brinkkemper, Frank Harmsen (Ed.) No. 93-32, Univ. of Twente, Enschede, the Netherlands.

Harmsen, F., S. Brinkkemper and H. Oei (1994), "A language and tool for the engineering of situational methods for information systems development," pp. 206--214 in *Proceedings of the Fourth International Conference on Information Systems Development*, J. Zupansis and S. Wrycza (Ed.), Moderna Organizacija, Kranj, Slovenia.

Harmsen, Frank, Sjaak Brinkkemper and Han Oei (1994), "Situational Method Engineering for Information System Project Approaches," pp. 169--194 in *Methods and Associated Tools for the Information Systems Life Cycle (A-55)*, A. A. Verrijn-Stuart and T. W. Olle (Ed.), Elsevier Science B.V. (North-Holland).

Heym, M., H. Österle (1992), "A Semantic Data Model for Methodology Engineering," in *Proceedings of the Fifth CASE '92 Workshop, Montreal*, G. Forte and N. Madhavji (Ed.), IEEE Computer Society Press, Los Alamitos.

Heym, M., H. Österle (1992), "A Reference Model of Information Systems Development," pp. 215--240 in *The Impact of Computer Supported Technologies on Information Systems Development*, K. E. Kendall, K. Lyytinen, J. L. DeGross (Ed.), North-Holland, Amsterdam.

Heym, M., H. Österle (1993), *"Computer-aided methodology engineering,"* INFORMATION AND SOFTWARE TECHNOLOGY 35(**6/7**) pp.345--354.

Hidding, Gezinus J., Gwendolyn M. Freund and Johan K. Joseph (1993), *"Modeling Large Processes with Task Packages,"* Workshop on Modeling in the Large, AAAI Conference, Washington, D.C..

Hofstede, A. H. M. ter, T. F. Verhoef, E. R. Nieuwland and G. M. Wijers (1992), *"Integrated Specification of Method and Graphic Knowledge,"* Proceedings of the Fourth International Conference on Software Engineering and Knowledge Engineering pp.307-316.

Hofstede, A. H. M. ter, T. F. Verhoef, E. R. Nieuwland and G. M. Wijers (1992), "Specification of Graphic Conventions in Methods," pp. 185--215 in *Proceedings of 3rd Workshop on Next Generation of CASE Tools*, B. Theodoulidis and A. Sutcliffe (Ed.), UMIST, Manchester, UK.

Hofstede, A. H. M. ter (1993), *"Information Modelling in Data Intensive Domains,"* PhD Thesis, University of Nijmegen, Nijmegen.

Hofstede, A. H. M. ter, Th. P. van der Weide (1993), *"Expressiveness in data modeling,"* Data & Knowledge Engineering (10) pp.65-100.

Hofstede, A. H. M. ter, Th. P. van der Weide (1993), *"Formalisation of techniques: chopping down the methodology jungle,"* Information & Software Technology 34(**1**) pp.57-65.

Hofstede, A. H. M. ter, E. R. Nieuwland (1993), *"Task structure semantics through process algebra,"* Software Engineering Journal (8) pp.14-20.

Hofstede, A. H. M. ter, H. A. Proper and Th. P. van der Weide (1993), *"Formal definition of of a conceptual language for the description and manipulation of information models,"* Information Systems 18 pp.489-523.

Hong, S., G. van den Goor and S. Brinkkemper (1993), "A Comparison of Six Object-Oriented Analysis and Design Methods," in *Proceedings of the 26th Hawaiian Conference on Systems Sciences*, IEEE Computer Science Press.

Hull, Richard, Roger King (1987), *"Semantic Database Modeling Survey, Applications, and Research Issues,"* ACM COMPUTING SURVEYS 19(**3**) pp.201--260.

ISDOS, (1985), *"System Encyclopedia Manager, Language Definition Manager: User Manual (SEM/LDM),"* Version 1.4 (June).

Jarke, Matthias, Manfred Jeusfeld and Thomas Rose (1990), *"A Software Process Data Model For Knowledge Engineering In Information Systems,"* Information Systems 15(**1**) pp.85--116.

Jarke, M., J. Mylopoulos, J. Schmidt and Y. Vassiliou (1991), *"DAIDA: An Environment for Evolving Information Systems,"* RWTH Aachen, Aachen.

Jenkins, A. M. (1985), "Research Methodologies in MIS Research," pp. 103-118 in *Research Methods in Information Systems*, E. Mumford, R. Hirschheim, G. Fitzgerald and A.T. Wood-Harper (Ed.), Elsevier Science Publishers.

Karrer, A., W. Scacchi (1993), *"Meta-Environments for software production,"* International Journal of Software Engineering and Data Engineering 3(**1**) pp.139-162.

Kelly, Steven (1994), *"A Matrix Editor for a MetaCASE Environment,"* Information and Software Technology 36(**6**) pp.361--371.

Kelly, Steven, Veli-Pekka Tahvanainen (1994), "Support for Incremental Method Engineering and MetaCASE," in *Proceedings of the 5th Workshop on the Next Generation of CASE Tools*, B. Theodoulidis (Ed.) No. Memoranda Informatica 94-25, Universiteit Twente, Enschede, the Netherlands.

Kelly, Steven (1995), "What's in a Relationship: on distinguishing property holding and object binding," in *Proceedings of 3rd International Conference on Information Systems Concepts, ISCO 3*, W. Hesse and E. Falkenberg (Ed.), University of Marburg, Lahn, Germany.

Kelly, Steven, Kari Smolander (1996), *"Evolution and Issues in MetaCASE,"* Information and Software Technology (to appear) .

Kinnunen, Kimmo, Mauri Leppänen (1994), "O/A Matrix and a Technique for Methodology Engineering," in *Proceedings of the Fourth International Conference on Information Systems Development*, J. Zupansis and S. Wrycza (Ed.), Moderna Organizacija, Kranj, Slovenia.

Kottemann, J. E., B. R. Konsynski (1984), "Dynamic Metasystems for Information Systems Development," pp. 187--204 in *Proceedings of the Fifth International Conference on Information Systems*.

Kumar, Kuldeep, Richard J. Welke (1992), "Methodology Engineering: A Proposal for Situation Specific Methodology Construction," pp. 257--269 in *Challenges and Strategies for Research in Systems Development*, Kottermann W. W. and Senn J. A. (Ed.), John Wiley & Sons, Washington.

Kusters, R. J., G. M. Wijers (1993), "On the Practical Use of CASE Tools: Results of a survey," pp. 2--10 in *Proceedings of the 6th International Workshop on Computer-Aided Software Engineering, CASE93*, Hing-Yan Lee, Thomas F. Reid and Stan Jarzabek (Ed.), IEEE Computer Society.

Leppänen, Mauri (1994), "Metamodelling: Concept, Benefits and Pitfalls," pp. 126--137 in *Proceedings of the Fourth International Conference on Information Systems Development*, J. Zupansis and S. Wrycza (Ed.), Moderna Organizacija, Kranj, Slovenia.

Liu, H. (1995), "A Visual Interface for Querying a CASE Repository," in *Proc. of the Eleventh IEEE Symposium on Visual Languages (VL'95)*, Darmstadt.

Lyytinen, Kalle (1987), "A Taxonomic Perspective of Information Systems Development: Theoretical Constructs and Recommendations," pp. 3--41 in *Critical Issues in Information Systems Research*, R. J. Boland Jr. and R. A. Hirschheim (Ed.), John Wiley & Sons Ltd..

Lyytinen, Kalle, Kari Smolander and Veli-Pekka Tahvanainen (1989), "Modelling CASE Environments in Systems Development," in *Proceedings of the first Nordic Conference on Advanced Systems*, SISU, Stockholm.

Marttiin, Pentti, Matti Rossi, Veli-Pekka Tahvanainen and Kalle Lyytinen (1993), "*A Comparative review of CASE shells: A preliminary framework and research outcomes,*" Information & Management 25 pp.11-31.

Marttiin, P. (1994), "Towards Flexible Process Support with a CASE shell," pp. 14--27 in *Advanced Information Systems Engineering, Proceedings of the Third International Conference CAiSE'94, Utrecht, The Netherlands, June 1994*, G. Wijers, S. Brinkkemper and T. Wasserman (Ed.), Springer-Verlag, Berlin.

Marttiin, Pentti, Kalle Lyytinen, Matti Rossi, Veli-Pekka Tahvanainen and Juha-Pekka Tolvanen (1995), "*Modeling requirements for future CASE: issues and implementation considerations,*" Information Resources Management Journal 8(**1**) pp.15--25.

Norman, Ronald J., Minder Chen (1992), "*Working Together to Integrate CASE,*" IEEE Software (March) pp.12--17.

Nunamaker, Jay F., Minder Chen and Titus D. M. Purdin (1991), "*Systems Development in Information Systems Research,*" Management Information Systems 7(**3**) pp.89--106.

Oei, J. L. H., L. J. G. T. van Hemmen, E. D. Falkenberg and S. Brinkkemper (1992), "*The Meta Model Hierarchy: A Framework for Information for Information Systems Concepts and Techniques,*" University of Nijmegen, Nijmegen.

Oei, J. L. H., E. D. Falkenberg (1994), "Harmonisation of information systems modelling and specification techniques," pp. 151--168 in *Methods and Associated Tools for the Information Systems Life Cycle*, A. A. Verrijn-Stuart and T. W. Olle (Ed.) No. A-55, Elsevier Science publishers.

Oei, J.L.H. (1995), "A meta model transformation approach towards harmonisation in information system modelling," pp. 106-127 in *Information System Concepts - Towards a consolidation of views*, E. D. Falkenberg, W. Hesse and A. Olivé (Ed.), Chapman & Hall, London.

Olle, T.W., H. Sol and A. Verrijn-Stuart (1983), "*Informations systems design methodologies: A feature analysis,*" North-Holland, Amsterdam.

Olle, T. W. (1992), "A Comparative Review of the ISO IRDS, the IBM Repository and the ECMA PCTE as a Vehicle for CASE Tools," pp. 147--165 in *CASE: Current Practice, Future Prospects*, Kathy Spurr and Paul Layzell (Ed.), Wiley.

Proper, H. A., Th. P. van der Weide (1994), "*EVORM: A conceptual modelling technique for evolving application domains,*" Data & Knowledge Engineering 10(**12**) pp.313-359.

Protsko, L. B., P. G. Sorenson and J. P. Tremblay (1989), "*Mondrian: system for automatic generation of dataflow diagrams,*" Information and Software Technology 31(**9**) pp.456-471.

Protsko, L. B., P. G. Sorenson, J. P. Tremblay and D. A. Schaefer (1991), "*Towards the Automatic Generation of Software Diagrams,*" IEEE TRANSACTIONS ON SOFTWARE ENGINEERING 17(**1**).

Rolland, C., C. Cauvet (1992), "Trends and Perspectives in Conceptual Modeling," pp. 27--48 in *Conceptual Modelling, Databases and CASE: An Integrated View of Information Systems Development*, P. Loucopoulos and R. Zicari (Ed.), Wiley, New York.

Rolland, C., C. Souveyet and M. Moreno (1995), "*An approach for defining ways-of-working,*" Information Systems 20(**4**) pp.337-359.

Rossi, M., M. Gustafsson, K. Smolander, L.-Å. Johansson and K. Lyytinen (1992), "Metamodeling editor as a front end tool for a case-shell," pp. 547--567 in *Advanced Information Systems Engineering*, P. Loucopoulos (Ed.), Springer Verlag, Berlin, Germany.

Rossi, M., J-P. Tolvanen (1995), "Using Reusable Frameworks in Development of a Method Support Envionment," in *Proceedings of The WITS 1995, Amsterdam, The Netherlands*, M. Jarke, S. Ram (Ed.), pp. 240-249.

Rossi, M., S. Brinkkemper (1995), "Metrics in Method Engineering," pp. 200-216 in *Advanced Information Systems Engineering, Proceedings of the 7th International Conference CAiSE'95*, J. Iivari, K. Lyytinen and M. Rossi (Ed.) No. 932, Springer-Verlag, Berlin.

Rossi, M. (1995), "*The MetaEdit CAME environment,*" Proceedings of the MetaCase 95, University of Sunderland press, Sunderland.

Russo, Nancy L., Judy L. Wynekoop and Diane B. Walz (1995), "The Use and Adaptation of System Development Methodologies," in *Proceedings of the 1995 International Resources Management Association Conference*, Atlanta.

Saeki, Motoshi, Kuo Wenyin (1994), "Specifying Software Specification & Design Methods," pp. 353--366 in *CAiSE '94 Proceedings*, Gerard Wijers, Sjaak Brinkkemper and Tony Wasserman (Ed.) Vol. Lecture Notes in Computer Science 811, Springer-Verlag, Berlin.

Slooten, Kees van, Sjaak Brinkkemper (1993), "A Method Engineering Approach to Information Systems Development," in *Procs. of the IFIP WG 8.1 Working Conference on the Information Systems Development Process*, N. Prakash, C. Rolland, B. Pernici (Ed.), North-Holland, Amsterdam.

Slooten, Kees van (1995), "*Situated Methods for Systems Development,*" PhD Thesis, University of Twente, Twente.

Smolander, Kari, Veli-Pekka Tahvanainen and Kalle Lyytinen (1990), "How to Combine Tools and Methods in Practice: a field study," pp. 195--214 in *Advanced Information Systems Engineering, proceedings of the Second Nordic*, B. Steinholz, A. Sölvberg, L. Bergman (eds) (Ed.), Springer-Verlag, Berlin.

Smolander, Kari, Kalle Lyytinen, Veli-Pekka Tahvanainen and Pentti Marttiin (1991), "MetaEdit --- A Flexible Graphical Environment for Methodology Modelling," pp. 168--193 in *Advanced Information Systems Engineering, Proceedings of the Third International Conference CAiSE'91, Trondheim, Norway, May 1991*, R. Andersen, J. A. Bubenko jr. and A. Solvberg (Ed.), Springer-Verlag, Berlin.

Smolander, Kari (1991), "OPRR: A Model for Modelling Systems Development Methods," in *Next Generation CASE Tools*, K. Lyytinen and V.-P. Tahvanainen (Ed.), IOS Press, Amsterdam, the Netherlands.

Sommerville, I., R. Welland and S. Beer (1987), *"Describing software design methodologies,"* The Computer Journal 30(**2**) pp.128-133.

Song, X., L. Osterweil (1992), *"Towards Objective and Systematic Comparisons of Software Design Methodologies,"* IEEE Software 18(**5**) pp.43--53.

Song, X., L. J. Osterweil (1994), "Experience with an Approach to Comparing Software Design Methodologies," IEEE Transactions on Software Engineering 20(5) pp.364--384.

Sorenson, Paul G., Jean-Paul Tremblay and Andrew J. McAllister (1988), *"The Metaview System for Many Specification Environments,"* IEEE SOFTWARE (March) pp.30--38.

Tagg, B. S. (1990), *"Implementing Tool Support for Box Structures,"* IBM Systems Journal 29(**1**).

Teichroew, D., P. Macasovic, III E. A. Hershey and Y. Yamamoto (1980), "Application of the entity-relationship approach to information processing systems modeling," pp. 15--38 in *Entity-Relationship Approach to Systems Analysis and Design*, P. P. Chen (Ed.), North-Holland.

Tolvanen, J.-P., P. Marttiin and K. Smolander (1993), "An integrated model for information systems modeling," pp. 470-479 in *Proceedings of 26th HICSS*, J. Nunamaker and H. Sprague (Ed.) Vol. 3, IEEE Computer Society Press, Los Alamitos.

Tolvanen, J.-P., K. Lyytinen (1993), *"Flexible method adaptation in CASE environments - The metamodeling approach,"* Scandinavian Journal of Information Systems 5(**1**) pp.51-77.

Tolvanen, J.-P. (1995), "Incremental Method Development for Business Modelling: An Action Research Case Study," pp. 79-98 in *Proceedings of the 6th Workshop on the Next Generation of CASE Tools, NGCT'95*, G. Grosz (Ed.), University of Paris 1, Paris.

Turner, W. S., R. P. Langerhorst, G. F. Hice, H. B. Eilers and A. A. Uijttenbroek (1988), *"SDM: system development methodology,"* North-Holland.

Verhoef, T. F., A. H. M. ter Hofstede and G. M. Wijers (1991), "Structuring modelling knowledge for CASE shells," pp. 502-524 in *Advanced Information Systems Engineering, Proceedings of the Third International Conference CAiSE'91*, R. Andersen, J. A. Bubenko and A. Solvberg (Ed.), Springer-Verlag.

Vlasblom, G., D. Rijsenbrij and M. Glastra (1995), *"Flexibilization of the methodology of system development,"* Information & Software Technology 37(**11**) pp.595-607.

Welke, R. J. (1988), "Metabase: A Platform for the Next Generation of Meta Systems Products," in *Proceedings of the Ninth Annual Conference on Applications of Computer-Aided Software Engineering Tools, May 23--27, 1988*, Meta Systems Ltd., Ann Arbor, MI.

Welke, R. J. (1992), "The CASE Repository: More than another database application," in *Challenges and Strategies for Research in Systems Development*, William W. Cotterman and James A. Senn (Eds.) (Ed.), Wiley, Chichester UK.

Wijers, G. M., H. E. van Dort (1990), *"Experiences with the use of CASE-tools in the Netherlands,"* Advanced Information Systems Engineering pp.5--20.

Wijers, G. M. (1991), *"Modelling Support in Information Systems Development,"* Ph.D. Thesis, Delft University of Technology, Thesis Publishers, Amsterdam.

Wijers, G. M., A. H. M. ter Hofstede and N. E. van Oosterom (1992), "Representation of Information Modelling Knowledge," in *Next Generation CASE Tools*, K. Lyytinen and V.-P. Tahvanainen (Ed.), IOS Press, Amsterdam, The Netherlands.

Wood-Harper, T. (1985), "Research Methods in Information Systems: Using Action Research," pp. 169-191 in *Research Methods in Information Systems*, E. Mumford, R. Hirschheim, G. Fitzgerald and A.T. Wood-Harper (Ed.), Elsevier Science Publishers.

Wynekoop, J. L., S. A. Conger (1991), *"A review of computer aided software engineering research methods,"* Information Systems Research, IFIP.

Wynekoop, J. D., N. L. Russo (1993), "System development methodologies: unanswered questions and the research-practice gap," pp. 181--190 in *Proceedings of the 14th ICIS*, J. I. DeGross, R. P. Bostrom and D. Robey (Ed.), ACM, Orlando, USA.

Yourdon, E. (1992), *"The Decline and Fall of the American Programmer,,"* Prentice-Hall, Englewood Cliffs, NJ.

8. BIOGRAPHY

The authors work as researchers in the MetaPHOR project at the Department of Computer Science and Information Systems in the University of Jyväskylä. Juha-Pekka Tolvanen received his Master's degree in 1992 and licentiate degree in 1994. His licentiate thesis and dissertation research focus on method engineering and especially on its organizational and methodical aspects. His other research interests include CASE tools, business modeling and business process re-engineering. Matti Rossi received his Master's degree in 1994 and completed his licentiate thesis in 1994. His research interests include database management, object-oriented data representation, metamodelling, transformations in metamodelling, and the applications of these to software engineering. Hui Liu received his Master's degree in Beijing and completed his licentiate thesis in 1996 in Jyväskylä. His research interests include metamodelling languages and query systems, in particular visual query languages in metaCASE environments.

20

Panel: Reengineering Method Engineering?

Panel Chair:
  Keng Siau, *University of Nebraska-Lincoln, USA*
Panelists:
  Lucas Introna, *London School of Economics, UK*
  Graham McLeod, *University of Cape Town, South Africa*
  Jeffrey Parsons, *Memorial University, Canada*
  Yair Wand, *University of British Columbia, Canada*

PANEL DESCRIPTION

Is there a need for method engineering when only 20% of the developers perform modeling work? Is there a future for method engineering when the majority of practitioners subscribe to their "home-made" methods or methodologies during information systems development? These are the issues that will be discussed and argued during the panel.

Panelist Lucas Introna advocates the abandonment of the notion of method and all of its rationalistic baggage. He argues that it is not possible to train designers in particular ways of developing systems. Designers have to become apprentices to existing system developers and learn their skill by socialization. Panelist Graham McLeod maintains that methods can never be fully prescriptive, since they operate in a social environment and the behavior of a complex system is not predictable, but emergent from the complex interaction of many autonomous agents.

Panelists Jeffrey Parsons, Keng Siau, and Yair Wand, on the other hand, believe that the unfortunate state of affairs in systems development method can be attributed partly to the lack of strong theoretical foundation and empirical work in the area. In this panel, Jeff Parsons will discuss the use of classification theory (i.e., how humans organize information in terms of categories or concepts) as a theoretical foundation for method engineering. Panelist Yair Wand will discuss method engineering from the ontological point of view and show how ontological concepts can be used in method engineering. Keng Siau will address the role of empirical research in method engineering.

21

Panel: Method Engineering: Experiences in Practice

Panel Chair:
   Gezinus J. Hidding, Andersen Consulting, USA
Panelists:
   James J. Odell, James Odell Associates, USA
   John Parkinson, Ernst & Young, USA
   Gerard M. Wijers, ID Research, the Netherlands

PANEL DESCRIPTION

Method Engineering is a topic of much research activity witness, for example, this conference. Much of the research focuses on contrasting and comparing various approaches, on repository design, or on design of Computer Aided Method Engineering (CAME) tools. Very little of the research focuses on whether methods are used or useful, let alone whether method engineering is used or valuable.

Some research, for example, by the Software Engineering Institute, suggests that much systems development work is being done without any formalized procedures for doing or managing the work (Masters and Kitson, 1992). Other researchers, e.g., Orr (1993), even argue that methodologies are not very useful. Ciborra (1993) argues that the a-conflictual and mechanistic nature of structured system development approaches does not even fit the current, and complex reality.

However, as Wynekoop and Russo (1993) argued, empirical results or research into experiences with methods (engineering) in practice are rare. Are practitioners using methods, let alone method engineering? Are there different practitioner segments, with different information needs? What are their experiences? What does it even mean to "use" methods? Research by the panel chair indicates that practitioners who use methods do so subconsciously. Their work reveals the method(s) they apply, but they don't read those methods actively anymore. How does methods use or non-use impact an organization's operations? How does it impact an organization's business results (e.g., better quality, faster turn around time, less cost, more productive)? Clearly, such questions are important, as investments in the development and training in such methods are substantial. The panelists, all close to practical applications of Method Engineering, will address these types of questions in their position statements.

REFERENCES

Ciborra, C., Teams, Markets and Systems: Business Innovation and Information Technology. Cambridge, Great Britain: Cambridge University Press, 1993.

Masters, S., and Kitson, D.H., An Analysis of SEI Software Process Assessment Results: 1987 - 1991. Technical Report CMU/SEI-92-TR-24. Software Engineering Institute, Carnegie Mellon University. Pittsburgh, PA. 1992.

Orr, J.E., Ethnography and Organizational Learning: In Pursuit of Learning at Work. In: Organizational Learning and Technological Change. Eds. Bagnara, S., C. Zucchermaglio and S. Stucky, New York and Berlin: Springer-Verlag, 1993.

Wynekoop, J.L., and Russo, N.L., System Development Methodologies: Unanswered Questions and the Research-Practice Gap. Proceedings of the Fourteenth International Conference on Information Systems. Orlando. Eds. J.I. DeGross, R.P. Bostrom and D. Robey, pp. 181 - 190, 1993.

INDEX OF CONTRIBUTORS

KEYWORD INDEX